STUDIES IN MEDIEVAL AND RENAISSANCE MUSIC 14

Music in Elizabethan Court Politics

Studies in Medieval and Renaissance Music

ISSN 1479-9294

General Editors
Tess Knighton
Helen Deeming

This series aims to provide a forum for the best scholarship in early music; deliberately broad in scope, it welcomes proposals on any aspect of music, musical life, and composers during the period up to 1600, and particularly encourages work that places music in an historical and social context. Both new research and major re-assessments of central topics are encouraged.

Proposals or enquiries may be sent directly to the editors or the publisher at the addresses given below; all submissions will receive careful, informed consideration.

Professor Tess Knighton, Institucio Mila i Fontanals/CSIC,
c/ Egipciaques, Barcelona 08001, Spain

Dr Helen Deeming, Department of Music, Royal Holloway College, University of London, Egham, Surrey TW20 0EX

Boydell & Brewer, PO Box 9, Woodbridge, Suffolk IP12 3DF

Previously published titles in the series are listed at the back of this volume.

Music in Elizabethan Court Politics

Katherine Butler

THE BOYDELL PRESS

© Katherine Butler 2015

All Rights Reserved. Except as permitted under current legislation no part of this work may be photocopied, stored in a retrieval system, published, performed in public, adapted, broadcast, transmitted, recorded or reproduced in any form or by any means, without the prior permission of the copyright owner

The right of Katherine Butler to be identified as the author of this work has been asserted in accordance with sections 77 and 78 of the Copyright, Designs and Patents Act 1988

First published 2015
The Boydell Press, Woodbridge
Paperback edition 2019

ISBN 978 1 84383 981 1 hardback
ISBN 978 1 78327 403 1 paperback

The Boydell Press is an imprint of Boydell & Brewer Ltd
PO Box 9, Woodbridge, Suffolk IP12 3DF, UK
and of Boydell & Brewer Inc.
668 Mt Hope Avenue, Rochester, NY 14620–2731, USA
website: www.boydellandbrewer.com

A CIP catalogue record for this title is available
from the British Library

The publisher has no responsibility for the continued existence or accuracy of URLs for external or third-party internet websites referred to in this book, and does not guarantee that any content on such websites is, or will remain, accurate or appropriate

Designed and typeset in Adobe Arno Pro by
David Roberts, Pershore, Worcestershire

Contents

List of Illustrations   vii
Editorial Note   viii
Acknowledgements   ix
List of Abbreviations   x

Introduction   1
    Appropriations of Court Music   2
    Tudor Perspectives on Music and Politics   6

CHAPTER 1   Music, Authority, and the Royal Image   15
    Sensuality and Rationality   19
    Musical Images of Political Authority   29
    A Harmonious Kingdom   33
    A Note of Discord   36

CHAPTER 2   The Politics of Intimacy   42
    Performance, Intimacy, and Power   43
    Political Performances   47
    Predecessors and Contemporaries   52
    Courting Royal Favour   55
    The Songs of Essex   65

CHAPTER 3   The Royal Household and its Revels   76
    Image and Diplomacy   79
    Control of Court Music   86
    Masqued Politics   89
    Counsel and the Choirboy Plays   94
    Morality, Mythology, and Flattery   100

CHAPTER 4   Noble Masculinity at the Tournaments   105
    The Performance of Noble Masculinity   108
    Philisides, The Shepherd Knight   114
    The Four Foster Children of Desire   121
    Sir Henry Lee's Retirement   129

CHAPTER 5   Politics, Petition, and Complaint on the Royal
            Progresses   143
                Praise and Ambition   148
                Love and Lament   161
                Catholic Complaints   165
                Performers' Petitions   170
                Moral Advice and Political Counsel   176
                Staging Harmony   184

            Conclusion   192

APPENDIX A Secular Musicians Employed in the Royal Household
            of Elizabeth I   197

APPENDIX B Extant Secular Songs Connected to Elizabeth and her
            Court   207

            Glossary of Musical Terms   220
            Bibliography   223
            Index   247

Illustrations

FIGURES

1.1 Nicholas Hilliard, 'Elizabeth I Playing the Lute' (*c.* 1580), Berkeley Castle. Image from the Photographic Survey, The Courtauld Institute of Art, London. Private collection. With grateful thanks to the Berkeley Will Trust.   16

5.1 *The First Anointed Queen I Am, within this Town which Ever Came* [1573], Houghton Library, Harvard University, STC 7582.5   188

MUSICAL EXAMPLES

2.1 Opening of John Dowland, 'Sorrow Stay, Lend True Repentant Tears', *The Second Book of Songs or Ayres* (London, 1600), sigs. C1v–C2r   70

2.2 Opening half of Daniel Bacheler, 'To Plead My Faith', *A Musical Banquet*, ed. Robert Dowland (London, 1610), sigs. D2v–E1r   71

2.3 Opening of John Dowland, 'Flow My Tears', *The Second Book of Songs or Ayres* (London, 1600), sigs. B2v–C1r   73

2.4 Richard Martin, 'Change Thy Mind Since She Doth Change', *A Musical Banquet*, ed. Robert Dowland (London, 1610), sigs. B2v–C1r   74

4.1 Opening of John Dowland, 'Time's Eldest Son' (Part 1), *The Second Book of Songs or Ayres* (London, 1600), sigs. D2v–E1r   132

4.2 Opening of William Byrd, 'The Trumpets', *The Battle*, GB-Lbl: MS Mus. 1591 [My Lady Nevell's Book], fol. 21r   133

4.3 John Dowland, 'Time's Eldest Son' (Part 1), bars 11–14   134

4.4 John Dowland, 'Time's Eldest Son' (Part 2), *The Second Book of Songs or Ayres* (London, 1600), sigs. E1v–E2r, bars 1–5   135

4.5 John Dowland, 'Time's Eldest Son' (Part 3), *The Second Book of Songs or Ayres* (London, 1600), sigs. E2v–F1r, bars 8–10   136

4.6 William Byrd, 'Second Preces', bars 16–19   136

4.7 William Byrd, 'Second Preces', bars 21–3   137

4.8 John Dowland, 'Time's Eldest Son' (Part 3), bars 19–22   137

4.9 John Dowland, 'Time's Eldest Son' (Part 3), bars 1–7   138

4.10 John Dowland, 'His Golden Locks', *The First Book of Songs or Ayres* (London, 1597), sigs. I2v–K1r, bars 1–13   140

4.11 John Dowland, 'His Golden Locks', bars 18–24   141

4.12 John Dowland, 'Humour Say What Mak'st Thou Here', *The Second Book of Songs or Ayres* (London, 1600), sigs. M2v–N1r, bars 14–20   142

5.1 William Byrd, 'This Sweet and Merry Month of May', *The First Set of Italian Madrigals Englished*, ed. Thomas Watson (London, 1590), no. XXVIII, bars 59–65   150

5.2 Edward Johnson, 'Elisa is the Fairest Queen', GB-Lbl: Add. MSS 30480–4, vol. 1, fol. 65r; vol. 2, fol. 68v; vol. 3, fol. 63v; vol. 4, fol. 65v; vol. 5, fol. 10v   152

5.3 Edward Johnson, 'Come Again', GB-Lbl: Add. MSS 30480–4, vol. 1, fol. 65r; vol. 2, fol. 68v; vol. 3, fol. 63v; vol. 4, fol. 65v; vol. 5, fol. 10v   154

5.4 Robert Jones, 'Cynthia Queen of Seas and Lands', *Ultimum Vale, with a Triplicity of Music* (London, 1605), sigs. E2v–F1r, bars 19–35   159

5.5 John Dowland, 'My Heart and Tongue were Twins', *A Pilgrim's Solace* (London, 1612), sigs. K2v–L1r, bars 1–5   175

5.6 John Dowland, 'My Heart and Tongue were Twins', bars 18–27 (with lyrics from the progress)   175

5.7 Opening of Nicholas Strogers, 'Mistrust Not Truth', GB-Och: Music MSS 984–8 [Dow Partbooks], no. 121   181

5.8 Nicholas Strogers, 'Mistrust Not Truth', bars 11–14   181

5.9 Opening four lines of *A Famous Ditty of the Joyful Receiving of the Queen's Most Excellent Majesty* (London 1584), set to the tune of Wigmore's Galliard   189

Editorial Note

For consistency and clarity, the spelling and capitalisation of quotations and titles of pre-nineteenth-century texts have been modernised throughout and contractions have been expanded. Dates have also been adjusted to the modern calendar. The musical examples maintain original pitches and note values, except where the addition of regular bar-lines has required the use of ties. Time signatures and clefs have been adjusted to those in current use and tablature has been transcribed into staff notation. Editorial accidentals are placed above the stave. Some additional annotations are given to assist readers from outside of musicology in following the more analytical arguments.

Acknowledgements

I AM most grateful for the encouragement and guidance I have received from numerous people throughout the research and writing of this book. Special thanks go to Stephen Rose and Elizabeth Eva Leach, who have both been invaluable in discussing my ideas, making perceptive suggestions, and providing generous and insightful feedback on my research. Owen Rees fostered my initial interest in Elizabethan court music, and I have also benefitted from the comments and suggestions of many other friends and colleagues, including Peter Holman, Susan Doran, Anna Whitelock, Paulina Kewes, Catherine Bradley, Adeline Mueller, Matthew Thomson, Henry Hope, Matthew Cheung Salisbury, Abigail Ballantyne, Andrew Cichy, Matthew Laube, and Nicola Clark. I am grateful for all their thoughts and advice. Thanks are also due to those who have listened and responded to the various conference and seminar papers I have given, and to the students of my course on Elizabethan court music who shared their thoughts with me.

On a more practical note, Henry Hope, Till Biskup, and Holly Kennard assisted with me with the sixteenth-century French and German. The staff at the Bodleian and British Libraries and the National Archives have always been most helpful. At Boydell & Brewer I have been fortunate to work with Caroline Palmer, who has been most supportive throughout the development of this book, as well as an excellent team of copy editors, typesetters and other assistants. Jeanne Roberts polished up the typesetting of my musical examples, and I also thank the reviewers for their suggested improvements.

I have been privileged to receive grants from the Arts and Humanities Research Council, the British Academy, and St John's College, Oxford, to support various stages of the research, writing, and publishing of this book, for which I am most thankful. An early version of Chapter 1 appeared as '"By Instruments her Powers Appeare": Music and Authority in the Reign of Queen Elizabeth I' in *Renaissance Quarterly* 65 (2012), and I am grateful for permission to include and expand on this work.

Finally, I have been sustained throughout this project by the love and encouragement of friends and family. My parents, especially, have always encouraged my musical and academic pursuits, while my husband Chris has been unfailing in his support and consistently willing to listen to my concerns or excitement.

Abbreviations

BRO	Bristol Records Office
CSP Spain	Royall Tyler *et al.* (eds.), *Calendar of Letters, Despatches and State Papers Relating to Negotiations between England and Spain*, 13 vols. (London, 1862–1954)
CSP Venice	Rawdon Brown *et al.* (eds.), *Calendar of State Papers Relating to English Affairs in the Archives and Collections of Venice*, 38 vols. (London, 1864–1947)
F-Pn	Paris, Bibliothèque Nationale
GB-AB	Aberystwyth, National Library of Wales
GB-CF	Chelmsford, Essex County Record Office
GB-Cfm	Cambridge, Fitzwilliam Museum
GB-Ckc	Cambridge, Kings College, Rowe Music Library
GB-EU	Edinburgh, University Library
GB-Lam	London, Royal Academy of Music Library
GB-Lbl	London, The British Library
GB-Lcm	London, Royal College of Music
GB-Lna	London, National Archives
GB-Oas	Oxford, All Souls College
GB-Ob	Oxford, Bodleian Library
GB-Och	Oxford, Christ Church Library
GB-WCc	Winchester College, Warden and Fellows Library
NG2	*The New Grove Dictionary of Music and Musicians*, ed. Stanley Sadie and John Tyrrell, 29 vols. (Oxford, 2004). Also available online through <www.oxfordmusiconline.com>
IRL-Dtc	Dublin, Trinity College Library
L&P Henry VIII	J. S. Brewer, R. H. Brodie, and James Gairdner (eds.), *Letters and Papers, Foreign and Domestic, of the Reign of Henry VIII*, 21 vols. (London, 1864–1920)
L&P Simancas	Martin Hume (ed.), *Letters and State Papers Relating to English Affairs Principally Preserved in the Archives of Simancas*, 4 vols. (London, 1892–9)
ODNB	*Oxford Dictionary of National Biography*. Online at <www.oxforddnb.com>
OED	*Oxford English Dictionary*. Online at <www.oed.com>
REED	*Records of Early English Drama*
RECM	Andrew Ashbee (ed.), *Records of English Court Music*, 9 vols. (Aldershot, 1986)
US-CA	Cambridge, MA, Harvard University, Harvard College Library
US-NH	New Haven, CT, Yale University, Irving S. Gilmore Music Library

Introduction

IN 1593 the poet Michael Drayton pictured Queen Elizabeth I of England (1558–1603) as the nymph Beta being entertained in state on the banks of the Thames in honour of her Accession Day (17 November):

> How merrily the Muses sing,
> That all the flowery meadows ring,
> And Beta sits upon the bank, in purple and in pall,
> And she the Queen of Muses is, and wears the coronal.[1]

Courtly revels are translated into an idealised pastoral English countryside. Courtiers become nymphs and shepherds; Muses and birds form choirs; swans serve for a guard of honour; Apollo's laurel and a coronet of flowers become the royal crown. In short, Drayton's poetic tableau resembles many of the real-life entertainments presented to Elizabeth at noble houses during her summer progresses, where she was entertained by a cast of sea and wood nymphs, fairies, ploughmen, and shepherds.[2]

For Drayton, Elizabeth was 'Queen of Muses': the prime spectator of the revels and receiver of the nymphs' and Muses' tributes.[3] This epithet evoked Elizabeth's dual role: as Queen *over* the Muses she was their ruler, akin to Apollo and a wise and noble patron of the arts; as Queen *among* Muses she was the inspiration of her courtiers and poets, who were driven to celebrate her in elaborate musical and poetic entertainments. For Richard Mulcaster, Headmaster of the Merchant Taylors' School, the epithet also captured her personal qualities:

> It is for our most worthy Princess, to have the presidency over nine men, the paragons of virtue: and yet to be so familiarly acquainted with the nine Muses, as they are in strife who may love her best, for being best learned.[4]

Elizabeth's intelligence, eloquence, and musicality made her the best of the Muses. Moreover, by contrasting the female Muses with an evocation of the male Nine Worthies – an assembly of Pagan, Jewish, and Christian warrior-kings formed in the medieval period – Mulcaster attributed to Elizabeth the twin virtues of just

---

[1] Michael Drayton, *Idea the Shepherd's Garland Fashioned in Nine Eclogues. Rowland's Sacrifice to the Nine Muses* (London, 1593), p. 16.

[2] *The Honourable Entertainment Given to the Queen's Majesty in Progress, at Elvetham in Hampshire, by the Right Honourable the Earl of Hertford* (London, 1591); Joseph Barnes (ed.), *Speeches Delivered to her Majesty this Last Progress at the Right Honourable the Lady Russels, at Bisham, the Right Honourable the Lord Chandos at Sudley, at the Right Honourable the Lord Norris, at Ricote* (Oxford, 1592), sigs. B1r–C1r.

[3] Drayton, *Idea the Shepherd's Garland*, p. 16.

[4] Richard Mulcaster, *Positions wherin those Primitive Circumstances be Examined, which are Necessary for the Training Up of Children* (London, 1581), pp. 173–4.

leadership and learned eloquence.[5] The political significance of music within the Elizabethan court relied on all these aspects of Elizabeth's image as 'Queen of Muses': her personal talents, her role as patron, and her position as inspiration for music, theatre, and poetry.

APPROPRIATIONS OF COURT MUSIC

YET the Muses did not always dance to Elizabeth's tune. In January 1595 the Muses were to accompany the entry of Arthur Throckmorton. His family had incurred royal displeasure because Arthur's sister Bess (one the Queen's Maids of Honour) had become pregnant by, and subsequently married, Sir Walter Ralegh. In a letter written to fellow courtier Robert Cecil in January 1595, Throckmorton outlined his plan to return himself and his family to royal favour. He had devised a masque of nine Muses, 'whose music, I hope, shall so modify the easy softened mind of her Majesty as both I and mine may find mercy'.[6] Meanwhile he would 'lie prostrate at her Majesty's feet till she says she will save me', and upon her acquiescence she would be presented with a copy of the song, allowing her to read and reflect on its message. Whether Throckmorton gained permission to execute this plan is unclear. It was due to take place during the wedding celebrations of Elizabeth de Vere, daughter of the Earl of Oxford, to William Stanley, Earl of Derby: a court occasion at which the Queen was present and for which she had appointed the masquers. Nevertheless Throckmorton's plan illustrates how individual courtiers employed musical entertainments to influence the Queen for their own personal advancement. In particular he saw the affective powers of music as a potent means of altering Elizabeth's opinions and moods. His none-too-flattering reference to Elizabeth's 'easy softened' mind was typical of sixteenth-century views that women were particularly susceptible to music's charms (as shown in Chapter 1).

Court musicians also recognised the political importance of music. Dedicating their *Cantiones, quae ab argumento sacrae vocantur* (1575) to Elizabeth, William Byrd and Thomas Tallis claimed that music was 'indispensable to the state' (*necessarium reipub.*).[7] Despite containing solely sacred music, the purpose of the *Cantiones sacrae* was more political than religious. The collection commemorated the seventeenth year of Elizabeth's reign and her Accession Day on 17 November with each composer contributing seventeen items.[8] The prefatory material hardly mentions the sacred nature of the contents, but rather emphasises the reputation of Elizabeth

---

[5] Mulcaster deliberately emphasises the virtues rather than the military prowess of the Nine Worthies, and the traditional comparison of arms versus letters is altered to make allowance for Elizabeth's gender and consequent lack of military role.

[6] R. A. Roberts (ed.), *Calendar of the Manuscripts of the Most Hon. the Marquis of Salisbury, Preserved at Hatfield House, Hertfordshire*, 23 vols. (London, 1894), vol. 5, p. 99.

[7] William Byrd, *Cantiones sacrae (1575)*, ed. Craig Monson, Byrd Edition 1 (London, 1977), pp. xvii, xxv.

[8] The composers sometimes counted the two parts of a motet as separate pieces to achieve this: ibid., pp. v–vi (Craig Monson's preface to the edition).

and English music: the opening page states that 'blessed with the patronage of so learned a ruler, she [English music] fears neither the boundaries nor the reproach of any nation.'[9] Music enhanced both Elizabeth's image and the international reputation of England. At the same time, the *Cantiones sacrae* was the first fruit of the monopoly on printed music and lined music paper granted by Elizabeth to Byrd and Tallis in response to their petition for a source of additional income in 1573.[10] Such a reward to two Catholic composers illustrates the privileged status that skilled court musicians enjoyed (especially as Byrd had only been a member of the Chapel Royal since 1572, though Tallis had served since c. 1543). This collection was representative of the pursuit of royal rewards and status common to all court servants from noblemen to humble musicians.

The premise of this book is that music at the Elizabethan court not only promoted the image and authority of its Queen, but was also appropriated by her courtiers, noblemen, and even musicians, to serve their personal and political ambitions. Such appropriations were not necessarily detrimental to Elizabeth's authority – courtiers and musicians played an essential role in creating and disseminating her image – but they did mean that musical performances were frequently serving multiple political interests.

Opportunities for appropriation arose because the music performed at court consisted of more than just performances by the royal music establishment.[11] In the royal palaces court music was enhanced by visiting musicians and external ensembles, complemented by the commissions of noblemen, and supplemented by the amateur music-making of the Queen and her courtiers (Chapters 2–4). As the court travelled to towns and noble estates during Elizabeth's summer progresses further opportunities arose for both noblemen and civic authorities to influence the music it heard (Chapter 5). Moreover the creation of an elaborate musical entertainment involved the collaboration of numerous individuals: patrons, writers, composers, and performers. From this perspective it becomes easier to see how secular court music might support a medley of political interests, sometimes complementary and at other times competing. Elizabeth was an active participant in creating a musical reputation both for herself and for her court; however, courtiers,

---

[9] Ibid., pp. xvii, xxv.
[10] Paul Doe and David Allinson, 'Tallis, Thomas', NG2.
[11] The Elizabethan royal musical establishment has been the subject of several studies: Andrew Ashbee and David Lasocki, *A Biographical Dictionary of English Court Musicians, 1485–1714*, 2 vols. (Aldershot, 1998); David Lasocki and Roger Prior, *The Bassanos: Venetian Musicians and Instrument Makers in England, 1531–1665* (Aldershot, 1995); Peter Holman, *Four and Twenty Fiddlers: The Violin at the English Court, 1540–1690*, Oxford Monographs on Music (Oxford, 1993); Roger Prior, 'Jewish Musicians at the Tudor Court', *The Musical Quarterly* 69 (1983), 253–65; David Lasocki, 'Professional Recorder Players in England, 1540–1740', 3 vols., PhD dissertation, University of Iowa, 1983. See also the insightful overview of music-making at the Elizabethan court in Craig Monson, 'Elizabethan London', in *The Renaissance: From the 1470s to the End of the 16th Century*, ed. Iain Fenlon, Man and Music 2 (London, 1989), pp. 304–40 (pp. 305–13, 316–26, 330–3).

noblemen, civic leaders, playwrights, and performers also had the opportunity to shape the political meanings of musical performances. Moreover their political intentions were not necessarily aimed solely at the Queen; it could be equally important to enhance one's reputation among one's peers or impress one's views on topical issues on Elizabeth's advisors and most influential statesmen. The result was entertainments whose political meanings were multi-layered, multi-purpose, and aimed at multiple audiences.

This perspective complicates the typically monarch-centred approaches to Renaissance court music, focussed on royal musical establishments or how music projected the power of the ruler.[12] Certainly music's role as an instrument of royal image-making and authority, and its influence on international relations were vital parts of its political significance.[13] I too explore such themes within the distinctive dynamic of Elizabeth's female-governed court (Chapters 1–3). Nevertheless, a re-evaluation of the roles and influences of court music is necessary, particularly in light of the musico-political machinations that have been identified in Byrd's Catholic networks and in printed song collections associated with the Earl of Essex's circle and the composer John Dowland.[14] Revealing how courtiers and musicians

---

[12] This includes both older, documentary accounts of court music, and more recent studies on music in the royal image: Allan Atlas, *Music at the Aragonese Court of Naples* (Cambridge, 1985); Lewis Lockwood, *Music in Renaissance Ferrara, 1400–1505: The Creation of a Musical Centre in the Fifteenth Century* (Oxford, 1984); Paul Merkley and Lora L. M. Merkley, *Music and Patronage in the Sforza Court*, Studi sulla storia della musica in Lombardia 3 (Turnhout, 1999); Mary Tiffany Ferer, *Music and Ceremony at the Court of Charles V: The Capilla Flamenca and the Art of Political Promotion*, Studies in Medieval and Renaissance Music 12 (Woodbridge, 2012); Andrew Weaver, *Sacred Music as Public Image for Holy Roman Emperor Ferdinand III: Representing the Counter-Reformation Monarch at the End of the Thirty Years' War*, Catholic Christendom, 1300–1700 (Farnham, 2012). Weaver's introduction recognises that the royal image was forged by courtiers and artists with their own agendas, but returns to a monarch-centred perspective on the grounds of a lack of evidence and a desire to elucidate the monarch's strategies of self-representation. Holman's *Four and Twenty Fiddlers* focusses on one ensemble, but does include a chapter on the violin 'outside the court', which includes the instrument's use in mixed consorts in pageants commissioned by the aristocracy (pp. 132–5).

[13] On image-making: Ferer, *Music and Ceremony*; Weaver, *Sacred Music as Public Image*; Peter Walls, *Music in the English Courtly Masque, 1604–1640*, Oxford Monographs on Music (Oxford, 1996), p. 304. On royal authority and absolutism: Kate Van Orden, *Music, Discipline, and Arms in Early Modern France* (Chicago, 2005). On international relations and diplomacy: Theodor Dumitrescu, *The Early Tudor Court and International Musical Relations* (Aldershot, 2007).

[14] Including: Joseph Kerman, 'On William Byrd's *Emendemus in Melius*', in *Hearing the Motet: Essays on the Motet of the Middle Ages and Renaissance*, ed. Dolores Pesce (Oxford, 1997), pp. 329–47; Craig Monson, 'Byrd, the Catholics, and the Motet: The Hearing Reopened', ibid., pp. 348–74; Joseph Kerman, 'Music and Politics: The Case of William Byrd (1540–1623)', *Proceedings of the American Philosophical Society* 144 (2000), 275–87; Jeremy Smith, '"Unlawful Song": Byrd, the Babington Plot and the Paget Choir', *Early Music* 38 (2010), 497–508;

manipulated performances within the court itself traces such political music-making back to the presence of the Queen and the heart of her government.[15] It also follows current trends in the interpretation of the art, literature, and pageantry of the Elizabethan court, which has moved away from seeing the artistic creations of the court as part of a 'cult of Elizabeth' created and maintained by the Queen herself, towards a more complex picture that recognises the motivations and ambitions of the individual courtiers who commissioned these flattering representations.[16]

It is literary historians (particularly so-called 'new historicists') who have led the way both in treating the arts as constructive acts rather than mere reflections of contemporary politics, and in unpicking the political significance of the arts to the Elizabethan court with increasing complexity. They have charted the role of court drama in debating pressing political issues, highlighted how pageantry became a means of political persuasion, explored the impact of gender on royal authority, and analysed the construction of Elizabeth's image through literary and political discourses.[17] Most, however, have little or nothing to say about music and

Lillian Ruff and D. Arnold Wilson, 'The Madrigal, the Lute Song and Elizabethan Politics', *Past & Present* 44 (1969), 3–51, and, 'Allusion to the Essex Downfall in Lute Song Lyrics', *The Lute Society Journal* 12 (1970), 31–6; Jeremy Smith, 'Music and Late Elizabethan Politics: The Identities of Oriana and Diana', *Journal of the American Musicological Society* 58 (2005), 507–58; Kirsten Gibson, '"So to the Wood Went I": Politicizing the Greenwood in Two Songs by John Dowland', *Journal of the Royal Musical Association* 132 (2007), 221–51, and, 'John Dowland and the Elizabethan Courtier Poets', *Early Music* 41 (2013), 239–53.

[15] Craig Monson briefly suggests that music might be an 'essential means of treating with Elizabeth' for courtiers seeking favour ('Elizabethan London', pp. 332–3), a suggestion on which I build in Chapter 2.

[16] Roy Strong, *The Cult of Elizabeth: Elizabethan Portraiture and Pageantry*, new edn (London, 1999), pp. 16, 115–16; Sydney Anglo, '"Image-Making": The Means and the Limitations', in *The Tudor Monarchy*, ed. John Guy, Arnold Readers in History (London, 1997), pp. 16–42 (p. 36); Susan Frye, *Elizabeth I: The Competition for Representation* (Oxford, 1993), pp. 4, 8–10.

[17] Just a few representative examples from this extensive literature are, on drama and persuasion: Greg Walker, *The Politics of Performance in Early Renaissance Drama* (Cambridge, 1998); Marie Axton, *The Queen's Two Bodies: Drama and the Elizabethan Succession*, Royal Historical Society Studies in History 5 (London, 1977). On gender: Louis Montrose, '"Shaping Fantasies": Figurations of Gender and Power in Elizabethan Culture', *Representations* 2 (1983), 61–94; Carole Levin, *The Heart and Stomach of a King: Elizabeth I and the Politics of Sex and Power*, New Cultural Studies (Philadelphia, 1994); Philippa Berry, *Of Chastity and Power: Elizabethan Literature and the Unmarried Queen* (London, 1989). On image: Helen Hackett, *Virgin Mother, Maiden Queen: Elizabeth I and the Cult of the Virgin Mary* (Basingstoke, 1996); Frye, *Elizabeth I*; Louis Montrose, *The Subject of Elizabeth: Authority, Gender, and Representation* (Chicago, 2006); Kevin Sharpe, *Selling the Tudor Monarchy: Authority and Image in Sixteenth-Century England* (New Haven, CT, 2009). Historians too have shown increasing interest in the politics behind the pageantry, for example Susan Doran, 'Juno versus Diana: The Treatment of Elizabeth I's Marriage in Plays and Entertainments, 1561–1581', *The Historical Journal* 28 (1995), 257–74; Mary Hill Cole, *The Portable*

song, despite music's presence in the majority of court plays and entertainments.[18] Basic questions about music's contribution to Elizabethan court politics remain unanswered: What influence did Elizabeth's musicality have on her royal authority, and to what extent did she create and control her musical image? How might music have assisted in negotiating the complex issues of gender and power in a female-governed court? How did courtly songs engage with the controversial issues of the day, including the royal marriage, the succession, and foreign policy? How did song compare to other literary and artistic modes of expression used by courtiers or the Queen?[19] In short, how and why was music useful within Elizabethan court politics?

TUDOR PERSPECTIVES ON MUSIC AND POLITICS

An Elizabethan faced with questions of music's purpose and value at court might have provided several quite different answers, though it was widely accepted that it could have a profound political effect. When court musicians William Byrd and Thomas Tallis claimed that music was 'indispensable to the state' in their *Cantiones sacrae* (1575), they referred to 'Philosophers, Mathematicians, Statesmen' whose arguments they might have summoned had they not been assured that their dedicatee Elizabeth was in agreement.[20] They perhaps had in mind Aristotle's *Politics* and Plato's *Republic*, two works with particular influence on Elizabethan attitudes to music and the state. Particularly relevant to the composers' argument would have been Plato's notion that the character of the state could be moulded by the modes and rhythms that were permitted (preferably a mode of bravery and adversity for wartime, and one of prudence and freedom

---

Queen: *Elizabeth I and the Politics of Ceremony*, Massachusetts Studies in Early Modern Culture (Amherst, 1999).

[18] Notable exceptions include Susan Anderson, 'Music and Power at the English Court, 1575–1624', PhD dissertation, University of Leeds, 2006; Gavin Alexander, 'The Musical Sidneys', *John Donne Journal* 25 (2006), 65–105; Daniel Fischlin, *In Small Proportions: A Poetics of the English Ayre, 1596–1622* (Detroit, 1998); David Lindley, 'The Politics of Music in the Masque', in *The Politics of the Stuart Court Masque*, ed. David Bevington and Peter Holbrook (Cambridge, 1998), pp. 273–95; Katherine Duncan-Jones, '"Melancholie Times": Musical Recollections of Sidney by William Byrd and Thomas Watson', in *The Well-Enchanting Skill: Music, Poetry, and Drama in the Culture of the Renaissance: Essays in Honour of F. W. Sternfeld*, ed. John Caldwell, Edward Olleson, and Susan Wollenberg (Oxford, 1990), pp. 171–80.

[19] For analyses of other modes of courtly expression see: Catherine Bates, *The Rhetoric of Courtship in Elizabethan Language and Literature* (Cambridge, 1992); Patricia Fumerton, *Cultural Aesthetics: Renaissance Literature and the Practice of Social Ornament* (Chicago, 1991); Richard McCoy, *The Rites of Knighthood: The Literature and Politics of Elizabethan Chivalry*, New Historicism 7 (Berkeley, CA, 1989).

[20] Byrd, *Cantiones sacrae* (1575), pp. xvii, xxv: 'necessarium reipub.'

for peacetime).[21] As the Elizabethan author of *The Praise of Music* interpreted it: 'the changing of musical notes hath caused an alteration of the common state.'[22]

Music might also inspire virtue in the governor of a state, who 'delighting in it and receiving it into his soul … will feed on it and so become noble and good'.[23] Plato suggested that music had the capacity to penetrate the soul and promote gracefulness, nobility, goodness, and an appreciation of beauty, though conversely excessive music-making might soften and dissolve the spirit, making one feeble.[24] Aristotle too noted music's effect on character and virtue, but he also took a less moralistic approach, recommending music not because it was 'necessary' or 'useful' in the way of letters, but for 'intellectual enjoyment in leisure'. 'There is a sort of education in which parents should train their sons', he argued, 'not as being useful or necessary, but because it is liberal or noble.'[25] Music was a mark of status, culture, and learning necessary for any young man being prepared for public life and a role in the government of the city.

Plato and Aristotle's comments on musical or political life influenced numerous sixteenth-century authors, including Count Baldassarre Castiglione, with his *Il libro del cortegiano* (1528, translated into English as *The Courtier* in 1561), and Sir Thomas Elyot's *The Book Named the Governor* (1531). Offshoots of the advice-to-princes and courtesy literature traditions, these were two of the most widely read books on courtly and political conduct in Elizabethan England, as well as those with the most extensive discussions of music.[26] Sir Thomas Elyot was a courtier in the reign of Henry VIII and had dedicated his *The Governor* to his King. The book was very successful, with eight editions printed between 1531 and 1580. Castiglione's *The Courtier* was translated by English courtier Sir Thomas Hoby and reprinted twice during Elizabeth's reign, as well as in a trilingual (Italian, French, English) edition in 1588. There was also an elegant Latin edition by Bartholomew Clerke,

---

[21] Plato, *The Republic*, ed. G. R. F. Ferrari, trans. Tom Griffith, Cambridge Texts in the History of Political Thought (Cambridge, 2000), book 3, 398c–399c.

[22] *The Praise of Music wherein Besides the Antiquity, Dignity, Delectation, and Use Thereof in Civil Matters, is also Declared the Sober and Lawful Use of the Same in the Congregation and Church of God* (Oxford, 1586), p. 62.

[23] Plato, *The Republic*, book 3, 401e–402a.

[24] Ibid., book 3, 401d–402a, 411a–c

[25] Aristotle, *The Politics of Aristotle*, trans. Benjamin Jowett (Oxford, 1885), book 8, ch. 3, 1338a13–30, ch. 5, 1340a7–b10. For a comparison of Plato's and Aristotle's views on music that emphasisies the similarities in their approaches see: Mary B. Schoen-Nazzaro, 'Plato and Aristotle on the Ends of Music', *Laval théologique et philosophique* 34 (1978), 261–73.

[26] On the classical roots and medieval forerunners in the 'advice to princes' literature see: Lester Kruger Born's introduction to Desiderius Erasmus, *The Education of a Christian Prince*, ed. and trans. Born, 2nd edn (New York, 1968), pp. 44–93, 99–128; Jean-Philippe Genet (ed.), *Four English Political Tracts of the Later Middle Ages* (London, 1977), pp. ix–xviii; Donald W. Rude (ed.), *A Critical Edition of Sir Thomas Elyot's 'The Boke Named the Governour'* (New York, 1992), pp. xlii–xlv.

which saw six editions and was dedicated to Queen Elizabeth herself. Moreover, noblemen owned copies of the Italian or French edition too, and courtiers such as Thomas Sackville (Lord Buckhurst), Henry Howard (Earl of Northampton), Edward de Vere (Earl of Oxford), Sir Thomas Knyvett, and Sir Christopher Hatton are all believed to have read Castiglione's book.[27]

The classical notion of politics inherited by the Elizabethans revolved around the governance of people, the necessary qualities of governors, and how the state should be ordered such that people lived together harmoniously. Thomas Elyot's explanation of music's utility in *The Governor* was still based on this tradition of politics as harmonious governance. He justified musical knowledge as:

> Necessary ... for the better attaining the knowledge of a public weal, which ... is made of an order of estates and degrees, and by reason thereof containeth in it a perfect harmony.[28]

Elyot was drawing on contemporary beliefs that music promoted social and political harmony, reflecting in microcosm the harmony which governed the motions of the celestial spheres. These were inherited from classical authors such as Plato, Aristotle, and Cicero, and transmitted particularly through Boethius's *De institutione musica* (sixth century), which remained an authority on music throughout the sixteenth century. Boethius's notions of *musica mundana* and *musica humana* (the universal music created by the movement of the planetary spheres, and the harmonious nature of the human soul and body) had been extended to regard the commonwealth as a similar, political harmony.[29] The hierarchical ordering of the estates was seen as mirroring the hierarchy of tones or voices in a composition. In the encyclopaedic *French Academy* (1586) – another popular translation of a Continental book with four English editions in Elizabeth's reign – Pierre de la Primaudaye described how from a multitude of estates 'an harmonical agreement ariseth by due proportion of one towards another in their divers orders and estates, even as the harmony in music consisteth of unequal voices or sounds agreeing equally together.'[30] This was not

---

[27] Peter Burke, *The Fortunes of the Courtier: The European Reception of Castiglione's 'Cortegiano'* (Cambridge, 1995), pp. 56, 60–1, 74–7, 86–9, 144–5, and appendix 2; Mary Partridge, 'Images of the Courtier in Elizabethan England', PhD dissertation, University of Birmingham, 2008, pp. 38–81.

[28] Sir Thomas Elyot, *The Book Named the Governor* (London, 1531), fol. 24r.

[29] John Hollander, *The Untuning of the Sky: Ideas of Music in English Poetry, 1500–1700* (Princeton, NJ, 1961), pp. 24–31; Boethius, *Fundamentals of Music*, trans. Calvin M. Bower, ed. Claude V. Palisca, Music Theory Translation Series (New Haven, CT, 1989), pp. 9–10; Calvin Bower, 'Boethius', *NG2*.

[30] Pierre de La Primaudaye, *The French Academy wherein is Discoursed the Institution of Manners, and whatsoever else Concerneth the Good and Happy Life of All Estates and Callings*, trans. T. B. (London, 1586), p. 743 (an English translation of Pierre de La Primaudaye's *L'Académie françoise* (1577)). This harmony is explicitly compared to that of the planets in Shakespeare's *Troilus and Cressida* (1601–2), act 1 scene 3, lines 85–111: William Shakespeare, *The Norton Shakespeare*, ed. Walter Cohen, *et al.* (New York, 1997), p. 1847.

merely a metaphorical notion; Elyot seriously recommended musical knowledge as a preparation for political understanding.

In a similar vein, political harmony or discord was often symbolised in art by musical instruments. Hans Holbein's *The Ambassadors* depicts a lute with a broken string to symbolise the religious discord in Europe, the English Church's potential split from Rome being a concern of both diplomats (Jean de Dinteville and Georges de Selves).[31] Images equating lutes and men's hearts were common in emblem books such as Alciato's *Emblematum liber* (1534), punning on the Latin words *cor* (heart) and *cordae* (strings). Alciato's emblem of a lute symbolised an alliance of princes in Italy, with the accompanying verses declaring that only a skilful man could 'tune so many strings'. If only one were out of tune 'all the music of the instrument is lost and its lovely song disjointed'.[32]

Yet the language of 'politics' was also undergoing a significant change during the sixteenth century. Politics was no longer just the art of virtuous governance and the maintenance of a harmonious state, but increasingly referred to 'reason of state' or the art of preserving dominance over people, a change exemplified by Machiavelli's *The Prince* (1532).[33] In contrast to the Aristotelian concept of politics as working for the common good, the word 'politics' increasingly came to be applied to the scheming, deceitful, and selfish actions of the élite. Thomas Nashe, playwright and writer for the popular press, characterised a 'politic' statesman as influenced by 'spirits of the air' who 'blear the worlds eyes with clouds of commonwealth pretences, to broach any enmity or ambitious humour of their own, under a title of their country's preservation', and 'make it fair or foul when they list to procure

---

[31] John North, *The Ambassadors' Secret: Holbein and the World of the Renaissance* (London, 2004), pp. 159–62, 299–305. North similarly interprets the case of flutes with one missing as a symbol of discord (p. 162). See also Mary Rasmussen, 'The Case of the Flutes in Holbein's *The Ambassadors*', *Early Music* 23 (1995), 115–23.

[32] Andrea Alciato, *Emblematum liber* (Augsburg, 1534), sig. A2v. 'Difficile est nisi docto homini tot tendere chordas,/ Unaque si fuerit non bene tenta fides./ Ruptave (quod facile est) perit omnis gratia conchae,/ Illeque praecellens cantus ineptus erit.' This particular emblem by Alciato was known to George Whitney, who used its picture in a manuscript collection of emblems he presented to Robert Dudley, Earl of Leicester, in 1585 (though with very different verses): see John Manning, 'Continental Emblem Books in Sixteenth-Century England: The Evidence of Sloane MS. 3794', *Emblematica* 1 (1986), 1–11; 'Geffrey Whitney's Unpublished Emblems: Further Evidence of Indebtedness to Continental Traditions', in *The English Emblem and the Continental Tradition*, ed. Peter Daly, AMS Studies in the Emblem 1 (New York, 1988), pp. 83–107; 'An Unedited and Unpublished Sixteenth-Century English Translation of Some Alciato Emblems: British Library Additional MS. 61822', *Emblematica* 7 (1993), 181–2.

[33] Maurizio Viroli, *From Politics to Reason of State: The Acquisition and Transformation of the Language of Politics, 1250–1600*, Ideas in Context 22 (Cambridge, 1992), p. 2. Machiavelli's *The Prince* circulated in England in manuscript translations and in an unauthorised Italian version printed by John Wolfe in 1584: Felix Raab, *The English Face of Machiavelli: A Changing Interpretation, 1500–1700*, Studies in Political History (London, 1964), pp. 52–3.

popularity'.[34] Elizabethan England lay poised on the transition from Aristotelian to Machiavellian notions of politics; both formed the framework within which Elizabethans conceived of music's functions in court politics.

In contrast to Elyot's emphasis on harmonious government, Castiglione's *The Courtier* advocated the politically manipulative uses of music at court. At their most virtuous, courtly arts might be used to influence a monarch to accept good counsel, as the character Lord Octavian suggests:

> In this wise may he lead him through the rough way of virtue (as it were) decking it about with bows to shadow it and strewing it over with sightly flowers, to ease the grief of the painful journey in him that is but of a weak force. And sometime with music … and with all those ways that these Lords have spoken of, continually keep that mind of his occupied in honest pleasure: imprinting notwithstanding therein always beside (as I have said) in company with these flickering provocations some virtuous condition, and beguiling him with a wholesome craft.[35]

Counsel was believed to be essential to good government, and monarchs had a moral obligation to seek advice. In their turn, counsellors had a duty to offer the monarch good counsel. For Elyot the giving of good counsel was his governor's primary aim.[36] The monarch was to receive such counsel graciously, but was not bound to follow it.[37] Octavian, however, portrayed his prince as morally weak, perhaps a tyrant, and one who must be beguiled by pleasurable pursuits and persuaded into virtuous governance by his courtiers. Court music was justified as a way of surreptitiously providing the prince with a moral education and encouraging him to govern virtuously. Just such a beguiling took place at Woodstock in 1575, where the chronicler of the entertainments suggests that delight in the excellent music of 'voice and instrument' bred in Elizabeth 'a great liking with a willing ear to the purport'.[38]

Though Lord Octavian couches his manœuvres in the language of virtue, his suggestion that they be applied to help 'purchase a man the favour of a prince' also had more self-interested connotations.[39] This potential for music to be a means of influence for personal gain was brought to the fore in Christopher Marlowe's play *Edward II* (1593). Piers Gaveston, a royal favourite, considers his plan to manipulate the King:

---

[34] Thomas Nashe, *The Terrors of the Night or, A Discourse of Apparitions* (London, 1594), sig. C2r.

[35] Count Baldassarre Castiglione, *The Courtier of Count Baldessar Castilio*, trans. Thomas Hoby (London, 1561), sig. Nn3r.

[36] Elyot, *The Governor*, fol. 254r.

[37] John Guy, 'The Rhetoric of Counsel in Early Modern England', in *Tudor Political Culture*, ed. Dale Hoak (Cambridge, 1995), pp. 292–310.

[38] *The Queen's Majesty's Entertainment at Woodstock* (London, 1585), sig. C2v.

[39] Castiglione, *The Courtier*, sig. Pp3v.

> I must have wanton poets, pleasant wits,
> Musicians that, with touching of a string,
> May draw the pliant king which way I please.
> Music and poetry is his delight ...[40]

Gaveston will rely both on the King's love of music and on music's affective powers to influence his moods and actions. Gaveston's image of the 'pliant king' is comparable to Arthur Throckmorton's belief in Elizabeth's 'easy softened mind', while the use of 'poetry' and the 'touching of a string' chimes with some Elizabethan courtiers' political use of lute songs, discussed in Chapter 2.[41] Unsurprisingly the majority who expressed their views publically in print advocated the use of music to benefit the monarch, though in practice more selfish motivations are often apparent.

For Elizabethans, then, music became political first as an audible harmony comparable to political concord; second as a sign of education, social status, and even virtue (if correctly used); and third as a means of persuasion. As such it was not only performances but also the ideas surrounding music that held political significance, as these could either fashion courtly identities or be manipulated to convey political views. Indeed, the two were often intimately connected: a courtier might employ music to create a particular persona for himself as a means to persuade the Queen of his worthiness of favour or reward.

Monarchs and courtiers alike applied these methods. The following chapters contain examples of music participating in the construction of courtly identities that were individual and communal, royal and aristocratic. These identities could be either the product of 'self-fashioning' – the conscious construction of a persona for one's own ends[42] – or representations created by others. In particular, music's associations with both masculinity and femininity assisted the Queen and her courtiers in negotiating the distinctive gender dynamic of a female-governed court and kingdom. Yet its flexibility was also its danger. Perceived as either virtue or vice, as a sign of education or foolishness, as heavenly or licentious, as promoting eloquence or causing effeminacy, musicality was a quality open to subversion, and to be evoked with caution (Chapters 1 and 4).

Musical persuasion, too, was a careful balancing act between getting one's message across and avoiding offence. Musical entertainments were an opportunity to have the ear of the Queen and were seen as an acceptable outlet for petition and criticism, tolerated by Elizabeth. Such songs encompassed the pursuit of

---

[40] Christopher Marlowe, *Edward II*, ed. Charles R. Forker (Manchester, 1994), p. 144 [act 1 scene 1, lines 50–3].

[41] Dennis Kay argues that *Edward II* invites its readers to find parallels with the Elizabethan court. Gaveston is presented as the quintessential Elizabeth courtier, while Edward was intended as a negative example in deliberate antithesis to Elizabeth: Dennis Kay, 'Marlowe, *Edward II*, and the Cult of Elizabeth', *Early Modern Literary Studies* 3.2 (1997), 1.1–30, online at <http://purl.oclc.org/emls/03-2/kaymarl.html> [accessed 19 July 2014]; Roberts, *Calendar of the Manuscripts ... at Hatfield*, vol. 5, p. 99.

[42] Stephen Greenblatt, *Renaissance Self-Fashioning: From More to Shakespeare* (Chicago, 1980).

personal advancement or royal favour, the offering of political advice on topical issues, and the presenting of petitions or complaints. Even the Queen herself used music for manipulative purposes as she sought to encourage or prolong diplomatic negotiations.

The difficulty in exploring this political music-making, however, is that only a handful of manuscripts linked to the Elizabethan court are extant, all preserving instrumental repertory.[43] Although numerous songs can be connected to the Queen or her courtiers (an extensive, though not necessarily exhaustive, list is provided in Appendix B), all survive in printed collections or manuscript copies that preserve the music at some remove from its initial context. As the specific meaning of a song relies heavily on the political circumstances and theatrical setting in which it was performed, so the original meanings of the first performances of these songs are obscured. For my purposes, it is also important to distinguish between songs written for direct political effect on a particular occasion, and those merely about a significant figure or reflecting upon court life.[44] Yet a picture of political music-making at the Elizabethan court can be formed by drawing together records of entertainments, surviving lyrics, and accounts of private music-making, with the small number of notated songs attributable to court occasions found in print or manuscript collections. The political significances surrounding specific performances and individual musical reputations can then be reconstructed in the light of both contemporary conceptions of music and topical issues at court.

Music had little role in the day-to-day administrative and governmental aspects of the court, but it nevertheless contributed to political life. I focus on the secular entertainments of the Elizabethan court, complementing previous discussion of the royal and diplomatic significance of the Chapel Royal's service music.[45] (Limitations of space require the making of such a separation, although in practice Elizabeth's

---

[43] GB-Lbl: Royal Appendix MSS 74–6 were connected with the violin consort in the 1550s–60s, and US-NH: Filmer 2 contains compositions by court musicians from c. 1600. The Stuart manuscript GB-Cfm: Mu. MS 734 also contains some wind consort repertory from Elizabeth's reign. The Mynshall Lute Book (GB-Lam: The Robert Spencer Collection, MS 601) has Elizabeth's royal arms on the cover but seems to have been a blank royal lute book which became the property of Richard Mynshall. The Winchester Partbooks (GB-WCc: MS 153) may have been commissioned as a gift for Elizabeth by Erik XIV of Sweden; however, the songs are all Continental pieces (with the exception of ten pieces added in the seventeenth century) not written specifically for the English court. Holman, *Four and Twenty Fiddlers*, pp. 90–9, 144–8; Matthew Spring, *The Lute in Britain: A History of the Instrument and its Music*, Early Music Series (Oxford, 2001), p. 129; Kristine K. Forney, 'A Gift of Madrigals and Chansons: The Winchester Partbooks and the Courtship of Elizabeth I by Erik XIV of Sweden', *The Journal of Musicology* 17 (1999), 50–75.

[44] For example the 'Bonny Boots' songs exemplify the practice of writing songs about a courtier, and John Mundy's 'Were I a King' reflects on political life (see below, Appendix B).

[45] Peter Le Huray, *Music and the Reformation in England 1549–1660*, Cambridge Studies in Music (Cambridge, 1978), pp. 33–4; Monson, 'Elizabethan London', pp. 305–10.

position as head of both the Church and the kingdom meant that religious issues were not confined to the ecclesiastical sphere, and nor was the Chapel Royal immune to political influence.) Moreover, while I will concentrate specifically on Elizabeth's court, this should not imply that hers was unique in its use of music. Courts across Europe employed musicians in their households and chapels, including loud and soft instruments for both public and private entertainments. The general pattern of court ritual for Elizabeth was similar to that enjoyed by other monarchs, with its tournaments, royal entries, plays with music, and both choreographed and informal dancing. Even attitudes to music shared many broad similarities, shaped by the cross-continental popularity of courtesy books such as Castiglione's *The Courtier* (translated into at least five different languages).[46] Yet each court was also individually characterised by a combination of the tastes of the particular monarch, changing political and religious circumstances, and localised customs or attitudes. In England one might point to elements such as Elizabeth's personal performances, her Protestantism, her preference for plays performed by choirboy companies, her regular royal progresses hosted by the nobility, her interaction with the crowds during royal entries, and the effects of a limited royal family (no husband, children or siblings) in restricting occasions for ceremonies such as marriages and births and focussing royal patronage in the hands of the Queen. As a ruler, Elizabeth's gender was unusual, too, though not unique (following her sister Mary I, and soon being joined by Mary Queen of Scots and Catherine de' Medici as regent of France). Overall, there remained a significant degree of shared culture among Europe's courtly élite, and so the approaches presented here are likely to offer avenues for comparative research at other Renaissance courts.

The following chapters trace the political use of music from intimate spaces to the most public occasions in court life. Accompanying this is a gradual shift in focus from music's political value for the Queen to its functions for the nobility, and finally for civic hosts and performers. The account begins in Chapter 1 with Elizabeth's royal image, considering the potential advantages and pitfalls of musicality for queens. Ultimately Elizabeth's musical image blended feminine sensuality with masculine rationality and governance as her personal talents became an outward sign of her political powers. Yet the harmonious persona could be all too easily subverted into discord by the discontented.

Peering into the intimate spaces of the court, Chapter 2 exposes the most private performances of Elizabeth and her closest courtiers. In these performances music's connotations of intimacy were engaged to fashion both diplomatic and courtly relationships, either influencing the course of negotiations or manipulating royal favour. Moving into the more open spaces of the royal palaces – those accessible to all Englishmen of sufficient social status as well as ambassadors and visiting foreign nobility – Chapter 3 considers the extent of Elizabeth's control over the musical institutions and revels of the royal household. From the personnel employed to the display of instruments, music portrayed the magnificence, prosperity, and cosmopolitanism of the court and, by extension, England. Yet Elizabeth allowed considerable latitude in the tone of the court's revels, which were not mere vehicles

---

[46] Burke, *Fortunes of the Courtier*, appendix 1.

for royal flattery, but also an outlet for moral and political debate. This sets the stage for the final chapters, in which the magnificence and image-making of the nobility begins to rival Elizabeth's own.

The last two chapters consider the most public occasions for courtly musical performance: tournaments (Chapter 4) and progresses (Chapter 5). The tournaments were usually performed at Whitehall, but were open to paying spectators as well as the court. The focus of these occasions was the competing knights and it was they who arranged the musical elements as part of their elaborate entries into the tiltyard. These were therefore ideal opportunities for the performance of noble masculinity. Noblemen drew not only on music's military associations, but also on its religious and pastoral connotations to demonstrate aspects of their characters or aspirations.

Elizabeth's progresses best illustrate how music could simultaneously encapsulate multiple political messages aimed at different kinds of audiences. These summer travels around parts of England brought her into contact with the widest spectrum of her subjects, though they did contain more exclusive entertainments too. As an honoured guest Elizabeth was to be entertained and flattered, so her hosts commissioned some of the most elaborate royal image-making of her reign. Yet noble hosts took the chance not only to seek royal favour, but also to enhance their status among their peers and to present their political petitions or complaints to Elizabeth. Civic authorities responded similarly, using their street pageants to promote the city and to comment on current issues. Even the musicians employed during these occasions might capitalise on having royal attention by making a bid for a court position. Simultaneously a tool of authority for the monarch and an instrument of persuasion and criticism for the political élite, music was a valuable means for both the tactful influencing of policies and patronage, and the construction of political identities and relationships.

CHAPTER 1

Music, Authority, and the Royal Image

NICHOLAS Hilliard's portrait of Queen Elizabeth I playing the lute presents an enigma (Figure 1.1).[1] As a portrait miniature it is highly unusual; whereas a miniature typically depicts just the head and shoulders, this portrait extends to the waist. Moreover, Elizabeth is not only sitting, but actively playing a lute, a rarity among portraiture of upper-class women. In the few exceptions (seventeenth-century portraits of Lady Mary Wroth, Lady Isabella Rich and Lady Anne Clifford) the instrument is held symbolically rather than played, as an emblem of sensibility or marriageability.[2] By contrast, the iconography of women playing lutes invited erotic interpretations, particularly on the Continent, as Venetian courtesans used the lute as the badge for their trade.[3] The European travels undertaken by young noblemen, the services undertaken abroad by Elizabeth's ambassadors, and the cosmopolitan nature of the Elizabethan court made such imagery familiar in English culture too. Such connotations of lust were hardly appropriate for an image of the Virgin Queen.

Yet Hilliard makes a conscious effort to distance Elizabeth from such negative associations. She is not pictured in one of the open-breasted dresses that were the fashion for young, unmarried women, although other paintings and descriptions by ambassadors and travellers suggest she wore these throughout her life, even in old age.[4] The high-necked dress – splendid and regal with its silver trim, but also dark, a colour associated with chastity and modesty – is designed to lessen such connotations. Moreover, the elaborate throne with crowned globes that forms the backdrop to the performance thrusts political resonances to the fore, suggesting that the lute functions symbolically, as in Holbein's *The Ambassadors* (see p. 9),

---

[1] This is an expanded and adapted version of an earlier article: Katherine Butler, '"By Instruments her Powers Appeare": Music and Authority in the Reign of Queen Elizabeth I', *Renaissance Quarterly* 65 (2012), 353–84 © 2012 by the Renaissance Society of America, Inc.

[2] Julia Craig-McFeely, 'The Signifying Serpent: Seduction by Cultural Stereotype in Seventeenth-Century England', in *Music, Sensation, and Sensuality*, ed. Linda Phyllis Austern, Critical and Cultural Musicology 5 (New York, 2002), pp. 299–317 (pp. 312–15).

[3] Ibid., pp. 300–1, 312; Carla Zecher, 'The Gendering of the Lute in Sixteenth-Century French Love Poetry', *Renaissance Quarterly* 53 (2000), 769–91 (pp. 772–4).

[4] In 1598 Paul Hentzner recorded how she had her 'breast uncovered, because it is a sign of virginity among English nobles; for married women are covered': Paul Hentzner, *Itinerarium Germaniae; Galliae; Angliae; Italiae* (Nuremberg, 1612), pp. 135–6: 'pectore erat nuda, quod virginitatis apud Anglos Nobiles signum est; nam maritatae sunt tectae.' Hentzner was tutor to a young Silesian nobleman with whom he toured Europe, visiting England in 1598.

Figure 1.1   Nicholas Hilliard, 'Elizabeth I Playing the Lute' (c. 1580), Berkeley Castle

representing political harmony or discord.⁵ While Holbein's lute was a symbolic object displayed on a shelf, in Hilliard's miniature it is a functioning musical instrument in the hands of an admired player. The imagined sensuous sound of music-making is not subdued: rather speculative and practical music, monarch and musician, are fused.

In combining the symbolic representation of political harmony with an evocation of her practical performances in life, Hilliard's miniature alludes to the blend of personal music-making and literary or artistic representations that formed the Queen's musical image. Little is known about Elizabeth's musical education and tutors, or any childhood performances; however, as Queen she played the virginals and the lute, she sang, danced, and on one occasion claimed to have composed dance music.⁶ She also played an instrument with 'strings of gold and silver' which may have been an orpharion, bandora, or cittern, or perhaps the poliphant, as described by the seventeenth-century music publisher John Playford.⁷ While a musical education was typical for women of royal and noble birth, Elizabeth's unusual position as a ruling queen allowed her music-making to gain political significance.⁸

Elizabeth projected her own musical image by using performances to manipulate political relationships and diplomatic negotiations (the subject of the next chapter); however, few people had the honour of hearing Elizabeth perform, so for the wider dissemination of her musical image she depended on the flattering conceits of courtiers, poets, musicians, and artists. This conceptualisation of Elizabeth's musicality by others is the focus of the current chapter. She was not in direct control of the majority of these representations (if she commissioned Hilliard's miniature this was an exceptional case); however, the desire of most creators of royal imagery to earn her favour in the hope of future rewards gave her

---

⁵ John North, *The Ambassadors' Secret: Holbein and the World of the Renaissance* (London, 2004), pp. 159–62, 299–305.

⁶ André Hurault de Maisse, *A Journal of All that was Accomplished by Monsieur de Maisse, Ambassador in England from King Henri IV to Queen Elizabeth Anno Domini 1597*, ed. Robert Arthur Jones and G. B. Harrison (London, 1931), p. 95; David Scott, 'Elizabeth I, Queen of England', *NG2*. Scott questions the evidence for Elizabeth playing the lute, but this is more extensive than he allows: see pp. 44 and 49.

⁷ William Brenchley Rye (ed.), *England as Seen by Foreigners in the Days of Elizabeth and James the First, Comprising Translations of the Journals of the Two Dukes of Wirtemberg in 1592 and 1610* (London, 1865), p. 12. Frederick Duke of Württemberg's travels were recorded by his private secretary: Jacob Rathgeb, *Warhaffte Beschreibung zweier Reisen* (Tübingen, 1603), fol. 15v: 'ihrem Instrument, welches Saiten dann von Gold und Silber sind.' John Playford, *An Introduction to the Skill of Music in Two Books* (London, 1674), sig. A7v.

⁸ For example: Janet Pollack, 'Princess Elizabeth Stuart as Musician and Muse', in *Musical Voices of Early Modern Women: Many Headed Melodies*, ed. Thomasin K. LaMay, Women and Gender in the Early Modern World (Aldershot, 2005), pp. 399–424; Linda Phyllis Austern, 'Women's Musical Voices in Sixteenth-Century England', *Early Modern Women: An Interdisciplinary Journal* 3 (2008), 127–52 (pp. 135–8, 141–6).

a powerful indirect influence. Once the musical conceit had been well received it gained momentum as a tried-and-tested theme for earning royal approval, imitated and developed by further artists and patrons. Nevertheless, Elizabeth's popularity and authority were not sufficient to prevent hints of discord and criticism from emerging on occasion.

Hilliard captured in miniature the blend of sensuality and authority that music brought to Elizabeth's royal image, though his attempt also exposes the problems of representing a woman as both musician and queen. Music's connotations of femininity and political harmony interacted with issues of gender and authority that underlay Elizabeth's reign. In the very year of her accession, 1558, John Knox had published his polemical *The First Blast of the Trumpet Against the Monstrous Regiment of Women*, claiming that 'Nature ... doth paint [women] forth to be weak, frail, impatient, feeble and foolish: and experience hath declared them to be inconstant, variable, cruel and lacking the spirit of counsel and regiment.'[9] Writing in Elizabeth's defence, John Aylmer did not deny Knox's representation, but merely distinguished between the female sex and womanish behaviour. He condemned women who were 'triflers, wavering, witless, without counsel, feeble, careless, rash, proud, dainty, nice, talebearers, eavesdroppers, rumour raisers, evil tongued, [and] worse minded'; but he admitted that there were women who were 'better learned, discreeter, constanter, then a number of men'.[10] In other words, one could be a woman in sex and yet masculine in one's qualities (or vice versa). He placed Elizabeth among the biblical heroines Deborah, Judith, and Esther as 'women in sex' but with no womanish 'feebleness of wit'.[11] More than forty years later, anxieties still remained about Elizabeth's gender, with Robert Cecil reflecting shortly after her death that she was 'more than a man, and (in troth) sometime less than a woman'.[12]

Elizabeth and her image-makers responded creatively to such gendered perceptions of her governance. According to Carole Levin, she was able to 'capitalise on the expectations of her behaviour as a woman and use them to her advantage', yet placed herself 'beyond gender expectations by calling herself King'.[13] Moreover, Louis Montrose identifies a tendency for representations of the Queen to politicise traditional images of womanhood while simultaneously eroticising the political sphere through the rhetoric of courtly love that characterised her relationships with

---

[9] John Knox, *The First Blast of the Trumpet Against the Monstrous Regiment of Women* (Geneva, 1558), p. 10.

[10] John Aylmer, *An Harborowe for Faithful and True Subjects Against the Late Blown Blast, Concerning the Government of Women* (London, 1559), sig. G3v.

[11] Ibid.

[12] Sir John Harington, *Nugae Antiquae: Being a Miscellaneous Collection of Original Papers, in Prose and Verse; Written during the Reigns of Henry VIII, Edward VI, Queen Mary, Elizabeth, and King James*, ed. Henry Harington and Thomas Park, 2 vols. (London, 1804), vol. 1, p. 345 [26th May 1603].

[13] Carole Levin, *The Heart and Stomach of a King: Elizabeth I and the Politics of Sex and Power* (Philadelphia, 1994), p. 1.

her courtiers.[14] Enabled by music's capacity to evoke both feminine and masculine qualities, Elizabeth's musical image similarly spanned the domestic and political spheres and both exploited and subverted gender stereotypes. On the one hand, music was considered sensual, feminine, and frivolous. It was associated with the attractiveness and marriageability of young women and charged with making young men effeminate. Conversely, music could evoke masculine attributes of rationality and order through its traditional basis as a mathematical art and the belief that musical harmony governed the heavens, the political world, and the human soul. If the positive attributes of music's sensuality and rationality were combined, music could therefore act as a symbolic means to reconcile Elizabeth's female gender with her masculine position of political authority. Over the next two chapters I suggest that, rather than escaping gender expectations, music allowed Elizabeth to fuse them, simultaneously exploiting music's traditional femininity to shape her relationships with courtiers and ambassadors, yet also appropriating its connotations of power and harmony as a symbol of authority.

SENSUALITY AND RATIONALITY

DESPITE the fundamental association of sensuality with femininity and rationality with masculinity, in practice these connotations existed on a continuum. For both genders music-making combined elements of both these qualities, and the virtue of an individual's musicality depended on holding both elements in careful balance, as well as using music in moderation. Nor was sensuality versus rationality merely a shorthand for vice versus virtue.

Although the sensuality of music provoked the greatest anxieties, if positively channelled it could also inspire effects of the highest virtue and admiration. The flexibility of music's connotations, widened further still by Elizabeth's position as both woman and monarch, offered plenty of inspiration for her image-makers; yet the potential for others to interpret her musicality in less flattering ways also set constraints.

Music was one of the talents expected of well-educated and broadly accomplished young women of royal or noble birth. These women were to become the eloquent, attractive centrepieces of Renaissance courts, with a duty to charm and entertain foreign visitors. The Headmaster of the Merchant Taylors' School, Richard Mulcaster, argued in a work dedicated to Elizabeth that princesses needed the talents of 'reading well, writing fair, singing sweet, playing fine' in order to 'honour themselves, and to discharge the duty, which the countries committed to their hands, do daily call for, and besides what match is more honourable, than when desert for rare qualities, doth join itself, with highness in degree?'[15] One of these duties, described by Lord Julian in Castiglione's *The Courtier*, was to

---

[14] Louis Montrose, '"Shaping Fantasies": Figurations of Gender and Power in Elizabethan Culture', *Representations* 2 (1983), 61–94.

[15] Richard Mulcaster, *Positions wherin those Primitive Circumstances be Examined, which are Necessary for the Training Up of Children* (London, 1581), pp. 180–1.

'entertain accordingly both with jests and feat conceits meet for her, every person that commeth in her company'.[16] Singing or playing on the lute and virginals could provide such entertainment.

In addition to such innocent charm and entertainment, music also assisted a woman in attracting a suitable husband. According to Mulcaster, 'young maidens being well trained are very soon commended to right honourable matches, whom they may well beseem, and answer much better, their qualities in state having good correspondence, with their matches of state … for the procuring of their common good.'[17] Although Mulcaster justified the advantages of music for young women using the gender-neutral notion of 'common good', it was not only music's status as a social accomplishment which made it useful in attracting a husband, but also its sensual connotations. Analysing music's role in causing love melancholy, the academic Robert Burton noted that music was 'the way their parents think to get them husbands', because ''tis a great allurement as it is often used, and many are undone by it'. Music was a tool of courtship through which a young woman might make herself desirable to a young gentleman, because 'to hear a fair young gentlewoman to play upon the virginals, lute, viol, and sing to it, must needs be a great enticement.'[18]

This sensual relationship of music with beauty and feminine attractiveness was captured in the courtier Sir John Harington's epigram 'In Praise of a Lady and Her Music':

> Upon an instrument of pleasing sound
> A lady played more pleasing to the sight.
> Being asked in which of these I found
> Greatest content, my senses to delight?
> Ravished in both at once, as much as may be,
> Said, sweet was music, sweeter was the lady.[19]

The poem offers a stereotypical situation where a man is captivated by an attractive woman's eloquent and beautiful music. Music facilitates an intimate bond between the lady and the male listener. Within the sphere of respectful courtly love the sensuality of music was admired, and at its most positive the love inspired by the music of women might even be likened to that of angel musicians, stirring the listener to thoughts of heaven.[20]

---

[16] Count Baldassarre Castiglione, *The Courtier of Count Baldessar Castilio*, trans. Thomas Hoby (London, 1561), sig. Cc2r.

[17] Mulcaster, *Positions*, p. 180.

[18] Robert Burton, *The Anatomy of Melancholy, what it is with All the Kinds, Causes, Symptoms, Prognostics, and Several Cures of it* (London, 1621), pp. 580, 586.

[19] Sir John Harington, *The Most Elegant and Witty Epigrams of Sir John Harington* (London, 1618), sig. K1v. Elsewhere said to be written about Lady Penelope Rich: see Sir John Harington, *The Epigrams of Sir John Harington*, ed. Gerard Kilroy (Farnham, 2009), p. 215.

[20] Elena Calogero, '"Sweet Aluring Harmony": Heavenly and Earthly Sirens in Sixteenth-Century Literary and Visual Culture', in *Music of the Sirens*, ed. Linda Phyllis Austern and Inna Naroditskaya (Bloomington, IN, 2006), pp. 140–75

Yet female musicians were also frequently accused of inciting lust, and were compared with courtesans and the Homeric Sirens in their threat to male self-control.[21] Such a paradoxical attitude arose from the close association of women's music with sensuality. Music's appeal to the senses caused concern over its ability to bypass reason and inflame bodily desires, but it could equally be said to appeal beyond human wisdom as a foretaste of divine harmony. Such contradictory notions were representative of debates over music's position as virtue or vice that had raged since classical antiquity, and controversy over the use of polyphony in churches (as opposed to plainchant) in 1470s had set many of the terms for sixteenth-century debates over music's sensuality or rationality, moderation or excess, and sinfulness or virtue.[22] Accusations of vice were made towards both genders, but it was female performers who were most readily assumed to be lustful and licentious, and for whom accusations of a lack of chastity were most dishonourable.

A particular fear was that the sensuality of women's music could undermine male rationality and authority. In Harington's epigram above, the delight in a lady's music is non-threatening, reinforcing rather than destabilising the gender hierarchy. Although 'ravished', the male listener maintains his wits and position of power, acting as judge and observer of the sweetness of the music and the lady. By contrast, the Sirens were frequently used as a warning of the dangerous power of women's music, as in Thomas Salter's advisory book on the bringing up of daughters, *The Mirror of Modesty* (1579):[23]

> from the false sweetness of the Sirens' songs, Ulysses, a prince famous among the Greeks, and said to be nourished with heavenly food in the very bosom of Sapience, Jupiter's daughter, could hardly escape, and shall we then without fear, give so much trust to a young maiden, daintily and tenderly trained up, that she not only by hearing, but by learning so wanton an art, will not become wanton and effeminate.[24]

Not only is the hearing and learning of music detrimental to the young woman, but her music, like that of the Sirens, will be hazardous for the young men who hear her. The reference to Ulysses as fed by 'Sapience, Jupiter's daughter' (who was Athena,

---

(pp. 140–6); Linda Phyllis Austern, '"Sing Againe Syren": The Female Musician and Sexual Enchantment in Elizabethan Life and Literature', *Renaissance Quarterly* 42 (1989), 420–48 (pp. 421–3).

[21] Calogero, 'Sweet Aluring Harmony', pp. 140–1; Austern, 'Sing Againe Syren', pp. 424, 427, 431–4; Zecher, 'Gendering of the Lute', pp. 772–4.

[22] Rob C. Wegman, *The Crisis of Music in Early Modern Europe, 1470–1530* (London, 2005), p. 179.

[23] See Calogero, 'Sweet Aluring Harmony'.

[24] Thomas Salter, *A Mirror Meet for All Mothers, Matrons, and Maidens, Entitled the Mirror of Modesty* (London, 1579), sig. C7r. This was an adaptation of Giovanni Michele Bruto's *La institutione di una fanciulla nata nobilmente* (Antwep, 1555), of which a proper translation was made in 1598. See Janis Butler Holm, 'Thomas Salter's *The Mirrhor of Modestie*: A Translation of Bruto's *La institutione di vna fanciulla nata nobilmente*', *The Library* s6–5 (1983), 53–7.

goddess of wisdom) implies that it is masculine intelligence and rationality which is threatened.[25]

Concerns were also raised about the effect of music on the virtue of women – whether as performers or listeners – and these informed the musical education received by both Elizabeth and her sister Mary. Juan Luis Vives's *The Instruction of a Christian Woman* was written for the education of Mary at the request of her mother, Catherine of Aragon, and later used for Elizabeth.[26] Vives objected both to the frivolity and the sensuality of music. He did not want a woman to be 'idle as were the women of Perseland, drowned in voluptuousness and pleasures, sitting among the company of gelded men, singing and banqueting continually'.[27] Here music is represented as part of the orientalised Other of Persia, where sensual pleasures such as music and indulgent feasting corrupted young women and emasculated young men. Furthermore, Vives believed that 'the mind, set upon learning and wisdom … shall leave all such light and trifling pleasures, wherein the light fantasies of maids have delight, as songs, dances, and such other wanton and peevish plays.'[28] The problem with Vives's advice was that these were just the kind of activities which did take place at court. Elizabeth's would be no exception, with plays, banquets, masques, and tournaments celebrating events like Christmas, Shrovetide, Accession Day, or her progresses. To Vives enjoyment of such activities signalled a lack of seriousness and intelligence, and threatened the virtue of a queen.

While men were not immune, for Vives it was women's minds that were most likely to be 'enticed and snared' by these sensuous pleasures of 'the kingdom of Venus and Cupid'.[29] Castiglione's character Count Lewis concurred, explaining that a woman's 'tender and soft breasts are soon pierced with melody and filled with sweetness'.[30] Yet in contrast to Vives's criticism of women's susceptibility, in *The Courtier* this enabled women's role as the inspiration for male music-making; Lord Cesar asks, 'Who learneth to dance featly for other, but to please women? Who applieth the sweetness of music for other cause, but for this?'[31] With even sensitivity to music characterised contrastingly as either evidence of licentiousness

---

[25] This tale was frequently used as a moral exemplar for shutting out not only sensuous music but all the sinful temptations of life, particularly through a popular variant of Homer's narrative in which Odysseus stopped his own ears as well as those of his crew. See Harry Vredeveld, '"Deaf as Ulysses to the Siren's Song": The Story of a Forgotten Topos', *Renaissance Quarterly* 54 (2001), 846–82.

[26] Charles Fantazzi, 'Vives, Juan Luis (1492/3–1540)', *ODNB* (online edn, 2008); Juan Luis Vives, *A Very Fruitful and Pleasant Book, Called the Instruction of a Christian Woman*, trans. Richard Hyrde, 7th edn (London, 1585). It was first published in 1524, and translated into English in 1529, with numerous subsequent editions published right up until 1592.

[27] Vives, *Instruction of a Christian Woman*, p. 10.

[28] Ibid., p. 27.

[29] Ibid., p. 137.

[30] Castiglione, *The Courtier*, sig. I2r.

[31] Ibid., sig. Iiiv.

or of a lady's role as Muse, the instability of the connotations of musicality for women as performers or listeners is clear.

Yet despite the colourful admonitions of authors like Salter and Vives, the perceived dangers of music could be mitigated through conventions of modesty and moderation. The majority of courtiers would not go as far as Vives in arguing that women should avoid all enjoyment of music. Even Salter, despite his anxieties about educating women in music, admitted its necessity for those who 'overworn with grief, sorrow, trouble, cares, or other vexation have need of recreation', or those who 'have not wherewith better to employ or pass out their idle time', though he thought it preferable for women to be listeners rather than performers.[32] Moderate use of music for personal recreation was acceptable. Furthermore, for female performers, Castiglione's Lord Julian advised that a gentlewoman should play only in private gatherings, being 'brought to it with suffering herself somewhat to be prayed and with a certain bashfulness, that may declare ... noble shamefastness', and avoiding 'those hard and often divisions that declare more cunning then sweetness'.[33] Displays of virtuosity indicated a lack of modesty and excessive time spent in practice. Such moderation was equally applicable to monarchs. In a commonly cited story, Philip of Macedon reproved his son Alexander (the Great) that 'he had profited too much in music, and was therein become too excellent, and that to other it might seem meet to be a musician, and not to a prince'; this served as a warning to monarchs lest musicality obscure their image as serious governors.[34] Perhaps for this reason, John Clapham described Elizabeth as, 'in matters of recreation, as singing, dancing and playing upon instruments ... not ignorant nor excellent: a measure which in things indifferent best beseemeth a prince.'[35]

Furthermore, even at their most powerful and subversive, the particularly potent powers attributed to women's music were not necessarily viewed negatively but could rather be regarded as evidence of the exceptionality of women. The same myth of the Sirens cited by Salter was retold as a positive example of female musical talent in *A Woman's Worth, Defended Against All the Men in the World* (1599). Here the Sirens 'had songs so wonderful sweet and melodious: as they could out ear the winds, and rob all mouths of their natural offices', while 'the Greeks returning from the wars of Troy, rested themselves a long while in those Isles ... little caring for return home to their own country, by being rapt, or rather charmed by such an harmonious delight'.[36] In this retelling of the Sirens' story, music gives women the

---

[32] Salter, *The Mirror of Modesty*, sigs. C6v, C8r.

[33] Castiglione, *The Courtier*, sig. Cc1v. 'Divisions' refers to a type of ornamentation where the melody is divided into notes of smaller values.

[34] Salter, *The Mirror of Modesty*, sig. C8r. Also cited by Sir Thomas Elyot, *The Book Named the Governor* (London, 1531), fol. 23v.

[35] John Clapham, *Elizabeth of England: Certain Observations Concerning the Life and Reign of Queen Elizabeth by John Clapham*, ed. Evelyn Plummer Read and Conyers Read (Philadelphia, 1951), p. 89.

[36] Alexandre de Pontaymeri, *A Woman's Worth, Defended Against All the Men in the World Proving them to be More Perfect, Excellent, and Absolute in All Virtuous Actions, than Any Man of what Quality Soever* (London, 1599), fols. 24r, 26v. This

power to control not only men, but also mythological heroes and even the winds. Furthermore, the traditional gender hierarchy was inverted by acknowledging music as a skill in which 'the glory which women have gotten thereby [is] over-far beyond men'. This manipulation of mythological stories to create divergent representations of musical women illustrates the flexibility of music's gendered connotations. Moreover, such positive images of female power might be usefully appropriated by a ruling queen.

Sensuality, however, was only one aspect of how music's power and social functions were perceived. The sensuality of music derived from its ability to move the passions, but music was also understood as a mathematical art associated with order, logic, and universal harmony. Moreover, music's status as a respected social accomplishment depended not just on performance ability, but also on good musical judgement.

For this reason a princess's musical education was intended not just to enable her to perform, but also to give her the knowledge to judge the performances of others and to prepare her to be a patron of musicians. Dietrich Helms has argued that 'Henry VIII's Book' – a selection of well-known Continental songs, pieces from court festivals, and compositions by Henry VIII – was compiled to instruct the royal children in forms of secular music.[37] By getting acquainted with such models they would gain what Castiglione termed the 'knowledge to praise and make of Gentlemen more and less according to their deserts' in the context of a musical performance.[38] Isabella d'Este, Marchioness of Mantua (1474–1539), exemplifies the high reputation courtly women might earn through their musical talent and patronage, and was perhaps a model for Castiglione's ideas on the conduct of gentlewomen. As well as being renowned as a performer, she was also a sophisticated patron, responsible for setting the direction of musical culture at the Mantuan court and aiding in the development of a new genre of song, the frottola.[39] Through her exceptional musicality she earned herself a fame usually only achievable by men. Musical taste was just as necessary for a ruler's respectability. Sir Thomas Elyot recommended that governors should be able to hear 'the contention of noble musicians' and 'give judgement in the excellency of their cunnings'.[40]

Elizabethan beliefs in speculative harmony meant that musicality was also perceived as an outward manifestation of virtue and the harmony of one's soul. Lucy Russell, Countess of Bedford (1581–1627), was praised by John Dowland for her 'well tuned … mind' when he dedicated to her his *Second Book of Songs or Ayres* (1600). Dowland's praise was founded both on her reputation as an important,

---

was an English translation of *Paradoxe apologétique, où il est fidellement démonstré que la femme est beaucoup plus parfaite que l'homme en toute action de vertu* (1594).

[37] Dietrich Helms, 'Henry VIII's Book: Teaching Music to Royal Children', *Musical Quarterly* 92 (2009), 118–35. Henry VIII's Book is GB-Lbl: Add MS 31922.

[38] Castiglione, *The Courtier*, sig. Cc1v.

[39] William Prizer, 'Una "virtù molto conveniente a Madonna": Isabella d'Este as a Musician', *The Journal of Musicology* 17 (1999), 10–49 (pp. 10–12).

[40] Elyot, *The Governor*, fol. 23v. See also the condemnation of the musically ignorant King in John Lyly's *Midas* (pp. 101–2)

intelligent, and musically talented noblewoman, and on her role as a patroness to musicians, dramatists, and translators including Michael Drayton, John Florio, Samuel Daniel, John Donne, and Ben Jonson, as well as Dowland himself.[41] Yet the notion of Lucy's well-tuned mind, founded on the notion *musica humana*, evoked not only her intelligence and artistic judgement, but also her piety and virtue. The dedicatory poem (an acrostic) explicitly praises the 'flowering treasure' of her 'spirit' which:

> **D** oth sweetest harmony express,
> **F** illing all ears and hearts with pleasure
> **O** n earth, observing heavenly measure.[42]

Not only Lucy's mind, but also her soul is harmonious, and this harmony is divine. The sweetness of her music and the pleasure it gives to 'ears and hearts' evoke a sensual realm, yet in stark contrast to Vives and Salter, for whom enjoyment of practical music's sensual pleasures signified a lustful and frivolous character, Lucy's musicality inspires spiritual devotion and implies her virtue. This was the challenge for musical women – pinning down music's significations in light of underlying disagreements over whether music was virtue or vice – and it could be achieved through balancing the connotations of rationality and sensuality, and a reputation as a performer with one as a discerning patroness.

As Elizabeth's posthumous reputation has become so positive, it is easy to assume that all aspects of her royal image were assured of such an interpretation by her contemporaries. Surely Elizabeth would always be portrayed like Lucy, Countess of Bedford, and not as the idle, lascivious woman of Vives and Salter? Yet Elizabeth's performances to male ambassadors or guests and the festivities of her court all provided potential opportunities not only for her womanly virtue to be criticised, but also her seriousness as a ruler. Now the flexibility of the imagery surrounding musical women became its central problem, as it allowed music to evoke less flattering interpretations just as easily as positive ones. Similar difficulties surrounded Elizabeth's visual image: while portraiture intended to display her glory and power, Nanette Salomon shows how her elaborate clothing, jewellery, and hairstyles played into the hands of the discourse of Vanity, a vice particularly associated with women.[43] Nor did this go unremarked at the time: John Foxe's praise of the young Elizabeth for taking 'so little delight in glistering gazes of the world, in gay apparel, rich attire, and precious jewels' was a backhanded criticism of the style of opulent display Elizabeth had adopted by the time Foxe was writing in 1563.[44]

---

[41] Helen Payne, 'Russell, Lucy, Countess of Bedford (bap. 1581, d. 1627)', *ODNB* (online edn, 2008).

[42] John Dowland, *The Second Book of Songs or Ayres, of 2, 4 and 5 Parts with Tablature for the Lute or Orpharion, with the Viola de Gamba* (London, 1600), sig. A3v.

[43] Nanette Salomon, 'Positioning Women in Visual Convention: The Case of Elizabeth I', in *Attending to Women in Early Modern England*, ed. Betty Travitsky and Adele F. Seeff (Newark, DE, 1994), pp. 64–95 (pp. 71–5).

[44] John Foxe, *Acts and Monuments of these Latter and Perilous Days* (London, 1563), p. 1710.

No direct condemnation of Elizabeth's musicality by her contemporaries survives; yet the potential for criticism and dire consequences are clear from the low reputations of other musical queens. Elizabeth's own mother, Anne Boleyn, was accused of having an affair with the musician Mark Smeaton. He pleaded guilty to 'violation and carnal knowledge of the Queen' and was executed in 1536 along with several courtiers and Anne herself.[45] Investigations surrounding the infidelity of another of Henry VIII's wives, Katherine Howard, collected an account of her premarital misconduct with her music tutor, Henry Monoxe, including details of the exchanging of love tokens, unchaperoned meetings, and Monoxe's claim that Katherine had promised him her maidenhead.[46] The sexually charged dynamic between artistically accomplished, unmarried, male tutor and young, female pupil in the intimate music room (often close to the bedchamber), the physical nature of the skill being taught, and the learning of fashionable love songs all made the music lesson fraught with social risk.[47] In Scotland, the court criticised the close relationship of Elizabeth's cousin Mary Queen of Scots with the singer David Rizzio, who later became Mary's Secretary for French Affairs. In his historical memoirs John Maxwell, Lord Herries, wrote of the rumours which were spread around the court: 'Tales were sometimes minced out, as though David Rizzio was many times too intimate with the Queen, more than was fitting', and, 'it was openly said that she took more pleasure in his company than in the King's, her husband's; that she made him sit at her table with her, and [he] had free access to her bedchamber, at all hours.' Lord Herries was sceptical of the truth of these claims, but they were nevertheless 'cried out with open mouth, to defame her and incense her husband'.[48] Such criticism was largely the result of the nobility's jealousy over the power given to a foreigner and someone of such low birth, but ultimately it led to Rizzio's murder by Mary's husband Lord Darnley and members of her nobility.

A queen's association with musicians could so easily become a symbol of her immorality and unfaithfulness once her reputation became tarnished, or even if

---

[45] *L&P Henry VIII*, vol. 10, pp. 351–2 ['Trial of Weston, Norris and Others', 12 May 1536]. The courtiers were Sir Henry Norris, Sir William Bryerton, and Sir Francis Weston.

[46] William Fitzwilliam, Earl of Southampton, 'About Katharine Howard: 5 November 1541', GB-Lna: SP1/167, State Papers Henry VIII: General Series, fols. 110r–113r, 117r–120v.

[47] Katie Nelson, 'Love in the Music Room: Thomas Whythorne and the Private Affairs of Tudor Music Tutors', *Early Music* 40 (2012), 15–26; Christopher Marsh, *Music and Society in Early Modern England* (Cambridge, 2010), pp. 199–203. The autobiography of the music tutor Thomas Whythorne reveals several occasions on which he was subject to amorous advances from his students or the mistress of the house, and in his own courtships he writes and performs songs to charm his lady: Thomas Whythorne, *The Autobiography of Thomas Whythorne*, ed. James Marshall Osborn (Oxford, 1961), pp. 30–2, 38–60, 76–9, 93–113.

[48] John Maxwell, Lord Herries, *Historical Memoirs of the Reign of Mary Queen of Scots, and a Portion of the Reign of King James the Sixth*, ed. Robert Pitcairn (Edinburgh, 1836), pp. 69, 75. These survive in a mid-seventeenth-century abridgement of an original manuscript.

she had simply become unpopular. Once the damage to a queen's reputation was done it did not matter that it was normal for a queen to have musicians (particularly singers and keyboard-players) among her Privy Chamber staff to give private performances for her entertainment and to offer musical tuition to members of the royal family. The intimate and private settings of performances by Privy Chamber musicians provided the opportunity for rumours to be spread, and the association of music with lust, wantonness, and prostitutes made such accusations all the more plausible for a musical or music-loving lady.

Elizabeth never became unpopular enough for her musicality to become a source of scandal, but when considered alongside contemporary slanderous rumours of her having had a child with Robert Dudley, the potential for a very different image of an immoral and licentious queen is evident.[49] Nor was Elizabeth entirely immune to criticisms of her love of music and dancing. In 1563 Francis Challoner condemned it as part of the court's inactivity (writing this critical comment to his brother – English ambassador to Spain – in Latin in a letter otherwise in English):

> The Queen is entirely given over to love, hunting, hawking, and dancing; consuming day and night with trifles; nothing is treated earnestly; and though all things go wrong they jest, and he who invents most ways of wasting time is regarded as one worthy of honour.[50]

A musical reputation could act to reinforce stereotypes of weak, foolish, and frivolous womankind, rather than establishing Elizabeth's image as a wise and capable monarch. Disapproval was similarly implied by Lodowick Lloyd, one of Elizabeth's sergeants-at-arms. In *The Pilgrimage of Princes* (1573) he argued that whereas in ancient times 'Mars claimed music in the field', now 'Venus occupies music in chambers' with 'that kind of gentle and soft music the Egyptians forbad the youth to be taught therein, lest from men they would become again women'.[51] As a soldier, Lloyd's disapproval of effeminate music was intended as an indirect criticism of the atmosphere in Elizabeth's court, where he worked. This was necessarily less warlike because, as a woman, Elizabeth could not participate directly in military affairs. For Lloyd feminine musicality was a sign of the impotence and frivolity of a queen's court.

Both these criticisms of the jollity or sensuality of Elizabeth's court belong to the first fifteen years of her reign. They reflect the scepticism of courtiers and

---

[49] Adam Fox, *Oral and Literate Culture in England, 1500–1700*, Oxford Studies in Social History (Oxford, 2000), p. 362.

[50] Francis Challoner, 'Letter to Sir Thomas Challoner: 18 December 1563', GB-Lna: SP70/66, Secretaries of State: State Papers Foreign, Elizabeth I, fol. 94v: 'Regina tota amoribus dedita est venationis aucupiis choreis et rebus ludicris insumus dies noctesque, nihil serio tractatur, quanque omnia adverse cedant tamen iocamur hic perinde ac si orbem universum debellati fuerimus et qui plures vere nugandi modos ridiculo studio excogitaverit (quasi vir summio premio dignus) suspicitum.' Translated in Joseph Stevenson et al. (eds.), *Calendar of State Papers, Foreign Series, of the Reign of Elizabeth*, 23 vols. (London, 1863–1950), vol. 6, pp. 623–5 (p. 624).

[51] Lodowick Lloyd, *The Pilgrimage of Princes* (London, 1573), fol. 115r.

ambassadors concerning a woman's suitability to rule more than any real flaw in Elizabeth's style of court. Yet the volatile meanings associated with musical women explain why Elizabeth, her courtiers, and her poets sought to control her musical image, ensuring it worked to her favour rather than her detriment. One strategy was to emphasise music's connotations of rationality and harmony, like those applied to the Countess of Bedford; another approach was provided by Elizabeth's position as a monarch, through the affinity between musical ability and political skill. The process of government was frequently characterised in musical terms (pp. 8–9), as by the Duke of Exeter in William Shakespeare's *Henry V*:

> For government though high or low, being put into parts,
> Congrueth with a mutual consent like music [52]

Political authority stemmed from an ability to maintain the harmony of the different social orders to create a concordant kingdom. As Sir Thomas Elyot had specifically recommended a musical education for his governor to better understand the workings of social harmony (p. 8), musicality could be regarded as an outward manifestation of knowledge and ability in governance. These connotations of music proved particularly useful to Elizabeth's monarchical image, and distinguished her musical identity from those of other women.

While to modern sensibilities sixteenth-century attitudes to music are frustratingly contradictory, to Elizabethan writers and image-makers this was instead a catalyst for creativity. The result was a union of contrarieties, a *concordia discors*, in which the fusion of opposites – sensuality and rationality, femininity and masculine authority – created a musical image of queenship that held its opposites in perfect balance and transcended the limitations of either. This paradigm, favoured by Renaissance writers, was the same principle that underlay the ideal of harmonious governance itself – the union of diverse people and estates in order to create the unity of a kingdom.[53] Elizabeth's image-makers – courtiers, poets, and musicians – simultaneously emphasised her charm and sensual powers as a musical woman while attributing to her the political authority, constancy, and rationality conventionally granted only to men. In doing so they forged an image of effective, harmonious queenship from the chaos of potential connotations surrounding her musicality.

---

[52] William Shakespeare, *The Chronicle History of Henry the Fifth with his Battle Fought at Agincourt in France* (London, 1602), sig. A3v.

[53] See for example: Edgar Wind, *Pagan Mysteries in the Renaissance*, new edn (London, 1968), pp. 76–8, 85–9, 97; Jean-Claude Margolin, 'Sur un paradoxe bien tempéré de la Renaissance: Concordia discors', in *Concordia discors: Studi su Niccolò Cusano e l'umanesimo europeo offerti a Giovanni Santinello*, ed. Giovanni Santinello and Gregorio Piaia, Medioevo e umanesimo 84 (Padova, 1993), pp. 405–32.

MUSICAL IMAGES OF POLITICAL AUTHORITY

ELIZABETH'S court musicians were among the first to turn Elizabeth's musicality into an inspiration for royal panegyric. In the dedication to their *Cantiones sacrae* (1575), Byrd and Tallis claimed that the Queen 'symbolise[d] practical skill' and praised 'the refinement of [her] voice' and 'the nimbleness of [her] fingers'.[54] Emphasising practical talents and bodily qualities was a typical way to praise the feminine attractiveness of musical women; however, Tallis and Byrd also credited Elizabeth with musical judgement, claiming that she was a fitting dedicatee because her practical skill made her able to appraise their work. Musical judgement was more highly esteemed than practical skill. According to Boethius's *De institutione musica*, it is not performers or composers reliant on physical skill and natural instinct who will 'rightly be esteemed as musical', but rather those with the ability to judge music, because they are 'totally grounded in reason and thought'. Consequently 'that person is a musician who exhibits the faculty of forming judgments'.[55] Tallis and Byrd therefore associated Elizabeth with the highest form of musicianship, where music is no longer merely sensual but allied with reason. Elsewhere Elizabeth's image as patroness and inspiration for music-making was evoked by comparing her to the Muses (pp. 1–2).

Elizabeth's abilities as performer and patroness increasingly became external signs of her personal character and virtues. John Bennet's 'Eliza, Her Name Gives Honour' (a consort song) was most likely performed during a court entertainment during the 1590s. Its lyrics attributed Elizabeth's ability to judge the singer's earthly music to her capacity to hear heavenly harmonies inaudible to ordinary ears, and ended with the conceit that earthly music was not good enough for her:

> I sing adoring,
> Humbly imploring
> That my rude voice may please her sacred ears,
> Whose skill deserves the music of the spheres.[56]

The audible harmony of the singer and his consort was paralleled with the inaudible music of the celestial spheres. The implication that Elizabeth's 'sacred ears' could hear such usually inaudible music imbued her with pious or even divine qualities (perhaps subtly evoking the divine right of kings).

Focussing on her intelligence, Sir John Davies compared Elizabeth's mind to both earthly instruments and heavenly spheres in his poem 'Of the Organs of her Mind' (an acrostic on Elizabeth's name) from his *Hymns of Astraea* (1599), a collection published in her honour:

---

[54] William Byrd, *Cantiones sacrae (1575)*, ed. Craig Monson, Byrd Edition 1 (London, 1977), pp. xvii, xxv: 'qua ... es peritia', and, 'vel vocis elegantia, vel digitorum agilitate facile'.

[55] Boethius, *Fundamentals of Music*, trans. Calvin M. Bower, ed. Claude V. Palisca, Music Theory Translation Series (New Haven, CT, 1989), p. 51.

[56] John Bennet, 'Eliza, Her Name Gives Honour', GB-Lbl: Add. MSS 17786–91, fol. 9 (17790, fols. 5–6). For a modern edition see Philip Brett (ed.), *Consort Songs*, 2nd rev. edn, Musica Britannica 22 (London, 1974), p. 76.

B y instruments her powers appear
E xceedingly well tun'd and clear:
T his lute is still in measure,
H olds still in tune, even like a sphere,
A nd yields the world sweet pleasure.[57]

Combining practical and speculative music, lutes and instruments evoke Elizabeth's own lute-playing and the ensembles of her court musicians, while simultaneously symbolising her well-tuned mind. Although 'her powers' refers to those of Elizabeth's mind, the choice of word recalls the authority which this particular mind held as a queen. The repeated word 'still' stresses constancy, a quality which women were typically accused of lacking.[58] In granting this virtue to Elizabeth, Davies mirrors her own motto, *semper eadem* (always the same). Although, like Byrd and Tallis, Davies was concerned with portraying Elizabeth's intellectual virtues above her feminine attractiveness, the description of these as bringing 'sweet pleasure' nevertheless continues to evoke conventional portrayals of the sensual delights of women's musical performances. Praise of Elizabeth's practical musicality emphasised her virtues as a woman, not as a queen; while it made her a model of femininity, eloquence, and charm, it also made her conform to female stereotypes.

So far, Elizabeth's image is not unique. Similar imagery was lavished on other intelligent and musically talented noblewomen. Yet whereas for other women this praise extended only to their personal virtues, Elizabeth's musicality became an image of power, presenting her as an exceptional woman, divinely appointed, and with God-given abilities to rise above the weakness traditionally associated with her gender. In musical terms, this was made possible via an expansion of the metaphors used when describing Elizabeth's musicality. Elizabeth was presented not only as a musician, patroness, and pious woman, but also as the bringer of heavenly harmony to earth, and the controller of political concord.

The earliest portrayal of Elizabeth as bringer of harmony employed classical mythology rather than the idea of the music of the spheres. In *The Shepherd's Calendar* (1579), the poet Edmund Spenser traced Elizabeth's harmonious persona back to her birth and parentage, portraying her as 'Syrinx daughter without spot,/ Which Pan the shepherds' god of her begot.'[59] In the myth, Pan attempted to seduce the nymph Syrinx. She was turned into reeds to preserve her chastity, so Pan cut the reeds and turned them into his pipes. The commentary published alongside Spenser's poem explained that Pan represented Henry VIII, a fitting persona because of Pan's position as god of the shepherds.[60] Spenser was creating a mythic reinterpretation of Elizabeth's birth, compensating perhaps for her

---

[57] Sir John Davies, *Hymns of Astraea* (London, 1599), p. 19. The poem is an acrostic on Elizabeth's name. Davies was a servant-in-ordinary to Elizabeth from 1594.

[58] The Earl of Essex complained in 1597 that, 'they laboured under two things at this court, delay and inconstancy, which proceeded chiefly from the sex of the Queen': Maisse, *A Journal*, p. 115.

[59] Edmund Spenser, *The Shepherd's Calendar Containing Twelve Eclogues Proportionable to the Twelve Months* (London, 1579), fol. 12v.

[60] Ibid., fol. 14v.

rather less-than-spotless parentage. Elizabeth's mother (Anne Boleyn) had been beheaded for adultery and Elizabeth declared a bastard. Furthermore, many Catholics refused to accept the legitimacy of Henry's annulment of his marriage to Catherine of Aragon, which had allowed his union with Anne, and in 1570 a Papal Bull of Excommunication also declared Elizabeth illegitimate.[61] Spenser's creation of a divine parentage and an immaculate conception for the Virgin Queen compensated for this uncertain legitimacy. Yet a further interpretation is suggested by casting Elizabeth as the music produced by playing on the Syrinx reeds.[62] While music could signify social and political harmony, Pan, by contrast, was not just god of shepherds but also associated with disorder, lust, and chaos. Such associations were equally applicable to Henry for those who recalled the disruptions of the Reformation and Henry's stream of wives. In this light, the mythical birth created a narrative in which Elizabeth was the peaceful harmony born out of the disorder of Henry's reign.

Making Elizabeth the embodiment of harmony credited her with the capacity to transform chaos into ordered paradise, a theme which was enacted on Elizabeth's arrival at Bisham during her 1592 progress. Lady Elizabeth Russell commissioned a series of tableaux, performed as Elizabeth travelled towards the house, in which various characters underwent a metamorphosis in the Queen's presence. Moreover, Elizabeth's powers of transformation were presented as musical powers. First, at the top of the hill, cornetts (probably along with sackbuts) sounded in the wood.[63] A Wild Man appeared claiming to have 'followed this sound, as if enchanted, neither knowing the reason why, nor knowing how to be rid of it'.[64] The Wild Man's speech ended predictably with his transformation to civility, as had occurred in several earlier progresses;[65] however, here music initiated the change. In the middle of the hill, Elizabeth saw Pan attempting (unsuccessfully) to seduce two maidens. The end of this device returned to the musical theme when upon the sight of Elizabeth Pan declared, 'here I break my pipe, which Apollo could never make me do; and follow that sound which follows you.'[66] The sound was presumably the cornetts following Elizabeth's procession towards the house. Pan also promised to make the

---

[61] Carole Levin, *The Reign of Elizabeth I* (Basingstoke, 2002), pp. 7, 41, 83.

[62] Philippa Berry, *Of Chastity and Power: Elizabethan Literature and the Unmarried Queen* (London, 1989), p. 79.

[63] Not a modern cornet, but rather a curved wooden instrument with a lip-vibrated mouthpiece.

[64] Joseph Barnes (ed.), *Speeches Delivered to her Majesty this Last Progress at the Right Honourable the Lady Russels, at Bisham, the Right Honourable the Lord Chandos at Sudley, at the Right Honourable the Lord Norris, at Ricote* (Oxford, 1592), sig. A2r.

[65] For example at the progresses to Kenilworth in 1575 and Cowdray in 1591: George Gascoigne, 'The Princely Pleasures at Kenilworth Castle', in *The Pleasantest Works of George Gascoigne Esquire* (London, 1587), sigs. A1r–C8v (sigs. A3r, A7v); *The Speeches and Honourable Entertainment Given to the Queen's Majesty in Progress, at Cowdray in Sussex, by the Right Honourable the Lord Montague* (London, 1591), sigs. A4v–B2v.

[66] Barnes (ed.), *Speeches Delivered*, sig. A4r.

landscape peaceful and safe during Elizabeth's visit: 'Green be the grass where you tread: calm the waters where you row: sweet the air where you breathe ... During your abode, no theft shall be in the woods: in the field no noise, in the valleys no spies, my self will keep all safe.'[67] The third and final tableau, while not explicitly musical (at least in the text – if in performance the cornetts were still following Elizabeth then the transformation may have seemed just as musical as the previous two), showed Ceres being transformed from being 'Queen of heaven', the only one on whom Phoebus shines, to become a servant of Cynthia/Elizabeth through a whispering in her ears.[68]

Both Pan and the Wild Man represent disordered and barbarous nature, and both were civilised by the presence of the Queen. Peter Davidson and Jane Stevenson interpret the 'image of concord' in terms of Pan 'abandon[ing] his essential nature, civilised (or emasculated) by one glance from the Queen's eyes', and his breaking of the pipe as 'his wild notes giv[ing] way to the lyre of Apollo; controlled court music'.[69] Yet as Pan submitted not to Apollo (who is not present), but to Elizabeth's music, the tableau represented rather more than rustic music giving way to the courtly. At the beginning of this tableau, Pan mocked both his own and Apollo's music by comically comparing their respective instruments to farmyard sounds: 'I cannot tickle the sheep's guts of a lute, bid, bid, bid, like the calling of chickens, but for a pipe that squeaketh like a pig, I am he.'[70] Rather than presenting Apollo's music as superior, the author had Pan denigrate both. While each of these gods represents only one genre of music – either courtly strings or rustic wind instruments – Elizabeth transcended their dichotomy as ruler of the whole kingdom, holding both court and country in harmony (a particularly appropriate message as Elizabeth moved her court through the English countryside on progress).[71] Furthermore, Elizabeth's music was not simply the *musica instrumentalis* of Pan and Apollo. In this pageant Elizabeth did not produce this music but instead it followed her and she commanded it. This was political harmony made audible: it was Elizabeth's music, not Apollo's, which represented harmony and order. Significantly, it is a music that is sensual and 'enchanting' for the Wild Man, yet simultaneously a transformative power of order. It was through these layers of *concordia discors*, and her association with speculative music, that Elizabeth's music was made to exceed even that of Apollo, god of music.

---

[67] Ibid.

[68] Ibid., sigs. A4r–v.

[69] Peter Davidson and Jane Stevenson, 'Elizabeth I's Reception at Bisham (1592): Elite Women as Writers and Devisers', in *The Progresses, Pageants, and Entertainments of Queen Elizabeth I*, ed. Jayne Elisabeth Archer, Elizabeth Goldring, and Sarah Knight (Oxford, 2007), pp. 207–26 (p. 220).

[70] Barnes (ed.), *Speeches Delivered*, sig. A2v.

[71] Wind, *Pagan Mysteries*, pp. 36, 86. The classical gods were often perceived as combining contrary characters in balance within themselves: Harmony, for example, inherits the contrary characters of Mars and Venus so that 'Harmonia est discordia concors', while Venus combines the diverse qualities of the three Graces.

These tableaux assigned to Elizabeth all the powers traditionally associated with music. Elizabeth's music could turn wild men civilised, convert lustful gods to chastity, and even make goddesses submit to her authority. The transformations reworked conventional myths of musical power such as Orpheus taming wild beasts with his music, or Plato and Aristotle's beliefs that music could incline people to virtue. Music was also believed to induce chastity: the aptly named treatise *The Praise of Music* recalled how Agamemnon sought to keep his wife chaste by hiring the musician Demodocus to play music in Dorian mode to her.[72] Another progress entertainment at Cowdray the previous year had seen Elizabeth credited with the powers of Amphion (who built the walls of Thebes by moving the stones with music), as walls which had only been kept from crumbling through music were supposedly magically restored by her harmonious presence.[73] As musical magic could potentially control all of creation, these progresses amplified Elizabeth's authority to divine levels. Music made Elizabeth's powers audible: those present could 'sense' Elizabeth's power through their ears.

A HARMONIOUS KINGDOM

An alternative to focussing on the musical qualities of Elizabeth herself was instead to represent the harmonious effect of this governance on her kingdom. The initial example of this approach came not from an Englishman, but from the French Huguenot printer Thomas Vautrollier, in one of the earliest polyphonic music publications in England: the *Recueil du mélange d'Orlande de Lassus* (1570).[74] As a refugee from religious persecution in France dedicating his book to the Earl of Arundel Henry Fitzalan, a nobleman of Catholic sympathies, Vautrollier saw Elizabeth's England as the fulfilment of the ideal of *concordia discors* in its religious tolerance. He praised the 'admirable beauty of the harmony' in states that temper the 'unified diversity of their various parts', and compared England to a motet in which 'thanks to the leading of one part, all others hold to a similar measure', making no discord despite their differences.[75] The leading part is that 'wise and virtuous queen', Elizabeth.[76] Unlike the majority of poets and musicians involved in the creation of Elizabeth's musical image, Vautrollier had no connection with the

---

[72] *The Praise of Music wherein Besides the Antiquity, Dignity, Delectation, and Use Thereof in Civil Matters, is also Declared the Sober and Lawful Use of the Same in the Congregation and Church of God* (Oxford, 1586), p. 57.

[73] *Speeches ... at Cowdray*, p. 2.

[74] Orlando di Lasso, *Recueil du mélange d'Orlande de Lassus* (London, 1570).

[75] Richard Freedman, *The Chansons of Orlando di Lasso and their Protestant Listeners: Music, Piety, and Print in Sixteenth-Century France*, Eastman Studies in Music (Rochester, NY, 2001), pp. 188–90: 'Je me figure la beauté admirable de l'harmonie, dont les republiques sagement administrées, temperent l'accordante diversité de leur états ... aussi se represente-elle au vif dans un motet musical, au quel sous la conduite d'une partie, toutes les autres tiennent tellement mesure, qu'estant toutes diverses entres-elles, elles ne discordent en rien.' (Translations used are Freedman's.)

[76] Ibid., p. 189: 'l'empire d'une sage et vertueuse règne'.

court, and his choice of metaphor was inspired not by his knowledge of Elizabeth's musicianship, but by the polyphonic music of his collection (although largely chansons rather than motets): Lassus's music, he argues, exemplifies the musical proportions of Plato's political harmony through the 'perfection of his art'.

Also unusual in Vautrollier's dedication is the impersonality of the relationship between the Queen and her subjects. Elizabeth presented herself (and desired others to present her) as a monarch who loved and was loved by her people. According to Kevin Sharpe, she 'never ceased to mention the reciprocal love between Queen and people which she claimed was a special hallmark of her reign (and perhaps her sex)', and, although this rhetoric was not new, she 'reiterated and personalized the conceit in hundreds of phrases, gestures and signs, and so made the relation with her people the centrepiece of her representation to princes abroad and to any who sought to challenge her at home'.[77] One expression of this relationship was the country-wide celebrations for Elizabeth's Accession Day which emerged and gradually spread from the mid-1560s onwards. These sparked the fiction of a harmonious isle celebrating its Queen through music and festivity. The celebrations and the literary outpourings that accompanied them reached a peak in the 1590s, coinciding with the similar increase in portrayals of Elizabeth as the bringer of harmony.[78]

The theme of 'unified diversity' found in Vautrollier's dedication now combined with idealised images of subjects united in song and dance to portray both the concord among English subjects and their supposedly loving relationship with the monarch they praised. Maurice Kyffin's commemoration for Accession Day, *The Blessedness of Britain* (1587), contrasted the 'ennobled Knight' honouring the Queen through martial feats with the 'country folk', whom he urges:

> Loud carols sing, to celebrate this time;
> Show signs of joy (as country manner yields),
> In sporting games, with dance, and rural rhyme:
> Each swain, and shepherd, sound his piping reed,
> For joy enjoying fields, and flocks to feed.[79]

Here the conventional associations of musical and social harmony were articulated through the pastoral topos in which shepherds were typically represented pursuing the pastimes of singing and dancing. Kyffin's appropriation of the pastoral genre for political purposes was in keeping with the tradition of poets who used 'the veil of homely persons, and in rude speeches to insinuate and glance at greater matters'.[80]

---

[77] Kevin Sharpe, *Selling the Tudor Monarchy: Authority and Image in Sixteenth-Century England* (New Haven, CT, 2009), p. 347.

[78] Katherine Butler, 'Creating Harmonious Subjects? Ballads, Psalms, and Godly Songs for Queen Elizabeth I's Accession Day', *Journal of the Royal Musical Association* (forthcoming); Roy Strong, 'The Popular Celebration of the Accession Day of Queen Elizabeth I', *Journal of the Warburg and Courtauld Institutes* 21 (1958), 86–103.

[79] Maurice Kyffin, *The Blessedness of Britain, or A Celebration of the Queen's Holiday* (London, 1587), sigs. B3v–B4r.

[80] George Puttenham, *The Art of English Poesy* (London, 1589), p. 31.

Furthermore, many pastoral images of harmony had a particularly English quality, reflecting their particular socio-economic significance in England where sheep farming was the foundation for the important wool trade.[81] In another Accession Day tribute, *Anglorum Feriae* (1595), George Peele called on England's nymphs to 'Wear eglantine/ And wreathes of roses red and white' – representing Elizabeth's flower and the Tudor Rose – while they 'paeans sing and sweet melodious songs', and lead the shepherds in a dance 'Along the chalky cliffs of Albion'.[82] Moreover, in Kyffin's poem nature itself begins to resound with Elizabeth's praise:

> Let hills, and rocks, rebounding echoes yield,
> Of Queen Elizabeth's long lasting fame;
> Let woody groves, and watery streams be filled,
> And creeks, and caves, with sounding of the same:
> O Cambria, stretch, and strain thy utmost breath,
> To praise, and pray for Queen Elizabeth.[83]

We have moved from the traditional music-making of shepherds to a biblically inspired image of hills and rocks praising Elizabeth, as well as the myth of Orpheus being able to move inanimate objects with his music.[84] Such are Elizabeth's harmonious powers that even the land (hills, woods, streams, and caves) is united and stirred by her reign. The reference to Cambria (Wales) reflects Kyffin's Welsh roots – he was born in Oswestry on the Welsh Border, then a largely Welsh-speaking town – and evokes the extent of Elizabeth's kingdom; praises come from even the distant corners of her realm. With two Welshman having been implicated in the recently foiled Babington plot, Kyffin perhaps felt a special need to reassure Elizabeth of the steadfast loyalty of himself and his fellow countrymen.[85]

Images of Englishmen united in song to praise Elizabeth spilled over into madrigals and canzonets of the period too. John Mundy's 'Turn About and See Me' (1594) is reminiscent of the numerous occasions on which Elizabeth was hailed by gods, wild men or shepherds while walking in the grounds of a nobleman's house, and may have originated in such an occasion (Mundy was an organist at St George's Chapel, Windsor). The singer calls out to Elizabeth to turn and see his joyful nature, caused by his 'mighty prince and excellent/ sweet eglantine the best'.[86]

---

[81] Louis Montrose, 'Of Gentlemen and Shepherds: The Politics of Elizabethan Pastoral Form', *English Literary History* 50 (1983), 415–59 (pp. 421–3).

[82] George Peele, *Anglorum Feriae: England's Holidays Celebrated the 17th Novemb. Last, 1595* (London, 1595; rept. Ipswich, 1840), sig. B1r.

[83] Kyffin, *Blessedness of Britain*, sigs. B3v–B4r.

[84] When the Pharisees commanded Jesus to rebuke his disciples, who were joyfully praising God in loud voices, he replied that if they kept quiet, the stones would cry out (Luke 19:40).

[85] Peter Roberts, 'Tudor Wales, National Identity and the British Inheritance', in *British Consciousness and Identity: The Making of Britain, 1533–1707*, ed. Brendan Bradshaw and Peter Roberts (Cambridge, 1998), pp. 8–42 (p. 34).

[86] John Mundy, *Songs and Psalmes Composed in 3, 4, 5 Parts*, ed. Edmund Fellowes and Thurston Dart, English Madrigalists 35b (London, 1961), pp. 10–14.

The poem does not reveal the status of the protagonist, but low-class characters such as shepherds, fishermen, and ploughmen often sang during Elizabeth's progresses, and a rustic persona is suggested by the simple tone of the language (for example, lines such as 'as glad as anything').[87]

Mundy's singer ends by calling everyone present to 'joy with me both great and small' because they are united in that fact that 'her life brings joy unto us all'.[88] It was the nature of pastoral to 'impl[y] a beautiful relationship between rich and poor', but in praises of Elizabeth the theme was frequently expanded to suggest the unifying of people not only across boundaries of social class, but also of place.[89] In Peele's *Anglorum Feriae*, 'court and country carol in her praise/ And in her honour tune a thousand lays', while Kyffin evoked the musical tributes of elaborate civic and courtly festivities which commonly used bell-ringing, consort music, drums, and trumpets.[90] As well as symbolising the joy of her subjects, for Mundy, Peele, and Kyffin music was the force that united the land, townspeople, country-dwellers, and courtiers.

A NOTE OF DISCORD

YET this image of England as a unified, harmonious kingdom was always a fiction. The English continued to be divided by loyalties to religion, localities, or social class that competed with their unified portrayal as Englishmen and Elizabethan subjects. The irony behind Vautrollier's praise of England's 'unified diversity' was that only a year earlier Elizabeth had faced an uprising of several of her Northern noblemen led by the Earls of Westmoreland and Northumberland, one of their aims being the restoration of the Catholic faith.[91] Similarly, though London had seen unrest on Shrove Tuesday, riots over the price of fish and butter, and a march of a thousand apprentices on Tower Hill that resulted in the city being placed under martial law for the rest of the summer in 1595, George Peele's Accession Day tribute

---

[87] *The Honourable Entertainment Given to the Queen's Majesty in Progress, at Elvetham in Hampshire, by the Right Honourable the Earl of Hertford* (London, 1591), sig. D3r; *Speeches ... at Cowdray*, pp. 9–12; Barnes (ed.), *Speeches Delivered*, sigs. B3r–C1r.

[88] Thomas Morley, 'Blow, Shepherds, Blow', is another three-part song which presents a group of shepherds greeting Elizabeth as 'shepherds queen and lovely sweet mistress' in their music: Thomas Morley, *Canzonets for Two and Three Voices*, ed. Edmund Fellowes and Thurston Dart, English Madrigalists 1 (London, 1956), pp. 39–43.

[89] William Empson, *Some Versions of Pastoral* (London, 1935), p. 11; Louis Montrose, '"Eliza, Queene of Shepheardes", and the Pastoral of Power', *English Literary Renaissance* 10 (1980), 153–82 (pp. 179–80).

[90] Peele, *Anglorum Feriae*, sig. C1v. Peele also makes the same contrast as Kyffin between martial nobility and the musical country people earlier in the poem. Kyffin, *Blessedness of Britain*, sig. B3v.

[91] K. J. Kesselring, *The Northern Rebellion of 1569: Faith, Politics, and Protest in Elizabethan England* (Basingstoke, 2007), pp. 1–3.

for the year is a picture of harmony.[92] The mayor, 'London's shepherd, guardian of his flock':

> Tunes his true joy for all those days of peace
> Those quiet days that Englishmen enjoy,
> Under our Queen, fair Queen of Brute's New Troy.
> With whom in sympathy and sweet accord,
> All loyal subjects join.[93]

Elsewhere Londoners also sing in praise and thanksgiving for their Queen; yet the disconnection between the poem and political reality could not be more marked.[94] In 1595 London would have felt quite the opposite to this image of perfect concord.

The 1590s was a decade of increasing political uncertainty across the whole country: high food prices, unemployment, and heavy taxation caused social unrest, while the court saw increasingly bitter factional disputes and Elizabeth continued to refuse to name her successor.[95] Vautrollier and Peele's approach was a whitewash, reinforcing a harmonious image despite the discordant reality. Yet as problems mounted, strains did appear within the praise of Elizabeth's harmonious government.

On the surface royal flattery was still the aim. Sir John Davies's poem 'To the Queen' appears to extol Elizabeth's pious governance, but tensions begin to show in the musical metaphors describing her rule. The opening question of Davies's poem seems initially to refer to practical music-making, before the poem quickly moves into the realm of political harmony and sounds a note of scepticism. It begins:

> What music shall we make to you,
> To whom the strings of all men's hearts
> Make music of ten thousand parts
> In tune and measure true,
> With strains and changes new?
>
> How shall we frame a harmony
> Worthy your ears, whose princely hands
> Keep harmony in sundry lands,

---

[92] Ian W. Archer, *The Pursuit of Stability: Social Relations in Elizabethan London*, Cambridge Studies in Early Modern British History (Cambridge, 1991), pp. 1–2.

[93] Peele, *Anglorum Feriae*, sigs. C1v–r. Brutus was the legendary Trojan who supposedly founded Britain: see also pp. 102–3 and 149.

[94] Peter Davidson and Jane Stevenson note a similar incongruity between image and political reality in their interpretation of the Bisham entertainment of 1592: the continued use of the fertile pastoral imagery of Elizabeth's youth despite her age, and images of concord despite warfare and strained domestic politics. See Davidson and Stevenson, 'Elizabeth I's Reception at Bisham', p. 220.

[95] John Guy, 'The 1590s: The Second Reign of Elizabeth I?', in *The Reign of Elizabeth I: Court and Culture in the Last Decade*, ed. John Guy (Cambridge, 1995), pp. 1–19. This poem exists only in manuscript but was probably written after 1594, when Sir John Davies was first presented at court by Lord Mountjoy and sworn in as servant-in-ordinary to Elizabeth. See Sean Kelsey, 'Davies, Sir John (bap. 1569, d. 1626)', *ODNB* (online edn, 2008).

> Whose people divers be
> In faction and degree?
> Heavens tunes may only please,
> And not such airs as these.[96]

These stanzas make commonplace comparisons between lute strings and heartstrings (p. 9), punning on the Latin words '*cor*' (heart) and '*cordae*' (strings). Davies pictured Elizabeth maintaining a well-tuned and rhythmic 'music of ten thousand parts' among the diverse peoples throughout her kingdom. He explained her harmonious political powers by turning her into an almost Christ-like figure:

> For you which down from heaven are sent
> Such peace upon the earth to bring,
> Have heard the choir of angels sing,
> And all the spheres consent,
> Like a sweet Instrument.

Evoking the notion of divinely appointed monarchy, Davies presented Elizabeth as heaven-sent. Her ability to instil concord in her kingdom stemmed from her capacity to hear that celestial harmony believed normally to be inaudible to human ears, thereby enabling her to recreate it on earth.

Yet in the final stanza of 'To the Queen' Davies juxtaposed his positive images of harmonious governance with allusions to 'harsh tunes' and 'troubled air' (punning on the dual sense of musical ayre and troubled atmosphere):

> How then should these harsh tunes you hear,
> Created of the troubled air,
> Breed but distaste when they repair
> To your celestial ear?
> So that this centre here
> For you no music finds,
> But harmony of minds.

This threatening dissonance evokes the economic crisis, social strain, political rivalry, and warfare of the 1590s. Earlier reference to 'faction' in the second stanza would have called to mind the conflicts between Robert Cecil and Robert Devereux, Earl of Essex, which John Chamberlain similarly described in musical terms in 1599: 'the jars continue as they did, if not worse, by daily renewing, and our music runs so much upon discords, that I fear what harmony they will make of it in the end.'[97] Similarly the 'strains and changes new' evoke the changing makeup of the Elizabethan court following the deaths of Robert Dudley, Earl of Leicester (1588), Ambrose Dudley, Earl of Warwick (1590), Sir Walter Mildmay (1589), Sir Francis Walsingham (1590), Sir Christopher Hatton (1591), and William Cecil,

---

[96] Sir John Davies, 'To the Queen', GB-EU: MS Laing III 444, fols. 33v–34r. For a modern edition see Sir John Davies, *The Poems of John Davies*, ed. Robert Krueger (Oxford, 1975), pp. 242–3.

[97] John Chamberlain, *The Letters of John Chamberlain*, ed. Norman Egbert McClure, 2 vols. (Philadelphia, 1939), vol. 1, p. 67.

Lord Burghley (1598), and their replacement by men such as Sir Walter Ralegh, Robert Cecil, and the Earl of Essex.[98] Such a sudden change in the key political figures would have had a destabilising effect and caused increased uncertainty as to the balance of power among leading political figures.

Other 'harsh tunes' might be those of warfare. In marked contrast to the first twenty-seven years of the reign, England was now at war with Spain (1585–1604), while further forces were committed in the Netherlands (from 1585), France (1589–94), and later Ireland (1594–1603).[99] The 'troubled air' calls to mind the problems of four successive harvest failures in 1594–7, which caused famine and a sharp rise in food prices; the outbreaks of plague and influenza; the heavy taxation levied to pay for the war; the large-scale unemployment as overseas trade diminished; the increased crime and vagrancy; and fears of civil unrest, which threatened to materialise in the Oxfordshire Rising of 1596.[100] Davies may also have had in mind the uncertainties caused by Elizabeth's refusal to name a successor.[101] Numerous tracts circulated discussing the merits of as many as thirteen domestic and foreign candidates for the succession, causing concern as to the chaos that might ensue on Elizabeth's death.[102] The succession crisis may even have sparked a literal musical response: if Jeremy Smith's interpretation is correct, Thomas Morley's *The Triumphs of Oriana* (1601) was originally intended as supportive of the Essex circle and their attempts to engineer the succession of James VI of Scotland (Oriana being Anna of Denmark, James's wife, and Diana being Penelope Rich, the Earl of Essex's politically active sister).[103]

Although Davies's final lines evoke the 'harmony of minds', the troubling references to discord remain unresolved. He suggests that only the loyalty and unity of English subjects can be music to Elizabeth's ears. Yet Elizabeth's potential as a bringer of harmony is juxtaposed against the realities of unrest, and the poem may be read not as praise, but as a criticism that Elizabeth is failing in her divinely appointed duty to bring heavenly order to her earthly kingdom.

Davies was not the only poet in the 1590s to mix images of harmony and discord in this way. In *A Musical Consort of Heavenly Harmony ... called Churchyard's Charity*

---

[98] Guy, 'The 1590s', pp. 2–4.
[99] Wallace MacCaffrey, *Elizabeth I: War and Politics, 1588–1603* (Princeton, NJ, 1992), pp. 3–9; Guy, 'The 1590s', p. 1.
[100] Archer, *Pursuit of Stability*, pp. 9–14; Guy, 'The 1590s', pp. 8–11.
[101] Brink suggests that Davies addressed this topic in his *Orchestra or a Poem of Dancing* (1596): J. R. Brink, 'Sir John Davies's Orchestra: Political Symbolism and Textual Revisions', *Durham University Journal* n.s. 41 (1980), 195–201.
[102] Joel Hurstfield, 'The Succession Struggle in Late Elizabethan England', in *Freedom, Corruption and Government in Elizabethan England*, ed. Joel Hurstfield (London, 1973), pp. 104–34; Nick Myers, 'The Gossip of History: The Question of the Succession in the State Papers', in *The Struggle for the Succession: Politics, Polemics and Cultural Representations*, ed. Jean-Christophe Mayer, Astraea Texts 11 (Montpellier, 2004), pp. 49–64; Susan Doran, 'Three Late-Elizabethan Succession Tracts', ibid., pp. 100–17.
[103] Jeremy Smith, 'Music and Late Elizabethan Politics: The Identities of Oriana and Diana', *Journal of the American Musicological Society* 58 (2005), 507–58.

(1595), Thomas Churchyard presented Elizabeth as personified through music, but the tensions of the period are still subtly evoked:

> O treble Queen, the sweet and highest part
> That we like best, and shrillest voice doth sound
> The only mean, to show deep music's art
> Where all the skill; of well set song is found.
> Grant silly man, a grace that means to sing
> Of heavenly love, and of none other thing.
> He sings of peace, a song should lull asleep
> The fellest fiends, and fearful bugs below.[104]

As an author of civic entertainments for Elizabeth's progresses and also a frequent writer of broadside ballads and poetic collections for the popular press, Churchyard represented a more populist type of poet than Davies. Churchyard drew on the musical imagery through which Elizabeth was increasingly portrayed in the 1590s, but adapted its themes to be accessible to a wider audience via print by abandoning the more learned topics of the music of the spheres or the classical gods. Through a series of puns, Elizabeth becomes 'treble Queen', 'the only mean', and 'deep music's art' ('deep' referring both to pitch and the exceptional quality of the music). As treble, mean, and bass – the upper, middle, and lower parts of a polyphonic song – she therefore had 'all the skill of well set song'. Elizabeth represented the total harmony; as Queen she was the highest part and the one with the skill to maintain the whole song, ordering the harmony of the lower estates. Furthermore, the song that she created and taught men to sing was one of 'peace' and 'heavenly love'. Yet, as shown above, 1595 was hardly peaceful, and Churchyard's 'fellest fiends' and 'fearful bugs' introduced a sense of discord. This juxtaposition of harmonious image and dissonant reality highlighted the gap between Churchyard's royal praise and the turbulent political situation.

As Elizabeth's natural body grew visibly older and weaker (she was almost sixty years old in 1592), as England remained at war with Spain, and as social and economic problems mounted, it was increasingly important to Elizabeth and her government that authors of court pageantry and literature represented her royal power as stronger than ever. Poets could amplify that power through musical metaphors that evoked political authority over men and nature, emphasised the shared heavenly source of both harmony and divinely appointed monarchy, and depicted the concord of her supposedly loving subjects. The intention was probably not merely to praise Elizabeth; some images may have been aimed at foreign nations as a statement of the strength of England. Poems aimed at a wide distribution like Churchyard's and Peele's may have been intended to encourage future stability and to inspire English subjects to loyalty and affection for their monarch. They may even reveal continued widespread and genuine affection for Elizabeth despite the uneasy times. Certainly Davies was content to glorify Elizabeth in his *Hymns to Astraea* of 1599, even if his 'To the Queen' was more ambivalent in mixing praise

---

[104] Thomas Churchyard, *A Musical Consort of Heavenly Harmony (Compounded Out of Many Parts of Music) Called Churchyard's Charity* (London, 1595), sig. A[4]r.

with expressions of discontent. Nevertheless, images of concord were increasingly distant from the political reality, and the temptation to hint at troublesome discords to express dissatisfaction was growing.

Although rulers across Europe were celebrated through metaphors of musical and political harmony, these were rarely applied with the same frequency and close relationship to the monarch's personal talents and qualities as they were to Elizabeth.[105] Her musical royal image was exceptional for the degree to which it combined audible practical music and speculative music harmony. Frequently intimate in tone, poets evoked her musical talents and natural body: the praise of her 'worthy ears', 'princely hands', and her mind by Davies, or her 'sacred ears' and 'skill' by Bennet.[106] Furthermore, images of political concord merged with the sensual delights of female music-making as Elizabeth's harmonious rule was described as 'sweet pleasure' or enchantment, and the Queen as 'the sweet and highest part/ that we like best'.[107] It was this interconnection of all levels of harmony – practical and speculative – as well as the combination of music's rationality and sensuality that was central to representations of Elizabeth's musicality. By blending the talents of Elizabeth's natural body with those of her political body, and by merging practical musicianship with speculative harmony, poets and musicians created an image of effective queenship. Yet this was not a final antidote to potential criticism. Music had the capacity to undermine as well as enhance the royal image, and this inherent instability of music's meanings left Elizabeth's harmonious persona open to the subversive undertones of the discontented.

---

[105] For some European spectacles on the theme of musical and political harmony see, for example, the 1589 Medici wedding festivities in Florence, and Henry IV's entries into Lyon and Rouen in 1595–6: James M. Saslow, *The Medici Wedding of 1589: Florentine Festival as Theatrum Mundi* (New Haven, CT, 1996), pp. 30–3, 151–8; Kate Van Orden, *Music, Discipline, and Arms in Early Modern France* (Chicago, 2005), pp. 176–82; Flora Dennis, 'Music in Ferrarese Festival: Harmony and Chaos', in *Court Festivals of the European Renaissance: Art, Politics, and Performance*, ed. J. R. Mulryne and Elizabeth Goldring (Aldershot, 2002), pp. 287–93.

[106] Davies, 'To the Queen', fols. 33v–34r; Davies, *Poems*, pp. 242–3; Davies, *Hymns of Astraea*, p. 19; Bennet, 'Eliza, Her Name Gives Honour'.

[107] Davies, *Hymns of Astraea*, p. 19; Barnes (ed.), *Speeches Delivered*, sig. A2r; Churchyard, *Churchyard's Charity*, sig. A[4]r.

CHAPTER 2

The Politics of Intimacy

MANY musical images of Elizabeth were public or semi-public in nature, being circulated in print or produced during grand occasions like the progresses. By contrast, Hilliard's miniature of Elizabeth playing the lute (Figure 1.1) was a private, personal possession. It belonged to Henry Carey, Lord Hunsdon, and was probably a gift from Elizabeth.[1] The Carey family were close to the Queen and would have been accustomed to hearing her play for recreation in her private apartments. Hunsdon was her cousin, and responsible for the famous incident in which the Scottish ambassador was caught eavesdropping on Elizabeth's virginal-playing (pp. 45–7).[2] His sister and two of his daughters were ladies of Elizabeth's Privy Chamber.[3] As well as depicting the royal image, the miniature was an expression of the Carey family's privileged relationship with the Queen.

The intimate quality of the miniature reflects the private nature of Elizabeth's own music-making. Her performances were reserved for distinguished guests, royal favourites, personal servants, and family relations, as was proper for an upper-class amateur musician. Like Hilliard's portrait, Elizabeth's music-making counterpointed her image as monarch and her private self as musician. Through her performances she not only portrayed a particular royal persona but also shaped her courtly relationships. Men like Hunsdon with regular, close access to the Queen's recreation were in the minority: for the majority of courtiers and all foreign visitors, Elizabeth's performances were a rare honour. Aware of their political potential, Elizabeth employed the intimacy of private music-making to charm foreign visitors, develop relations with courtiers and ambassadors, and influence the course of diplomatic negotiations. Moreover, Elizabeth's courtiers began to follow her example, singing or commissioning intimate performances of their own poetry to the Queen in the hope of renewed or continued favour at the expense of their rivals. This 'politics of intimacy' was characteristic of the workings of Tudor government, in which political power depended on access to the monarch and a courtier or diplomat's personal relationship with the Queen.[4] In such circumstances recreational activities like music gained political significance as a means through which personal relationships could be fostered, which in turn would lead to power and influence.

---

[1] Roy Strong, *The English Renaissance Miniature* (London, 1983), p. 95.

[2] Sir James Melville, *The Memoirs of Sir James Melville of Halhill*, ed. George Scott (London, 1683), p. 50.

[3] Wallace MacCaffrey, 'Carey, Henry, First Baron Hunsdon (1526–1596)', *ODNB* (online edn, 2013); Simon Adams, 'Howard, Katherine, Countess of Nottingham (1545×50–1603)', *ODNB* (online edn, 2008).

[4] David Starkey, 'Introduction: Court History in Perspective', in *The English Court: From the Wars of the Roses to the Civil War*, ed. David Starkey (London, 1987), pp. 1–24 (p. 13).

Yet this intimacy was not necessarily sincere. Instead the play of intimacy and politics could become a '"game" of secrecy', as Patricia Fumerton has termed it, in which the appearance of granting access to the private self was in fact carefully staged. This involved 'representing through "public" forms (of ornament, convention, rhetoric) the "private" and "true" self'.[5] For Elizabeth these games of secrecy took on political significance because of how she blurred the boundaries between her royal and private selves, 'handling threats from foreign princes by dangling the possibility of marriage with herself and managing her courtiers at home by encouraging the revival of courtly love'.[6] While Fumerton considered sonnets and portrait miniatures, this staged intimacy was also characteristic of private musical performances at court. Although both Elizabeth's performances and the songs of courtiers gave the appearance of revealing intimate thoughts and personal qualities, they did so through the conventional genres and rhetoric of the courtly love topos and musical sensuality. Amorous rhetoric frequently encoded desires, ambitions, and frustrations of a political or social kind.[7] The relationship between appearance and reality – or sincerity and deception – was deeply ambivalent.

PERFORMANCE, INTIMACY, AND POWER

For the music historian, interpreting Elizabeth's performances is much like viewing Hilliard's miniature: letters and ambassadors' reports describe the occasions, but the sound is lost along with any knowledge of what tunes Elizabeth played. For these men who heard Elizabeth it was the fact that she played and the context in which she chose to do so that was most noteworthy (they either did not know what she played or did not consider it worth reporting). Once the sound had faded it was the symbolism of the performance that remained and shaped its longer-term political significance.

Elizabeth's performances became games of secrecy through her deliberate creation of conditions of intimacy and sensuality and because of her underlying intentions: to fashion particular images of her private self and to influence her relationships with ambassadors. The creation of intimacy began with the performance space. For Elizabeth's performances this was typically the Privy Chamber and her private rooms. This was where her virginals would have been set up and these small chambers were most suitable for the soft tones of the lute. Yet intimacy could be staged even in more unusual settings, as when Caspar Breuner, Baron of Rabenstein (Imperial Ambassador from Ferdinand I), heard Elizabeth perform on the river in 1559:

---

[5] Patricia Fumerton, '"Secret" Arts: Elizabethan Miniatures and Sonnets', *Representations* 15 (1986), 57–97 (p. 59).

[6] Ibid., pp. 58–9.

[7] Arthur F. Marotti, '"Love is Not Love": Elizabethan Sonnet Sequences and the Social Order', *English Literary History* 49 (1982), 396–428; Catherine Bates, *The Rhetoric of Courtship in Elizabethan Language and Literature* (Cambridge, 1992).

I, after supper, to refresh myself, took a boat on the river, and the Queen came there too, recognized and summoned me. She spoke a long while with me, and invited me to leave my boat and take a seat in that of the Treasurer's. She then had her boat laid alongside and played upon the lute.[8]

Through the positioning of boats and the Queen's music-making, Breuner was brought into the circle of intimates around Elizabeth. These performances created both a physical closeness between the Queen and her audience, and a social one with the small, select audience emphasising the favoured status of the listeners.

Elizabeth maintained a sense of exclusivity around her music-making. As Elizabeth's performances largely took place in the female-dominated space of the Privy Chamber, it was a privilege for the men of the court to hear her play. For courtiers, hearing Elizabeth's music-making was a symbol of their familiarity with the Queen. William Cecil, Elizabeth's chief political councillor, drew attention to the more personal side of their relationship by likening himself to the Queen's lute and presenting himself as an instrument for Elizabeth's entertainment.[9] Likewise the fallen royal favourite Sir Walter Ralegh aimed to elicit sympathy for his current misfortune by emphasising his past status as one who had been 'wont to behold her ... sometime singing like an angel, sometime playing like Orpheus'.[10] Exiled from court for his secret marriage to one of Elizabeth's Maids of Honour, Ralegh hoped that his correspondent, Robert Cecil, might intercede on his behalf, perhaps even showing Elizabeth this letter with its impassioned lament for past intimacy. Diplomatic performances were even more of a rarity. When Don Virginio Orsino, Duke of Bracciano, saw Elizabeth dance in 1601, he was told by 'those informed of this court' that this was 'the greatest honour she could do me', while the French ambassador Monsieur de Boissise considered Elizabeth's performances a mark of royal esteem, commenting that Elizabeth 'looked most favourably upon [the Duke], danced, played and sang for love of him'.[11]

Elizabeth's performances also drew on the sensuality of music. Lute performances in particular were believed to draw attention to the physical appearance of the performer. Mary Burwell's seventeenth-century lute tutor stressed the visual enticements of a woman playing the lute:

---

[8] Victor Klarwill (ed.), *Queen Elizabeth and some Foreigners: Being a Series of Hitherto Unpublished Letters from the Archives of the Hapsburg Family* (London, 1928), p. 96.

[9] Thomas Wright (ed.), *Queen Elizabeth and her Times: A Series of Original Letters*, 2 vols. (London, 1838), vol. 2, p. 428 [7 December 1593].

[10] Sir Walter Ralegh, *The Letters of Sir Walter Ralegh*, ed. Agnes M. C. Latham and Joyce A. Youings (Exeter, 1999), p. 70 [July 1592].

[11] Leslie Hotson, *The First Night of Twelfth Night* (New York, 1954), pp. 210–11, 232. 'Sua Maestà fû contenta di ballare, che è maggiore onore, che ella mi potessi fare, secondo il detto di questi informati di questa corte' (p. 232), and, 'Ladicte Dame aussi l'a vu de très bon oeil, là festoyé, à dansé, sonné, chanté pour l'amour de lui' (p. 211).

> All the actions that one does in playing of the lute are handsome, the posture is modest free and gallant ... The beauty of the arms, of the hands and of the neck are advantageously displayed in playing of the lute. The eyes are employed only in looking upon the company ... Of all the arts that I know there is none that engages more the inclination of men than the lute ... ravishing the soul by the ear and the eyes by the swiftness and neatness of all the fingers.[12]

Elizabeth's performances focussed attention on her person, her 'body natural' rather than her 'body politic'. They were deliberately charming and enticing as she aimed to impress with her beauty as well as her art. The reactions of those who saw and heard Elizabeth's performances often echo typical tropes of the female musician's sensual powers. The Scottish ambassador Sir James Melville excused his trespassing into her chamber by claiming: 'I heard such melody as ravished me, whereby I was drawn in ere I knew how' (see below).[13] Similarly in 1601, Don Virginio evoked the fantasy world of romances to describe the experience of Elizabeth's musical performance: 'it seemed to me I had become one of the paladins who used to go to those enchanted palaces.'[14] Whereas for Vives oriental connotations were symbolic of vice (p. 22), for Don Virginio these exotic resonances symbolised the captivating sumptuousness of Elizabeth and her court. The conventional erotic and musical power which women had over men became a political tool as part of the personal charm through which she shaped relationships with courtiers, foreign guests, and ambassadors.

Despite the atmosphere of intimacy, these diplomatic occasions were not meant to be wholly private. Rather, they were politically motivated and intended to be reported to a wider audience through the publication of travel diaries or in the dispatches sent back to foreign courts. While they were made to appear spontaneous and intimate, they were in fact carefully staged and framed in conventional rhetoric so that little of Elizabeth's personal self was revealed. An extreme but telling case was that of the Scottish ambassador Sir James Melville, who was embarrassingly caught eavesdropping on Elizabeth's virginal-playing in 1564. Yet he believed the compromising situation to have been staged by the Queen herself. He had been brought up to the 'quiet gallery' by Lord Hunsdon (a cousin of the Queen)

---

[12] Julia Craig-McFeely, 'The Signifying Serpent: Seduction by Cultural Stereotype in Seventeenth-Century England', in *Music, Sensation, and Sensuality*, ed. Linda Phyllis Austern, Critical and Cultural Musicology 5 (New York, 2002), pp. 299–317 (pp. 303–4). This contrasts with the opinion among modern performers that the instrument is not good for posture as it encourages the player to hunch over the instrument.

[13] Melville, *Memoirs*, pp. 50–1.

[14] Hotson, *The First Night of Twelfth Night*, p. 210: 'che mi p[arve di] essere diventato uno di quei paladini, che andavan[o in] quei palazzi incantati' (p. 232). Don Virginio's accounts are vague (he tells his wife he is saving the details until his return), but his comment follows a meeting in which Elizabeth had specifically promised to perform, and the French ambassador confirms that she danced, played and sang for the Duke (p. 211).

to listen in on Elizabeth's playing, but had given away his presence by stepping into her chamber. According to Melville, however, Elizabeth, only '*appeared* to be surprised to see me, and came forward, seeming to strike me with her hand, *alleging* she used not to play before men' [my italics].[15]

Melville was right to be suspicious; Elizabeth had previously performed for Breuner with no such play-acting and was to do so for other men. Furthermore, this incident took place following an audience in which Elizabeth had asked Melville 'whether my Queen's hair or hers was best, and which of them two was fairest … which of them was of highest stature?' Significantly the audience had ended with Elizabeth asking what kind of recreational activities Mary enjoyed. Melville had told Elizabeth that Mary played the lute and the virginals. Being asked if Mary played well, he had responded 'reasonably for a Queen'. On this occasion, Melville had tactfully avoided choosing between the two Queens by pointing out the exceptional qualities of each. After his eavesdropping, however, Melville felt 'obliged to give her the praise'. Melville was also forced to remain at the court for two more days to see Elizabeth dance. Again he had to concede that Mary 'danced not so high, and disposedly as she [Elizabeth] did'.[16]

The apparent intimacy of Elizabeth's performances was offset by the conventional rhetoric of her responses. Elizabeth's feigned modesty about playing before men alluded to Castiglione's prescription that a gentlewoman should 'show her music with suffering herself to be first prayed somewhat and drawn to it' (p. 23).[17] Elizabeth also used this topos when she performed for Frederick, Duke of Württemberg, in 1592 only after his escort, the French ambassador Monsieur de Beauvois, 'so far prevailed upon her'.[18] More conventional rhetoric was employed when Elizabeth told Melville that she played 'when she was solitary to shun melancholy', mirroring Salter's prescription of music for those 'over worn with grief, sorrow, trouble, cares, or other vexation'.[19] Although Elizabeth's comment to Melville seems to be revealing information about her personal temperament and the strains of governance, in fact she has told Melville nothing more than impersonal commonplaces concerning the use of music by women; in the game of secrecy, all and nothing must be revealed.

---

[15] Melville, *Memoirs*, p. 50.

[16] Ibid., pp. 50–1.

[17] Count Baldassarre Castiglione, *The Courtier of Count Baldessar Castilio*, trans. Thomas Hoby (London, 1561), sigs. Zz3v.

[18] William Brenchley Rye (ed.), *England as Seen by Foreigners in the Days of Elizabeth and James the First, Comprising Translations of the Journals of the Two Dukes of Wirtemberg in 1592 and 1610* (London, 1865), p. 12; Jacob Rathgeb, *Warhaffte Beschreibung zweier Reisen* (Tübingen, 1603), fol. 15v: 'Ihre Majestät so weit gebracht daß sie eines auf ihrem Instrument … sehr lieblich kunstreich geschlagen.'

[19] Melville, *Memoirs*, p. 50; Thomas Salter, *A Mirror Meet for All Mothers, Matrons, and Maidens, Entitled the Mirror of Modesty* (London, 1579), sig. C6v.

POLITICAL PERFORMANCES

So what did Elizabeth intend to achieve through such elaborate musical games of secrecy? The performances of music and dance for Melville were an expression of political rivalry staged to gain an admission from the ambassador of Elizabeth's superiority compared to the Scottish Queen. Such rivalry stemmed not from mere personal vanity or jealousy: there were important political reasons for Elizabeth to defend her reputation relative to Mary that explain the especially elaborate manipulation surrounding this performance. Mary was a rival claimant for the throne of England. In 1558 she had claimed to be the rightful Queen of England and until 1560 had used the English royal arms. The danger Mary posed was fully realised when she became the focus of several Catholic plots in the 1570s and 80s.[20] To be seen as a better queen than Mary was necessary to reinforce Elizabeth's political authority.

Furthermore, Elizabeth and Mary were also rivals in the marriage market. The Imperial Ambassador, negotiating for a marriage with Archduke Charles in 1565, reminded Elizabeth of the comparisons taking place across Europe:

> I told the Queen that I myself had heard the French Ambassador when he came to Vienna, praise the Queen of Scotland, saying that she was very beautiful and the heir to the throne of England and therefore worthy of such a Prince as the Archduke. The Queen answered that she was superior to the Queen of Scotland.[21]

The themes of beauty, music, and dancing on which Elizabeth had sought Melville's opinions were all related to female attractiveness and marriageability. Elizabeth had good reason to be concerned. Mary had been brought up at the Valois court in France, a centre of Renaissance culture and courtliness, while Elizabeth had had to make do with native tutors and spent many of her formative years away from court life as she tried to survive the Catholic regime of Mary I. Elizabeth had grounds to fear that she might be inferior to Mary Queen of Scots in some of these talents expected of princesses and queens. Elizabeth's use of music and dance in this diplomacy shows her desire to be recognised as superior not just in regal power but also in the cultural and social skills expected of a royal woman. Placing Melville in a compromising position and manipulating his loyalties by forcing him to admit that Elizabeth was a better musician and dancer than his own queen was a show of power. Furthermore, by overtly displaying her marriageability, Elizabeth may also have been indicating her own ability to provide for the English succession, therefore suggesting that Mary should not hope to become her heir.

Music's diplomatic influence was rarely as direct as in Melville's case, but it had had a role in marital negotiations since the beginning of Elizabeth's reign. These were important in the long term for potential political alliances and if she was going to produce an heir, but even in the short term they fostered cordial diplomatic relations. Elizabeth's musical performances encouraged these useful yet difficult

---

[20] Julian Goodare, 'Mary [Mary Stewart] (1542–1587)', *ODNB* (online edn, 2007).
[21] Klarwill (ed.), *Queen Elizabeth and some Foreigners*, p. 215.

negotiations, signalling her availability for courtship and implying that it was worthwhile persevering with these suits.

From her earliest known diplomatic performance – her lute-playing for Breuner on the river (p. 44) – Elizabeth found music a useful means of prolonging such negotiations. Breuner was undertaking marital discussions on behalf of Emperor Ferdinand I's son, Archduke Charles of Austria.[22] At the time of the performance talks were stalling because Elizabeth would neither make any firm commitment to marry, nor was she prepared to break off the talks. On 3 June Breuner thought that Elizabeth had rejected this suit altogether; but then it appeared that she was keen for him to stay, as she informed him that: 'she would not like to say that my being here on account of the marriage question was disagreeable to her … for she was well content with me.'[23] Breuner's letter of 13 June (in which he describes her musical performance) contains an even greater mix of frustration and optimism at Elizabeth's behaviour. Referring to the negotiations he writes, 'God knows what a sorry business that is'; however, he also observes that 'although the Queen affects a certain strangeness, she is quite otherwise in conversation', and since he has continued the marriage negotiations she has been behaving 'more confidingly' every day.[24] The musical performance is one of a series of stories Breuner relates to demonstrate the Queen's increasing openness and to indicate that continued negotiations might not be in vain. Music allowed Elizabeth to honour the ambassador with renewed intimacy and to hint that she might yet be open to negotiations, thereby maintaining a stalemate that avoided a firm decision on the marriage proposal yet sustained relations with the powerful Hapsburgs (both Emperor Ferdinand I and his brother, King Philip II of Spain).

As a statement of marriageability Elizabeth's performance on the lute was a particularly appropriate choice of instrument. Characterised by Julia Craig-McFeely as 'a weapon of last resort for the girl who was in danger of spinsterhood', the lute also symbolised marital harmony.[25] In his eighth sonnet, Shakespeare characterised each lute string as 'husband to another', referring to the stringing of lutes in pairs, or courses, that provide sympathetic resonance. Expanding the metaphor to illustrate familial concord he portrayed the harmoniously resonant strings as 'Resembling sire and child and happy mother/ Who all in one, one pleasing note do sing'.[26] Alternatively two lutes strung in unison, so that 'striking the strings of the one, straws will stir upon the strings of the other', could be compared to 'two minds linked in love [such that] one cannot be delighted but the other rejoyceth', as in John Lyly's court play

---

[22] Susan Doran, *Monarchy and Matrimony: The Courtships of Elizabeth I* (London, 1996), pp. 26–31, 73–98.
[23] Klarwill (ed.), *Queen Elizabeth and some Foreigners*, pp. 84–5.
[24] Ibid., pp. 95–6.
[25] Craig-McFeely, 'Signifying Serpent', p. 312.
[26] William Shakespeare, *Shakespeare's Sonnets*, ed. Katherine Duncan-Jones, Arden Shakespeare, rev. edn (London, 2010), pp. 126–7.

Sappho and Phao (1584).[27] Yet notions of matrimony were not the only meaning that lute playing might evoke: perhaps Elizabeth was merely demonstrating her eloquence and education, honouring the ambassador, or symbolising harmony between their two nations? A musical performance might imply matrimonial possibilities but was also ambiguous enough to simply encourage diplomatic relations. This uncertainty was its advantage for Elizabeth, who wished to allude to the possibility of marriage yet not appear too committed.

Breuner's suit was unsuccessful, but a marriage was looking increasingly likely when another of the Imperial ambassadors, Adam Zwetkovich, Baron of Mitterburg, wrote that he had seen Elizabeth dance and play on the lute as well as at the keyboard on 31 May 1565.[28] Now Elizabeth was taking the negotiations seriously rather than being evasive, and on 30 May she had written her terms for inclusion in the marriage treaty.[29] This time her performance came at a highpoint in negotiations and was more sincere in its intentions. The performance deliberately paraded her feminine attractiveness and marriageability, demonstrating her commitment to the negotiations with the aim of encouraging the Emperor Maximilian (Ferdinand's successor) to accept her terms. Another performance by Elizabeth on 1 June was recorded in a summary of dispatches from the Spanish ambassador Guzman da Silva: 'On Ascension Day she summoned the King's Ambassador … in whose presence she played privately on a lute and a spinet, which she does very well.'[30] As the Spanish were supporting the Austrian match (which would ally England with the Hapsburgs rather than France) while the French were promoting Charles IX as an alternative suitor, this performance may have been designed to signal her preference for the Hapsburgs.[31]

Similar optimism surrounded Elizabeth's performance for the French ambassadors Sieur de La Mothe-Fénélon and Sieur de La Mole, who were negotiating a potential marriage with Francis, Duke of Alençon (later Anjou), in August 1572. Following an audience in which Elizabeth had declared her willingness to marry and requested a meeting with the Duke, she asked the ambassadors to stay for supper and played for them on the spinet.[32] Given Elizabeth's changeable attitude to matrimonial matters the performance served to underline the seriousness of her request, so the ambassadors reported the occasion as an indication of Elizabeth's favour towards the Duke and the significant progress of the marriage negotiations.

---

[27] John Lyly, *Sappho and Phao, Played Before the Queen's Majesty on Shrove-Tuesday by her Majesty's Children and the Boys of Paul's* (London, 1584), sig. F1r [act 4, scene 3].

[28] Klarwill (ed.), *Queen Elizabeth and some Foreigners*, pp. 228.

[29] Doran, *Monarchy and Matrimony*, p. 79.

[30] *L&P Simancas*, vol. 1, pp. 434–5 [8 June 1565].

[31] Doran, *Monarchy and Matrimony*, pp. 65–6, 77–80. It is also possible, given the closeness of the dates and the similarity of the instruments played, that both the Imperial and Spanish ambassadors heard the same private performance.

[32] Bertrand de Salignac de La Mothe-Fénélon, *Correspondance diplomatique de Bertrand de Salignac de La Mothe Fénélon*, ed. Charles Purton Cooper, 7 vols. (Paris, 1840), vol. 5, pp. 91–112 (p. 96) [28 August 1572].

Yet this optimism proved fleeting: the ambassador's next letter reports the court's horrified reaction to the news of the St Bartholomew's Day Massacre that had taken place on 24 August, ending current hopes for the marriage.

Negotiations did resume, but when Elizabeth performed for French ambassadors in 1581 she had little intention of encouraging marital possibilities. By 1581 Anjou's Catholicism, and widespread domestic opposition to the match, were making a marriage impossible. The growing power of Spain meant that Elizabeth and her councillors were interested in a defensive pact with France instead, but the ambassadors had no authority to negotiate one. This performance came at the height of the stalemate, as on 28 April Elizabeth had warned the ambassadors of the difficulties preventing the marriage and declared herself unwilling to make a decision until she had heard Anjou's response to these problems. During a private musical evening in her Privy Chamber on May Day (with entertainment provided by her ensemble of three lutes) Elizabeth gave her own performance on the spinet.[33] She was surely not so much promoting the marriage as smoothing over difficult relations and drawing out the talks while they awaited word from Anjou and perhaps the hope of some diplomatic development.[34] Despite music's strong connotations of desire and marriageability, it was equally capable of performing less amorous roles.

By the time of the failed Anjou match in 1581 Elizabeth was forty-seven years old, but she persisted with her performances throughout the 1590s and beyond, well into her sixties. In continuing to display her musical talents in later life, Elizabeth was departing radically both from the example of her predecessors and from contemporary attitudes about music and age. The majority of Henry VIII's performances had taken place in 1513–17 when he was still in his twenties. This followed Castiglione's advice that music's connotations of love made it an inappropriate pastime for old men (except for their own private recreation) because 'in old men love is a thing to be jested at.'[35] Given music's connotations of beauty and marriageability, Castiglione's recommendation would hold equally well for women. Yet Elizabeth played to various young men who were touring Europe: Frederick, Duke of Württemberg, in 1592; Don Virginio Orsino, Duke of Bracciano, in 1601; and the French ambassador Charles de Gontaut, Duke of Biron, in 1601.[36]

---

[33] 'Journal des négociations des commissaires et ambassadeurs français de 24 Avril au 1er Mai 1581', GB-Lna: PRO 31/3/28, fol. 306r–v.

[34] Doran, *Monarchy and Matrimony*, pp. 179–82; Mack P. Holt, *The Duke of Anjou and the Politique Struggle during the Wars of Religion*, Cambridge Studies in Early Modern History (Cambridge, 1986), pp. 149–50.

[35] Castiglione, *The Courtier*, sig. M4v. Examples of Henry's performance can be found in: John Stevens, *Music and Poetry in the Early Tudor Court*, Cambridge Studies in Music (Cambridge, 1979), pp. 275–6; *CSP Venice*, vol. 2, p. 139; *L&P Henry VIII*, vol. 2, p. 117 [30 April 1515].

[36] Rathgeb, *Warhaffte Beschreibung*, fol. 13v; Rye (ed.), *England as Seen by Foreigners*, p. 12; Hotson, *The First Night of Twelfth Night*, pp. 211–12; Friedrich Ludwig von Raumer, *The Political History of England, during the 16th, 17th, and 18th Centuries*, trans. Hannibal Evans Lloyd (London, 1837), vol. 1, p. 414.

In these later years, Elizabeth's musical image reinforced the fiction of the ageless Queen. In accordance with her motto, *semper eadem*, Elizabeth did all she could to keep up the illusion of eternal youth. This was a new strategy to protect her authority against accusations of frailty, questions of succession, and Elizabethan society's disparaging attitude to single women past child-bearing age.[37] Even in the early years of her reign William Cecil, Lord Burghley, had long recognised the threat of popular contempt for an old, unmarried woman if Elizabeth remained a spinster.[38] There were no positive images of ageing women that Elizabeth could employ. Portraits of ageing men communicated experience, wisdom, and power; however, old women were associated with sin, vice, and decay, as opposed to the virtuous Virgin Mary who was always depicted young.[39] From the early 1590s, Elizabeth no longer sat for portraits and in July 1596 an Act of the Privy Council ordered the seeking out of 'unseemly' likenesses of the Queen, with no further portraits to be produced without the approval of the Queen's Sergeant Painter. Nicholas Hilliard's miniatures showed Elizabeth as increasingly youthful and his 'mask of youth' became the pattern for future portraits.[40] Images of timeless youth were similarly presented in poetry and music, including John Dowland's lute song, 'Time Stands Still with Gazing on her Face', and a song ('Ode of Cynthia') commissioned by the Earl of Cumberland for a 'show on horseback' in 1600, which claimed that 'Time's young hours attend her still'.[41]

In the latter part of her reign Elizabeth's music-making and dancing were frequently interpreted as attempts to deny her old age. In 1589, the courtier John Stanhope reported that 'the Queen is so well as I assure you VI or VII galliards in a morning besides music and singing, is her ordinary exercise.'[42] A letter from the Londoner John Chamberlain to Dudley Carleton, reporting rumours from the court about the Queen's entertaining of Don Virginio (1601), similarly suggested that she danced galliards 'to show that she is not so old as some would have her'.[43] A woman in her late sixties, Elizabeth went out of her way to impress Don Virginio

---

[37] Susan Frye, *Elizabeth I: The Competition for Representation* (Oxford, 1993), pp. 100–3.
[38] Louis Montrose, *The Subject of Elizabeth: Authority, Gender, and Representation* (Chicago, 2006), pp. 211–12.
[39] Nanette Salomon, 'Positioning Women in Visual Convention: The Case of Elizabeth I', in *Attending to Women in Early Modern England*, ed. Betty Travitsky and Adele F. Seeff (Newark, DE, 1994), pp. 64–95 (pp. 82–3).
[40] Strong, *English Renaissance Miniature*, pp. 118–21; Daniel Fischlin, 'Political Allegory, Absolutist Ideology, and the "Rainbow Portrait" of Queen Elizabeth I', *Renaissance Quarterly* 50 (1997), 175–206 (pp. 178–81); Montrose, *Subject of Elizabeth*, pp. 215–28; Frye, *Elizabeth I*, pp. 101–3.
[41] John Dowland, *The Third and Last Book of Songs or Airs Newly Composed to Sing to the Lute, Orpharion, or Viols* (London, 1603), sigs. B2v–C1r; Frye, *Elizabeth I*, p. 101; Elizabeth Goldring et al. (eds.), *John Nichols's The Progresses and Public Processions of Queen Elizabeth I: A New Edition of the Early Modern Sources*, 5 vols. (Oxford, 2014), vol. 4, pp. 120–1.
[42] Goldring et al. (eds.), *John Nichols's The Progresses*, vol. 3, p. 508 [22 December 1589].
[43] Hotson, *The First Night of Twelfth Night*, pp. 211–12.

(then in his early twenties) with her singing, playing, and dancing, and she seems to have succeeded (p. 45). Equally, her music-making kept up the illusion of her eternal youth and demonstrated that her mental and physical faculties were still sharp: 'It is a strange thing to see how lively she is in body and mind and nimble in everything she does', wrote Monsieur de Maisse in 1597.[44] Yet the fiction was not accepted by all. The Spanish ambassador complained in 1599 that 'on the day of Epiphany the Queen held a great feast, in which the head of the Church of England and Ireland was to be seen in her old age dancing three or four galliards.'[45] While religious impropriety seems to be the ambassador's main criticism (as well as a cultural disapproval of the lack of decorum compared to the strict protocol of the Spanish court), he also suggests that dancing is inappropriate for her age. He was doubtless not the only one to see Elizabeth's youthful persona for the fiction it was. Nevertheless, old age was a sign of weakening authority, while attraction and desire were part of Elizabeth's style of government. Therefore the reality of ageing had to be disguised by pretence.

PREDECESSORS AND CONTEMPORARIES

IT was not unusual for Renaissance royalty to be musical: Catherine de Medici, Charles IX and Henry III of France, Margaret of Valois, Isabella d'Este, Emperor Charles V, and Margaret of Austria were all among those esteemed for their musical talents or judgement in the sixteenth century, not to mention Elizabeth's own father and siblings.[46] Nevertheless, upon Elizabeth's accession to the throne, few could have predicted the political significance that her music-making was to gain during her reign. When she was sixteen, her tutor Roger Ascham even commented that, although she was talented, she did not take much pleasure in music.[47] In her late teens she perhaps found music-making unbefitting to her current image of 'Puritan Maid', designed to proclaim her virtue in answer to the scandal of her early teens over her relationship with the forty-year-old Thomas Seymour. The

---

[44] André Hurault de Maisse, *A Journal of All that was Accomplished by Monsieur de Maisse, Ambassador in England from King Henri IV to Queen Elizabeth Anno Domini 1597*, ed. Robert Arthur Jones and G. B. Harrison (London, 1931), p. 26.

[45] *L&P Simancas*, vol. 4, p. 650 [24 January 1599].

[46] Jeanice Brooks, *Courtly Song in Late Sixteenth-Century France* (Chicago, 2000), pp. 10–12; Mary Tiffany Ferer, *Music and Ceremony at the Court of Charles V: The Capilla Flamenca and the Art of Political Promotion*, Studies in Medieval and Renaissance Music 12 (Woodbridge, 2012), pp. 41–3; William Prizer, 'Una "virtù molto conveniente a Madonna": Isabella d'Este as a Musician', *The Journal of Musicology* 17 (1999), 10–49.

[47] Edward Grant (ed.), *Disertissimi viri Rogeri Aschami, Angli, Regiae maiestati non ita pridem a Latinis epistolis, familiarium epistolarum libri tres magna orationis elegantia conscripti* (London, 1571), p. 18: 'Musicae ut peritissima, sic ea non admodum delectate.' The modern translators of these letters demonstrate the strength of Elizabeth's reputation as a musical monarch when they mistranslate this as 'she is as skilled in Music as she is delighted by it': Roger Ascham, *Letters of Roger Ascham*, trans. Maurice Hatch and Alvin Vos (New York, 1989), p. 167.

early-seventeenth-century historian William Camden reported that Edward VI called Elizabeth 'Sweet sister Temperance' while criticising Mary's attendance at 'foreign merriments and dances' (though this view may be influenced by Camden's own Protestantism).[48] Yet within the first year of her reign, Elizabeth began performing for ambassadors.

The strongest influences on Elizabeth would have been her family, and particularly other female rulers. Yet neither the reign of her predecessor and sister Mary I, nor that of her cousin Mary Queen of Scots, offered any model. Although Mary I was musically talented, she showed little concern with making constructive political use of performances during her reign. There are no known diplomatic performances and very few comments on Mary's musical abilities, even during marriage negotiations with Philip II of Spain.[49] According to the Venetian ambassador Giovanni Michieli, by 1557 she played rarely, though she still 'surprised the best performers, both by the rapidity of her hand and by her style of playing'.[50] Mary's failure to exploit the political potential of her musicality cannot be attributed to ignorance of the political significance of the arts – the elaborate symbolism of both Mary's coronation and her marriage to Philip suggests otherwise.[51] Rather it appears to have been a conscious choice. Mary's decision may have been based on her age: she was thirty-seven on her accession in 1553. After her marriage in July 1554 there were even fewer reasons for performances. She may also have been wary of the criticism of music's frivolity, avoiding public musical performances and dances as a sign of her Catholic piety and her seriousness and wisdom as a ruler in answer to those who were sceptical about whether a woman could be a virtuous and capable monarch. These risks became a reality for Mary Queen of Scots, who attracted the criticism of John Knox. His misogynistic, xenophobic, and Presbyterian attitudes

---

[48] David Starkey, *Elizabeth: Apprenticeship* (London, 2000), pp. 85, 87; William Camden, *Annales rerum Anglicarum, et Hibernicarum, regnante Elizabetha, ad annum salutis M.D.LXXXIX* (London, 1615), p. 9: 'dulcis sororis Temperantiae'.

[49] *CSP Spain*, vols. 11–12.

[50] *CSP Venice*, vol. 6, pp. 1043–85 (p. 1055) [11 May 1557]; Eugenio Albèri (ed.), *Relazione degli ambasciatori Veneti al senato*, 15 vols. (Florence, 1839–63), vol. 4, p. 323. In 1554 Venetian ambassador Giacomo Soranzo reported that Mary was a 'very good performer' on the lute and spinet, and that before her accession she had taught many of her Maids of Honour. Yet he did not indicate that he had heard Mary play, and his reference to music-making before her reign suggests his knowledge was gained from talking to members of her household. See *CSP Venice*, vol. 5, pp. 532–64 (p. 533) [18 August 1554]; Albèri, *Relazione degli ambasciatori*, vol. 8, p. 323.

[51] Paulina Kewes, 'Godly Queens: The Royal Iconographies of Mary and Elizabeth', in *Tudor Queenship: The Reigns of Mary and Elizabeth*, ed. Anna Whitelock and Alice Hunt, Queenship and Power (New York, 2010), pp. 47–62; Alexander Samson, 'Changing Places: The Marriage and Royal Entry of Philip, Prince of Austria, and Mary Tudor, July–August 1554', *The Sixteenth Century Journal* 36 (2005), 761–84 (pp. 761–7). This more recent work contrasts with the earlier view of David Loades that 'although she enjoyed ceremony and splendour [Mary] seems to have had no notion of how to put it to constructive political use.' David Loades, *Mary Tudor: A Life* (Oxford, 1989), pp. 333–4.

led him to see her love of music and dance as a sign that she lacked both piety and the seriousness required for rule.[52] Yet she too gave her talents little political role when she became Queen of Scotland, despite the high regard for her musicality held by those who knew her during her upbringing at the French court and her marriage to the dauphin (later Francis II).[53]

The musical reputation of Elizabeth's father, Henry VIII, must have had some influence. Yet whereas Elizabeth's musical talents were wholly conventional, Henry deliberately cultivated more unusual abilities. Alongside the singing and playing on the lute, virginals, and organs that were typically learnt by courtly amateurs, Henry performed for ambassadors on the recorder (*li flavuti*), gitteron-pipe (*flauto de cythara*), the lute-pipes (*lira de' flauti*) and the cornett (*corno*), despite wind instruments usually being considered unfitting for upper-class amateur performers.[54] Breaking with convention allowed Henry to display his exceptional talents (for a monarch and amateur): his ability to play instruments usually associated with professional musicians and to perform in consort (recorders and cornetts being ensemble rather than solo instruments). Another ambassador also recorded Henry's ability to 'sing from book at sight', a further indication of his high standard of musical literacy.[55] John Stevens likens Henry's musical showing-off to his spectacular feats on the tiltyard, where he 'performed supernatural feats, changing his horses, and making them fly rather than leap'.[56] Henry flaunted an exceptional musicality to inspire splendour and wonder without regard to convention in a way that would have been hard for a queen to pull off without accusations of licentiousness and immodesty. Elizabeth's performances were quite different in character: more modest and intimate, evoking feminine qualities of sensuality and beauty.

Perhaps most akin to Elizabeth's musical politics, however, are the childhood performances of her sister Mary. As heir to the throne, from the age of just four Mary's musical talents were being employed to impress ambassadors, and parade her marriageability. In July 1520 during her betrothal to Francis, the French Dauphin, the four-year-old Mary entertained three French gentlemen with such 'pleasant pastime in playing at the virginals, that they greatly marvelled and rejoiced the same, her young and tender age considered'.[57] During negotiations in 1527

---

[52] John Knox, *The Works of John Knox*, ed. David Laing, 6 vols. (Edinburgh, 1846–64), vol. 2, p. 294.

[53] Antonia Fraser, *Mary Queen of Scots* (London, 2004), p. 177. Pierre de Bourdeilles, Seigneur de Brantôme, 'Vies des dames illustres françoises et étrangères', *Œuvres complètes du Seigneur de Brantôme*, 8 vols. (Paris, 1823), vol. 5, pp. 1–349 (p. 86).

[54] Stevens, *Music and Poetry*, pp. 275–6; *CSP Venice*, vol. 2, p. 139. Stevens suggests that the ambassador may have got his instruments slightly muddled here (perhaps itself a sign of the strangeness of Henry's performance), because an inventory of Henry VIII's instruments records that it held 'two gitteron pipes of ivory tipped with silver and gilt; they are called cornetts'. The gitteron-pipes and the cornett would therefore seem to be the same instrument.

[55] *L&P Henry VIII*, vol. 2, p. 117 [30 April 1515].

[56] Stevens, *Music and Poetry*, p. 275 [citing the Venetian ambassador, 11 July 1517].

[57] *L&P Henry VIII*, vol. 3, pp. 322–3 [2 July 1520].

for a marriage to either Francis I or his second son, Henry, Duke of Orléans, the French ambassador's secretary Dodieu heard her play on the spinet, judging her 'the most accomplished person of her age'.[58] Yet Mary was only a child during these negotiations and a mere pawn of international diplomacy throughout these betrothals. Her performances are more likely to have been instigated by her parents and carers than to have been conscious political acts on her part. By contrast, Elizabeth was in full control of when and how she performed, and calculating in her diplomatic use of performances to draw out negotiations or manipulate ambassadors.

Nevertheless, the parallel reveals how much Elizabeth's use of music was based on the conventional musical practice of royal and noble women, despite appearing so different in comparison to Mary I and Mary Queen of Scots. The initial catalyst for Elizabeth's performances was the numerous and protracted marriage negotiations in the first decades of the reign, and if her decision to perform into her old age was unusual, it was fully in keeping with the image of youthful beauty she was trying to project. Whereas the royal image created in literature, portraiture, and song emphasised music's political connotations as much as its sensual ones, by contrast Elizabeth's performances largely depended on typical ideas of female music-making, exploiting its connotations of marriageability, beauty, and attractiveness. The political overtones were provided by virtue of her status and through the situations in which she chose to perform. Her musical queenship melded femininity and intimacy with political calculation and intent.

COURTING ROYAL FAVOUR

While Elizabeth drew on the desirability of the female performer to charm foreign diplomats and guests, her courtiers similarly employed music to praise, charm, and entertain, attempting to be personally attractive to the Queen. Sir Francis Bacon recognised this performance of courtly love as a strategy actively encouraged by Elizabeth herself. As he explained in his *In felicem memoriam Elizabethae* (1606):

> She allowed herself to be wooed and courted, and even to have love made to her; and liked it; and continued it beyond the natural age for such vanities.[59]

Bacon compared Elizabeth with 'the accounts of romances, of the Queen in the blessed islands and her court and institutions', because she 'allow[ed] of amorous admiration but prohibit[ed] desire'. According to David Norbrook this culture of courtly love 'actualised a metaphor that was always latent in monarchical systems of government: relations between individual and authority were ... those of a subject, a dependent, to a single individual whose favour had to be "courted".'[60] Yet this was

---

[58] Ibid., vol. 4, pp. 1397–415 [8 May 1527].

[59] Francis Bacon, *The Works of Francis Bacon*, ed. James Spedding, Robert Leslie Ellis, and Douglas Denon Heath, 14 vols. (London, 1857), vol. 11, p. 460.

[60] David Norbrook, *Poetry and Politics in the English Renaissance*, rev. edn (Oxford, 2002), p. 104.

a 'frozen courtship' in which courtiers were perpetually courting their beloved, but never able to achieve the fulfilment of an amorous relationship.[61] Music's tradition as an art of love in which men serenaded their ladies (and *vice versa*) inspired courtiers to turn to its charms for their political courting of Elizabeth. Lute songs in particular were often a performance of intimacy and introspection, enacting seemingly personal confessions of melancholy or love to the lute's discreet tones, but in the presence of an audience.[62] Such conventions were ideal for courtiers wishing to perform their devotion to Elizabeth, or perhaps their distress at her disfavour. As with Elizabeth's performances, these songs were games of secrecy in which courtiers gave the appearance of revealing private thoughts, but used thoroughly conventional genres, themes, and rhetoric.

Courtly entertainments and recreational activities took on greater significance for male courtiers during Elizabeth's reign because of the impact her gender had on their opportunities to influence her. The court positions which offered the closest and most reliable access to the monarch were those in the Privy Chamber. Members of the Privy Chamber served the private needs of the monarch and enjoyed an intimacy that brought privileged opportunities to influence policies and patronage. Yet Elizabeth's Privy Chamber was largely staffed by women, many of whom were long-standing servants (such as Catherine Asteley or Blanche Parry) or relations of the Queen (like the Howard, Carey, or Knollys families).[63] The limited positions for men within the Privy Chamber meant fewer posts through which men could gain personal access to the monarch. With access to the Privy Chamber for those without an official position being at the pleasure of the Queen, courtiers could suddenly find their access removed if they were out of favour.[64] This state of affairs made active courtship of Elizabeth more important for male courtiers, placing greater significance on alternative means of gaining the Queen's attention, such as pageants, entertainments, poetry, and music.[65] Elaborate entertainments required long-term and large-scale planning, but courtiers could also create musical performances that were more private and spontaneous, responsive to

---

[61] Bates, *Rhetoric of Courtship*, pp. 46–8.

[62] Daniel Fischlin, 'The Performance Context of the English Lute Song, 1596–1622', in *Performance on Lute, Guitar, and Vihuela: Historical Practice and Modern Interpretation*, ed. Victor Coelho, Cambridge Studies in Performance Practice (Cambridge, 1997), pp. 47–71 (pp. 59–61).

[63] Pam Wright, 'A Change in Direction: The Ramifications of a Female Household, 1558–1603', in *The English Court: From the Wars of the Roses to the Civil War*, ed. David Starkey (London, 1987), pp. 147–72 (pp. 149–50, 158, 172); Kristin Bundesen, '"No Other Faction But My Own": Dynastic Politics and Elizabeth I's Carey Cousins', PhD dissertation, University of Nottingham, 2009; Natalie Mears, 'Politics in the Elizabethan Privy Chamber: Lady Mary Sidney and Kat Ashley', in *Women and Politics in Early Modern England, 1450–1700*, ed. James Daybell (Aldershot, 2004), pp. 67–82.

[64] Wright, 'Change in Direction', p. 160.

[65] Curtis Perry, 'Court and Coterie Culture', in *A Companion to English Renaissance Literature and Culture*, ed. Michael Hattaway, Blackwell Companions to Literature and Culture (Oxford, 2000), pp. 106–18 (pp. 112–13).

immediate circumstances and able to help sustain their close relationship with the monarch.

Simply performing music for the pleasure of the Queen was a means of gaining favour. In 1563 Henry Stewart, Lord Darnley, was described as a 'daily waiter' who 'playeth very often at the lute before the Queen, wherein it should seem she taketh pleasure, as indeed he plays very well'.[66] Darnley was an important figure because he was connected by birth to both the Scottish and English monarchies through his grandmother, Margaret Tudor, the sister of Henry VIII and widow of James IV. Darnley and his parents, Lord and Lady Lennox, had been imprisoned in 1561 for secret journeys to the French and Scottish courts made by Darnley and servants of the Lennox household attempting to gain favour with Mary Stuart (as Queen Consort of France and later Queen of Scots). Yet by 1563 the family had been forgiven and were being shown considerable favour at court by Elizabeth.[67] Darnley's performances were noted by Sir John Mason (a member of the Privy Council) and relayed to Thomas Challoner (English ambassador in Spain) as evidence of the surprising intimacy the Lennox family were gaining with the Queen. His favoured position was possibly being interpreted as suggesting Elizabeth's preference for the Lennox family's claim to be her successors over the Grey family, who were preferred by many Protestants.[68] The succession was a particular concern as Elizabeth had nearly died of smallpox in 1562. Though usually unrecorded, this use of courtly talents to entertain the monarch was probably common. Henry VIII had often invited Sir Peter Carew to sing songs with him for recreation.[69]

In the late 1580s, however, courtiers began a more intensive musical politics, composing their own lyrics either to sing themselves to ballad tunes, or to be set to music and performed by professional musicians on their behalf. While the intimacy of such performances shares similarities with music-making like Darnley's, the songs are more intense in their pleas or complaints and, where the context is known, respond to an immediate political situation that sparked the courtier's need to communicate with the Queen.

Although one might have expected courtiers to have been using songs to convey personal political messages throughout the reign, this practice depended upon courtiers writing their own political verses (if it was to be more spontaneous, rather than commissioned like an entertainment).[70] At the beginning of Elizabeth's reign English noblemen held poetry in low esteem. Very few courtiers seem to have written

---

[66] Sir John Mason, 'Sir John Mason to Challoner: 19 July 1563', GB-Lna: SP70/60, Secretaries of State: State Papers Foreign, Elizabeth I, fols. 99r–100v (fol. 100r).

[67] Elaine Greig, 'Stewart, Henry, Duke of Albany [Lord Darnley] (1545/6–1567)', ODNB (online edn, 2008).

[68] Caroline Bingham, *Darnley: A Life of Henry Stuart, Lord Darnley, Consort of Mary Queen of Scots* (London, 1995), pp. 78–83. In the alternative line of succession Catherine Grey had offended Elizabeth by secretly marrying Edward Seymour, Earl of Hertford and son of Protector Somerset, and giving birth to two sons.

[69] Stevens, *Music and Poetry*, p. 286.

[70] It is possible that they may have had a poet write lyrics for them, but this would diminish the personal nature of the lyrics and would be more akin to the producing of music for formal entertainments.

any poems, those who did wrote only a few, and no sixteenth-century courtesy book for the aristocracy suggested that a courtier should compose poetry.[71] This situation began to change in the 1570s, when Edward de Vere, Earl of Oxford, and Sir Edward Dyer began to compose personal poems to Elizabeth; however, political poems still constituted only the minority of these poets' outputs.[72] Most reflected a courtier's immediate experience of the court rather than addressing Elizabeth directly and were designed for the entertainment of a small group of family and friends to whom they would be read aloud, enclosed with letters, or circulated by manuscript.[73] In the 1580s, however, Steven May identifies the development of 'utilitarian poetics' which saw courtiers such as Sir Arthur Gorges, Sir Walter Ralegh, and Robert Devereux, Earl of Essex, writing poetry with the primary purpose of communicating with Elizabeth and maintaining their relationship with her for their individual advancement.[74] This created the opportunity for songs to be used in the same way.

Presenting a musical performance to the Queen was like the giving of a gift. Gifts from a courtier to a monarch signalled gratitude for past favours, demonstrated the worthiness of the giver, and anticipated future patronage. As well as being pleasing, the etiquette of giving and receiving created a social pressure for the recipient to receive the gift politely and to reciprocate in some way.[75] In the past Elizabeth had received gifts of song-books at New Year from court musicians Thomas Kent (1559) and Peter Lupo (1579), as well as a John Cavely (1559), whose status is unknown (for diplomatic gifts see p. 85).[76] A performance had neither the permanence nor the magnificence of a beautifully copied manuscript, but it had other advantages. While the copying of a special manuscript required time and planning, the performance of a song was informal and could be contrived more spontaneously in response to an immediate political need.

A song was also a gift which could deliver a specific message. Composer Thomas Whythorne employed songs to communicate his amorous intentions because he thought the recipient would be more attentive and also:

---

[71] Steven W. May, *The Elizabethan Courtier Poets: The Poems and their Contexts* (Columbia, MO, 1991), p. 45 (with the exception of an ambivalent reference in Castiglione's *The Courtier* to poetry's function in entertaining ladies).

[72] May, *Elizabethan Courtier Poets*, pp. 52–7, 97.

[73] Arthur F. Marotti, *Manuscript, Print, and the English Renaissance Lyric* (Ithaca, NY, 1995), pp. 1–3, 8.

[74] May, *Elizabethan Courtier Poets*, pp. 103–39.

[75] Ilana Krausman Ben-Amos, *The Culture of Giving: Informal Support and Gift-Exchange in Early Modern England*, Cambridge Social and Cultural Histories 12 (Cambridge, 2008), pp. 5–9, 205–7.

[76] Jane A. Lawson, 'The Remembrance of the New Year: Books Given to Queen Elizabeth as New Year's Gifts', in *Elizabeth I and the Culture of Writing*, ed. Peter Beal and Grace Ioppolo (London, 2007), pp. 133–72 (pp. 157–8, 164).

if it were not to be well taken, yet in as much as it was sung there could not so much hurt be found as had been in the case of my writing being delivered to her to read, for singing of such songs and ditties was a thing common.[77]

Convention provided safeguards against causing undue offence, while the ephemeral nature of performance might also allow the courtier to be more daring in his petitions or complaints than one might in writing.

The courtier could also shape the song's reception through varying the relationship between himself, his message, and his recipient. Songs written to ballad tunes were performable by the courtier himself, allowing him to deliver his message personally. Conversely, employing a professional musician (either to improvise or to compose and perform a musical setting) added formality to the occasion and distanced the delivery of the message from its writer. This method allowed courtiers to address the Queen indirectly through a professional musician when personal access might have been denied, or when they were unsure of the reception they might receive. Moreover, the courtier might hope to benefit from the better quality of a professional singer and the recognition of his effort in arranging such a composition and performance.

The earliest example of this political song-writing for personal gain – Sir Walter Ralegh's 'Fortune Hath Taken Thee Away My Love' – appears to have been written to fit a pre-existing melody. The theme and metre suggest that the lyrics were probably written to fit the fit the popular ballad tune 'Fortune My Foe', a melody that Robert Naunton specifically connected with Ralegh.[78] Describing Ralegh's rise and later decline in favour in *Fragmenta regalia*, Naunton writes that:

> he had gotten the Queen's ear at a trice ... which nettled them all, yea those that he relied on, began to take this his sudden favour for an allarum, and to be sensible of their own supplantation, and to project his, which made him shortly after sing, *Fortune my foe, &c.*[79]

It is unclear whether Naunton meant to imply the literal use of the song for political ends, or whether he intended the statement metaphorically; however, the technique was one practised by other courtier-poets. Indeed, the making of contrafacta was widespread in Tudor culture, from the writing of new ballads to popular tunes, to the Englishing of Latin motets or Italian madrigals, to Dowland's creation of some songs from his previously written galliards and pavans.[80] William Webbe, author of *Discourse of English Poetry* (1586), claimed that there was not 'any tune or stroke ... which hath not some poetical ditties framed according to the

---

[77] Thomas Whythorne, *The Autobiography of Thomas Whythorne*, ed. James Marshall Osborn (Oxford, 1961), p. 51.

[78] Gerald Abraham, 'A Lost Poem by Queen Elizabeth I', *Times Literary Supplement*, 30 May 1968, 553.

[79] Sir Robert Naunton, *Fragmenta Regalia, or, Observations on the Late Queen Elizabeth, Her Times and Favorites* (London, 1641), p. 31.

[80] Gavin Alexander, 'The Elizabethan Lyric as Contrafactum: Robert Sidney's "French Tune" Identified', *Music & Letters* 84 (2003), 378–402 (pp. 378–84).

number thereof – some to Rogero, some to Trenchmore'.[81] Many miscellanies of courtly verse expected their contents to be sung, with Richard Edwards claiming that the verses in *The Paradise of Dainty Devices* (1576) were 'aptly made to be set to any song in five parts, or sung to Instrument' (and several settings survive).[82] More particularly, Sir Philip Sidney wrote several sonnets to fit European song tunes, while Robert Devereux, Earl of Essex's, 'Say, What is Love?' has a nonsense refrain that suggests it was written to fit a now-lost ballad tune.[83]

Composing lyrics to fit a pre-existing tune would allow Ralegh to perform himself without the mediation of professional musicians, enacting the poetic convention of a lover serenading his lady and creating an intimate plea to protect his favoured position. May believes that the lyrics were written in response to the Earl of Essex's rise in favour, threatening Ralegh's position as a royal favourite in 1587.[84] Although a conventional love lament, the lyrics allude to its political overtones by labelling the mistress as a 'princess'. The 'love' Ralegh has lost is Elizabeth:

> Fortune hath taken thee away my love
> My life's joy and my soul's heaven above.
> Fortune hath taken thee away my princess
> My world's joy and my true fantasy's mistress.[85]

Ralegh tactfully blames Fortune (which even 'conquers kings') rather than his mistress for his current distress. Yet this does not prevent him ending the poem by asserting the contrast between his constancy and Elizabeth's changing favour:

> With wisdom's eyes had but blind fortune seen
> Then had my love, my love for ever been.
> But love farewell: though fortune conquer thee
> No fortune base nor frail shall alter me.

---

[81] William Webbe, *A Discourse of English Poetry* (London, 1586), sig. F4v.

[82] Richard Edwards (ed.), *The Paradise of Dainty Devices Containing Sundry Pithy Precepts, Learned Counsels and Excellent Inventions* (London, 1576), sig. A2v; Edward Doughtie, *Lyrics from English Airs, 1596–1622* (Cambridge, MA, 1970), pp. 10–16; Matthew Spring, *The Lute in Britain: A History of the Instrument and its Music*, Early Music Series (Oxford, 2001), pp. 255–6.

[83] Sir Philip Sidney, *The Poems of Sir Philip Sidney*, ed. William A. Ringler (Oxford, 1962), p. xliii. Letter from Sir Philip Sidney to Edward Denny, 22 May 1580, printed in James Marshall Osborn, *Young Philip Sidney, 1572–1577*, Elizabethan Club Series 5 (New Haven, CT, 1972), p. 540; John Stevens, 'Sir Philip Sidney and "Versified Music": Melodies for Courtly Songs', in *The Well-Enchanting Skill: Music, Poetry, and Drama in the Culture of the Renaissance: Essays in Honour of F. W. Sternfeld*, ed. John Caldwell, Edward Olleson and Susan Wollenberg (Oxford, 1990), pp. 153–69 (pp. 157–66); Steven W. May, 'The Poems of Edward DeVere, Seventeenth Earl of Oxford, and of Robert Devereux, Second Earl of Essex: An Edition and Commentary', *Studies in Philology* 77.5 (1980), 46.

[84] May, *Elizabethan Courtier Poets*, p. 132.

[85] Walter Ralegh, *The Poems of Sir Walter Ralegh: A Historical Edition*, ed. Michael Rudick, Medieval and Renaissance Texts and Studies 209; Renaissance English Text Society 23 (Tempe, AZ, 1999), pp. 19–20.

Ralegh's suggestion that Elizabeth's love is changed by Fortune deliberately subverts her motto, *semper eadem*, and invokes those conventions of female inconstancy that Elizabeth sought to distance herself from. In a bid to persuade her to repay his love with favour, he challenges her to prove that she is constant by reaffirming his favoured position.

It is tempting to see the poetic answer to Ralegh's poem, 'Ah Silly Pug Wert Thou So Sore Afraid', as evidence of an intimate musical exchange between Queen and courtier. Attributed to Elizabeth in two sources, it directly answers Ralegh's arguments and reassures him that his position of favour is not under threat.[86] Responding to Ralegh's assertion that 'dead to all joys I only live in woe', the poem answers:

> Dead to all joys and living unto woe,
> Slain quite by her that ne'er gave wise man blow,
> Revive again and live without all dread.[87]

Answer-poems were common in manuscript verse exchanges between circles of family and friends in the upper classes. Yet they could often be humorous parodies and satires.[88] The Elizabeth poem mocks Ralegh's exaggerated tone, while the stereotypical lament and the intimate pet-names 'silly pug' and 'my Wat' could easily be the humorous inventions of a satirical answer-poem. Furthermore, the only source to contain both poems provides no attributions, further weakening the assumption that this poem is evidence for a genuine exchange of songs between Elizabeth and Ralegh.[89]

Yet an enigmatic incident between the Queen and Robert Cecil (her Secretary of State) on 18 September 1602 offers a firmer example of the playfulness with which Elizabeth and her courtiers engaged in these musical games of courtly love. Unlike Ralegh, Cecil had his lyrics set and sung by the singer-lutenist Robert Hales. A court employee, Hales was one the Queen's favourite musicians, though only one of his compositions is preserved: the lute song 'O Eyes Leave Off Thy Weeping' in Robert Dowland's *Musical Banquet* (1610).[90] Cecil's commissioning of the most talented musician available was fitting for his status as a significant patron of music. He employed his own full-time household musicians (relatively rare for the nobility at this period), owned music books and instruments, and received dedications in the publications of Thomas Morley, Robert Jones, and John Dowland.[91]

---

[86] It is ascribed to Elizabeth in two sources: George Puttenham's *The Art of English Poesy* (London, 1589) – which includes just a single couplet – and in MS Petyt 538.10 from the Inner Temple Library. Ralegh, *Poems*, p. 20.

[87] Ibid.

[88] Marotti, *Manuscript, Print*, pp. 159–70.

[89] Ralegh, *Poems*, pp. 22–3. The single source containing both poems is Wiltshire Record Office 865/500.

[90] Robert Dowland (ed.), *A Musical Banquet Furnished with Variety of Delicious Ayres* (London, 1610), sigs. C1v–C2r.

[91] Lynn Hulse, 'The Musical Patronage of Robert Cecil, First Earl of Salisbury (1563–1612)', *Journal of the Royal Musical Association* 116 (1991), 24–40.

According to Sir William Browne, the incident began when Elizabeth spotted Lady Derby wearing a portrait miniature of her uncle (Cecil):

> The Queen espying it asked what fine jewel that was the Lady Derby was curious to excuse the showing of it but the Queen would have it and opening it and finding it to be Mr Secretary's snatched it away and tied it upon her shoe, and walked long with it there, then she took it thence and pinned it on her elbow and wore it sometimes there also, which Mr Secretary being told of, made these verses, and had Hales to sing them in his chamber, it was told her majesty that Mr Secretary had rare music and songs she would needs hear them and so this ditty was sung, which you see first written, more verses there be likewise whereof some or all were likewise sung.

Writing to George Talbot, 17th Earl of Shrewsbury, Browne claimed that he would not send them to anyone else because:

> I hear they are very secret, some of the verses argue that he repines not though her ma[jesty] please to grace others, and contents himself with th[e fav]our he hath.[92]

Modern scholars have interpreted the meaning of Elizabeth's actions in strikingly different ways. David Price described Elizabeth's action as arising from jealousy so that Cecil 'could only appease Elizabeth with a song'.[93] Similarly, Lynn Hulse suggested that Cecil wrote the song to 'flatter', 'appease', and 'placat[e]' Elizabeth.[94] In contrast, May suggested that the incident was a rare glimpse of Elizabeth 'playfully teasing her courtiers' and the seizure of the portrait was 'a manifest sign of her fondness for him'.[95] The occasion demonstrates the difficulty courtiers must have had in interpreting the Queen's mood towards them. Courtly expression was ambivalent, and while this added to its richness and subtlety, it was easy for these signs and gestures to be misunderstood.[96] Elizabeth could not have taken any severe offence at Lady Derby wearing a portrait of her uncle, but the placing of Cecil's portrait on her shoe was hardly a flattering way to treat it. Alternatively, this may have been a means of hiding the image, perhaps as part of a game to see how long it would take Cecil to notice (which Elizabeth made easier when Cecil failed to notice by placing the miniature at her elbow).

Although the verses sent by Browne have not survived alongside his letter, Cecil's lyrics have recently been found by Joshua Eckhardt in two early-seventeenth-century

---

[92] Facsimile given in Joshua Eckhardt, '"From a Seruant of Diana" to the Libellers of Robert Cecil: The Transmission of Songs written for Queen Elizabeth I', in *Elizabeth I and the Culture of Writing*, ed. Peter Beal and Grace Ioppolo (London, 2007), pp. 115–31 (pp. 124–5).

[93] David Price, 'Gilbert Talbot, Seventh Earl of Shrewsbury: An Elizabethan Courtier and his Music', *Music & Letters* 57 (1976), 144–51 (p. 147).

[94] Hulse, 'Musical Patronage', p. 35.

[95] May, *Elizabethan Courtier Poets*, pp. 133–4.

[96] Bates, *Rhetoric of Courtship*, pp. 43–4.

miscellanies.[97] The poem 'From a Servant of Diana' begins by describing Elizabeth taking the picture and then how she would 'wear it at her elbow, though first tied at her shoe', before offering an interpretation of the Queen's actions.[98] In light of the lyrics, Eckhardt reads the situation as one of 'harmony and mutual trust' in which 'the Queen silently registered the courtier's devotion and the courtier's verses explicated her actions accordingly.'[99] To my mind, however, Cecil's second verse explicitly addresses the possibility of Elizabeth's disfavour, asking the very question that must have been on both his own mind and that of all the other courtiers who had seen Elizabeth wearing the miniature:

> What meant that angel-like Queen to wear the picture so?
> Meant she to scorn her servant, or to disgrace him?[100]

He completes the line by giving the firm answer 'no'. At this point Cecil takes control of the meaning of this courtly performance:

> She at her elbow wore it, to signify that he
> To serve her at her elbow, doth ever love to bee.
>
> And at her foot she plac'd it where he would prostrate lie
> To show where he resolved even at her feet to die.

Cecil acted to ensure that his reputation among his fellow couriers would not be damaged by disseminating a positive interpretation of the Queen's actions. His interpretation was also aimed at Elizabeth, presenting himself as her devoted servant in case she should have taken offence. Yet he simultaneously responds to the possibility that Elizabeth's actions were merely courtly teasing and flirtation with his own tool of courtly love, a song.

Intriguingly, Cecil may not have acted alone in engineering his musical tribute. Cecil's poem hardly fits Browne's description of arguing that 'he repines not though her ma[jesty] please to grace others, and contents himself with th[e fav]our he hath.' Yet in both miscellanies Cecil's verses are preceded by the poem 'My Love Doth Fly with Wings of Fear', with no more than a line break between the two. This poem is a much closer fit to Browne's description, particularly in its second and third verses:

> My love doth see and doth admire
> Admiring breedeth humbleness
> Blind love is bold, but my desire
> The more it loves presumes the less.

---

[97] Eckhardt, 'From a Seruant of Diana', pp. 115–16: GB-Ob: MS Don. c. 54 [Richard Roberts's Miscellany], fol. 7v, and GB-Oas: MS 155 [Sir Christopher Yelverton's Miscellany], fols. 127v–128r.
[98] GB-Ob: MS Don.c.54, fol. 7v
[99] Eckhardt, 'From a Seruant of Diana', p. 119.
[100] GB-Ob: MS Don.c.54, fol. 7v

> My love seeks not reward, nor glory
> But with itself, itself contenting
> Is never sullen, never sorry
> Never repining, never repenting.[101]

In the miscellany of the Welsh judge Richard Roberts, this poem is entitled 'Of the Last Queen by the Earl of Clanricarde'. Richard Burke, the Fourth Earl of Clanricarde, was an Irish nobleman who was raised in England and well connected with the English court and nobility: in his diary on 10 October 1602 John Manningham described Clanricarde as 'well esteemed of by her Majesty, and in special grace at this time'.[102] Roberts's attribution is plausible, then, as by this date Clanricarde was at court and enjoying the Queen's favour.[103]

Eckhardt suggests either that this is an example of musical and poetic rivalry in which Cecil was defending his position against Clanricarde's success at court, or that Cecil and Clanricarde cooperated to have their songs performed together.[104] If the former were the case, we might expect the rivalry between the Cecils and Essex in the 1590s to have prompted similar poetic and musical competition, but no other verses by Cecil survive. Furthermore, Robert Cecil's position of favour with the Queen was built on his usefulness to her as a minister following in his father's footsteps, so he had little need at this stage in his career to feel under threat from a young earl. Instead the circumstances described in Browne's letter suggest that Cecil needed a helper to tell the Queen about the songs being performed in his chamber and persuade her to hear them. The most plausible situation is that Clanricarde acted as Cecil's accomplice in exchange for having his own lyrics performed too.

Finally, the incident exemplifies courtly 'games of secrecy' not only in its playful courtship and collaborative scheming, but also in the way it counterpoints the public and the private. Although William Browne's letter claims that these matters are 'very secret', his information is already second-hand and he is spreading the tale further still. The performance was the subject of common court gossip, and the lyrics, at least, circulated widely enough to reach the miscellanies of two gentlemen outside of the court. Music was always more public than a sonnet or miniature, as it was harder to control who overheard a live performance than who read or looked at an object; however, this inherent lack of secrecy may have been an advantage to courtiers. Leaked details of intimate performances spread word of the courtier's closeness to the Queen and, by extension, his power to influence and petition her.

---

[101] Ibid.

[102] Colm Lennon, 'Burke, Richard, Fourth Earl of Clanricarde and First Earl of St Albans (1572–1635)', *ODNB* (online edn, 2004); John Manningham, *The Diary of John Manningham of the Middle Temple, 1602–1603*, ed. Robert Parker Sorlien (Hanover, NH, 1976), p. 59.

[103] Eckhardt, 'From a Seruant of Diana', p. 121.

[104] Ibid.

THE SONGS OF ESSEX

PERHAPS the most prolific musical politician was Robert Devereux, Earl of Essex. According to Sir Henry Wotton, one of the Earl's secretaries, it was Essex's 'common way' to write lyrics to the Queen and have them set to music.[105] Wotton's illustrative situation concerns a case of political rivalry from c. 1590–2 when the Earl of Southampton was particularly prominent at court.[106] Spotting 'some weariness in the Queen, or perhaps (with little change of the word, though more in the danger) some wariness' towards Essex, Sir Fulke Greville seized the opportunity to put forward the Earl of Southampton as a challenger to Essex's supremacy as the royal favourite. Having discovered the threat, Essex chose to 'evaporate his thoughts in a sonnet', and (like Cecil) to have this sung to the Queen by Robert Hales. Impressing and entertaining her with this special musical offering would certainly address Elizabeth's supposed weariness. Furthermore, a couplet cited by Wotton suggests that Essex tackled her potential wariness towards him by presenting himself as an unshakeably loyal admirer:

> And if thou should'st by her be now forsaken,
> She made thy heart too strong for to be shaken.

According to Wotton, however, 'the complot ... had as much of the hermit as of the poet', and it was 'as if he had been casting one eye back at the least to his retiredness'. Although the hermit was a conventional courtly persona (see Henry Lee in Chapter 4), it captured Essex's inclination towards the contemplative life. He referred to his own bookish nature in his early years, and had been a keen scholar before his participation in the conflict in the Netherlands. His Accession Day pageantry of 1595 saw him petitioned (unsuccessfully) by a Hermit to reject the active life to return to one of study and artistic pursuits.[107] Furthermore, withdrawing from court when he felt rejected by Elizabeth became one of Essex's particular political tactics.[108] If Wotton's comment describes Essex's actual self-presentation as a rejected courtly lover turned hermit on this occasion, then the image implicitly threatened the Earl's retirement from court life if he did not continue in Elizabeth's favour. The result was apparently successful: 'all this likewise quickly vanished, and there was a good while fair weather over head.'[109] While the song on this occasion does not survive, extant musical settings of other lyrics by Essex offer rare glimpses into how his daring and impassioned complaints were

---

[105] Henry Wotton, *Reliquiae Wottonianae or a Collection of Lives, Letters, Poems with Characters of Sundry Personages and Other Incomparable Pieces of Language and Art*, 3rd edn (London, 1672), pp. 165–6.

[106] May, 'Poems', p. 88.

[107] Ibid., p. 18; Edward Doughtie, 'The Earl of Essex and Occasions for Contemplative Verse', *English Literary Renaissance* 9 (1979), 355–63 (pp. 358–9).

[108] Wotton, *Reliquiae Wottonianae*, p. 166; Paul E. J. Hammer, *The Polarisation of Elizabethan Politics: The Political Career of Robert Devereux, 2nd Earl of Essex, 1585–1597*, Cambridge Studies in Early Modern British History (Cambridge, 1999), pp. 122, 318, 339–40, 379, 386.

[109] Wotton, *Reliquiae Wottonianae*, pp. 165–6.

contained within the bounds of decorum by musical convention and restrained stylistic choices as he sought to maintain his position as a favourite of the Queen.

Wotton's anecdote, Essex's musical patronage, and the Earl's status as a figurehead for the Catholic sympathies of musicians have led musicologists to connect numerous songs to the Earl. Most extensive was Lillian Ruff and Arnold Wilson's linking of Essex's career with the changing moods and fluctuating frequency of the entire output of madrigal and lute-song collections.[110] They argued that the words of John Dowland's lute songs, particularly ones like 'If My Complaints', 'Would my Conceit', 'Shall I Sue', and 'Die Not Before Thy Day', formed a commentary on the unfolding relationship of Elizabeth and Essex, his downfall, rebellion, and execution.[111] As a well-known figure of the court, songs are likely to have been written about him (in the same way as the 'Bonny Boot' madrigals were written about a courtier thought to be Sir Henry Noel).[112] Yet in practice few songs and texts have any direct connection with the Earl. Instead most reflect more widely on the experience of being a courtier, as Kirsten Gibson illustrated in her analysis of the greenwood trope as a metaphor for political alienation and withdrawal in John Dowland's 'Can She Excuse' and 'O Sweet Woods the Delight of Solitariness'.[113] Although the turbulent career of Essex and the anecdote from Wotton's memoirs make it tempting to attribute such political love songs to the Earl, he was perhaps only the most prominent exemplar of the frustrated ambitions and falls from royal favour that were common experiences for courtiers.

In any case, to determine if any of the Essex-related songs functioned in the kind of context Wotton described, it is necessary to distinguish between songs which merely reflected on his career and misfortunes, and those designed for direct political persuasion. Essex's authorship of the lyrics is the most convincing factor for determining potential candidates for these actively political songs, and this limits the possibilities to five. Of these, three remain questionable. Diana Poulton has argued for Essex's authorship of the lyrics to Dowland's 'Can She Excuse' on the basis of poetic style and the fact that the tune of 'Can She Excuse' became known as the 'Earl of Essex's Galliard'.[114] The stylistic grounds, however, have been disputed by the literary scholar Steven May, while the tune name cannot distinguish between whether Essex was the author or subject.[115] Indeed, as it was only after

---

[110] Lillian Ruff and D. Arnold Wilson, 'The Madrigal, the Lute Song and Elizabethan Politics', *Past & Present* 44 (1969), 3–51, and, 'Allusion to the Essex Downfall in Lute Song Lyrics', *The Lute Society Journal* 12 (1970), 31–6.

[111] Ruff and Wilson, 'The Madrigal', pp. 31, 36–7.

[112] David Greer, '"Thou Court's Delight": Biographical Notes on Henry Noel', *The Lute Society Journal* 17 (1975), 49–59. An alternative suggestion for the identity of Bonny Boots is Christopher Morley (possibly a relation of the composer Thomas Morley): Sukanta Chaudhuri, 'Marlowe, Madrigals, and a New Elizabethan Poet', *Review of English Studies* n.s. 39 (1988), 199–216 (pp. 213–15).

[113] Kirsten Gibson, '"So to the Wood Went I": Politicizing the Greenwood in Two Songs by John Dowland', *Journal of the Royal Musical Association* 132 (2007), 221–51.

[114] Diana Poulton, *John Dowland*, rev. edn (London, 1982), pp. 152, 226–9.

[115] May, 'Poems', pp. 114–15.

the Earl's death that the galliard took his name, it is not even possible to conclude whether these lyrics were originally written about Essex or if they only later became associated with his well-known plight.[116] Similarly, while Poulton attributes the lyrics of Dowland's 'O Sweet Woods' to Essex on the basis of the reference to Wanstead (where Essex had withdrawn to from court in 1597), this only provides convincing evidence that the song is about Essex, not of his authorship.

Finally, there is John Dowland's 'It Was a Time When Silly Bees', whose lyrics are attributed to either Essex or his secretary, Henry Cuffe, in poetic sources.[117] As Essex is known to have collaborated closely with his secretariat in the production of semi-public letters and Accession Day pageantry, both men may have contributed to the poem's creation.[118] Yet the text consists of an allegorical narrative and reads more as a reflection on the futility of appealing to the monarch than a direct petition. In particular, the song already contains the monarch's response. When the bee complains to the King about his lack of favour or reward, the King responds, 'Peace peevish bee,/ Thou'rt bound to serve the Time, the thyme not thee'.[119]

Two songs emerge as most likely to provide an insight into the kind of musical performance described by Wotton. Both Richard Martin's 'Change Thy Mind Since She Doth Change' and Daniel Bacheler's 'To Plead My Faith' have lyrics directly attributed to Essex (Examples 2.2 and 2.4). Furthermore, both were printed in Robert Dowland's *Musical Banquet* (1610), a collection with close connections to the courtly and artistic circles surrounding the Earl.[120] The attributions of the two lyrics are not challenged elsewhere and are especially convincing in the case of Bacheler: he was a musician in the Earl's household, had previously been employed by Sir Philip Sidney, and had been an apprentice at court in the 1580s.[121] Richard Martin may have been the member of the Chapel Royal of that name.[122] Both the genre (love complaint) and the composers' connections to Essex or the court make these songs plausible candidates for intimate musical petition to Elizabeth.

'To Plead My Faith' has a very similar sentiment to the couplet quoted by Wotton. Essex stresses his faith while lamenting his mistress's lack of regard for his loyalty. Although more sorrowful in tone than complaining, the mistress is accused

---

[116] Gibson, 'So to the Wood Went I', pp. 11–12.

[117] May, 'Poems', p. 113.

[118] Paul E. J. Hammer, 'The Earl of Essex, Fulke Greville, and the Employment of Scholars', *Studies in Philology* 91 (1994), 167–80.

[119] John Dowland, *The Third and Last Book of Songs*, sigs. K2v–L1r. Edition: John Dowland, *The Third Booke of Songs* (1603), ed. Edmund Fellows and Thurston Dart, The English Lute Songs 3 (London, 1970; rept., 2005), pp. 36–7.

[120] Dowland (ed.), *A Musical Banquet*, sigs. B2v–C1r, D2v–E1r. The producer Robert Dowland and the courtier poets and composers represented in the collection were all closely associated with the Sidney–Essex circle: Gavin Alexander, 'The Musical Sidneys', *John Donne Journal* 25 (2006), 65–105 (pp. 72–85).

[121] Katherine Duncan-Jones, *Sir Philip Sidney: Courtier Poet* (London, 1991), pp. 279, 298–9; Robert Spencer, 'Bacheler, Daniel', *NG2*.

[122] Doughtie, *Lyrics from English Airs*, p. 583.

of having rejected his love: 'Forget my name since you have scorn'd my love.'[123] 'Change Thy Mind', however, is openly critical. The first verse advises the lover to abandon his false mistress because 'Thy untruth cannot seem strange/ When her falsehood doth excuse thee.' The verses feel less like a lament than an expression of anger. Whereas most courtiers expressed fear at losing royal favour, Essex's verses threaten to abandon his attendance on the Queen. The final verse of the poem goes as far as suggesting that Elizabeth's virtue, honour, and status were diminished by her treatment of him:

> Die, but yet before thou die,
> Make her know what she hath gotten;
> She in whom my hopes did lie,
> Now is chang'd, I quite forgotten,
> She is chang'd, but changed base,
> Baser in so vild a place.[124]

If May is correct that the poem dates from 1597–8, its daring critical tone stemmed from Essex's particular grievances beginning in late 1596 with Elizabeth's lack of gratitude for his victory at Cadiz and her granting of the position of Secretary of State to his rival, Robert Cecil, while he was away fighting.[125] The following year, during his absence on an expedition to the Azores, Elizabeth gave the Lord Admiral the title 'Earl of Nottingham', giving him precedence over Essex at the gathering of the new Parliament. To make matters worse, Nottingham's patent of creation gave him, rather than Essex, credit for the victory at Cadiz. Essex's response was to withdraw from court and claim illness. He refused to return to carry out his duties unless he was appointed Earl Marshal and Nottingham's patent was changed. Essex was finally created Earl Marshal late in December 1597.[126] His troubled relationship with the Queen continued in 1598, culminating in a dispute over appointing a new Lord Deputy for Ireland, during which Essex turned his back on the Queen. She struck him across the head for his insolence, while he had to be prevented from drawing his sword, before he again withdrew angrily from the court.[127]

Yet complaints as bold and as angry as 'Change Thy Mind' would be permissible, because they were understood in the context of the extravagant love complaints that had been present in courtly poetry since the 1570s. According to May, 'these hyperbolic passions must have been recognised for the exaggerations they were … the author's intentions were distanced from the face value of the poetry.'[128] The tone of love poetry had become less excessive in its rhetoric since the 1570s, but the sentiments remained larger-than-life. The songs of Essex (and also Ralegh's, above)

---

[123] May, 'Poems', p. 46.
[124] Ibid., pp. 45–6. 'Vild' is an obsolete form of 'vile'. The poem has five stanzas, though only the first two are printed by Robert Dowland.
[125] Ibid., pp. 90–1; Doughtie, *Lyrics from English Airs*, p. 582.
[126] Hammer, *Polarisation of Elizabethan Politics*, pp. 368, 384–6.
[127] Paul E. J. Hammer, 'Devereux, Robert, Second Earl of Essex (1565–1601)', *ODNB* (online edn, 2008).
[128] May, *Elizabethan Courtier Poets*, p. 57.

used an exaggerated rhetorical style that emphasised the artificiality of the situation even as it created a moving performance. This was underlined by the lack of direct reference to either Elizabeth or the courtier in the lyrics. Elizabeth had to infer that the professional singer represented the courtier, that the beloved was herself, and that the situation represented in highly exaggerated form some aspect of their courtier–monarch relationship.

This ambivalence was a common feature of courtly expression, which Catherine Bates describes as a play of deception and sincerity in which intimate communication is made through external, observable signs whose relationship to the real situation or private feelings is not easily decipherable.[129] These songs would be interpreted as rhetorical performances, exaggerated in tone, regardless of the extent to which they represented the true strength of the courtiers' feelings. Yet while sincerity was diminished through performance, the passion and persuasiveness of the representation was enhanced. The sentiments of abandonment and constant fidelity to an unfaithful mistress, descriptions of the physical effects of their woe, and expressions of their desire for death were typical of the complaints of courtly lovers, but nonetheless created a moving picture of grief supposed to elicit Elizabeth's sympathy. Convention and rhetoric allowed complaints to be made by creating distance from the real world to avoid offence, yet nevertheless enabling the message to be strongly conveyed.

The precautionary effect of rhetorical convention is enhanced by the relatively simple and understated musical settings of both songs in contrast with their highly emotional lyrics. Bacheler and Martin could have chosen to set their texts in the style of the most expressive, declamatory lute songs, like John Dowland's 'Sorrow Stay' (Example 2.1).[130] Here irregular rhythms, short phrases, and instrumental interjections, as well as extensive use of suspensions (marked with arrows on the score), create a style that is overtly rhetorical and expressive.

Instead, both composers chose an alternative style of lute song – the dance-form variety. This form was not without expression, but it was more subtle. Bacheler's song (Example 2.2) is based on one of his earlier galliards, adapting the first and last strains and composing new middle sections.[131] Such adaptation would be a practical method of setting lyrics quickly to meet the political needs of a patron. This

---

[129] Bates, *Rhetoric of Courtship*, p. 44.

[130] John Dowland, *The Second Book of Songs or Ayres, of 2, 4 and 5 Parts with Tablature for the Lute or Orpharion, with the Viola de Gamba* (London, 1600), sigs. C1v–C2r. A full edition can be found in John Dowland, *The Second Book of Songs (1600)*, ed. Edmund Fellowes and Thurston Dart, The English Lute Songs 2 (London, 1969), p. 13.

[131] Dowland (ed.), *A Musical Banquet*, sigs. D2v–E1r. The cantus part of the original is notated a tone higher than the lute and bassus parts, with a one-flat key signature. Christopher Morrongiello suggests that the cantus part has been transposed so that if the singer takes his pitch from the lute, he can read in an easier key; Dowland's preface states that the songs are 'sorted to the capacities of young practitioners'. The original galliard is no. 32 in Morrongiello's edition. Christopher Morrongiello, 'Edward Collard (d. 1600) and Daniel Bacheler (d. 1619): A Critical Study and Edition of their Lute Music', 3 vols., DPhil dissertation, University of Oxford, 2005, vol. 1, pp. 170, 176–8; vol. 3, pp. 128–30, 227–8.

Ex. 2.1 Opening of John Dowland, 'Sorrow Stay, Lend True Repentant Tears', *The Second Book of Songs or Ayres* (London, 1600), sigs. C1v–C2r

Ex. 2.2 Opening half of Daniel Bacheler, 'To Plead My Faith', *A Musical Banquet*, ed. Robert Dowland (London, 1610), sigs. D2v–E1r

Ex. 2.2 continued

particular galliard may have been chosen for its mood: Christopher Morrongiello has pointed out that the opening phrases of both the galliard and song are closely related in melody and harmonic progression to the falling fourth motifs that open Dowland's 'Flow my Tears' (Example 2.3) and 'Lachrimae'.[132] While possibly a tribute to Dowland, who made the motif a personal trope, the figure also had clear melancholic associations.[133] Along with the Phrygian cadences at the end of the first phrase (as well as phrases 6 and 7, not shown) it established the lamenting tone (the Phrygian mode being associated with lament by theorists such as Zarlino).[134] On the other hand, the song avoids any madrigalian touches, including obvious opportunities for word-painting on the lines 'and my vain hope, which far too high aspired/ Is dead and buried for ever gone'. Only the subtle effect of repeated B flats at 'I loved her whom all the world admir'd', and 'I was a fond as ever she was fair' adds a slight insistent quality to the text as the protagonist pleads his faithful love. Furthermore, the song has a particularly regular construction, with six of the eight phrases identical in rhythm, which adds to the contrast between the emotive lyrics and a more constrained musical setting.

---

[132] Morrongiello, 'Edward Collard', vol. 1, pp. 171–2. Dowland also uses similar falling fourths in the opening two lines of 'My Thoughts are Wing'd with Hopes' (probably another courtier complaint, though anonymous), but in a different harmonic context and with the perfect and diminished versions reversed: Kirsten Gibson, 'The Order of the Book: Materiality, Narrative and Authorial Voice in John Dowland's *First Booke of Songes or Ayres*', *Renaissance Studies* 26 (2012), 13–33 (p. 29). Dowland, *The Second Book of Songs or Ayres*, sigs. B2v–C1r. For a full edition of 'Flow My Tears' see Dowland, *Second Book of Songs (1600)*, pp. 10–12.

[133] Gibson, 'Order of the Book', pp. 29–30; Anthony Rooley, 'New Light on John Dowland's Songs of Darkness', *Early Music* 11 (1983), 6–22 (pp. 19–20).

[134] Claude Palisca, 'Mode Ethos in the Renaissance', in *Essays in Musicology: A Tribute to Alvin Johnson*, ed. Lewis Lockwood and Edward H. Roesner (Philadelphia, 1990), pp. 126–39 (p. 133).

Ex. 2.3 Opening of John Dowland, 'Flow My Tears',
The Second Book of Songs or Ayres (London, 1600), sigs. B2v–C1r

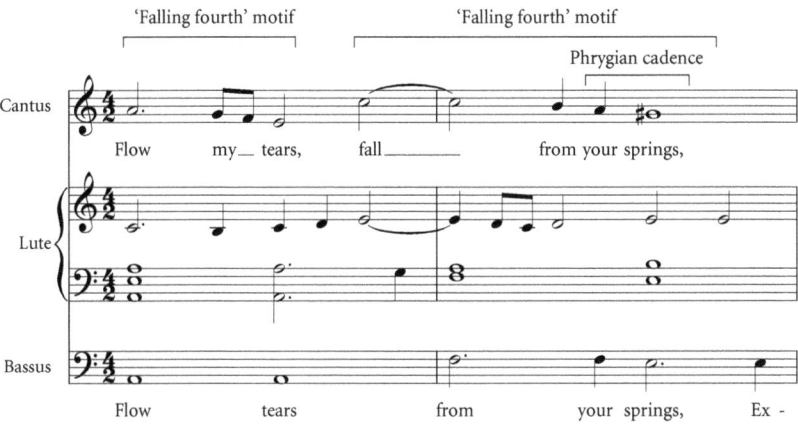

Martin's setting (Example 2.4) is an almand and could also have been quickly composed.[135] Martin chose to compose just eight bars of music, by setting the first four lines of each verse to the same two musical phrases. Furthermore, the harmonies of bars 5–6 are almost identical to bars 1–2. This harmonic progression, with its bass line descending through a fourth and ending in a Phrygian cadence, would, as in Bacheler's setting, be appropriate to the mood of lament. Yet the emotional portrayal is again unembellished by any word-painting or expressive use of dissonance. There is nothing to draw attention to the critical tone of the lyrics. Rather, the song is rhythmically very regular (with four two-bar phrases and limited rhythmical diversity in the vocal part) and melodically simple (proceeding largely in stepwise motion), with just subtle use of register to stress the climax point of each verse: at 'thou art free' in the first stanza.

Bacheler and Martin chose a style of musical setting which encloses Essex's complaints within conventional forms: the hyperbolic passions of the lyrics are contrasted with regularity of rhythm and melody, and a strophic or otherwise repetitive form. Conjunct and repetitive melodies enhance the memorability, potentially increasing the impact of the song by allowing fragments of the tune and lyrics to be recalled by Elizabeth after the performance ended. This simpler style would also have had some practical advantages in allowing the lyrics to be set to music quickly to take advantage of a particular opportunity or pressing situation. Message and timing were more important than sophisticated musical artistry on such occasions.

With their style a mixture of pragmatism and shrewd political intention, these songs offered a 'refined form of protest' in which potentially offensive texts were

---

[135] Dowland (ed.), *A Musical Banquet*, sigs. B2v–C1r; also edited in Robert Dowland, *A Musical Banquet (1610)*, ed. Peter Stroud, trans. Edward Filmer and Keith Statham, The English Lute Songs 16 (London, 1968), p. 6. The bassus part is texted and so could either be sung or played on a viol.

Ex.2.4 Richard Martin, 'Change Thy Mind Since She Doth Change', *A Musical Banquet*, ed. Robert Dowland (London, 1610), sigs. B2v–C1r

contained safely within artistic forms and conventions.[136] Mixing the intimate and the public, the conventional and the critical, and combining personal sentiments with rhetoric, love songs offered complex and polyvalent means of political manœuvring as courtiers sought renewed or continued favour, often at the expense of their rivals. Elizabeth permitted such musical politics because it emphasised her position as the central focus of her courtiers' lives, while offering courtiers an outlet for their complaints and petitions. Just as Elizabeth's performances enhanced the reputation of her recipient as well as her own, she would have been aware that as courtiers fashioned their own identities, they also enriched her own image. While she risked occasionally being painted as the cold-hearted and cruel mistress rather than the virtuous, unattainable beloved, the overall effect only added to her image of eternal youth and charm. In these musical games of secrecy both the Queen and her courtiers could count themselves winners.

---

[136] Hammer, *Polarisation of Elizabethan Politics*, p. 318.

CHAPTER 3

The Royal Household and its Revels

INTIMATE and informal performances were only heard by a select group of courtiers and ambassadors. The outward face of court music-making was the royal musical establishment and its provision for both daily ceremonies and grand seasonal revels. These performances in the Presence Chamber and the Great Hall were open to English nobility and gentry, as well as ambassadors and visiting foreign nobility. Music was essential to the image of a court, and Elizabeth's was no exception. Aside from offering entertainment, musicians had to produce the aural equivalent of the magnificent visual effects of portraits, architecture, jewellery, courtly dress, or silverware that conveyed the prosperity and richness of the court to English and foreign visitors alike. Whether grand and ceremonial or the height of innovation and sophistication, music's political purpose was to display the prosperity and sophistication of Queen, court, and kingdom in the best possible light.

Having considered Elizabeth the performer, this chapter turns to Elizabeth the patron. How active and innovative a musical patron was she, and to what extent was she in control of all the music performed at her court? It was not only Elizabeth who commissioned entertainments, and nor was it only court employees who performed in them. In addition to enriching the royal image, what other messages were musical entertainments in the royal household projecting?

Like most Renaissance courts, Elizabeth's musical establishment consisted of musicians for the Chapel Royal and for the royal household, though in practice these boundaries were blurred when special occasions called for extended resources in either space. The Chapel Royal employed thirty-two gentlemen and twelve boys, who might also be used as singers and even actors in secular court entertainments. The majority of the secular music, however, was performed by the musicians of the royal household. The largest group were the consorts of viols or violins, flutes, recorders, and sackbuts with shawms, typically each with six or seven members.[1] The consort of sackbuts with shawms and the drum and fife band were those most suitable for outdoor music or performances in large halls during noisy events, while the softer ensembles such as the recorders and violins played mainly in indoor settings (such as the Presence Chamber) on quieter occasions.[2]

The violin consort's primary role was to accompany dancing, including practices, formal events, and informal social occasions.[3] The recorder consort, too, played

---

[1] The term 'consort' is used throughout this book in its modern sense of an ensemble of instrumentalists and their instruments, though in Elizabethan times 'consort' most commonly meant the mixed consort: Warwick Edwards, 'Consort', *NG2*.

[2] Peter Holman, *Four and Twenty Fiddlers: The Violin at the English Court, 1540–1690*, Oxford Monographs on Music (Oxford, 1993), pp. 36–7.

[3] Ibid., pp. 111–18.

dance music, but its repertory of fantasias and wordless madrigals suggests that it was also used for dinner music or in concert.[4] Trumpeters and a band of drums and fifes provided fanfares for entrances and exits on state occasions or accompanied processions. Unlike the other consorts, their music was largely memorised or improvised, but it was not necessarily always monophonic. Trumpet ensembles across Europe used a method by which a single notated part was doubled at one harmonic below and sounded over two drone parts (a fifth apart). At the top of the texture, the *clarino* part provided ornamental divisions or memorised melodic material using the uppermost harmonics.[5]

Players of soft instruments generally performed in the smaller Privy Chamber.[6] These included lutenists (who also tended to be singers) and virginal-players, while early in the reign a harpist, a viol-player, and a rebec-player were also employed.[7] These performers were probably invited to the Privy Chamber when a performance was required for Elizabeth's personal entertainment or when she entertained honoured guests. Only a select group of musicians held posts which gave them the privilege of permanent access to Privy Chamber.[8] Identifying musical members of the Privy Chamber staff is difficult as they were usually employed as personal servants, not specifically musicians. Thomas Lichfield, Ferdinando Heybourne, and Alfonso Ferrabosco I were all Gentlemen or Grooms of the Privy Chamber with musical talents; however, only the Keeper of Instruments with his assistant (who required free access to tune and maintain instruments) and lutenist Mathias Mason seem to have had access to the Privy Chamber primarily through their posts as musicians.[9] Additionally, there were further extraordinary Gentlemen of the Privy Chamber who were unpaid and are therefore hard to trace.[10] This may explain the

---

[4] David Lasocki, 'Professional Recorder Players in England, 1540–1740', 3 vols., PhD dissertation, University of Iowa, 1983, vol. 1.1, p. 96.

[5] Edward Tarr, 'The Trumpet before 1800', in *The Cambridge Companion to Brass Instruments*, ed. Trevor Herbert and John Wallace, Cambridge Companions to Music (Cambridge, 1997), pp. 84–102 (pp. 84–5); Michael Gale, 'Remnants of Some Late Sixteenth-Century Trumpet Ensemble Music', *Historic Brass Society Journal* 14 (2002), 115–31 (pp. 115–16); Margaret Sarkissian and Edward Tarr, 'Trumpet', *NG2*.

[6] Holman, *Four and Twenty Fiddlers*, pp. 36–8.

[7] The rebec was a small, bowed instrument with gut strings.

[8] Mason is described as 'Lute of the Privy Chamber' in Elizabeth's funeral accounts. See Andrew Ashbee, 'Groomed for Service: Musicians in the Privy Chamber at the English Court, c. 1495–1558', *Early Music* 25 (1997), 185–97 (pp. 186–8).

[9] *RECM*, vol. 4, p. 1.

[10] Pam Wright, 'A Change in Direction: The Ramifications of a Female Household, 1558–1603', in *The English Court: From the Wars of the Roses to the Civil War*, ed. David Starkey (London, 1987), pp. 147–72 (p. 155). Steven May suggests that this practice of making unpaid 'extraordinary' appointments explains how John Lyly could be appointed as an Esquire of the Body even though there is no record of payments: Steven W. May, *The Elizabethan Courtier Poets: The Poems and their Contexts* (Columbia, MO, 1991), p. 35.

case of Antony Holborne, a composer who claimed to be a 'gentleman and servant' to Elizabeth but who is never listed as an employee of the court.[11] These men were often of a different class from other musicians, more courtier than professional performer.[12] Many of the women in Elizabeth's Privy Chamber were also musical, including the Maids of Honour Lady Penelope Rich and Cicely Ridgeway.[13] No account of their making music either with or for the Queen survives, but an elegy for Cicely Ridgeway implies that she was taught to play the lute and bandora by the Queen.[14] It would seem likely that informal female music-making took place in the Privy Chamber, but no specific evidence survives.

Despite being a music-loving monarch and maintaining this sizable musical staff, Elizabeth was neither as active nor as innovative a patron as her father and grandfather had been. Henry VII began the process of employing foreign musicians, including tutors for his children.[15] The musical tastes and abilities Henry VIII gained from these tutors made him active in bringing new Continental musicians to the court throughout his reign. He continually updated his ensembles: the shawms and sackbuts, for example, saw three or four different consorts come and go during the reign, as first a Flemish group (in the late 1510s), then an Italian band (c. 1521–5), and finally the members of the Bassano family (in the early 1530s) were employed. Henry attracted Benedictus de Opiciis and Dionysius Memo as virtuoso organists, the van Wilder family as lutenists and viol-players, and introduced a violin/viol consort from Venice in 1540, followed by another of recorders (the return of members of the Bassano family again, in 1540).[16] Henry VIII's musical establishment was constantly changing and expanding to keep up with the latest European trends and encompass the best musical talent available.

---

[11] Brian Jeffrey, 'Antony Holborne', *Musica Disciplina* 22 (1968), 129–205 (pp. 129, 133–6).

[12] Holman, *Four and Twenty Fiddlers*, p. 38.

[13] Violet A. Wilson, *Queen Elizabeth's Maids of Honour and Ladies of the Privy Chamber* (London, 1922), pp. 6, 10, 54–5; Charlotte Merton, 'The Women who Served Queen Mary and Queen Elizabeth: Ladies, Gentlewomen and Maids of the Privy Chamber 1553–1603', PhD dissertation, University of Cambridge, 1992, p. 98; Sylvia Freedman, *Poor Penelope: Lady Penelope Rich, An Elizabethan Woman* (Abbostbrook, 1983), p. 10.

[14] Andrea Brady '"Without Welt, Gard, or Embroidery": A Funeral Elegy for Cicely Ridgeway, Countess of Londonderry (1628)', *Huntington Library Quarterly* 72 (2009), 373–95 (pp. 380, 385). Mary I is also known to have taught her Maids of Honour to play the lute and spinet prior to her accession. *CSP Venice*, vol. 5, pp. 532–64 (p. 533) [18 August 1554]; Eugenio Albèri (ed.), *Relazione degli ambasciatori Veneti al senato*, 15 vols. (Florence, 1839–63), vol. 8, p. 323.

[15] Theodor Dumitrescu, *The Early Tudor Court and International Musical Relations* (Aldershot, 2007), pp. 63, 115–16; Holman, *Four and Twenty Fiddlers*, p. 59.

[16] Dumitrescu, *Early Tudor Court*, pp. 63–116; Holman, *Four and Twenty Fiddlers*, pp. 62–3, 79–87; John Stevens, *Music and Poetry in the Early Tudor Court*, Cambridge Studies in Music (Cambridge, 1979), pp. 296–328; Lasocki, 'Professional Recorder Players', vol. 1, pp. 23–8.

By contrast, Elizabeth made few changes to the musicians employed in the royal household (see Appendix A).[17] Although several musicians in the Privy Chamber were retired or replaced at her accession and a few old-fashioned instruments disappeared, the structure of the consorts remained the same and their membership changed only gradually.[18] The violin consort saw just nine changes of personnel in Elizabeth's forty-four-year reign, and this stability was typical of other ensembles and their members.[19] The only significant alteration was the creation of a small lute consort in the late 1580s, when John Johnson, Mathias Mason, and Walter Pierce began to be described as 'the three lutes'.[20] Elizabeth's lack of husband or children contributed to this stasis in musical personnel, as there were no additional royal households through which new musicians could enter court service. Furthermore, with the Tudor dynasty now well settled there was not the same impetus to develop the musical establishment as under her father and grandfather, especially as Elizabeth had inherited an extensive and distinguished set of musicians. She proudly told the French ambassador in 1597 that she 'entertained at least sixty musicians', and she presumably felt that this was enough to create the desired effect.[21] While no longer perhaps as stunning as Henry VIII's establishment when continually attracting the latest talent, Elizabeth's skilful musicians were nonetheless more than sufficient to fulfil the court's public and private musical needs and to display its prosperity and sophistication. Their performances helped to create the distinctive magnificence of the monarchy in the eyes of her noble subjects, but also served important diplomatic functions.

IMAGE AND DIPLOMACY

CONVEYING the sophistication of the court depended on both displaying English arts and music, and establishing the court's cosmopolitan nature. Italian culture was the primary mark of sophistication in the Elizabethan period,

---

[17] In discussing the music of Elizabeth's royal household I draw particularly on: RECM; Andrew Ashbee and David Lasocki, *A Biographical Dictionary of English Court Musicians, 1485–1714*, 2 vols. (Aldershot, 1998); Holman, *Four and Twenty Fiddlers*; Lasocki, 'Professional Recorder Players'.

[18] Older Privy Chamber musicians such as Walter Earle and Peter van Wilder retired. A group of singers was disbanded (William Mapperley, who continued to serve in the Chapel Royal, Thomas Kent and John Temple).

[19] Holman, *Four and Twenty Fiddlers*, p. 104; Craig Monson, 'Elizabethan London', in *The Renaissance: From the 1470s to the End of the 16th Century*, ed. Iain Fenlon, Man and Music 2 (London, 1989), pp. 304–40 (p. 317).

[20] Matthew Spring, *The Lute in Britain: A History of the Instrument and its Music*, Early Music Series (Oxford, 2001), pp. 46, 103. A performance by the three lutes is described by French ambassadors: 'Journal des négociations des commissaires et ambassadeurs français de 24 Avril au 1er Mai 1581', GB-Lna: PRO 31/3/28, fol. 306r–v.

[21] André Hurault de Maisse, *A Journal of All that was Accomplished by Monsieur de Maisse, Ambassador in England from King Henri IV to Queen Elizabeth Anno Domini 1597*, ed. Robert Arthur Jones and G. B. Harrison (London, 1931), p. 95.

and analogous processes of cultural imitation occurred at other European courts. At Dresden, for example, the Electors of Saxony sought to establish themselves as rulers of European importance through the patronage of Italian architects, craftsmen, artists, and musicians. The Italianisation extended to education with the teaching of Italian dancing, riding, conversation, and etiquette.[22] To impress on the European stage, the English court too had to demonstrate its participation in European standards of court culture, including music.

The secular musical establishment and the Chapel Royal presented two complementary images of music-making in England. The Gentlemen of the Chapel Royal were Englishmen, and their Protestant polyphony represented the artistic heights of English sacred song. The Chapel Royal, meanwhile, was designed both to impress foreign ambassadors and underplay the difference between the Anglican and Catholic Churches. Its rich ceremonies (including crucifixes, candles, and lavish vestments), use of Latin, and elaborate polyphony aimed to persuade foreign visitors of the moderate nature of Elizabeth's Protestantism, thereby smoothing diplomatic relations.[23] By contrast, much of the court's secular music promoted its cosmopolitanism. The household musicians Elizabeth inherited were an international establishment: the violinists were mostly Jews from Italy (the Galliardellos and Kellims) or Spain and Portugal (the Lupos and possibly the Comeys). The Bassano family (also Jewish) came from Venice, while the flautists were largely French or Dutch.[24] The trumpeters and the drums and fifes, however, were mostly English, while the sackbut consort also contained some Englishmen (such as Raphe Greene and Robert Howlett). By the 1590s, however, the consorts were looking rather less international. Places in the violins, recorders, and flutes began to be filled with Englishmen (for example, Robert Baker joined the recorder consort and William Warren the violins), and as the musicians hired by Henry VIII retired, the descendants who replaced them were now English-born. Elizabeth maintained the structure of her father's musical establishment, but not his continued efforts to seek out the best musicians from across Europe. By the end of her reign the international credentials of her musicians were less impressive.

Nevertheless, these foreign musicians were important for their potential to bring in new genres and performing styles, keeping Elizabeth's court up to date with the latest European fashions. The Frenchman Nicholas Lanier I may have had a role in teaching the flute ensemble to play cornetts, while Alfonso Ferrabosco I has been credited with establishing of the lute fantasia and influencing the development of the English madrigal.[25] Even as fewer musicians were recruited from abroad, the

---

[22] Helen Watanabe-O'Kelly, *Court Culture in Dresden: From Renaissance to Baroque* (Basingstoke, 2002), pp. 37–59.

[23] Peter Le Huray, *Music and the Reformation in England 1549–1660*, Cambridge Studies in Music (Cambridge, 1978), pp. 33–4; Monson, 'Elizabethan London', pp. 305–10.

[24] Roger Prior, 'Jewish Musicians at the Tudor Court', *The Musical Quarterly* 69 (1983), 253–65; Holman, *Four and Twenty Fiddlers*, pp. 81–5.

[25] David Lasocki and Roger Prior, *The Bassanos: Venetian Musicians and Instrument Makers in England, 1531–1665* (Aldershot, 1995), p. 175; Spring, *Lute in Britain*, p. 145; Christopher Field, 'Fantasia', *NG2*; Richard Charteris, *Alfonso Ferrabosco*

international connections of court musicians continued to provide a route for new Continental music and ideas to be imported. The Bassano family still owned a house in Bassano, maintained business connections, and made several visits back to Italy.[26] Similarly the Galliardello family (from Brescia) had branches in Antwerp (a significant centre for music printing) and Paul Galliardello owned a house there. A relative of Joseph Lupo seems to have been a cittern- and violin-maker in Amsterdam.[27]

The few extant court manuscripts hint at the international styles and repertory used at court. GB-Lbl: Royal Appendix MSS 74–6 (a manuscript thought to be connected with the violin ensemble in the 1550s and 60s) includes Flemish and Italian dances, and divisions (variations created by splitting the tune into shorter notes) applying techniques similar to Italian *viola bastarda* pieces. While the English versions employ the technique to dance rather than vocal music, and a treble instrument rather than the bass viol, they are nearly contemporary with the earliest Italian *bastarda* pieces and must have been written by someone with direct experience of Italian music (possibly Peter Lupo).[28] Manuscript US-NH: Filmer 2, which contains dance music composed by court musicians *c.* 1600, also includes textless Italian madrigals that were played by court ensembles, while George Peele's play *The Arraignment of Paris* (performed by the Chapel Royal children and published in 1584) included the Italian song 'Si Diana nel cielo è una stella', sung by Helen of Troy (possibly a madrigal, as Helen is described as having four attendants).[29]

The royal musicians performed not only for the Queen and English nobility, but also for foreign ambassadors. The Swedish ambassador Duke Johan, for example, gave gratuities on an almost daily basis to musicians ranging from the trumpeters, the fifes and drums, and the shawms, to the violin consort, lutenists, a harpist, and a bagpiper.[30] The mix of loud and soft instruments, consorts and soloists, suggests

---

the Elder (1543–1588): A Thematic Catalogue of his Music with a Biographical Calendar, Thematic Catalogues 11 (New York, 1984), pp. 11, 151–63; Joseph Kerman, 'An Italian Musician in England', in *Write All These Down: Essays on Music* (Berkeley, CA, 1994), pp. 139–51 (pp. 142–6). Ferrabosco's extant Italian madrigals of the 1560s–70s were probably written for an Italian patron during his departure from the court in 1569–71, and he left court a decade before the fashion for English madrigals developed in the late 1580s. Yet it would be surprising if he was not involved in bringing Italian madrigals and madrigalian techniques into the English court, particularly given his known involvement with court entertainments in 1572 and 1576, and the continued presence of his illegitimate son living with royal flautist Gommar van Oostrewijk.

[26] Lasocki, 'Professional Recorder Players', vol. 2, p. 606; Lasocki and Prior, *The Bassanos*, pp. 211, 245.

[27] Holman, *Four and Twenty Fiddlers*, pp. 105, 121.

[28] Ibid., pp. 90–9.

[29] Ibid., p. 145; George Peele, *The Arraignment of Paris a Pastoral. Presented before the Queen's Majesty, by the Children of her Chapel* (London, 1584), sig. C1r–v.

[30] Kia Hedell, 'Musical Contacts of the Swedish Royal Court during the Early Vasa Dynasty (1521–1611): Towards a Changed View of Swedish Particpation

a range of public and private performances. This might have included attending formal entertainments such as masques, plays, and tournaments (discussed later), or more informal, personal recreation.

Even when not important enough to be personally entertained by the Queen or her musicians, foreign visitors might experience the court's secular music-making by attending a ceremonial serving of dinner in the Presence Chamber. (A visit to the Chapel Royal to hear English sacred music was also common.)[31] Although Elizabeth was not usually present (she took dinner in her Privy Chamber), this was a grand affair with processions of people bearing the various dishes to the accompaniment of trumpets and drums. It was designed both to look and sound impressive. German lawyer Paul Hentzner spoke of twelve trumpeters and two drummers who made the hall resound with a great noise for an hour and a half.[32] Trumpeters playing in the higher registers would have improvised around a given theme played in a middling register, over open fifths provided by the kettledrums and lower trumpet parts.[33] Swiss student Thomas Platter heard not only trumpets, but also shawms. These would not have performed with the trumpets, but rather in a consort with sackbuts.[34] This ceremony was less concerned with presenting the eloquence of English music than with arousing wonder at the splendour of the occasion. Hentzner came away with the impression that the English were 'greatly delighted with sounds that fill the ears, such as the firing of cannons, drums, and the ringing of bells'.[35]

When the court was not present, the instruments on display at the royal palaces evoked its quality and splendour. During tours of the royal palaces, foreign travellers seem to have had instruments pointed out to them by their guides, who emphasised their connections with Elizabeth's talents or patronage. Baron

in European Cultural Life', in *Early Music: Context and Ideas: International Conference in Musicology, Kraków, 18–21 September 2003*, ed. Karol Berger, Lubomir Chalupka, and Albert Dunning (Kraków, 2003), pp. 103–9 (pp. 105–6).

[31] Le Huray, *Music and the Reformation*, pp. 33–4; Monson, 'Elizabethan London', pp. 305–10.

[32] Paul Hentzner, *Itinerarium Germaniae; Galliae; Angliae; Italiae* (Nuremberg, 1612), p. 137: 'Dum satellites isti … supradictos cibos ad portarent, erant in Aulae area XII Tubicines, et duo Tympanistae, qui tubis, buccinis, et tympanis magno sonitu per sesqui horam clangebant.'

[33] Don L. Smithers, *The Music and History of the Baroque Trumpet before 1721*, 2nd edn (Buren, 1988), p. 111; Sarkissian and Tarr, 'Trumpet'.

[34] Thomas Platter, *Beschreibung der Reisen durch Frankreich, Spanien, England und die Niederlande, 1595–1600*, ed. Rut Keiser, 2 vols. (Basel, 1968), vol. 2, pp. 829–30: 'Musik von Trompeten und Schalmeien'. English translation: P. E. Razzell (ed.), *The Journals of Two Travellers in Elizabethan and Early Stuart England* (London, 1995), p. 62. Thomas Platter was a Swiss medical student who travelled in England in 1599.

[35] Hentzner, *Itinerarium*, p. 156: 'delectantur quoq: valde sonitibus, qui ipsis aures implent, uti explosionibus tormentorum, typanis et campanarum boatu'. Hentzner's experience of bell-ringing was not at the court, but the drums and canon evoke courtly pomp and his experience of ceremonial dinner cited above.

Waldstein was shown 'ivory flutes which are used by the Queen's musicians'.[36] Frederick, Duke of Württemberg, noted that 'her Majesty is particularly fond of' organs and other keyboard instruments, while Thomas Platter was shown 'a lovely positive organ' (*schöne positiv*) and spinets (*spinetten*) on which Elizabeth might play.[37] Many instruments were specifically engraved with references to the Queen. Waldstein noted at Hampton Court a 'most interesting and ingenious musical instrument made in Germany', within whose case was written:

> *Cantabis moneo, quisquis cantare rogaris,*
> *Vivat ut aeternos* ELISABETHA *dies.*

[Whoso is asked, I tell you, sing 'May Elizabeth live for ever'.]

Then over the keyboard it read:

> *Phoebe ades et modulos cum tractat pollice princeps*
> *Fac resonent plaidum tinula corda melos.*

[Phoebus be present; and when Her Grace's finger strikes the keys make the tingling strings resound with tuneful melodies.][38]

These instruments evoked the music-making of both the Queen and her courtiers, encouraging the beholder to imagine the musicality and culture of the absent court, singing the praises of its Queen.

Other instruments were notable for their novelty, including one that made music by itself; one that looked like a large, high box and contained various other instruments (Wedel); and one on which two people could perform at the same time (Hentzner).[39] This last instrument might have been a 'mother and child' virginal of the kind made by Ruckers, which had two keyboards, the second being

---

[36] Zdenek Brtnický z Valdštejna, *The Diary of Baron Waldstein, a Traveller in Elizabethan England*, ed. and trans. G. W. Groos (London, 1981), p. 151. Baron Waldstein was born in Iglau, in the present day Czech Republic, and visited London in 1600 during his European travels.

[37] William Brenchley Rye (ed.), *England as Seen by Foreigners in the Days of Elizabeth and James the First, Comprising Translations of the Journals of the Two Dukes of Wirtemberg in 1592 and 1610* (London, 1865), p. 18; Jacob Rathgeb, *Warhaffte Beschreibung zweier Reisen* (Tübingen, 1603), fol. 18v: 'Orgeln [und] auch Instrumenten (derer Ihre Königliche Majestät ein besondere Liebhaberin ist).' In German usage of the period, the term 'Instrumenten' refers to small keyboard instruments such as spinets or virginals. Platter, *Beschreibung der Reisen*, vol. 2, p. 790; Razzell, *Journals of Two Travellers*, p. 26.

[38] Valdštejna, *Diary of Baron Waldstein*, pp. 154–5 (Groos's translations).

[39] Lupold von Wedel was a young German nobleman who spent twenty years travelling around Europe, visiting England in 1584–5. Gottfried von Bülow, 'Journey through England and Scotland made by Lupold von Wedel in the Years 1584 and 1585', *Transactions of the Royal Historical Society* 9 (1895), 223–70 (p. 237); Lupold von Wedel, *Lupold von Wedels Beschreibung seiner Reisen und Kriegserlebnisse, 1561–1606*, ed. Max Bär (Stettin, 1895), p. 325: 'Es ist fast in einem jeden Gemach ein Instrument … darunter eines, welches wie ein großer hoher Kasten anzusehen [ist], in dem viele Instrumente gewesen auf mannigerlei Art,

a smaller octave keyboard.[40] Other instruments were singled out for their beauty or richness: Frederic Gerschow noted the loveliness of one 'in the Queen's cabinet', which was 'a virginal or other keyboard instrument of glass, so artistically made as if it were set with pearls and precious stones'.[41] This instrument may have been similar to an example made in Innsbruck, *c.* 1600 (now in the Victoria and Albert Museum), whose case is highly decorated with glass.[42]

Gerschow's reference to the 'Queen's cabinet' relates these instrument collections to the trend for cabinets of curiosities. Several cabinets were founded across Europe in the 1560s–70s, made up of natural or manmade objects which were intended to elicit wonder. Manmade objects were collected for their skill of manufacture, for their beauty, or for the richness of their materials.[43] Cabinets of curiosity were considered by the mock court of the Prince of Purpoole established for the *Gesta Grayorum*: the Christmas and Shrovetide Revels of the Gentlemen of Gray's Inn (1594/5). The Mock-Prince was advised by one of his counsellors that the study of philosophy would advance his honour, and that for this he needed a 'goodly huge cabinet, wherein whatsoever the hand of man, by exquisite art or engine, hath made rare in stuff, form, or motion, whatsoever singularity, chance and the shuffle of things hath produced, whatsoever nature hath wrought in things that want life, and may be kept, shall be sorted and included'. This would cause people to 'wonder at the prince's reason and knowledge' and 'when all other miracles and wonders shall cease, by reason that you shall have discovered their natural causes, your self shall be left the only miracle and wonder of the world.'[44] Cabinets of curiosity, including Elizabeth's collection of striking musical instruments, promoted

---

darunter eines, welches selbst schlagen und hofieren [Musik machen] konnte'; Hentzner, *Itinerarium*, p. 128: 'unum in quo duo simul et una vice ludere possunt'.

[40] Edward L. Kottick, *A History of the Harpsichord* (Bloomington, IN, 2003), pp. 60–1.

[41] Gottfried von Bülow and Wilfred Powell, 'Diary of the Journey of Philip Julius, Duke of Stettin-Pomerania, through England in the Year 1602', *Transactions of the Royal Historical Society* 6 (1892), 1–67 (pp. 52–4): 'In der Königin Cabinet stand ein Virginal oder Instrument von Glas, so künstlich ausgearbeitet, als ob es mit Perlen und Edelsteinen versetzet wäre.' Frederic Gerschow was the tutor of a young German nobleman, Philip Julius, Duke of Pomerania-Wolgast, who ordered him to keep a record of his tour of Europe.

[42] Victoria and Albert Museum, 'The Glass Virginal', *V&A Collections*, online at <http://collections.vam.ac.uk/item/O58892> [accessed 19 July 2014].

[43] Watanabe-O'Kelly, *Court Culture in Dresden*, pp. 71–2.

[44] William Canning (ed.), *Gesta Grayorum, or, The History of the High and Mighty Prince, Henry Prince of Purpoole … who Reigned and Died, A.D. 1594: Together with a Masque, as it was Presented (by His Highness's Command) for the Entertainment of Q. Elizabeth* (London, 1688), pp. 34–5. 'Trismegistus' literally means 'Thrice-greatest' and was an epithet applied to the Egyptian god Thoth, who was equated with the Greek god Hermes and known as Hermes Trismegistus. Hermes Trismegistus was considered 'the father and protector of all knowledge': M. C. Howatson and Ian Chilvers, 'Hermes Trismegistus', in *The Concise Oxford Companion to Classical Literature* (Oxford, 1996), p. 262.

the court as a place of wealth, knowledge, and discovery. The wonder they evoked was intended to rub off on the possessor of the objects, too, encouraging viewers to be in awe of the sovereign who owned them.

Many of Elizabeth's instruments may have been diplomatic gifts representative of her international connections and reputation abroad. Keyboard instruments were common diplomatic gifts because they displayed craftsmanship, art (in the painting of the case), and mechanical ingenuity at a reasonable cost.[45] The German keyboard instrument described by Waldstein was probably one such present.[46] Elizabeth also received music manuscripts as gifts. In 1559, noting Elizabeth's pleasure in 'la diversité de chansons en musique', François de Montmorency sent her a dozen chansons and some galliards obtained from the King's violin consort.[47] In addition, the Winchester Partbooks may have been presented to Elizabeth by King Erik XIV of Sweden as one of the final gifts of his courtship.[48] As well as flattering Elizabeth's musicality and promoting favourable diplomatic relations, such gifts were another means by which the Elizabethan court gained fashionable music from across Europe to perform.

Elizabeth also sent musical instruments as gifts.[49] In league with the Levant Company, she commissioned the organ-maker Thomas Dallam to build an organ for Sultan Mahomed III, to secure their continued ability to trade in Turkey. This was not just a musical instrument, but a feat of English engineering able to be played or to play itself, with its clock and moving pieces creating a visual accompaniment to the varied sounds. Dallam describes its first performance for the Sultan:

> First the clock struck 22; then the chime of 16 bells went off, and played a song of 4 parts. That being done, two personages which stood upon two corners of the second storey, holding two silver trumpets in their hands did lift them to their heads, and sounded a tantara. Then the music went off and the organ played a song of 5 parts twice over. In the top of the organ, being 16 foot high, did stand a holly bush full of black birds and thrushes, which at the end of the music did sing and shake their wings.[50]

---

[45] Ian Woodfield, 'The Keyboard Recital in Oriental Diplomacy, 1520–1620', *Journal of the Royal Musical Association* 115 (1990), 33–62 (p. 33).

[46] Valdštejna, *Diary of Baron Waldstein*, pp. 154–5.

[47] François de Montmorency, 'Montmorency to Throgmorton: 14 August 1559', GB-Lna: SP70/6, Secretaries of State: State Papers Foreign Elizabeth I, fol. 76 (fol. 76r).

[48] Kristine K. Forney, 'A Gift of Madrigals and Chansons: The Winchester Part Books and the Courtship of Elizabeth I by Erik XIV of Sweden', *The Journal of Musicology* 17 (1999), 50–75. The Winchester Partbooks are GB-WCc: MS 153.

[49] Woodfield, 'The Keyboard Recital', pp. 37–40. There was also a bass lute delivered by an embassy to Morocco in 1577 to secure the Barbary Company's trading rights, and the Russia Company presented organs and virginals to the Tsar in 1586, though the extent of Elizabeth's involvement with these gifts is less clear.

[50] Thomas Dallam, 'The Diary of Master Thomas Dallam, 1599–1600', in *Early Voyages and Travels in the Levant*, ed. J. Theodore Bent (London, 1893), pp. 1–98 (pp. 67–8).

The importance of this gift extended beyond Turkey and the Levant Company's trade interests; it enhanced England's reputation in Europe too. Londoner John Chamberlain wrote to Dudley Carleton in January 1599 that 'a great and curious present is going to the Grand Turk, which will scandalize other nations, especially the Germans', while the Venetian ambassador in Constantinople also reported on the 'organ very cunningly designed, which serves as a clock and can play several airs by itself'.[51]

While the German diarists tended to be impressed with the music of the English court, not everyone was so complimentary.[52] The Mantuan ambassador, Il Schifanoya, was dismissive of the music at banquets after Elizabeth's coronation, declaring that 'much music was performed, but it not being remarkable and having heard better I will say nothing about it.'[53] While this is the only surviving critical reaction to English court music, it raises the possibility that the German gentlemen, nobles, and minor princes may have been more easily impressed than ambassadors from Italy, France, or Spain. Paired with Elizabeth's limited interventions in the musical set-up of her court and her scarce attempts to source musicians from abroad in the latter decades of her reign, we should be cautious about overestimating the musical reputation of Elizabeth's court. She succeeded in gaining the admiration of at least some foreigners, though often as much through the splendour and noise of the ceremonial occasions or the beauty and novelty of the instruments, as through the skill of the players and composers. While Elizabeth's court may not have been the envy of all others, it was nevertheless sufficient to convey magnificence, cultural and economic prosperity, native talents, and internationalism. In doing so, music assisted in presenting England as a significant participant in Europe's culture and, by extension, its politics.

CONTROL OF COURT MUSIC

WHILE court music served Elizabeth's political and diplomatic needs, she was not in direct control of every musical performance within her court and these did not unequivocally communicate her political will. A monarch had more important matters to deal with than the day-to-day organisation of the music and so the majority took place without her involvement. Instead the court ensembles were answerable to the Lord Chamberlain (who also appointed the musicians) and his

---

[51] John Chamberlain, 'John Chamberlain to Dudley Carleton: 31 January 1599', GB-Lna: SP12/270, Secretaries of State: State Papers Domestic, Elizabeth I, fol. 41r–v (fol. 41v); *CSP Venice*, vol. 9, p. 375 [18 September 1599].

[52] Hentzner, *Itinerarium*, p. 156: 'in saltationibus et arte Musica excellunt; sunt enim agiles et alacres' ('They excel in dances and the art of music for they are agile and lively'). Rye, *England as Seen by Foreigners*, p. 11; Rathgeb, *Warhaffte Beschreibung*, fol. 15r: 'eine solche herzliche, liebliche Musik (die, wie zu vermuten, der Königin zugehört) gehabt, daß sich höchlich daran zu verwundern'. Wedel, *Lupold von Wedels Beschreibung*, p. 360, describes the music at dinner as 'gar herrlich und gut' (very magnificent and good). Translation differs slightly from Bülow, 'Journey through England and Scotland', p. 264.

[53] *CSP Venice*, vol. 7, p. 18 [23 January 1559].

staff.[54] Some organisational role also seems to have been taken by Thomas Lichfield, a Groom of the Privy Chamber, who was described as the supervisor of the Queen's music by the cofferer who paid his wages.[55] What this position entailed is not clear, and nor do we know who continued the role when Lichfield resigned his post in the Privy Chamber in December 1575. Not until the reign of Charles I was there a formal post of 'Master of the Music' (the singer-lutenist Nicholas Lanier II), and the resentment caused by his attempts to exercise authority over other ensembles suggests the independence that the consorts had previously enjoyed.[56] Since much of the musical provision on a day-to-day basis was routine, these ensembles could be granted a high degree of autonomy. They would probably have been told where and when they should perform, but not exactly what to provide. In any case, it would be difficult for their instrumental music to be politically controversial.

Examples of Elizabeth directing a performance by her musicians for political ends are rare. On one occasion, while entertaining the Spanish ambassador Guzman da Silva at dinner in July 1564, Elizabeth ordered her musicians to play the 'Battle of Pavia', telling the ambassador that it was 'the music she enjoyed most'.[57] Her choice of piece was not only designed to show her cosmopolitan musical tastes, but also had diplomatic significance. The French ambassador was also at court at this time and the relative treatment of the two ambassadors was being carefully observed. Da Silva notes in his letter that the French ambassador had not been invited to dinner and had been made to wait for Elizabeth's reply to a letter delivered that morning. The Battle of Pavia commemorated in the music Elizabeth chose had been a decisive Spanish victory over the French in Italy on 24 February 1525. The piece Elizabeth was referring to was probably Hermann Matthias Werrecore's widely circulated secular song, 'La bataglia tagliana', a piece which told the story of the battle (though three motets also commemorated the event). It was designed to answer the French composer Clément Janequin's 'La Guerre', from which it borrowed musical material and stylistic features, especially in mimicking the sounds of the battle.[58] Whether or not the 'Battle of Pavia' really was one of Elizabeth's favourites, her decision to ask for it must have been designed to flatter the Spanish ambassador and signal the greater honour she was showing da Silva over the French diplomat. On another exceptional occasion – the post-Armada celebrations of November 1588 – Elizabeth wrote a thanksgiving prayer 'Look and Bow Down', which was set to music by William Byrd and performed by the Children of St Paul's during her procession through London.[59] This, however, was a public display of piety and thanksgiving, rather different from courtly diplomacy within the royal palaces.

---

[54] Holman, *Four and Twenty Fiddlers*, p. 229.
[55] Ashbee and Lasocki, *Biographical Dictionary*, vol. 2, pp. 722–4.
[56] Holman, *Four and Twenty Fiddlers*, pp. 232–4.
[57] *L&P Simancas*, vol. 1, p. 367.
[58] Christine Suzanne Getz, *Music in the Collective Experience in Sixteenth-Century Milan* (Aldershot, 2005), pp. 4–30.
[59] William Byrd, *Madrigals, Songs and Canons*, ed. Philip Brett, Byrd Edition 16 (London, 1976), pp. 197–8; Arthur F. Marotti and Steven W. May, 'Two Lost

More typically Elizabeth's influence over musical performances stretched only to directing the choice of performers rather than their politics. The Lord Chamberlain's memorandum for Twelfth Night 1601 notes Elizabeth's requests for a carol to be sung at dinner by the Children of the Chapel Royal, and for music to be appointed for the Queen and the play in the hall, which would include 'great variety and change of music and dances' and a place for Robert Hales to sing.[60] While Elizabeth indicated which ensembles and musicians she wanted to hear and when, she said very little about their actual music, leaving this to the Chamberlain, the Master of the Revels, and the musicians to determine.

Rather than maintaining firm control over court performances, Elizabeth was willing to receive musical entertainments performed by external groups and commissioned by her courtiers (whether the intimate songs of the previous chapter or the more elaborate pageants at tournaments seen in the next). The court's festivities at Christmas, New Year, and Shrovetide might include the London waits, Gentlemen from the Inns of Court, and professional acting companies.[61] The most musical of the acting troupes were the choirboys who performed plays, including those of Elizabeth's Chapel Royal, St Paul's Cathedral, and until 1577, St George's Chapel, Windsor. Not only were these boys trained singers, they could also provide their own accompaniment, being proficient on instruments such as the lute and viol.[62] The plays, masques, and songs were an opportunity for political comment by the authors and their patrons. Plays were approved by the Master of the Revels, but his job was not primarily one of censorship, but rather to make sure that the entertainments would suit the tastes of the Queen.[63] He potentially had influence over the way in which music was used in these plays or the musical styles and genres performed, but probably made little alteration to the political content.

Elizabeth tolerated court performances that expressed ideas and themes contrary to her own desires. Following a dramatic debate in March 1565 between Juno (advocating marriage) and Diana (representing chastity) in which Jupiter ruled in

---

Ballads of the Armada Thanksgiving Celebration [with texts and illustration]', *English Literary Renaissance* 41 (2011), 31–63. Another of Elizabeth's poems, 'Deliver me, O Lord my God', was set by John Bull. It appeals to God for England's deliverance from the Armada, though it is less clear when this was performed.

[60] Leslie Hotson, *The First Night of Twelfth Night* (New York, 1954), pp. 180–1.
[61] Ibid., p. 181.
[62] Harold Newcomb Hillebrand, *The Child Actors: A Chapter in Elizabethan Stage History*, Illinois Studies in Language and Literature 11 (Urbana, 1926), pp. 40–4, 75–151; G. E. P. Arkwright, 'Elizabethan Choirboy Plays and their Music', *Proceedings of the Musical Association* 40 (1913/14), 117–38; W. Reavley Gair, *The Children of Paul's: The Story of a Theatre Company, 1553–1608* (Cambridge, 1982), pp. 33–6, 75–112; Michael Shapiro, *Children of the Revels: The Boy Companies of Shakespeare's Time and their Plays* (New York, 1977).
[63] Richard Dutton, *Mastering the Revels: The Regulation and Censorship of English Renaissance Drama* (Basingstoke, 1991), pp. 34–7, 89.

favour of marriage, Elizabeth told the Spanish ambassador Guzman da Silva, 'this is all against me.'[64] Under pressure to marry and produce an heir, Elizabeth read the dramatic portrayal of marriage and chastity as a direct comment on her own situation. As such, the music of the royal household could do far more than merely promote the magnificence of the Queen and court. Drawing on two particularly musical forms of court entertainment – the masque and the plays of choirboy companies – I show how these genres combined royal praise with the staging of political counsel and moral advice. They touched on topical issues and promoted the interests of ambitious individuals or the external groups who brought shows to court.

MASQUED POLITICS

THE grandest musical festivity performed in the royal palaces was the masque. As masques could either be put on by the royal household or brought to court from the Inns of Court, they exemplify how musical entertainments served the interests of both Elizabeth and the political élite.[65] The Elizabethan masque was not as formalised, elaborate, or large-scale as its more well-known Jacobean successor. Its essence was the arrival of a procession of masked or disguised people to present a dance or a gift to the Queen.[66] Music was central to the masque, for the focal processions and dances all required musical accompaniment. This was provided by professional musicians, usually those of the royal household. The masquers, however, were ladies and gentlemen of the court rather than professional dancers, though again the speaking parts were often given to actors. A speech presented the pretext for the arrival of the masquers, though this introduction could be expanded into an elaborate scene with conversations between mythical or allegorical characters and even songs. Dance was not yet a defining element. A masque presented to the Queen at Norwich, for example, was simply a procession of classical gods accompanied by torchbearers who presented speeches and gifts.[67] Where dances did follow the procession these might include formal, practised dances by the masquers, as well as social dancing in which the masquers took partners from among the spectators. This moment where the masque-world dissolved into the court so that the spectators became part of the spectacle was characteristic of the masque and also influenced plays

---

[64] *CSP Simancas*, vol. 1, pp. 404–14.

[65] The royal household put on masques during the first twenty-five years of the reign, but left these to external groups towards the end of the reign (meaning fewer were performed). A useful compilation of references to performances of plays and masques, in chronological order, is Mary Susan Steele, *Plays and Masques at Court during the Reigns of Elizabeth, James and Charles* (New Haven, CT, 1926).

[66] Enid Welsford, *The Court Masque: A Study in the Relationship between Poetry and the Revels* (New York, 1962), p. 3.

[67] B[ernard] G[arter], *The Joyful Receiving of the Queen's Most Excellent Majesty into her Highness' City of Norwich* (London, 1578), sigs. E1r–E3v.

(such as Peele's *The Arraignment of Paris*) and entertainments for Elizabeth's progresses.[68]

As masques were ephemeral, one-off performances they leave limited records, especially in this early period when the theatrical introductions were less developed.[69] Most masques are known only through the Revels Accounts, which do no more than list the characters (for example, masques of barbarians, Italian women, astronomers, Moors and Amazons, or fishermen, fishwives, and market-wives) and the costs of providing costumes and scenery.[70] As the music was provided by the musicians of the royal household virtually no record of it appears in the Revels Accounts except for an occasional description of a musician among the masquers. The masque of fishermen, fishwives, and market-wives in February 1559, for example, included a fisherman with 'drum and fife' and six 'minstrels' to accompany the fishwives and market-wives.[71] In 1565, a 'masque of hunters and divers devices' included the singing of Muses, while in 1579 cornetts accompanied the entry of Amazons.[72]

The more extensive research surrounding the better-preserved and more highly developed Jacobean masque suggests that the genre was a performance of royal authority and a 'ritual embodiment of the mythology of monarchy'.[73] Music and dance were essential parts of this mythology. Masque texts frequently depicted good governance as mirroring divine harmony, so music and dancing became manifestations of social order and musical power represented princely authority.[74] Yet there were also contesting voices: favourites and royal consorts whose self-display challenged the policies and image of the King, individual

---

[68] For Orgel this dissolving of the boundary between spectacle and the court is sufficient to define an entertainment as a masque. I limit my discussion to shows designated as masques by their authors, but note that forms were fluid enough that one courtly genre could borrow and incorporate techniques from another. Stephen Orgel, *The Jonsonian Masque* (New York, 1981), pp. 6–7.

[69] On the music and dance of the Stuart masque see particularly Peter Walls, *Music in the English Courtly Masque, 1604–1640*, Oxford Monographs on Music (Oxford, 1996); Barbara Ravelhofer, *The Early Stuart Masque: Dance, Costume, and Music* (Oxford, 2006); Mary Chan, *Music in the Theatre of Ben Jonson* (Oxford, 1980), pp. 138–304.

[70] Steele, *Plays and Masques*, pp. 4–5, 7–10, 69.

[71] Albert Gabriel Feuillerat, *Documents Relating to the Office of the Revels in the Time of Queen Elizabeth*, Materialien zur Kunde des älteren Englischen Dramas 21 (Louvain, 1908), pp. 25, 28.

[72] Ibid., pp. 117, 287.

[73] Stephen Orgel, *The Illusion of Power: Political Theater in the English Renaissance*, Quantum Books (Berkeley, CA, 1975), inside cover.

[74] Walls, *Music in the English Courtly Masque*, pp. 7–10, 13, 103–8, 113; Kristin Rygg, *Masqued Mysteries Unmasked: Early Modern Music Theater and its Pythagorean Subtext*, Interplay 1 (Hillsdale, NY, 2000), pp. xx–xxv, 25–6; Skiles Howard, *The Politics of Courtly Dancing in Early Modern England*, Massachusetts Studies in Early Modern Culture (Amherst, 1998), pp. 20–5, 27–45, 60–8; Ravelhofer, *Early Stuart Masque*, pp. 102–8.

virtuosic performances that threatened the image of collectivity and submission to the monarch's will, and topical issues whose tensions needed to be diffused.[75] Many of these themes already appear in the Elizabethan masques, which similarly encompassed both extravagant royal praise and the self-interest of participants.

The royal household masques are the least well recorded in Elizabeth's reign, but one that reveals how masque music served Elizabeth's aims was planned for a meeting between Elizabeth and Mary Queen of Scots in York in 1562.[76] Though neither the meeting nor the masque took place, this spectacle was intended to enact the creation of a harmonious relationship between the two Queens and their kingdoms. On the first night Prudentia and Temperantia were to lock Report and Discord into the prison of Extreme Oblivion, after which the English ladies were to dance with the Scottish nobles. On the second night the goddess Pallas was to send Peace and Friendship along with two porters, Ardent Desire and Perpetuity, signifying that 'by ardent desire and perpetuity, perpetual peace and tranquillity may be had and kept through the whole world.' Then the English lords were to masque with the Scottish ladies. On the third night Malice and Disdain were to be sent by Pluto, but Jupiter was to counter these vices by sending Discretion and Valiant Courage. After the defeat of Disdain and Malice in a mock battle, lady masquers were to enter with a song 'that shall be made hereupon, as full of Harmony, as maybe be devised'.[77] The diplomatic display of concord was depicted allegorically in the shows, while the mixing of the Scottish and English nobility in dance would have both represented and helped to create cordial relations. The instruction to produce a song 'full of harmony' seems to imply that the music too was intended to signify political concord, as well as to impress the assembled Scots with English music of the highest quality.

Masques also enhanced Elizabeth's image through the singing of extravagant royal praise. John Manningham (a student in the Middle Temple) recorded a masque song in his diary ('Song to The Queen at the Masque at Court,

---

[75] Martin Butler, *The Stuart Court Masque and Political Culture* (Cambridge, 2008), pp. 4–7, 22–33; David Lindley, 'The Politics of Music in the Masque', in *The Politics of the Stuart Court Masque*, ed. David Bevington and Peter Holbrook (Cambridge, 1998), pp. 273–95; David Bevington and Peter Holbrook, 'Introduction', ibid., pp. 1–19; Sara Pearl, 'Sounding to Present Occasions: Jonson's Masques of 1620–5', in *The Court Masque*, ed. David Lindley, Revels Plays Companion Library (Manchester, 1984), pp. 60–77.

[76] 'Devices to be Showed Before the Queen's Majesty by way of Masking at Nottingham Castle After the Meeting of the Queen of Scots', GB-Lbl: Lansdowne MS 5/38 (1562), fol. 126. Transcription in E. K. Chambers and W. W. Greg (eds.), 'Dramatic Records from the Lansdowne Manuscripts', *Malone Society Collections*, 16 vols. (Oxford, 1908), vol. 1, pt. 2, pp. 143–215 (pp. 144–8). For music-making at The Inns of Court see: Robert W. Wienpahl, *Music at the Inns of Court during the Reigns of Elizabeth, James, and Charles* (Ann Arbor, MI, 1979); David Price, *Patrons and Musicians of the English Renaissance*, Cambridge Studies in Music (Cambridge, 1981), pp. 27–31.

[77] 'Devices to be Showed … at Nottingham Castle'; Chambers and Greg (eds.), 'Dramatic Records', pp. 144–18.

Nov. 2.')[78] No other record of this masque survives so the context of the song is lost, but the lyrics are presented as 'tributes due' and praise Elizabeth for her beauty, eternal youth, and good governance, having brought peace and prosperity to her realm. The song heralds her as 'Mighty Princess of a fruitful land' who brings 'the death of war the life of peace', and ends by asserting that she will 'live/ Till Time it self must die'.

Aside from producing visions of royal authority and courtly harmony, masques also served the interests of those who participated in them. As Elizabeth would pick the masquers, being chosen was a mark of favour.[79] For outsiders bringing a masque to court, participation was a means of coming to royal attention. Henry Helmes from Gray's Inn found favour while dancing in the *Masque of Proteus* (1595) and became a Gentleman Pensioner at the court.[80]

Masques commissioned by courtiers or brought to the court by outside groups were particularly likely to combine the ambitions of participants with their vision of princely harmony. Arthur Throckmorton, introduced at the opening of this book, hoped a masque might stage a reconciliation between himself and the Queen (p. 2). In addition many courtiers had connections to the Inns of Court and used the entertainments these gentlemen brought to court as opportunities to further their political aims. Robert Dudley, Earl of Leicester, collaborated with the gentlemen of the Inner Temple and Gray's Inn in January 1562 to produce a masque of Desire and Beauty, which Marie Axton suggests was designed to present himself as suitor to the Queen. Elizabeth was represented in the figures of Beauty and Pallas, and Leicester in Desire/Perseus, while the masque ended with dancing at the wedding of Beauty to Perseus (who was Desire metamorphosed).[81]

The most detailed description of music-making in an Elizabethan masque comes from the *Masque of Proteus* provided by the Gentlemen of Gray's Inn in 1595.[82] Bringing this masque to court ended an extensive Christmas Revels at Gray's Inn

---

[78] John Manningham, *The Diary of John Manningham of the Middle Temple, 1602–1603*, ed. Robert Parker Sorlien (Hanover, NH, 1976), p. 29.

[79] On Elizabeth choosing masquers, see Throckmorton's letter, p. 2.

[80] Marie Axton, *The Queen's Two Bodies: Drama and the Elizabethan Succession*, Royal Historical Society Studies in History 5 (London, 1977), p. 85.

[81] Marie Axton, 'The Tudor Mask and Elizabethan Court Drama', in *English Drama: Forms and Development: Essays in Honour of Muriel Clara Bradbrook*, ed. Marie Axton and Raymond Williams (Cambridge, 1977), pp. 24–47 (pp. 33–4).

[82] Canning (ed.), *Gesta Grayorum*, pp. 57–66. This was not printed until 1688 and the text is corrupt in several places (particularly in the songs). A manuscript version survives in GB-Lbl: MS Harley 541, fols. 138r–145r, which Greg believes may be in the hand of Francis Davison: W. W. Greg (ed.), *Gesta Grayorum, 1688*, Malone Society Reprints (London, 1914), pp. vii–viii. The manuscript only contains the text of the final hymn, but the first song appears in Francis Davison (ed.), *A Poetical Rhapsody Containing, Diverse Sonnets, Odes, Elegies, Madrigals, and Other Poesies* ... (London, 1602), sig. K8r (again in a version which makes better sense than the print). The 1688 publication does contain additional descriptions of the event, however. An edition and collation using both sources has recently been published in Elizabeth Goldring *et al.* (eds.), *John Nichols's The*

in which they had appointed a mock king, the Prince of Purpoole. The masque was topical with its nautical theme reflecting the continuing maritime warfare against Spain. References to a rock which 'draws the needle to the North' subtly alluded to the Scottish King, who was increasingly coming to be seen as Elizabeth's successor and receiving secret ingratiating letters from her courtiers.[83] The masque reassured Elizabeth of the unshakeable loyalty of her lawyers, who presented themselves as unswayed by the lesser powers of the Adamantine Rock.

The masque also furthered the personal aims of its specific creators and their patrons. Francis Davison (one of the main authors) was a supporter of the Earl of Essex, so this nautical masque may have been intended to promote the more aggressive naval policy towards Spain which Essex desired.[84] Davison himself was concerned with restoring the fortunes of his father, William Davison, who was the unfortunate person who delivered the signed death-warrant for Mary Queen of Scots and became a scapegoat for Elizabeth's guilt.[85] More generally it advertises the lawyers' ability to deal with any threat to Elizabeth's authority.[86] The complexity of the conceit was sufficient to serve these various purposes simultaneously, alongside the masque's customary royal tributes.

Music's role was theatrical: it was through the songs that the illusory world of the masque was first created and then dissolved. Yet there was also a political edge to the music. The opening song (written by Thomas Campion) heralds 'Neptune's Empery' in an explicit challenge to Elizabeth's frequent portrayal as Cynthia, the 'wide Ocean's Empress'.[87] Yet the Lawyer-Prince of Purpoole has plans afoot to unmask Neptune's false power. Doubt is immediately cast on the validity of the song by the Prince's Esquire, who raises philosophical concerns over whether fishes have a sense of hearing. The sea-god Proteus rebukes the Esquire for putting the 'dreaming guess' of philosophers who do not speak from experience ('that never held his idle buzzing head/ Under the water') above the 'old received story' of Arion being saved by a dolphin.[88] This moment gently mocks scholarly thought without practical application, the opposite of the lawyers whose education in law would be applicable to worldly politics. It transpires that Proteus has promised the Prince the Adamantine Rock that lies beneath the arctic pole on condition that he

---

Progresses and Public Processions of Queen Elizabeth I: A New Edition of the Early Modern Sources, 5 vols. (Oxford, 2014), vol. 3, pp. 843–55.

[83] Axton, 'Tudor Mask', p. 46; 'The Dialogue Between the Squire, Proteus, Amphitrite and Thamesis', GB-Lbl: MS Harley 541, fols. 138r–145r (fol. 143v).

[84] Richard C. McCoy, 'Lord of Liberty: Francis Davison and the Cult of Elizabeth', in *The Reign of Elizabeth I: Court and Culture in the Last Decade*, ed. John Guy (Cambridge, 1995), pp. 212–28 (p. 218).

[85] Ibid., p. 222.

[86] Axton, *Queen's Two Bodies*, p. 85.

[87] Davison (ed.), *A Poetical Rhapsody*, sig. K8r. As he was a composer as well as a poet, it is probable that Campion wrote the now-lost music as well as the lyrics. For other examples of Elizabeth as Cynthia see pp. 32, 51, 149 and 157.

[88] 'The Dialogue', GB-Lbl: MS Harley 541, fol. 139r.

first shows Proteus something which surpasses the power of the Rock. The Prince has requested that Proteus and the Rock should be brought to Elizabeth's court.

The masque depicts the moment when the Prince reveals Elizabeth as the 'true adamant of hearts'. Whereas Neptune was crowned with gems, Elizabeth is crowned with virtues. Neptune's source of power is an iron-attracting rock that can do nothing without the arms of men, while Elizabeth's authority attract the hearts of men (and 'arms of men from hearts of men do move'). In a series of puns surrounding the dual meaning of arms (body-parts or weapons), Neptune's power is revealed as founded on iron weaponry and warfare, and Elizabeth's on peace and 'purest zeal'.[89] Moreover, it is through the lawyers' peaceful means of wit, words and demonstrations that false authority has been unmasked.[90] The threatening power of Neptune and Proteus is banished as they disappear into the Rock. Meanwhile the knights of the Prince's court illustrate the restored harmony with specially devised dances. As the masquers then take their partners among the spectators for social dancing, Elizabeth's power as 'adamant of hearts' is made visible and audible in the harmonious music and collective dancing in her honour. Similarly the divisions over foreign policy or successors-in-waiting alluded to in the masque are symbolically resolved through an image of Elizabeth's ultimate authority.

The final song sees power restored to its rightful place. Not only is 'Neptune's Empery' replaced with the 'true majesty' of Elizabeth, but the mock-kingdom of the lawyers' Christmas revels also dissolves as they admit to being 'shepherds sometimes in lion's skins'.[91] As the final song described, 'Colours of false principality/ Do fade in presence of true majesty.'[92] While praising Elizabeth for her virtuous governance and enacting her princely power, the lawyers also evoked their abilities to see through falsehoods, challenge opposing powers, and put their wit to good use in protecting their monarch's interests.

COUNSEL AND THE CHOIRBOY PLAYS

As well as celebrating Elizabeth's authority and earning rewards for their performers, court entertainments also staged political counsel, advising both the monarch and her courtiers on how to govern wisely.[93] The clearest examples of music's role in imparting such advice come from the plays performed by the

---

[89] Ibid., fol. 143r.
[90] Orgel, *The Jonsonian Masque*, p. 15.
[91] 'The Dialogue', GB-Lbl: MS Harley 541, fol. 145r.
[92] Ibid. In Canning (ed.), *Gesta Grayorum*, 'colours' reads 'counsellors' (p. 66).
[93] See for example: Greg Walker, *The Politics of Performance in Early Renaissance Drama* (Cambridge, 1998); Greg Walker, *Plays of Persuasion: Drama and Politics at the Court of Henry VIII* (Cambridge, 1991); Ros King (ed.), *The Works of Richard Edwards: Politics, Poetry, and Performances in Sixteenth-Century England*, Revels Plays Companion Library (Manchester, 2001), pp. 55–62; Susan Doran, 'Juno versus Diana: The Treatment of Elizabeth I's Marriage in Plays and Entertainments, 1561–1581', *The Historical Journal* 28 (1995), 257–74; Axton, *Queen's Two Bodies*, pp. 38–60.

choirboy companies of the Chapel Royal, St Paul's, and Windsor, in which songs played a significant role.[94] Choirboy plays were frequently performed during the Christmas or Shrovetide revels between 1558 and c. 1590, and were a favourite entertainment of Elizabeth's until at least 1576.[95] Only in the 1580s, with the founding of the Queen's Men, did adult companies begin to perform as frequently as the choirboys, and their plays generally used far fewer songs.[96]

Plays provided a means through which sophisticated political debate could be sustained in a system where the decision-making ultimately lay with the monarch. This political debate frequently drew on the language of morality so that appeals to virtue were aimed at altering the monarch's views and policies.[97] Songs too were a recognised means of moral persuasion because music was credited with inspiring virtuous behaviour. Count Lewis, in Castiglione's *The Courtier*, argued that music is 'sufficient to bring into us a new habit that is good, and a custom inclining to virtue, which maketh the mind more apt to the conceiving of felicity'.[98] Though elsewhere castigated for causing vice, the affective powers of music could be harnessed to instil moral qualities. Moreover, pleasurable music could sweeten a didactic purpose. Sir Philip Sidney described how the poet comes 'with words set in delightful proportion, either accompanied with, or prepared for, the

---

[94] Detailed studies of these choirboy companies in the Elizabethan period include: Hillebrand, *The Child Actors*; Gair, *Children of Paul's*; Shapiro, *Children of the Revels*; Jeanne H. McCarthy, 'Elizabeth I's "Picture in Little": Boy Company Representations of a Queen's Authority', *Studies in Philology* 100 (2003), 425–62; Trevor Lennam, *Sebastian Westcott, The Children of Paul's, and The Marriage of Wit and Science* (Toronto, 1975).

[95] Elizabeth was not the only monarch to enjoy the performances of child actors. Many European rulers and their courtiers attended the plays (including music) of the Jesuit schools across the continent and in some capitals their playhouses became almost like minor court theatres: William H. McCabe, *An Introduction to the Jesuit Theater: A Posthumous Work*, ed. Louis J. Oldani (St Louis, MO, 1983), pp. 37–46, 63–4. Nor were English choirboys the only ones to be involved in dramatic performances: Juan Ruiz Jiménez, 'From *Mozos de coro* towards *Seises*: Boys in the Musical Life of Seville Cathedral in the Fifteenth and Sixteenth Centuries', in *Young Choristers, 650–1700*, ed. Susan Boynton and Eric Rice (Woodbridge, 2008), pp. 86–103 (pp. 99–101).

[96] The choirboy companies ceased to perform altogether between c. 1590 and 1597, as the Chapel Royal boys lost their Blackfriars theatre where they had rehearsed in 1584, and the St Paul's boys were banned in 1589/90 for their involvement in the Martin Marprelate controversy. Only in the final few years of Elizabeth's reign did the choirboys return to court. For a summary of the Marprelate controversy see Gair, *Children of Paul's*, pp. 110–12. On the later, post-1597 phase of choirboy plays see Linda Phyllis Austern, *Music in English Children's Drama of the Later Renaissance*, Musicology Series 13 (Philadelphia, 1992); Mary Chan, 'Cynthia's Revels and Music for a Choir School: Christ Church Manuscript Mus 439', *Studies in the Renaissance* 18 (1971), 134–72; Chan, *Music in the Theatre*, pp. 1–72.

[97] Walker, *Politics of Performance*, p. 224.

[98] Count Baldassarre Castiglione, *The Courtier of Count Baldessar Castilio*, trans. Thomas Hoby (London, 1561), sig. I2v.

well-enchanting skill of music ... and pretending no more, doth intend the winning of the mind from wickedness to virtue'.[99] In the plays of the 1560s–90s, songs frequently served to summarise the moral and political positions being presented, or to highlight the contrast between the joy of the virtuous and lamentations caused by vice.

Some songs were openly political but addressed topics that were typical throughout the Tudor period, such as those distinguishing self-serving flatterers from trustworthy counsellors.[100] Others presented general moral arguments that had immediate relevance to topical concerns. Songs on love or chastity, for example, could make a political statement on the Queen's marital status. Further songs were not political through their lyrics but through the mood they created and the wider context in which they occurred.[101] In the examples discussed below it is rarely possible to establish precisely who is offering the advice: the (often anonymous) author or a courtly patron, and with what influence from the Master of the Revels?[102] The intended audience could be equally diverse. These court plays were not only addressing Elizabeth, but also her courtiers. The Christmas revels were a popular time for young men and women from noble families to make an appearance at court, so plays that communicated principles of courtly behaviour were especially appropriate.[103] It was also a time when noblemen not in regular attendance at court might make the effort to appear, and ambassadors would also have been present. Political counsel might therefore be aimed at instructing the nobility as well as the Queen.

The ability of songs to state a moral position clearly and succinctly is a feature that is commonly exploited in allegorical plays such as *The Contention Between Liberality and Prodigality*. This was first performed in 1567/8, but is known from a revised version performed and published in 1602.[104] It concerns an argument between Prodigality and Tenacity as to who should have control of Money, the son of Fortune. Prodigality exploits Money until he is bare and thin to fund a lifestyle of feasting and merry-making, whereas Tenacity chains Money and allows him to

---

[99] Sir Philip Sidney, *An Apology for Poetry* (London, 1595), sig. E4v.

[100] See for example, the analysis of John Skelton's *Magnificence* (1515–6?) in Walker, *Plays of Persuasion*, pp. 133–68.

[101] For a broader survey of types of songs found in choirboy plays see Shapiro, *Children of the Revels*, pp. 232–55. Not all songs were political, but those whose purpose appears to be solely dramatic will not be considered here.

[102] Edward de Vere, the Earl of Oxford, for example, was patron of an amalgamation of the Chapel Royal and St Paul's boys in 1583/4. Gair, *Children of Paul's*, p. 98. Jeanne McCarthy argues that the companies portrayed Elizabeth's 'propaganda or rhetoric of rule' (McCarthy, 'Elizabeth I's "Picture in Little"', p. 459). Yet aside from Elizabeth's repeated patronage in inviting the companies to perform, there is no evidence that she dictated their content, and most contain counsel for the Queen as much as for her courtiers.

[103] John Astington, *English Court Theatre, 1558–1642* (Cambridge, 1999), p. 168.

[104] *A Pleasant Comedy, Showing the Contention Between Liberality and Prodigality as it was Played Before her Majesty* (London, 1602); Hillebrand, *The Child Actors*, pp. 128–30.

grow so fat he cannot move. Finally, Money is saved from these bad masters and delivered to Virtue who appoints Money to Liberality. Songs were used throughout the play to introduce the nature of these allegorical characters (though only the lyrics are now extant). Money's song, for example, describes how he is 'the spring of all joy', 'the medicine that heals each annoy', and 'the idol that women adore', while Fortune 'with twinkling of her eye … misers can advance to dignity/ And Princes turn to miser's misery'.[105]

Two further songs acted as a means of moral debate. Prodigality and Tenacity initially take part in a song contest to determine who will have Money. Prodigality says that the 'Princely heart' who spends freely 'getteth praise, he gaineth friends,/ And people's love procures therefore', while Tenacity responds, 'Thou liv'st for the most part by the spoil/ I truly labour day and night, To get my living by my toile.'[106] Later Virtue's song compares the easy road to vice with the difficult path of virtue:

> The passage first seems hard:
> To virtue's train: but then most sweet,
> At length is their reward.
> To those again that follow vice
> The way is fair and plain:
> But fading pleasures in the end,
> Are bought with fasting pain.[107]

This song acts as the moral conclusion to the play (the closing scenes simply wrap up the plot with Prodigality admitting to his crimes and appealing to the Prince's mercy). With their direct and succinct lyrics, these songs contain the strongest statement of the moral debate concerning the proper use of riches being explored in the play.

This moral point becomes a political issue first in the presentation of two contrasting courts ruled by women (Fortune and Virtue), and second when Prodigality's song associates his use of money with his 'princely heart'. The message for Elizabeth is that she must use money wisely to create a court which is governed by Virtue rather than Fortune. Yet the message also applied to courtiers, as liberality was equally a virtue to which the nobility were to aspire. Although warning of the dangers of 'excessive rewards … or else employing treasure … on persons unworthy, or on things … of small importance' (all illustrated by the actions of Prodigality), Thomas Elyot argued in *The Book of the Governor* that liberality was commended in noblemen as 'it acquireth perpetual honour to the giver' when he rewards 'honest and virtuous personages'.[108]

Other plays addressed issues of good governance more directly. Richard Edwards's *Damon and Pithias* told the story of two friends who visit the kingdom

---

[105] *Liberality and Prodigality*, sig. B3r–v [act 1, scenes 5 and 6].

[106] Ibid., sigs. C2v–C3r [act 2, scene 4].

[107] Ibid., sig. F1r–v [act 5, scene 3].

[108] Sir Thomas Elyot, *The Book Named the Governor* (London, 1531), fols. 130r, 140v–141r.

of the tyrant Dionisius.[109] Edwards was the Master of the Children of the Chapel Royal, and his play was performed in 1564 and published in 1571. Pithias is unfairly arrested and condemned to death for spying by King Dionisius, due to the efforts of the unscrupulous courtier Carisophus; however, the companions' friendship is so great that each would die for the other, and this touches the heart of Dionisius. He saves both Damon and Pithias and – finally understanding the value of true friendship rather than courtiers' flattery – he begs them to extend such amity to him.

Throughout the play, musical laments underscore the misery caused by the tyrant's actions. The first two laments emphasise the friendship and shared grief of Damon and Pithias at the unjust situation and impending death.[110] Pithias sings 'Awake Ye Woeful Wights' to the accompaniment of regals; and Damon calls on music to 'sound my doleful plaints when I am gone my way', following which 'regals play a mourning song'.[111] A setting of 'Awake Ye Woeful Wights' survives in an early-seventeenth-century manuscript arranged for lute and voice.[112] As is typical for sung laments of the 1560s–70s, the melody is subtle rather than overtly expressive, using predominantly stepwise motion and employing dissonances only sparingly (for example, a chromatic E flat for the phrase 'plaints and tears').[113] Such laments (which were typically consort songs) were a conventional song type in plays of this period; however, as few surviving songs can be connected to extant play texts, any potential political significance remains obscured.[114] In *Damon and Pithias* the accumulation of laments climaxes with the Muses' appearance in the lament of Eubulus (a good-hearted courtier from Dionisius's court). This lament aligns the good courtier with the two friends: his concern for the companions and the state of Dionysius's court is a contrast to the flattery and false friendship of his fellow courtiers Aristippus and Carisophus.

Having impressed upon the audience the tragedy of Dionisius's bad governance through these laments, Edwards also provided a sung epilogue to summarise the play's moral message (most likely either a consort song or a partsong). Beginning 'The strongest guard that Kings can have/ Are constant friends their state to save', the song concludes by emphasising the importance of a monarch having wise and

---

[109] Richard Edwards, *The Excellent Comedy of Two the Most Faithfullest Friends, Damon and Pithias* (London, 1571); King (ed.), *Works of Richard Edwards*.

[110] Tommy Waldo, 'Music and Musical Terms in Richard Edwards's "Damon and Pithias"', *Music & Letters* 49 (1968), 29–35 (pp. 33–4).

[111] Edwards, *Damon and Pithias*, sigs. D1r, E2r; King (ed.), *Works of Richard Edwards*, pp. 148–9 [scene 10, line 314; scene 11, opening instruction].

[112] The melody also appears on a broadside ballad of 1568 described as 'to the tune of Damon and Pithias'. John Long, 'Music for a Song in "Damon and Pithias"', *Music & Letters* 48 (1967), 247–50; Claude M. Simpson, *The British Broadside Ballad and its Music* (New Brunswick, 1966), pp. 157–9.

[113] [Richard Edwards?], 'Awake Ye Woeful Wights', GB-Lbl: Add. MS 15117, fol. 2.

[114] Arkwright, 'Elizabethan Choirboy Plays'; Philip Brett, 'Consort Song', *NG2*; Chan, *Music in the Theatre*, pp. 15–30. The extant consort songs are edited Philip Brett (ed.), *Consort Songs*, 2nd rev. edn, Musica Britannica 22 (London, 1974).

trustworthy counsellors.[115] The song outlines the qualities of such friends before praying that God might grant Elizabeth such good companions.

Friendship (*amicitia*) was recognised as the spirit of good counsel.[116] Such friendship gave the liberty to speak freely and provide honest opinions ('True friends talk truly'), which the monarch was to receive in a spirit of equality. As the song suggests, a good friend/counsellor for a monarch was trustworthy and sought the common good rather than his own advancement. Whereas the song emphasises the importance of constancy in both 'word and deed', courtiers were commonly suspected of being two-faced. Courtiers were frequently condemned for their manipulative behaviour, flattering and deceitful tongues, and self-seeking aims.[117] As George Puttenham wrote in his *Art of English Poesy*, a courtier 'dissemble[s] not only his countenances and conceits, but also all his ordinary actions of behaviour … whereby the better to win his purposes and good advantages'.[118] This was opposed to the ideal of good counsel, according to which one should 'gloze for no gain' (as Edwards's epilogue puts it). In *Damon and Pithias* the vice of such deceitful and self-serving behaviour had been demonstrated though the character Carisophus, the stereotypical evil courtier who is described as a 'flattering parasite'.[119] His motivation for falsely accusing Pithias of being a spy is a plan to achieve favour with the King by being credited with uncovering a plot. Dionisius is not blameless, however: his tyrannous rule based on fear encouraged such flattery and deception, and he failed to listen to the advice of the good counsellor, Eubulus. Edwards argues that it is only friendship that can prevent monarchy from becoming tyranny.[120] The song therefore summarised for courtiers what true service to the Queen entailed, while simultaneously reminding Elizabeth about the importance of maintaining the spirit of friendship that enabled good counsel to be freely offered, and distinguishing between true courtiers and self-serving flatterers. Furthermore, through its contrast with the preceding dialogue, the musical setting would draw the audience's attention to the parting message and signal the end of the play.

---

[115] Edwards, *Damon and Pithias*, sig. H4r; King (ed.), *Works of Richard Edwards*, p. 184. King reproduces these opening lines as stage directions, but as they sum up the song's point they seem intended to be heard. While not separated by line breaks, they are in a different metre from the rest of the song. They perhaps formed a short introductory phrase before the two six-line stanzas, which could have been either said or sung.

[116] John Guy, 'The Rhetoric of Counsel in Early Modern England', in *Tudor Political Culture*, ed. Dale Hoak (Cambridge, 1995), pp. 292–310 (p. 294).

[117] Mary Partridge, 'Images of the Courtier in Elizabethan England', PhD dissertation, University of Birmingham, 2008, pp. 134, 147–51.

[118] George Puttenham, *The Art of English Poesy* (London, 1589), p. 251.

[119] Edwards, *Damon and Pithias*, sig. B2r; King (ed.), *Works of Richard Edwards*, p. 117 [scene 1, line 110].

[120] King (ed.), *Works of Richard Edwards*, p. 61.

MORALITY, MYTHOLOGY, AND FLATTERY

IN the plays of the 1560s and 70s the songs often contain the most direct summary of the work's moral–political message. Not only could a tuneful setting aid the listener in remembering that message, it could also make the uncompromising moral contrasts and often formulaic poetic style more agreeable and entertaining. By the 1580s allegorical and morality plays were becoming less popular at court, and there was a shift towards mythological subjects and more overt royal flattery. Nevertheless, plays and their songs were still frequently the bearers of counsel.[121]

The foremost children's playwright of the 1580s was John Lyly, but unfortunately the first publishers of Lyly's plays felt no need to include the song lyrics, creating uncertainty as to the status of the lyrics surviving in Blount's seventeenth-century collected edition made after Lyly's death.[122] This makes it difficult to discuss the effect of the songs in the Elizabethan performances of these plays except in general terms. Many of Lyly's songs were given to low-class characters, where they tended to be primarily comic.[123] Music has its most substantial contribution to plot and political meaning in one of Lyly's later plays, *Midas* (performed by the Children of St Paul's on Twelfth Night 1589 and published in 1592).[124] Lyly's *Midas* differs from his earlier plays in not providing a character who creates flattering parallels with Elizabeth (as in *Campaspe*, *Sappho and Phao*, or *Endimion*).[125] Instead the King provides an allegory of tyranny and bad kingship, similar to Dionisius in Edward's

---

[121] See for example: Greg Walker, 'Courtship and Counsel: John Lyly's *Campaspe*', in *A New Companion to English Renaissance Literature and Culture*, ed. Michael Hattaway, 2 vols., Blackwell Companions to Literature and Culture (Oxford, 2010), vol. 1, pp. 320–8.

[122] On John Lyly see G. K. Hunter, *John Lyly: The Humanist as Courtier* (London, 1962). Song lyrics for Lyly's plays first appear in a collected edition produced by Edward Blount in 1632. It is unclear whether these texts are original to Lyly's plays or texts from later restaging. G. K. Hunter summarises the debate on this issue before concluding that Blount may have had access to the songs in the archives of the St Paul's boys: Hunter, *John Lyly*, pp. 367–72; John Lyly, *Six Court Comedies Often Presented and Acted Before Queen Elizabeth, by the Children of her Majesty's Chapel, and the Children of Paul's*, ed. Edward Blount (London, 1632).

[123] Hunter, *John Lyly*, pp. 104–5. A precursor to this is found in the song at the shaving of the Collier in Edwards's *Damon and Pithias*, sigs. F4v–G1v; King (ed.), *Works of Richard Edwards*, p. 169 [scene 13, lines 277–304].

[124] John Lyly, *Midas Played Before the Queen's Majesty Upon Twelfth Day at Night, by the Children of Paul's* (London, 1592), sigs. D3v–E2v [act 4, scene 1].

[125] See for example: Robin Headlam Wells, 'Elizabethan Epideictic Drama: Praise and Blame in the Plays of Peele and Lyly', *Cahiers Élisabéthains* 23 (1983), 15–33 (pp. 22–30); David Bevington, 'John Lyly and Queen Elizabeth: Royal Flattery in *Campaspe* and *Sapho and Phao*', *Renaissance Papers* 1 (1966), 56–67. Pincombe, however, argues that many of the parallels between particular characters and Elizabeth are less flattering than they may initially appear and illustrate Lyly's resistance to royal panegyric: Michael Pincombe, *The Plays of John Lyly: Eros and Eliza*, Revels Plays Companion Library (Manchester, 1996).

Damon and Pithias.[126] Midas is also given a topical edge: references to the sinking of the Spanish Armada, the gold of the New World sought by Spanish expeditions, and Midas's military ambitions against the island of Lesbos all suggest parallels with King Philip II of Spain.[127]

The musical scene relates the mythological tale in which Midas is given ass's ears for his inability to recognise the superiority of Apollo's lute song over Pan's piping. Whereas the nymphs recognise Pan's piping as 'neither keeping measure, nor time; his piping as far out of tune, as his body out of form', Midas foolishly declares that 'there's more sweetness in the pipe of Pan, than Apollo's lute'. He claims not to enjoy 'that nice tickling of strings', but rather music that 'makes one start', preferring the 'shrillness' and 'goodly noise' of the pipe.[128] Midas thus exposes his musical ignorance: although loud wind instruments were necessarily used for court ceremonial in large, outside spaces, they were regularly deemed uncouth and not regarded as fitting instruments for the aristocracy to play or enjoy in private. The anonymous *Praise of Music* (1586) describes how Minerva threw away her pipe after seeing how it disfigured her face and how Alcibiades argued that 'the harp is to be preferred before the whistling pipe or shawms, because it leaves room for the voice.'[129] In Castiglione's *The Courtier*, Sir Frederick forbids a courtier to play on shawms because they are 'noisome' (meaning annoying, unpleasant or offensive, though also punning on 'noisy').[130] Rather, music at court should be 'sweet and artificial'. Midas gets his ass's ears for failing to show the musical taste and judgement befitting a king.

The song contest between Apollo and Pan also had much in common with music's role in earlier morality plays. Just as the morality songs contrasted virtues and vices, so too Apollo and Pan represent contrasting positions: mostly obviously 'barbarous noise' versus 'sweet melody', and courtly versus rustic music.[131] On a deeper level the scene sees Apollo the sun-god contrasted with Pan, whose domain is the dark woods, and Apollo's music presented as divine order while Pan is described as excluded from heaven. Francis Guinle therefore argues that the contest is not solely a musical one, but symbolic of the struggle between darkness and light, good and evil, in which Midas's choice of Pan as the victor represents

---

[126] On *Midas* as allegory see: Stephen S. Hilliard, 'Lyly's *Midas* as an Allegory of Tyranny', *Studies in English Literature, 1500–1900* 12 (1972), 243–58.

[127] On *Midas* and Philip II see: David Bevington, Lyly's *Endymion* and *Midas*: The Catholic Question in England', *Comparative Drama* 32 (1998), 26–46 (pp. 37–41); Annaliese Connolly, '"O Unquenchable Thirst of Gold": Lyly's *Midas* and the English Quest for Empire', *Early Modern Literary Studies* 8.2 (2002), 4.1–36, online at <http://purl.oclc.org/emls/08-2/conngold.html> [accessed 19 July 2014].

[128] John Lyly, *Midas*, sig. E1v [act 4, scene 1].

[129] *The Praise of Music wherein Besides the Antiquity, Dignity, Delectation, and Use Thereof in Civil Matters, is also Declared the Sober and Lawful Use of the Same in the Congregation and Church of God* (Oxford, 1586), pp. 13, 17.

[130] 'Noisome', *OED* online; Castiglione, *The Courtier*, sig. M4v.

[131] Lyly, *Midas*, sigs. E1v–E2r, G3v [act 4, scene 1; act 5, scene 3].

a fall from grace.[132] This moral interpretation would only be enhanced by the Elizabethan belief that musicality was an outward manifestation of inner harmony (pp. 24–5). Midas's preference for noise over music is an indication not just of his foolishness, but also of his lack of virtue and ability to govern. The cause of his moral disorder is revealed in the final resolution: Apollo forces Midas to give up his military ambitions concerning Lesbos/England and his tyranny at home in order to be cured of his ass's ears.[133] This scene, then, simultaneously educates the audience on the importance of musical appreciation as a marker of courtliness, dignity, and virtue, while conducting a comic character assassination of the Spanish King and subtly flattering Elizabeth, whose own musical talents contrasted with Midas's ignorance.

More typical of the overtly flattering tone in 1580s plays was George Peele's *The Arraignment of Paris* (performed by the Children of the Chapel Royal, probably in 1581/2, and published in 1584). Here morality was no longer a means of counsel, but rather a servant to royal praise.[134] The play takes the myth of Paris having to judge whether Juno, Venus, or Pallas was the most beautiful, awarding the victor a golden ball. Despite having promised his love to the nymph Oenone, Paris chooses Venus in exchange for the love of the beautiful Helen. The other goddesses appeal to the court of the gods, who finally award the golden ball to the nymph Eliza (Queen Elizabeth) in a masque-like dismantling of the boundary between stage and court.

Louis Montrose describes the play as abounding in the 'ungoverned and destructive passions' which will ultimately lead to the fall of Troy. By contrast Eliza (a nymph of Diana) is creating the new Troy in her kingdom built on chastity, order, and the control of passions.[135] The play therefore offered counsel on the virtues of chastity and woes of love. It employed music as a means to distinguish between the ordered paradise of the chaste kingdoms of Diana and Eliza, and the unhappiness brought by the rule of unchecked passions. Diana's kingdom is a place of harmony,

---

[132] Francis Guinle, 'Rude Ditties to a Pipe and Sonnets to a Lute', in *The Show Within: Dramatic and Other Insets: English Renaissance Drama (1550–1642)*, ed. François Laroque, 2 vols. (Montpellier, 1992), pp. 417–26. Michael Pincombe, however, sees the presentation of Apollo and his fellow Olympians as far from flattering. He finds that Pan is successful in elevating his own status and attacking Apollo's superiority, and reads the passage as illustrating Lyly's growing disenchantment with the court, stemming from his inability to gain a position there through his service. To my mind, however, the audience's prior knowledge of this story will lead them to interpret Midas's choice as foolish and Apollo as the rightful victor. Pincombe, *Plays of John Lyly*, pp. 113–14, 123–6.

[133] Lyly, *Midas*, sig. G4v [act 5, scene 3].

[134] Carter Daniel, 'The Date of Peele's *Arraignment of Paris*', *Notes & Queries* 29 (1982), 131–2.

[135] Louis Montrose, 'Gifts and Reasons: The Contexts of Peele's *Araygnement of Paris*', *English Literary History* 47 (1980), 433–61 (pp. 444–5); Headlam Wells, 'Elizabethan Epideictic Drama', p. 21. See also Andrew Von Hendy, 'The Triumph of Chastity: Form and Meaning in *The Arraignment of Paris*', *Renaissance Drama* 1 (1968), 87–101.

characterised by the piping of Pan (here a follower of Diana rather than the figure of discord and excess passion seen elsewhere), by 'an artificial charm of birds' brought forth by Pomona, and by a dance song performed by the gods and Muses. Eliza's country is one where even nature is harmonious, where 'whistling winds make music 'mong the trees' and 'in honour of [her] name the Muses sing'.[136] As Diana's nymph declares, they know only:

> Some rounds or merry roundelays, we sing no other songs,
> Your melancholic notes not to our country mirth belongs.[137]

The melancholic notes the nymph refers to here are those of Vulcan and Bacchus, who have been chasing and lusting after her. The audience, however, has already been made aware of the melancholy notes caused by love in Act 3. Colin sings a lament and dies of unrequited love for Thestilis. Oenone laments the unfaithfulness of Paris. The shepherds carrying Colin's hearse sing a prayer to Venus that Thestilis may be similarly wounded by love, which Venus grants, singing a song called 'the wooing of Colman', presumably on the same theme of unrequited love. Thestilis also appears and sings her own lament of pain in love.[138] The piling up of lament upon lament for the tragedy of unrequited love creates an overwhelming sense of the disorder, pain, and even death caused by the ungoverned passions and the jealous arguments of Juno, Venus, and Pallas.

The contrast between these pastoral moods is specifically used to praise Elizabeth's chastity, which allows her country to avoid the troubles of love and remain in simple, innocent happiness. Whereas Paris's unchecked passions result in disorder and death (the Trojan War was sparked by Paris's abduction of Helen and the destruction of Troy is alluded to in the Prologue), Elizabeth's chastity maintains a happy harmony for the pleasure of all her subjects. The ending to Peele's play borrows from the court masque. The Fates make a procession to offer Elizabeth the tools through which they spin, measure, and cut the thread of human life, before Diana presents her with the golden ball.[139] The Fates' song carries connotations of concord appropriate to their gifts, which represent Elizabeth's ability to control rather than be prey to fate through her harmonious soul as one '*Corpore, mente, libro, doctissima, candida, casta*' ('Chaste in body, pure in mind, most skilled in learning').[140]

Yet praise was not just about celebrating the status quo; praise presented visions of ideals and challenged the recipient to live up to them.[141] If it was performed

---

[136] Peele, *The Arraignment of Paris*, sigs. A4r–v, E3r [act 1, scene 3; act 5, scene 1].
[137] Ibid., sig. D2r [act 4, scene 3].
[138] Ibid., sig. C4v [act 3, scenes 1–5].
[139] Ibid., sig. E4r–v [act 5, scene 1].
[140] Ibid. Translation from: *The Life and Works of George Peele*, ed. R. Mark Benbow, Elmer M. Blistein, and Frank S. Hook, 3 vols. (New Haven, CT, 1952), vol. 3, p. 131.
[141] Headlam Wells, 'Elizabethan Epideictic Drama', pp. 16, 31; Walker, *Plays of Persuasion*, p. 87; O. B. Hardison, *The Enduring Monument: A Study of the Idea of Praise in Renaissance Literary Theory and Practice* (Westport, CT, 1973), pp. 26–42, 51–60.

in the 1581/2 Christmas season then the play came just months after Elizabeth's fleeting betrothal to Francis, Duke of Anjou. This threw the court into turmoil with the Queen's ladies putting pressure on her to retract and her courtiers expressing strong criticism (Thomas Norton even ended up in the Tower for his words).[142] Whether Elizabeth's espousal was truly meant or whether she was playing a political game was a matter of debate at the time and still is among historians today.[143] Certainly it took the court by surprise and gave them recent experience of the political turbulence that might be caused by notions of love. While none of the portrayals of unhappy love in the middle scenes seems intended to parallel Elizabeth's actions specifically, her twenty-plus years of intermittent marriage negotiations, encouraging and disappointing various suitors, and even faithlessly breaking off a betrothal (a move she justified by the horrified reaction of her court) meant that a critical eye might equate Elizabeth as much with the turbulent world of love as with the chaste nymph Eliza. Indeed, it was only in the previous couple of years that the Virgin Queen image had been created, and this was by writers and opponents to the Queen's marriage negotiations with the Duke of Anjou. In 1581 Elizabeth was only just beginning to adopt the image for her own purposes.[144] Peele's harmonious chastity was as much an ideal which Elizabeth was called to live up to, as it was a celebration of her reign so far.[145]

If the masques and play songs of the royal household did not always depict flattering images of monarchy and were not solely designed to exalt the Queen, they did not threaten her authority either. Offering counsel to the monarch was considered a political duty and aimed to inspire virtuous governance in both the Queen and her advisors alike, while courtly self-promotion was reined in by an ultimate dependence on Elizabeth for status and reward. Nevertheless, this meant that, although their magnificent display might enhance her image at home and abroad, in no musical entertainment was Elizabeth's political agenda absolute; not even in her greatest sphere of influence, her own household. Though always preserving the outward trappings of royal compliment, the diverse interests and intentions jostling for position within courtly entertainments only intensified the further from her control they were. While it is tricky to determine the extent to which individual gentlemen influenced the politics behind the majority of masques and play songs, the situation becomes somewhat clearer with the self-fashioning of courtiers during tournament pageantry, or the petitions, complaints, and ambitious manœuvres that surfaced in entertainments staged for Elizabeth's progresses.

---

[142] Susan Doran, *Monarchy and Matrimony: The Courtships of Elizabeth I* (London, 1996), p. 187.

[143] Ibid., pp. 187–9; Mack P. Holt, *The Duke of Anjou and the Politique Struggle during the Wars of Religion*, Cambridge Studies in Early Modern History (Cambridge, 1986), pp. 161–3.

[144] Doran, 'Juno versus Diana', pp. 272–4.

[145] Similar themes of love versus reason or chastity can be found in Lyly's *Campaspe* and *Sappho and Phao*, also performed in the early 1580s: Walker, 'Courtship and Counsel', p. 321.

CHAPTER 4

Noble Masculinity at the Tournaments

THOMAS Campion's poem 'Faith's Pure Shield, the Christian Diana' tells the story of a spectacular Elizabethan tournament that was ironically brought to a premature end by a typical English downpour.[1] An 'angry tempest' drives away not only the fair weather, but also that metaphorical English sun, Elizabeth, so that the disappointed participants and spectators disperse. Campion's poem reveals Elizabeth as the focus of the day: she is hailed as the 'Christian Diana' and 'England's glory' while the crowds yearned for a glimpse of her, 'at [her] sight triumphing'. The lavish pageantry dramatised the knights' submission and service before her, competing for her favour as 'the wonder/ Whom Eliza graceth.' Yet much of Campion's poem also describes the splendour of the knights: their entry into the lists ready for combat, their 'rough steeds', and their 'plum'd pomp'. This balance of royal and noble display enacted what Richard McCoy has termed the 'chivalric compromise', in which the nobility enacted their submission to the Queen and paid her tribute, but were also permitted to celebrate their exalted status and demonstrate their honour.[2] Although such occasions were a stage for the creation of the monarch's identity, the aristocracy were also able to further their own political ambitions.

Elizabethan tournaments were usually held at the specially constructed tiltyard at Whitehall. A public challenge was issued in advance, calling the knights to take part. On the appointed day, each knight entered the tiltyard, acting out a fictional knightly persona through his themed armour and his accompanying pageant, train of supporters, and music. A page presented each knight's *imprese* (a shield displaying his emblem and motto) to the Queen with a speech or song. Music's role was comparable to early masques where music accompanied the entry of the masquers who then presented speeches, gifts, and songs to Elizabeth.[3] The following tournament consisted of three events: the tilt or joust where knights rode at each other with lances; the tourney, a mock combat between groups of knights on horseback; and barriers, where knights fought each other on foot.[4] By the

---

[1] Thomas Campion, *Observations in the Art of English Poesy* (London, 1602), p. 30.

[2] Richard C. McCoy, *The Rites of Knighthood: The Literature and Politics of Elizabethan Chivalry*, New Historicism 7 (Berkeley, CA, 1989), pp. 18, 62.

[3] As in the masque Henry Goldingham prepared for the Queen's visit to Norwich (1578): B[ernard] G[arter], *The Joyful Receiving of the Queen's Most Excellent Majesty into her Highness' City of Norwich* (London, 1578), sigs. E1r–E3v.

[4] For more details of the combats, devices and speeches: Alan R. Young, *Tudor and Jacobean Tournaments* (London, 1987); Roy Strong, *The Cult of Elizabeth: Elizabethan Portraiture and Pageantry*, new edn (London, 1999), pp. 129–54; Frances Amelia Yates, 'Elizabethan Chivalry: The Romance of the Accession Day Tilts', *Astraea: The Imperial Theme in the Sixteenth Century* (London, 1975), pp. 88–111.

sixteenth century the tournament no longer functioned as military training, and as the martial sports became more spectacle than practical in purpose, so the element of disguise and pageantry increased in importance and the opportunity for political comment was amplified.

What made these occasions so valuable for both royal and noble display was the admission of paying spectators. The traveller Lupold von Wedel noted that entrance to the stands for the Accession Day tournament cost 12*d* and that 'in the stands there were thousands of men, women and girls, not to mention those who were within the barrier and paid nothing.'[5] The court was on show to the people of London, and printed accounts such as those by George Peele and Henry Goldwell spread news of these events further still.[6]

For kings and princes, tournaments offered the opportunity to socialise with their noblemen and to gain the respect of the aristocracy by proving their skill at arms.[7] Henry VIII held numerous tournaments in his youth, and enjoyed participating in them himself, while Edward VI also delighted in participating in events such as 'running at the ring', which were considered suitable for his young age.[8] As a woman, however, Elizabeth was not expected to have martial skills and could not participate. Instead, for Elizabeth the importance of these events relied on the traditional aim of tournaments: to win the favour of ladies. The spectacle of noblemen loyally competing for her favour enhanced Elizabeth's image by demonstrating the devotion of her nobility and implying her popularity, especially as from 1577 the most common occasion for tournaments was her Accession Day (17 November).[9]

Yet the passive presence of the Queen contrasted with the active participation of the knights. The nobility held the reins (metaphorically and literally) to this courtly pageant and guided its political significance. Tournaments were a significant opportunity for the performance of aristocratic identity, first because of the traditional association of nobility with military valour, and second because

---

[5] Lupold von Wedel, *Lupold von Wedels Beschreibung seiner Reisen und Kriegserlebnisse, 1561–1606*, ed. Max Bär (Stettin, 1895), p. 354: 'auf den Ständen viele tausend Leute, von Männern, Weibern und Mädchen [Metlin] gestanden, ich geschwiege jene, die auf der Bahn gewesen und kein Geld für einen Stand geben durften.'

[6] George Peele, *Anglorum Feriae: England's Holidays Celebrated the 17th Novemb. Last, 1595* (London, 1595; rept. Ipswich, 1840); George Peele, *Polyhymnia Describing, the Honourable Triumph at Tilt, Before Her Majesty, on the 17 of November, Last Past* (London, 1590); Henry Goldwell, *A Brief Declaration of the Shows, Devices, Speechs, and Inventions, Done and Performed Before the Queen's Majesty, and the French Ambassadors, at the Most Valiant and Worthy Triumph, Attempted and Executed on the Monday and Tuesday in Whitson Week Last, Anno 1581* (London, 1581).

[7] Braden Frieder, *Chivalry and the Perfect Prince: Tournaments, Art, and Armor at the Spanish Habsburg Court*, Sixteenth Century Essays and Studies 81 (Kirksville, MO, 2008), pp. 4, 31.

[8] Young, *Tudor and Jacobean Tournaments*, pp. 21–31.

[9] Ibid., pp. 35–6.

the nobleman himself took the stage. The men were called upon to perform their nobility by taking to the tiltyard to prove their prowess and honour to the Queen, the court, and the spectators. This personal involvement intensified the performance of identity in comparison to plays or progress entertainments, where actors performed on behalf of the patron. Moreover, the knightly personae adopted by an Elizabethan nobleman signified not only his position in the noble community, but also his individual political disappointments and aspirations. In 1593 Robert Carey entered as the Unknown Forsaken Knight (illustrating his current disgrace and exile from court) in the hope of being able to regain Elizabeth's favour, while in 1600 the Earl of Cumberland was the Discontented Knight following his failure to obtain the governorship of the Isle of Wight.[10] Such personae aimed to register grudges or to elicit sympathy and future favours, yet within the constraints of the expected tributes of royal praise. It was the elaborate pageantry rather than the military sports which enabled such subtle manipulations of political duties and ambitions. On occasion the pageantry of courtiers even threatened to upstage the Queen. Paul Hammer suggests that Essex used the Accession Day celebrations of 1595 as an opportunity for public self-promotion that was not aimed at winning the Queen's favour, but at building up political momentum to force Elizabeth into accepting his policies. Although Elizabeth signalled her displeasure by leaving, Essex incurred no disfavour for his pageant.[11] She accepted that courtiers manipulated courtly entertainments in her honour for their own political desires, and simply put them in their place if they were too blatant.

Campion's poem, however, reveals that not all spectators were equally impressed by the artistic and sporting shows. The 'plum'd pomp' and 'rough steeds' were enjoyed by the 'vulgar heaps' while 'we', his educated readers, would 'close observe' the 'still devices ... the speeches and the musics/ Peaceful arms adorning'. Friction existed between the different classes of spectators at these events, and between the military spectacles and artistic pageantry of the tournaments. Spanning both spheres, music too reflected these tensions. George Peele's description of the sounds of the tiltyard in *Polyhymnia* (1590) evoked the military atmosphere with 'trumpets sounding shrill' signalling the start of the knights' combat and Sir Philip Butler entering the tiltyard followed by 'dub of drum';[12] however, the extant songs and lyrics from tournament pageantry are surprisingly un-militaristic in their styles and themes. Indeed, the relationship of music to masculinity and martial prowess was an uneasy one; music was a necessary courtly skill, signalling learning, culture, and virtue; yet it was also viewed as potentially effeminising, a threat to masculinity, and so to the military strength of England.

So what was music's role in the tournament, and why did noblemen find it a useful tool in fashioning noble identities? How did music enable noblemen to negotiate the underlying tensions of these events: between dutiful royal service

---

[10] Strong, *Cult of Elizabeth*, pp. 140–1.
[11] Paul E. J. Hammer, 'Upstaging the Queen: The Earl of Essex, Francis Bacon and the Accession Day Celebrations of 1595', in *The Politics of the Stuart Court Masque*, ed. David Bevington and Peter Holbrook (Cambridge, 1998), pp. 41–66.
[12] Peele, *Polyhymnia*, sigs. A4r, B2r, B3r.

and personal ambition, or the courtly and military arts? Answering these questions leads from the role of music in ideals of noble masculinity to the enacting of these values by individual courtiers in the tiltyard. Music was closely interwoven into the imagery of the tournaments, from Sir Philip Sidney's fusing of artistic and warlike qualities in his Shepherd Knight persona to the tensions between the male courtier's desire for military glory and the Queen's preference for peace in *The Four Foster Children of Desire* (1581). Finally, music initiated the transformation of identity required for the retirement of Sir Henry Lee as the Queen's Champion. While songs were frequently the vehicle for conveying the knight's praises to Elizabeth, they simultaneously served the nobleman's interests: to create a magnificent display appropriate to his status, to demonstrate his balance of military and courtly talents, and to create a striking and meaningful knightly persona that communicated his ambitions and desired self-image.

THE PERFORMANCE OF NOBLE MASCULINITY

For the aristocracy, the demonstration of their superior status was essential to their nobility. The internal quality of nobility needed to be manifested in outward signs and 'disclosed in appropriate gestures – literally to be acted out'.[13] Tournaments offered an ideal opportunity for such display. The first step in 'staging their distinctiveness' was the display of wealth and status.[14] Shows of magnificence, conspicuous consumption, and fashionable dress were seen as a privilege of the aristocracy. Sumptuary laws proclaimed by the monarch attempted to protect this privilege by restricting the fabric which could be worn by different classes, and limiting cloth of gold and silver to the nobility alone. Meanwhile, the splendour of noble entertainments, feasting, and wedding ceremonies could equally be markers of distinction.[15]

Music combined with elaborate pageantry to stage the distinctiveness of the nobility as a class for the London public, as well as promoting competition among its members. Knights aimed to make spectacular entrances using special effects such as hidden music that seemed to arise magically from thin air. Consorts of musicians might be hidden within elaborate pageant cars, as at a tournament in 1581 when musicians were concealed in eagles, while 'divers kind of most excellent music' were hidden in a rolling trench.[16] The choice of ensemble or instrument could also signal either fashion or novelty. The ensemble in the rolling trench was

---

[13] Fiona Dunlop, *The Late Medieval Interlude: The Drama of Youth and Aristocratic Masculinity* (York, 2007), p. 122.

[14] Susan Crane, *The Performance of Self: Ritual, Clothing, and Identity during the Hundred Years War*, Middle Ages Series (Philadelphia, 2002), p. 2.

[15] David Kuchta, 'The Semiotics of Masculinity in Renaissance England', in *Sexuality and Gender in Early Modern Europe: Institutions, Texts, Images*, ed. James Turner (Cambridge, 1993), pp. 233–46.

[16] Nallot, 'Tournoi', F-Pn: MS Dupuy 33 (1581), fols. 77r–81r (fol. 79r); Friedrich Ludwig von Raumer, *History of the Sixteenth and Seventeenth Centuries, Illustrated by Original Documents*, 2 vols. (London, 1835), pp. 432–4; Goldwell, *A Brief Declaration*, sig. A5v.

probably a mixed consort. Consisting of treble viol/violin, flute/recorder, bass viol, lute, cittern, and bandora this ensemble probably originated in aristocratic households and was a novelty in comparison to the ensembles of the court, which all consisted of instruments of the same family. Common in both tournaments and progress entertainments, it was also the first standardised mixed ensemble of soft instruments in Europe and would have displayed the innovation and excellence of aristocratic household music-making.[17] The quality of music could also distinguish the nobleman as a patron of discerning tastes with the wealth to hire the best available musicians. Sir Henry Lee certainly aimed to impress when he commissioned John Dowland to compose and Robert Hales (a favourite singer of the Queen) to perform the music for his entry and retirement pageant in 1590 (pp. 130–1, 138–9). The knights aimed to impress, or to inspire awe and wonder in the Queen, fellow courtiers, and the assembled crowds.

In addition to magnificent display, true nobility depended on honourable actions. According to *The Book of Honour and Arms* (1590), a man may be counted noble by birth, by virtue, or by a mixture of the two. This combination of 'ancient gentle race with virtue' was the most commendable because 'he ought be called man, in respect of his own virtue, and not the virtue of others.'[18] But it was not enough for a nobleman to merely undertake noble deeds; he needed to be observed doing them if they were to enhance his reputation. The court was therefore a vital location for the performing and receiving of honour, as opposed to the reality of battle where staging an honourable action in the sight of other noblemen or one's monarch would be much less reliable.[19] Yet what constituted honourable actions was more ambivalent, and so was music's relationship to noble quality.

The tensions in music's role in noble masculinity, and between courtly and military arts in Campion's poem, were symptomatic of contrasting Elizabethan ideals of nobility: the martial knight or the educated gentleman-courtier. The tournament's military sports primarily celebrated the nobleman as knight. Traditionally the nobility were a warrior class and they still maintained their martial aspirations, traditional notions of honour, and sense of autonomy.[20] As Count Lewis proposes

---

[17] Peter Holman, *Four and Twenty Fiddlers: The Violin at the English Court, 1540–1690*, Oxford Monographs on Music (Oxford, 1993), p. 131. The composition of the consort is clearly stated in the account of the Elvetham progress of 1591, but its use can be identified in earlier progresses because in the sixteenth century the word 'consort' was used to mean a mixed ensemble. *The Honourable Entertainment Given to the Queen's Majesty in Progress, at Elvetham in Hampshire, by the Right Honourable the Earl of Hertford* (London, 1591), sig. E1v; Warwick Edwards, 'Consort', NG2.

[18] *The Book of Honour and Arms* (London, 1590), p. 50. The work was printed by Richard Jones, who may also have been its author or compiler. Jones seems to have had particular interests in chivalry and aristocratic culture, publishing seven books on the subject. Kirk Melnikoff, 'Jones, Richard (*fl.* 1564–1613)', ODNB (online edn, 2004).

[19] Richard Wistreich, *Warrior, Courtier, Singer: Giulio Cesare Brancaccio and the Performance of Identity in the Late Renaissance* (Aldershot, 2007), pp. 227–8.

[20] McCoy, *Rites of Knighthood*, p. 3.

in Castiglione's *The Courtier*, 'the principal and true profession of a courtier ought to be in feats of arms.'[21] For the many courtiers with military ambitions and dreams of chivalry and honour, the tournaments were a significant public and courtly stage on which to build their knightly reputations. Although traditionally this reputation relied on military honour, in the sixteenth century that was changing.

Increasingly the ideal nobleman was a gentleman-courtier who combined learning and knowledge of the arts with skill at arms.[22] Courtiers were expected to be good all-rounders, with the greatest praise going to men like Sir Philip Sidney who combined intelligence, skill at arms, and inventiveness in court pageantry. Roger Ascham (once Elizabeth's tutor) listed the diverse skills necessary for a courtier as:

> to ride comely; to run fair at the tilt or ring; to play at all weapons; to shoot fair in bow, or surely in gun; to vault lustily; to run; to leap; to wrestle; to swim; to dance comely; to sing, and play of instruments cunningly; to hawk; to hunt; to play at tennis; and all pastimes generally, which be joined with labour, used in open place, and on the day light, containing either some fit exercise for war, or some pleasant pastime for peace.[23]

Notions of honour were being conceived more broadly, so that both artistic and military skills became means of performing nobility. Despite its title, *The Book of Honour and Arms* concluded that 'the commendation due unto learning is of no less desert, than that which belongeth to martial merit. And indeed very rarely doth any man excel in arms, that is utterly ignorant in letters.'[24] Moreover in many Italian treatises military pursuits and music were aligned as practical arts both of which could be performed in order to earn honour. In Annibale Romei's *Discorsi* (translated into English as *The Courtiers' Academy* in 1586) these practical arts were opposed to speculative knowledge and the intellectual activity of the sphere of letters. Music, like military deeds in battle, needed an audience to judge the performance and assign the reputation it deserves.[25] As ideals changed, courtiers had to negotiate conflicting opinions on the merits of various pursuits and become adept at an increasing list of courtly talents. In their combination of military sport with the poetic and musical devices of the knights' entries, these tournaments reflected the principles of both chivalric knight and gentleman-courtier, and required noblemen to excel at a combination of military prowes, intelligence, and creativity.

---

[21] Count Baldassarre Castiglione, *The Courtier of Count Baldessar Castilio*, trans. Thomas Hoby (London, 1561), sig. C4v.

[22] Diane Bornstein, *Mirrors of Courtesy* (Hamden, CT, 1975), p. 9; Ronald G. Asch, *Nobilities in Transition, 1550–1700: Courtiers and Rebels in Britain and Europe*, Reconstructions in Early Modern History (London, 2003), p. 5; Dunlop, *Late Medieval Interlude*, p. 124.

[23] Roger Ascham, *The Schoolmaster or Plain and Perfect Way of Teaching Children, to Understand, Write, and Speak, the Latin Tongue* (London, 1570), fols. 19v–20r.

[24] *Book of Honour*, p. 66.

[25] Wistreich, *Warrior, Courtier, Singer*, pp. 257–60.

Music was not necessarily at odds with the military sphere. In the culture of the French nobility, music was integrated with military ideals as the exercise of arms remained the primary mode through which to demonstrate noble qualities. The figure of Achilles playing his lute with still-bloodied hands after battle illustrated the heroic qualities of music, which was not merely a recreation after the business of war, but a demonstration that one was attuned with divine order. Music, therefore, could signal a knight's virtue, as important an element in his honour as his valour.[26] Music and arms became closely intertwined in France during the religious civil war (1562–1629), with military academies including music and dancing in their studies, martial themes appearing in the *ballets de court*, and the creation of genres such as the pyrrhic dance and equestrian ballet. Music and dance were means of instilling military discipline, and dramatised the consolidation of armed force in the command of the monarch, as well as creating a discipline of manners which would control violence and integrate a belligerent nobility into the royal court.[27]

Despite the pairing of knightly and musical pursuits in Romei's *Discorsi* and in France, the relationship between the two was not always so comfortable in English ideals of nobility. Here music suffered from ambivalent attitudes similar to those seen in relation to women and music. Music's martial connotations and its usefulness in warfare were certainly recognised in England. The anonymous treatise *The Praise of Music*, for example, recommended drums, fifes, and a marching beat to the captain to give his troops courage.[28] Yet in England it was more typical for arms and music to be conceptualised as opposites, with music as an art of peace and leisure, and arms as an art for war. The anonymous author of *The Institution of a Gentleman* (first printed in 1555) argued that a gentleman 'ought to be learned, to have knowledge in tongues, and to be apt in the feats of arms' as well as being adept in 'courtly behaviour'. He should be able to entertain men of all degrees and thus 'some knowledge in music, or to know the use of musical instruments is much commendable', so that the nobleman becomes 'a man fit for the wars, and fit for the peace'.[29] Although most treatises would not disagree that music could have military uses, the nobleman's musical education was designed primarily for courtly recreation in peacetime.

Whereas *The Institution of a Gentleman* portrays arms and music in a delicate balance as arts for contrasting times and places, it was equally possibly to see the two as in opposition. When music and arms were contrasted in this way it fuelled anxieties among some men about music's potential effects on their masculinity.

---

[26] Jeanice Brooks, *Courtly Song in Late Sixteenth-Century France* (Chicago, 2000), pp. 127–31, 133–50.

[27] Kate Van Orden, *Music, Discipline, and Arms in Early Modern France* (Chicago, 2005).

[28] *The Praise of Music wherein Besides the Antiquity, Dignity, Delectation, and Use Thereof in Civil Matters, is also Declared the Sober and Lawful Use of the Same in the Congregation and Church of God* (Oxford, 1586), pp. 88–90.

[29] *The Institution of a Gentleman*, 2nd edn (London, 1568), sigs. A8v–B1r. See also Sir Humphrey Gilbert, *Queene Elizabethes Achademy, a Booke of Precedence etc.*, ed. Frederick James Furnivall (London, 1869), p. 10; Ascham, *The Schoolmaster*, fols. 19v–20r.

Indicative was Lodowick Lloyd's fear in *The Pilgrimage of Princes* that 'gentle and soft music' might make men 'become again women' (p. 27).[30] Lloyd's concern was particularly with courtly music, such as the lutes that were recommended as a gentlemanly instrument, as well as the music men would hear, enjoy, and dance to at court.[31] This sensuous music was portrayed by some as weakening self-control and reason, threatening to revert men to a state of effeminate boyhood. Music's association with love and the pleasing of women was a particular concern, as the natural state of male lovers (typically portrayed as adolescent boys who had not achieved full adult masculinity) was considered to be one of effeminacy.[32]

This view was probably inspired by Italian sources such as Castiglione's *The Courtier*, in which Lord Gaspar argues that while 'meet for women', men 'ought not with such delicacies to womanish their minds'.[33] Similarly, in his courtly conduct-book *The Civil Conversation* (translated into English in 1581), Stefano Guazzo's character Annibal warns that, as it takes place in the company of women, music might undermine a man's ability to fight honourably in war:

> we must take heed that we be not so wrapped in it, that we never come out of it, least thereby we distemper the mind, and effeminate it in such sort, that it lose that courage which is proper to man.

There is a sense of paranoia in his statement that when partaking in music 'it may be said that we have been in the very jaws of Scylla, and drunk of Circe's cup, and yet have escaped both drowning and transforming.'[34] The emotional power of music was seen as overpowering, even addictive. In England, Protestant polemicist Phillip Stubbes argued indiscriminately that any music could cause a man to be 'transnatured into a woman, or worse', while even the author of *The Praise of Music* did not deny that music could make men effeminate, but merely defended music on the grounds that the fault lay with men for being corrupt in nature and prone to wantonness.[35]

At the same time arms had the potential to make men too masculine, for which courtly arts such as music and dance could be an antidote. Castiglione's character Count Lewis demonstrated this point with the tale of a courtier who offended

---

[30] Lodowick Lloyd, *The Pilgrimage of Princes* (London, 1573), fol. 115r.

[31] Gilbert, *Queene Elizabethes Achademy*, p. 7.

[32] Kirsten Gibson, 'Music, Melancholy and Masculinity in Early Modern England', in *Masculinity and Western Musical Practice*, ed. Ian D. Biddle and Kirsten Gibson (Farnham, 2009), pp. 41–66 (pp. 42, 61); Linda Phyllis Austern, '"Alluring the Auditorie to Effeminacie": Music and the Idea of the Feminine in Early Modern England', *Music & Letters* 74 (1993), 343–54.

[33] Castiglione, *The Courtier*, sig. I2r. Van Orden suggests that such anxiety was rarely present in French sources: Van Orden, *Music, Discipline, and Arms*, p. 13.

[34] Stefano Guazzo, *The Civil Conversation*, trans. George Pettie (London, 1581), fol. 71v.

[35] Phillip Stubbes, *The Anatomy of Abuses Containing a Discovery, or Brief Summary of Such Notable Vices and Imperfections, as Now Reign in Many Christian Countries of the World* (London, 1583), sig. O5r; *Praise of Music*, p. 58. See also Roger Ascham, *Toxophilus: The School of Shooting Contained in Two Books* (London, 1545), fol. 10r–v (reprinted 1571 and 1589).

a 'worthy gentlewoman' and became a laughing-stock for refusing to dance, hear music or partake in other entertainments, claiming that these were 'not to be his profession':

> at last the Gentlewoman demanding him, what is then your profession? He answered with a frowning look, to fight. Then said the Gentlewoman: seeing you are not now at the war nor in place to fight, I would think it best for you to be well besmeared and set up in an armoury with other implements of war till time were that you should be occupied, least you wear more rustier then you are. Thus with much laughing of the standers-by she left him with a mock in his foolish presumption.[36]

A man who was too masculine and did not have the skills to enjoy leisured pastimes in the company of women was a figure of ridicule. John Lyly's character Sir Tophas, from *Endimion* (performed at court by the children of the Chapel Royal in the 1580s), presented a similarly unflattering picture of over-masculine men to the English court. Sir Tophas is encouraged by three pageboys to boast of his valour and knowledge of military science. They ask mockingly simple questions to which he responds with exaggeratedly technical and pompous language:

> SAMIAS: But what is this; call you it your sword?
> TOPHAS: No, it is my scimitar, which I, by construction often studying to be compendious, call my smiter.
> DARES: What – are you also learned, sir?
> TOPHAS: Learned? I am all Mars and Ars.
> SAMIAS: Nay, you are all mass and ass.[37]

Sir Tophas suffers from the same obsession with military matters as the knight in Count Lewis's story. His language is humorous because he uses the technical vocabulary of a professional soldier, rather than that of a leisured noble who partakes in military pursuits for honour not necessity. Although he tries to act learned, the pageboys show that he is actually a fool, turning his Latin 'Mars and Ars' into 'mass and ass' to imply both foolishness and a less-than-athletic physique. Later even his honour and bravery are called into question as Sir Tophas describes his foe as a 'black and cruel enemy, that beareth rough and untewed locks upon his body, whose Sire throweth down the strongest walls, whose legs are as many as both ours, on whose head are placed most horrible horns, by nature, as a defence from all harms'.[38] Or in other words, a black sheep! Lyly mocks the exaggerated tales which soldiers tell of their exploits.

Had the tournament music consisted largely of military styles its role would have been less notable. Instead the music that accompanied the pageantry was more diverse, often including courtly and pastoral genres that were just the kind

---

[36] Castiglione, *The Courtier*, sig. D1r.
[37] John Lyly, *Endimion, The Man in the Moon Played Before the Queen's Majesty at Greenwich on Candlemas Day at Night, by the Children of Paul's* (London, 1591), sig. C1r [act 1, scene 3].
[38] Ibid., sig. D1v [act 2, scene 2].

of 'gentle and soft music' condemned by Lloyd. With military sport as the central event there was little danger of music becoming a sign of effeminacy, but there was perhaps a need to balance the overt martial masculinity of the tournament sports. A nobleman could not perform music himself as it was not considered appropriate for a nobleman to do so in public or before those of lower social status.[39] Yet as the patronage and appreciation of talented musicians were also signs of nobility, by commissioning music for a tournament entry the nobleman could present himself as a cultured, well-rounded individual. Given the potential for negative portrayals of military men and the expectation upon noblemen to demonstrate a breadth of courtly talent, music could provide an important counterbalance to the martial skills portrayed through the central sporting events.

PHILISIDES, THE SHEPHERD KNIGHT

THE paradox of Sir Philip Sidney's knightly persona, Philisides, the Shepherd Knight, brings to the fore these underlying tensions between music and the arts versus arms and military sport. As with Elizabeth's musical image, the Shepherd Knight is another striking example of the fusing of contrarieties: elements that seem frustratingly contradictory to modern eyes are synthesised so as to transcend the limitations of each and create a new, balanced perfection of opposites, a *concordia discors*. Sidney's Shepherd Knight persona combined the ideals of the noble knight and Renaissance courtier and blended praise of Elizabeth with enhancement of Sidney's own reputation. It was also cleverly designed to manipulate spectators' expectations and provide a supposedly humble disguise under which to parade Sidney's talents to best advantage. Music served as a characterising device, as well as symbolising the diversity of Sidney's noble qualities beyond the military sphere.

The tensions of the Shepherd Knight persona underlay Sidney's own courtly identities as courtier, diplomat, soldier, and poet. As the nephew and heir (until 1581) of the Queen's favourite, Robert Dudley, Earl of Leicester, Sidney was an ambitious and charismatic courtier. He was well travelled in France (where he had been part of the embassy to negotiate the Queen's marriage to Francis, Duke of Alençon, in 1572), as well as in Germany, Poland, Italy, and Austria, where he was highly admired and well received. Yet he was never particularly favoured by Elizabeth and failed to achieve any significant court position.[40] Instead he sought military glory as a solider, but although he had fought in Ireland, his military ambitions were also frustrated by the Queen's refusal to offer military support to the Dutch Protestants against the Spanish. He was not knighted until 1583, and only then because he had been named as Johann Casimir's proxy for installation in the Order of the Garter. When in 1585 Elizabeth finally agreed to send forces to the Netherlands, Sidney was among those appointed, and his death at Zutphen in 1586 earned him a reputation as a Protestant martyr. As well as soldier and courtier, he was also a poet and writer,

---

[39] Castiglione, *The Courtier*, sig. M4r.

[40] H. R. Woudhuysen suggests this was because 'he was irascible, ambitious, proud, and perhaps unreliable; his religious faith may not have been certain; he behaved and was received as a powerful figure abroad': H. R. Woudhuysen, 'Sidney, Sir Philip (1554–1586)', *ODNB* (online edn, 2005).

whose works included *The Arcadia*, the sonnet sequence *Astrophel and Stella*, and an entertainment for Elizabeth, *The Lady of May*, performed at Wanstead in May 1578.

Sidney developed the persona of Philisides both practically in the tiltyard and through his literary works. All that survives of the tournament appearance of Philisides is a song (in praise of Elizabeth) with an accompanying poem which explained the conceit of the pageant: that Philisides the good shepherd has called Menalcha and his ploughmen from their work to celebrate Elizabeth's Sabbath.[41] These may have been from Sidney's first known appearance at the Accession Day tilt of 1577.[42] In the literary works, Philisides appears first as a lovesick shepherd in the eclogues of the *Old Arcadia* (c. 1580). He is a mysterious figure, described as one 'who as a stranger sat among them ... having put himself in their company', suggesting that he might be an unhappy courtier who has retreated to the countryside.[43] This lovesick shepherd is similar to the Philisides of the Accession Day tournament, who is 'the Shepherd good and true' made 'pale and wan' by Mira's 'fair sweet looks.'[44]

Even more closely related to the tournament persona is the Philisides of the substantially different *New Arcadia* (published after Sidney's death as *The Countess of Pembroke's Arcadia*, 1590), a Shepherd Knight who opens the tilt at the Iberian yearly jousts for Queen Helen of Corinth.[45] The obvious parallel between the annual jousts for Queen Helen and the Accession Day tilts of Elizabeth has led to suggestions that the *New Arcadia* passage may be a representation of an actual tournament, particularly as Philisides's opponent, Laelius, was a pseudonym for Sir Henry Lee, Elizabeth's champion.[46] Lee and Sidney are known to have tilted against each other on Accession Day in 1581 and 1584, where they also opened the proceedings as they do in *New Arcadia*. Whatever the extent of their reality or fiction, however, these narratives were clearly part of the tradition and fantasy of the Accession Day tilts. Although probably only seen by friends and family during

---

[41] These are found in both the Ottley Manuscript in the National Library of Wales, and in St Loe Kniveton's Commonplace Book (GB-Ob: Harley MS 7392). Peter Beal, 'Poems by Sir Philip Sidney: The Ottley Manuscript', *The Library* 33 (1978), 284–95 (pp. 287–9). Sir Philip Sidney, *The Poems of Sir Philip Sidney*, ed. William A. Ringler (Oxford, 1962), pp. 356–8. Ringler includes both the song and poem under 'wrongly attributed poems', but Beal, while accepting that uncertainty remains, points to several arguments for Sidney's authorship.

[42] Young, *Tudor and Jacobean Tournaments*, pp. 128, 153.

[43] Sir Philip Sidney, *The Countess of Pembroke's Arcadia (The Old Arcadia)*, ed. Katherine Duncan-Jones, World's Classics (Oxford, 1985), p. 221.

[44] Sidney, *Poems*, pp. 357–8.

[45] Sidney, *Old Arcadia*, p. vii; Sir Philip Sidney, *The Countess of Pembroke's Arcadia* (London, 1590). For an explanation of the various versions of Arcadia see: Sidney, *Old Arcadia*, pp. vii–ix.

[46] Strong, *Cult of Elizabeth*, p. 149. James Hanford and Sara Watson, 'Personal Allegory in the *Arcadia*: Philisides and Lelius', *Modern Philology* 32 (1934), 1–10. Lelius was the name of one of Lee's estates, and a tribute to Lee by Joseph Sylvester in 1611 also uses the pseudonym.

Sidney's lifetime (especially as the revised *New Arcadia* was never completed), the literary works clarify the connotations of Sidney's Shepherd Knight persona and its associated musical pageantry.

The incongruity of a shepherd taking part in a military tournament would have been striking. The figure of the shepherd is the opposite of the knight, engaging in musical and poetic contests rather than feats of arms. This was emphasised aurally through the musical accompaniments, as well as visually through the costumes. Sidney's description of Philisides's entry in the *New Arcadia* contrasts the typical military pageantry with the rusticity of the shepherd's entry. Trumpets are replaced with bagpipes, shepherd-boys take the place of pages, lances are made to represent sheep-hooks, and his *imprese* was a sheep marked with pitch alongside the motto 'Spotted to be known'. Yet beneath the rustic trappings are signs of concealed nobility: Philisides's furnishings were 'dressed over with wool, so enriched with jewels artificially placed, that one would have thought it a marriage between the lowest and the highest'.[47] Similarly the 1577 poem highlights the incongruity of Philisides's ploughmen followers in the tiltyard: Menalcha's 'whip must be his spear', and a till-horse his noble steed.[48]

The music too was designed to emphasise this surprise. The Ottley Manuscript records that the poem 'Philisides the Shepherd' was 'to be said by one of the ploughmen after that I had passed the tilt with my rustical music and this freeman's song that followeth.'[49] Freemen's songs (or three-men's songs) were simple polyphonic songs, usually in three parts, which might be notated (as in Ravenscroft's collections) or improvised around a well-known melody.[50] Several contemporary sources suggest that low-status groups such as shearers, shoemakers, and Cornishmen sang these three-men's songs very well, so the ploughmen offered the best of their rustic talents in tribute to the Queen.[51] The 'rustical music' may have been like Philisides's entry in *Arcadia*, where shepherds 'sang an eclogue; one of them answering another, while the other shepherds pulling out recorders (which possessed the place of pipes) accorded their music to the others voice'.[52] This would have proved a stark contrast with the trumpets and drums usually associated with the entries of knights.

Yet the idea was not original to Sidney but rather derived from Castiglione's *The Courtier*. In a passage on the appropriate way for a courtier to display his talents in public, Sir Frederick suggests that a knight should disguise himself as a shepherd (though still 'well trimmed' and with an excellent horse) because:

> the mind of the lookers on runneth forthwith to imagine the thing that is offered unto the eyes at the first show, and when they behold afterward a far

---

[47] Sidney, *Countess of Pembroke's Arcadia*, fol. 196r.

[48] Sidney, *Poems*, pp. 356–7.

[49] Beal, 'Poems by Sir Philip Sidney', p. 287.

[50] Thomas Ravenscroft, *Deuteromelia: or the Second Part of Music's Melody* (London, 1609); Christopher Marsh, *Music and Society in Early Modern England* (Cambridge, 2010), pp. 190–1.

[51] Ibid.

[52] Sidney, *Countess of Pembroke's Arcadia*, fol. 196r.

greater matter to come of it than they looked for under that attire, it delighteth them and they take pleasure at it.[53]

The shepherd's pastoral arts served as a foil to Sidney's martial skill, while the shepherd costume led the spectators to anticipate a poor performance; but they could be pleasurably surprised when the knight performed well. The audience is entertained by the suspense and 'delayed disclosure', having to wait until the unmasking before the relationship of knightly skill and social status is reaffirmed.[54]

The song in Sidney's *Arcadia* created just such expectations, presenting Philisides as inexperienced but fortunate:

> Me thought some staves he missed: if so, not much amiss:
> For where he most would hit, he ever yet did miss.
> One said he brake across; full well it so might be:
> For never was there man more crossly crossed then he.
> But most cried, 'O well broke: O fool full gaily blest:
> Where failing is a shame, and breaking is his best.'[55]

He misses staves (fails to hit the target with his lance) and when he finally hits his target he does so through the inferior tilting move of breaking his lance across his opponent.[56] Nonetheless, most cheer him for succeeding in breaking his lance, though they judge it to be more beginner's luck than skill, and pun on the idea that whereas to break an object would usually be a mistake, in jousting breaking one's lance is a winning move. Similar sentiments are present in the Accession Day poem which made light of whether a knight performed well or badly, because either way his loyalty was expressed. The shepherd-knight persona would have been an excellent means of managing expectations to achieve an honourable outcome, however successful or not Sidney was at tilting in his first tournament.

The shepherd disguise also acted as a mask. According to Castiglione's Sir Frederick, masks brought the courtier 'a certain liberty and licence', allowing him to 'use bent study and preciseness' to show his particular talents without the 'certain recklessness' ordinarily required for a gracious courtly performance.[57] Masking temporarily separated the talent from the identity of the performer so that the action could be judged for itself, without the bias of knowing the performer. The nobleman could therefore seek honour without being accused of merely desiring fame and glory, because in hiding his identity he diverted attention away from the personal and self-seeking motives to his actions. The fine line between the virtuous pursuit of honour and the selfish desire for glory was created through image. Robert Ashley's *Of Honour* (c. 1596–1603) contrasts glory's emphasis on magnificence to honour's satisfaction with the good opinion of others, so that 'glory is accompanied with show and solemnity, pomp and magnificence; but honour only with the

---

[53] Castiglione, *The Courtier*, sig. M3v.
[54] Louis Montrose, 'Of Gentlemen and Shepherds: The Politics of Elizabethan Pastoral Form', *English Literary History* 50 (1983), 415–59 (pp. 444–5).
[55] Sidney, *Countess of Pembroke's Arcadia*, fol. 196v.
[56] On tournament moves see: Young, *Tudor and Jacobean Tournaments*, pp. 46–7.
[57] Castiglione, *The Courtier*, sigs. M3r–v.

approbation of a good and sound judgement directed by reason.'[58] Swapping trumpets and loud music for shepherd songs, a train of courtly servants for one of ploughmen, and shining knightly armour for a shepherd's appearance may also have been designed to lessen that 'show and solemnity, pomp and magnificence' associated with glory rather than honour. When the mask was removed the honour attached to the performance could be attributed to the nobleman himself, but the reputation had been virtuously attained.

The character of Philisides, however, was not a simple, uneducated herder of sheep. One *imprese* related to Sidney has a sheep marked with the planet Saturn, with the motto 'Macular modo noscar' (I am marked only that I may be recognised). Abraham Fraunce's verses for this *imprese* compared the shepherd and the King, presenting Agamemnon as 'shepherd of his people'.[59] The shepherd, like the King, is responsible for the lives and well-being of his flock. This idealised pastoral topos borrowed from classical and Italian Renaissance models, such as Virgil's *Eclogues* and pastoral dramas like Tasso's *Aminta* (1573). Shepherds were perceived here as intelligent and artistic figures, whose undemanding employment allowed them to develop their musical and literary talents, just as noblemen had the leisure time to pursue varied pastimes.[60] Shepherds were associated with poetic and musical talent through their performance of eclogues. These literary connotations were emphasised in Sidney's *imprese* by the juxtaposition of the sheep with the planet Saturn, which was considered particularly favourable to scholars and poets.[61] This sophisticated shepherd was appropriate for Sidney's poetic, literary, and musical interests. While in 1577 Sidney's literary pursuits were not so well known, in the years immediately following he wrote the *Lady of May* and the *Old Arcadia*, and was the dedicatee of Edmund Spenser's *The Shepherd's Calendar*. Although critical of his musical talents, Sidney was also an active patron of music, organising private performances for himself and a circle of aristocratic friends, and writing song lyrics. He employed the young Daniel Bacheler, and his family were connected with the Dowlands, William Byrd, and Thomas Morley.[62] The shepherd persona subtly reminded spectators of Sidney's cultural achievements.

---

[58] Robert Ashley, *Of Honour*, ed. Virgil Barney Heltzel (San Marino, CA, 1947), pp. 136–7.

[59] Abraham Fraunce, *Symbolicae philosophiae liber quartus et ultimus*, ed. John Manning, trans. Estelle Haan, AMS Studies in the Emblem 7 (New York, 1991), pp. 46, 49; Katherine Duncan-Jones, 'Sidney's Personal Imprese', *Journal of the Warburg and Courtauld Institutes* 33 (1970), 321–4 (p. 323).

[60] Montrose, 'Of Gentlemen and Shepherds', pp. 427–31.

[61] Fraunce, *Symbolicae philosophiae*, pp. 174–7. Saturn was also believed to foster success in petitions to princes.

[62] Bruce Pattison, 'Sir Philip Sidney and Music', *Music & Letters* 15 (1934), 75–81. Gavin Alexander, 'The Musical Sidneys', *John Donne Journal* 25 (2006), 65–105 (pp. 65–85); Katherine Duncan-Jones, *Sir Philip Sidney: Courtier Poet* (London, 1991), pp. 171, 279, 298–9. In May 1580 Sidney wrote to Edward Denny reminding him, 'with your good voice, to sing my songs for they will one well become another': James Marshall Osborn, *Young Philip Sidney, 1572–1577*, Elizabethan Club Series 5 (New Haven, CT, 1972), p. 540.

Music participated in creating this idealised version of the pastoral. In the tournament from *Arcadia*, the shepherds entered not with a rustic song, but with an eclogue, a classical literary form. The song from the Accession Day tournament is described as a freemen's song; however, it is unlike any those from Thomas Ravenscroft's *Deuteromelia* (1609). Many of those in Ravenscroft's publication are drinking or bawdy songs while others are character songs, such as 'We Be Soldiers Three' and 'We Be Three Poor Mariners'.[63] By contrast, the tournament song was not a character song, a drinking song, nor even a tale of shepherds or ploughmen, but a carol of praise.

The song begins by encouraging people to sing in celebration of Elizabeth's Accession Day:

> Sing, neighbours, sing, here you not say,
> This Sabbath day:
> A Sabbath is reputed,
> Of such a royal saint
> As all saints else confuted,
> Is love without constraint.[64]

In the second verse the rejoicing is given a pastoral feel with the exhortation to 'Sound up your pipes', and this is followed in later verses with the more generic 'Show forth your joy'. The overall tone is sacred, with Elizabeth figured as a saint and her Accession Day as a Sabbath (though in fact it was never an official holiday). The carol's refrain continues to worship Elizabeth as a saint:

> Let such a saint be praised,
> Which so her worth hath raised,
> From him that would not thus,
> Good Lord deliver us.[65]

The final line offers up a prayer using a response from the Litany in the *Book of Common Prayer*. The ploughmen are presented as honest, loyal, and pious country-folk, using their joyous music to worship their saint. It represents the nobility's idealised version of countryside song.

Sidney's lyrics were typical of the religious imagery associated with Accession Day that was increasingly being expressed in specially printed songs.[66] Yet they were also appropriate to his Shepherd Knight persona, through the religious overtones of the biblical Good Shepherd.[67] Furthermore, the shepherd was symbolic of the purity of the country rather than the corruption of court. Sidney's own poem,

---

[63] Ravenscroft, *Deuteromelia*, sigs. B2v–B3r, C1v–C2r.

[64] Sidney, *Poems*, pp. 357–8.

[65] Ibid.

[66] Katherine Butler, 'Creating Harmonious Subjects? Ballads, Psalms, and Godly Songs for Queen Elizabeth I's Accession Day', *Journal of the Royal Musical Association* (forthcoming).

[67] Roger Howell, *Sir Philip Sidney: The Shepherd Knight* (London, 1968), pp. 8–11.

'Dispraise of a Courtly Life', compared the natural love of a simple shepherd to the artful deceit of the courtier, arguing that:

> … shepherds wanting skill,
> Can love's duties best fulfil:
> Since they know not how to fain,
> Nor with love to cloak disdain,
> Like the wiser sort, whose learning
> Hides their inward will of harming.[68]

Such honesty and openness were the ideal characteristics for a courtier's role as adviser to the monarch, as opposed to the dissembling, factionalism, and selfishness of which courtiers were frequently accused.

Sidney's persona, therefore, demonstrated a balance of artistic and martial talents, presenting him as the ideal courtier, equipped with the best of skills for war and peace. He combined multiple pathways to honour: martial, learned, artistic, pious, and virtuous. As a knight he defended England and protected its people; the knight's chivalric code and the traditional innocence of shepherds implied his virtues; the shepherd's musical and literary talents suggested his appreciation of learning and the arts.

Yet his personal image-making also dovetailed neatly with his knightly duty to praise Elizabeth. The happiness of a peaceful and secure existence was an essential part of the pastoral ideal evoked in the Shepherd Knight persona, with music being the shepherd's expression of joy. The same image of a blissful England enjoying a golden age of peace and harmony that was common in representations of Elizabeth's reign was enacted in Sidney's tournament entry as Menalcha and the ploughmen joined in song to praise Elizabeth. The third verse of the ploughmen's carol specifically celebrated the 'peace' brought by her accession, 'Which she hath not adventured/ But kept for our increase'.[69] Although an alternative pastoral image of the melancholy, lovesick shepherd was evoked briefly at Sidney's entrance, this initial lovesickness becomes a foil to chaste jolliness. Philisides may be 'pale and wan' because of Mira's 'fair looks', but the Accession Day of Elizabeth, the Virgin Queen, is 'the chief of Cupid's Sabbath days' so the melancholy of love is set aside for rejoicing.[70] Sidney's combination of shepherd and knight, and of musical and military entertainment, therefore celebrated peace and stability at the same time as recognising the importance of the military in defending such prosperity. Pastoral themes and portrayals of the court as a kind of Arcadia were common in courtly literature, entertainments, and songs across sixteenth-century Europe.[71] In

---

[68] Sir Philip Sidney, 'Dispraise of a Courtly Life', in *A Poetical Rhapsody Containing, Diverse Sonnets, Odes, Elegies, Madrigals, and Other Poesies …*, ed. Francis Davison (London, 1602), sigs. B2v–B3r.

[69] Sidney, *Poems*, pp. 357–8.

[70] Ibid.

[71] See for example: Giuseppe Gerbino, *Music and the Myth of Arcadia in Renaissance Italy*, New Perspectives in Music History and Criticism (Cambridge, 2009); Brooks, *Courtly Song*, pp. 333–87.

Sidney's pageants, they participated in a synthesis of the warlike and the peaceful, military talent and cultured learning, as summed up in his description of Helen of Corinth's court in *Arcadia*, with its thinly veiled flattery of Elizabeth:

> She made her people by peace, warlike; her courtiers by sports, learned; her ladies by love, chaste. For by continual martial exercises without blood, she made them perfect in that bloody art. Her sports were such as carried riches of knowledge upon the stream of delight.[72]

Music functioned on multiple levels: completing the shepherd disguise, serving as a mask of modesty in the martial sphere of the tilts, symbolising Sidney's talents, and evoking the flourishing of the courtly arts in Elizabeth's peaceful reign. The success of this persona was proved by continuing celebration of Sidney as the Shepherd Knight even after his death. According to George Peele's commentary the Earl of Essex dressed all in black for the 1590 tournament to mourn for 'Sweet Sidney, fairest shepherd of our green/ Well lettered warrior'.[73] Actively fashioning himself as Sidney's heir (having been bequeathed his sword and then married his widow), the Earl of Essex was already assuming Sidney's Shepherd Knight image. Returning from military exploits in Portugal in 1589, Essex was now heralded as 'renowned shepherd of Albion's Arcadia'.[74]

THE FOUR FOSTER CHILDREN OF DESIRE

So far the Shepherd Knight has been interpreted in light of Sidney's personal and noble qualities, but like many tournament personae it also had a more particular political edge. In 1577 Sidney's political career was briefly looking more promising: in that year he had been sent on an official mission to seek support for a Protestant Alliance. The desires of Protestant noblemen such as Sidney and the Earl of Leicester to provide military assistance to Dutch Protestants against the

---

[72] Sidney, *Countess of Pembroke's Arcadia*, fol. 195r.
[73] Peele, *Polyhymnia*, sig. A4v.
[74] George Peele, *An Eclogue, Gratulatory. Entituled: To the Right Honorable, and Renowned Shepherd of Albion's Arcadia: Robert Earl of Essex and Ewe for his Welcome into England from Portugal* (London, 1589); Paul E. J. Hammer, *The Polarisation of Elizabethan Politics: The Political Career of Robert Devereux, 2nd Earl of Essex, 1585–1597*, Cambridge Studies in Early Modern British History (Cambridge, 1999), pp. 51–4, 215. For musical examples of the Earl of Essex's self-fashioning via Sidney's legacy see: Katherine Duncan-Jones, '"Melancholie Times": Musical Recollections of Sidney by William Byrd and Thomas Watson', in *The Well-Enchanting Skill: Music, Poetry, and Drama in the Culture of the Renaissance: Essays in Honour of F. W. Sternfeld*, ed. John Caldwell, Edward Olleson, and Susan Wollenberg (Oxford, 1990), pp. 171–80; Jeremy Smith, 'Music and Late Elizabethan Politics: The Identities of Oriana and Diana', *Journal of the American Musicological Society* 58 (2005), 507–58 (pp. 522, 529–35).

Spanish looked likely to come to fruition.[75] Indeed Sidney's emphasis on the peace and stability of England may have been intended to convince Elizabeth that her domestic affairs were secure enough to commit to military intervention, and the Shepherd Knight paradox a sign that domestic harmony could be combined with military action abroad.

Yet the hope of military service was short lived. Elizabeth's reluctance to undertake military missions and Sidney's continued failure to gain court office meant that he could not maintain the balance of military and courtly arts that was the ideal of his Shepherd Knight persona. In May 1578, his friend and advisor Hubert Languet responded to his complaints of 'too much leisure' by advising him not to 'long after a reputation founded on bloodshed' as most men of high birth, but rather to take pride in being 'adorned … by providence with all those splendid gifts of the mind'.[76] Yet Sidney saw poetry as his 'unelected vocation', having unintentionally 'slipped into the title of a poet', rather than the political and military role he aspired to as appropriate to his noble class.[77] For Sidney and his circle, virtue consisted of action and Sidney rebuked the 'over-faint quietness' of 'idle England'.[78]

By the time of the *Arcadia*, the character of Philisides had changed its significance and could now be seen as representative of Sidney's partial estrangement from court due to his failure to achieve a position there.[79] Regardless of its original connotations, the figure of the Shepherd Knight was now part of a wider discourse of frustrated martial ambition staged by courtiers who wanted England to play an active military role in defending the Protestant cause in Europe. The *Lady of May* entertainment, which Sidney wrote for the Queen's visit to Wanstead (a residence of the Earl of Leicester) in May 1578, invited Elizabeth to choose a husband for the May Lady: either Espilus, the shepherd, or Therion, the forester.[80] Like the paradox of the Shepherd Knight, these characters have been interpreted as representing the merits of the bold and active approach to life (portrayed by Therion) over the cautious and contemplative (Espilus). Indeed William Ringler went as far as to argue that the suitors directly represented peaceful foreign policy versus active military intervention, and were aimed to persuade Elizabeth to provide military

---

[75] Richard C. McCoy, *Sir Philip Sidney: Rebellion in Arcadia* (Sussex, 1979), pp. 12–13; Susan Doran, *Elizabeth I and Foreign Policy, 1558–1603*, Lancaster Pamphlets 20 (London, 2000), pp. 36–7.

[76] Steuart Adolphus Pears (ed.), *The Correspondence of Sir Philip Sidney and Hubert Languet: Now First Collected and Translated from the Latin with Notes and a Memoir of Sidney* (London, 1845), p. 147.

[77] Sir Philip Sidney, *An Apology for Poetry* (London, 1595), sig. B1v.

[78] Blair Worden, *The Sound of Virtue: Philip Sidney's 'Arcadia' and Elizabethan Politics* (New Haven, CT, 1996), pp. 61–7, 299–300; Sidney, *Apology for Poetry*, sig. I3r.

[79] McCoy, *Rites of Knighthood*, pp. 63–4.

[80] Sir Philip Sidney, 'Her Most Excellent Majesty Walking in Wanstead [The Lady of May]', *The Countess of Pembroke's Arcadia* (London, 1598), pp. 570–6; Elizabeth Goldring et al. (eds.), *John Nichols's The Progresses and Public Processions of Queen Elizabeth I: A New Edition of the Early Modern Sources*, 5 vols. (Oxford, 2014), vol. 2, pp. 542–65.

support for the Protestants in the Netherlands – a policy favoured by Sidney and the Earl of Leicester, but firmly resisted by Elizabeth herself.[81]

These tensions between the military ambitions of noblemen and the caution of the Queen came to the fore in a tournament known as *The Four Foster Children of Desire*, which was performed before Elizabeth and the French ambassadors in May 1581 (and to which Sidney may have contributed some of the speeches).[82] The tournament was based on the conceit that the Fortress of Beauty (Elizabeth) was being besieged by four Foster Children of Desire (Philip Howard, the Earl of Arundel; Lord Frederick Windsor; Philip Sidney; and Sir Fulke Greville), so called because they were acting with the encouragement and instruction of Desire. The first entry began with a variation on the medieval chivalric game of the 'storming of the castle of love', in which the ladies of the court defended a wooden castle against an opposing force of knights who attacked using the weapons of love: roses, rose water, and sonnets attached to arrows, all accompanied by highly allegorical love poetry. Eventually the ladies were expected to yield to be ransomed with kisses or favours.[83] In 1581, however, the ending was twisted so that Elizabeth as the Queen of Beauty refused to yield and the four Foster Children of Desire admitted defeat.

As the French ambassadors were in England to negotiate a possible marriage between Elizabeth and Francis, Duke of Anjou, the *Four Foster Children of Desire* allegory has most commonly been understood as a pageant designed to present the noblemen's opposition to the proposed marriage.[84] Yet Susan Doran pointed out that the courtiers who played the Foster Children included supporters of the marriage as well as those opposed to it. Instead it appears to have been an 'official statement of policy' commissioned by the Queen, in which courtiers on both sides of the debate cooperated to create this elaborate tournament.[85] The pageant's depiction of Elizabeth as unassailable by Desire, impervious to the arts of love

---

[81] Sidney, *Poems*, p. 362. Philippa Berry sees the wild man or forester as a signifier of militant Protestantism: Philippa Berry, *Of Chastity and Power: Elizabethan Literature and the Unmarried Queen* (London, 1989), p. 94.

[82] Goldwell, *A Brief Declaration*. A few additional words on the pleasantness of the songs are found in Raphael Holinshed's *The Third Volume of Chronicles, Beginning at Duke William the Norman, Commonly Called the Conqueror; and Descending by Degrees of Years to All the Kings and Queens of England in their Orderly Successions* (London, 1586), pp. 1317–8; Goldring et al. (eds.), *John Nichols's The Progresses*, vol. 3, pp. 80–1.

[83] Helmut Nickel, 'The Tournament: A Historical Sketch', in *The Study of Chivalry: Resources and Approaches*, ed. Howell D. Chickering and Thomas H. Seiler (Kalamazoo, MI, 1988), pp. 213–62 (pp. 234–6).

[84] Including Jean Wilson, *Entertainments for Elizabeth I*, Studies in Elizabethan and Renaissance Culture 2 (Cambridge, 1980), p. 62; McCoy, *Rites of Knighthood*, pp. 61–2; Norman Council, 'O Dea Certe: The Allegory of The Fortress of Perfect Beauty', *The Huntington Library Quarterly* 39 (1976), 329–42; Berry, *Of Chastity and Power*, p. 103; Young, *Tudor and Jacobean Tournaments*, p. 148.

[85] Susan Doran, 'Juno versus Diana: The Treatment of Elizabeth I's Marriage in Plays and Entertainments, 1561–1581', *The Historical Journal* 28 (1995), 257–74 (pp. 273–4).

(including music), and disinterested in marriage therefore represented a policy and royal image endorsed by the Queen herself.

Given the creativity with which royal and noble interests were negotiated in courtly entertainments, if the message of Elizabeth's chastity and the impossibility of her accepting a husband were designed by the Queen herself, then what were the courtiers' political intentions? Various suggestions have been made: for Catherine Bates, the complaint had a distinctly gendered tone as the courtiers performed in exaggerated form the submissive role forced upon them in the court of a ruling queen.[86] Alternatively, perhaps they performed a symbolic apology for their interference in the issue of her marriage, or criticised Elizabeth's cruel indifference to their loyal service (the Desire which Elizabeth rebuked being not only that of suitors like Anjou, but the love/loyalty of all Elizabeth's courtiers)?[87] Yet in addition to the marriage issue, the Duke of Anjou was significant to foreign policy because of his own campaigns in the Netherlands, and there was also hope of a potential defensive alliance with France against the increasing aggression of Spain. In May 1581 Elizabeth was still holding out on direct intervention in the Netherlands, and nor would she agree to grant Anjou funds for his campaign (though by August she had done so).[88] So the pageantry was also created against a backdrop of increasing fear at the military power of Spain, deliberation over supporting Dutch Protestants, and continuing tensions over the obstruction of the nobility's traditional military role. From this perspective the noblemen went beyond generic complaints over royal indifference to service and submission to a queen, to stage a defence of the value of martial masculinity as the threat of war increased.

The response of Elizabeth's courtiers to the Queen's anti-marriage pageant was to demonstrate to her that while she might not require a husband, nevertheless her noblemen were vital to defend her reign and protect her interests abroad. In this tournament the juxtaposition of music and courtly arts with arms and military sport underscored the limitations of Elizabeth's gender in the martial sphere and demonstrated the value and importance of noblemen to the kingdom. The courtiers presented themselves as willing and able to participate in the courtly arts of peace but also needing to maintain their role as knights practised in the art of war for Elizabeth's defence. Furthermore, with marriage negotiations over, the military role of these noblemen would be particularly important if political alliances were not achieved and England came under threat, as was indeed to happen in 1585 with the outbreak of war against Spain.

The opening pageantry began with the four Foster Children of Desire assaulting the Fortress of Perfect Beauty with the weaponry of love, before the entry of the defenders of the fortress initiated the military sports of the tiltyard as the defending knights fought on Elizabeth's behalf. The Foster Children appeared with a 'rolling

---

[86] Catherine Bates, *The Rhetoric of Courtship in Elizabethan Language and Literature* (Cambridge, 1992), pp. 72–5.

[87] McCoy, *Rites of Knighthood*, p. 62.

[88] Doran, *Elizabeth I and Foreign Policy*, pp. 39–41; Mack P. Holt, *The Duke of Anjou and the Politique Struggle during the Wars of Religion*, Cambridge Studies in Early Modern History (Cambridge, 1986), pp. 149–57.

trench': a wooden frame on wheels, made to look like earth ramparts with wooden cannons mounted on top, and with space inside to hide 'divers kind of most excellent music'.[89] This hidden music represented the challengers' divine assistance, as 'not only the heavens send their invisible Instrument to aid them', but also the 'very earth the dullest of all the elements' is stirred to move and rise up against the fortress.[90] In addition to creating spectacle and wonder through the hidden music, the choice of a mixed consort was also symbolic: an ensemble used in noble households rather than the court (p. 109), it underlined Desire as a force alien to Elizabeth's Fortress of Beauty.[91]

The knights' defence of martial nobility began with a pageboy's speech evoking the incongruity of a queen on a battlefield: her eyes, which have only seen 'the bowed knees of kneeling hearts', and her 'heavenly peace of a sweet mind', should not have 'their fair beams reflected with the shining of armour, should not now be driven to see the fury of Desire, nor the fiery force of fury'.[92] The speech drew on traditional gender contrasts between noble men and women. Pamphleteer Joseph Swetnam's *The Arraignment of Lewd, Idle, Froward, and Unconstant Women* (1613), for example, contrasted warlike masculinity and peace-loving femininity:

> for a man delights in arms, and in hearing the rattling drums, but a woman loves to hear sweet music on the lute, cittern, or bandora: a man rejoyceth to march among the murdered carcasses, but a woman to dance on a silken carpet: a man loves to hear the threatenings of his Prince's enemies, but a woman weeps when she hears of wars … a man triumphs at wars, but a woman rejoyceth more at peace.[93]

This contrast underlies the tournament pageant both in the distinction between the warlike knights and the female Beauty, and in the multiple assaults on the fortress and its defender: first with the weapons of love (including music with its close-knit associations with desire and women), and second by the military weapons of the tournament proper.

As the speech ended, the 'rolling trench' was drawn up to the fortress and the contrast between peaceful femininity and aggressive masculinity was continued in two songs, each sung by a boy accompanied by cornetts (who would perform in

---

[89] Goldwell, *A Brief Declaration*, sig. A5v.

[90] Ibid., sig. A8r.

[91] Assuming the consort was provided by the four Foster Children, it might have been recruited from the rich musical establishment at Nonesuch (as Philip Howard was the nephew of Lord Lumley); or from the Earl of Leicester's musicians, who had performed as a mixed consort at Kenilworth in 1575 (as Sir Philip Sidney had, until April, been his heir): Charles Warren, 'Music at Nonesuch', *Musical Quarterly* 54 (1968), 47–57; David Lasocki, 'Professional Recorder Players in England, 1540–1740', 3 vols., PhD dissertation, University of Iowa, 1983, vol. 1.1, pp. 176–7.

[92] Goldwell, *A Brief Declaration*, sig. A7v.

[93] Joseph Swetnam, *The Arraignment of Lewd, Idle, Froward, and Unconstant Women or the Vanity of them, Choose You Whether* (London, 1615), pp. 38–9.

consort along with sackbuts).[94] The first song was sung to Elizabeth and urged her to yield up the fortress. Yet even with the aid of heavenly music, Beauty proved unassailable. The second song, directed at the Foster Children, was an 'affectionate alarm' signalling the beginning of the assault on the fortress. Like the pageant itself, the songs presented the contrast between 'strong Desire' which 'no forces can withhold', and the 'feeble shield' of fairness and beauty.[95] The two songs form a contrasting pair, using the same metre and parallel structures. (In the following display, boldface indicates the parallel placing of 'yield' and 'alarm'; underlining highlights the repetition of themes and phrases.)[96]

Yield, yield, O yield, you that this Fort do hold, / which seated is, in spotless honour's field, / Desire's great force, no forces can withhold: / then to <u>Desire's desire</u>, **O yield, O yield**.

Alarm, alarm, here will no <u>yielding</u> be, / such marble ears, no cunning words can charge, / Courage therefore, and let the stately see / that naught withstands <u>Desire</u>, **Alarm, alarm**.

Yield, yield, O yield, trust not on <u>beauty's</u> pride, / fairness though fair, is but a feeble shield, / When strong Desire, which <u>virtue's love</u> doth guide, / claims but to gain his due, **O yield, O yield**.

Alarm, alarm, let not their <u>beauties</u> moue / remorse in you to do this Fortress harm, / For since war is the ground of <u>virtue's love</u>, / no force, though force be used, **Alarm, alarm**.

Yield, yield, O yield, who first this Fort did make, / did it for just Desires, true children build, / Such was his mind, if you another take: / defence herein doth wrong, **O yield, O yield**.

Alarm, alarm, companions now begin, / about these never conquered walls to swarm, / More praise to us, we never look to win, / much may that was not yet, **Alarm, alarm**.

Yield, yield, O yield, now is it time to <u>yield</u>, / Before th'assault begin, **O yield, O yield**.

Alarm, alarm when once the fight is warm, / then shall you see them <u>yield</u>, **Alarm, alarm**.

The first song called for Beauty to yield, while the second called the knights to action, with the 'Yield, yield' of the first song replaced by 'Alarm, alarm' in the second and the response that 'here will no yielding be'. Similarly, references to 'Desire', 'Beauty', and 'virtue's love' are all mirrored in corresponding lines of the two songs, so that where the first song commands, 'to Desire's desire, O yield, O yield', the second song responds, 'naught withstands Desire, Alarm, alarm'. Despite the poetic parallels, it is likely that two contrasting musical settings were used to illustrate the opposing themes. While the lyrics of the first song might suit the style of a love song with its conventional conceit of the lover persuading his beloved to yield to his desires, the second song was a call to war. Music was credited with the ability to ready troops for battle. The treatise entitled *The Praise of Music* (1586) challenged, 'Let them speak if the drum, fife, and trumpet do not excite their spirits, and make their hearts even to swell to the overthrow of their enemies.'[97] These songs acted both as the lover's means of persuasion and the knight's call to arms.

---

[94] The boy was probably one of the Chapel Royal choirboys, and the cornetts from the royal household musicians.
[95] Goldwell, *A Brief Declaration*, sig. A8v.
[96] Ibid., sigs. A8v–B1r.
[97] *Praise of Music*, p. 88.

Further music continued as the Foster Children had their retinue shoot sweet water, throw flowers, and scale pretty ladders so that 'the noise of shooting was very excellent consent of melody within the mount'.[98] The assault continued until the entry of the defending knights. Each of these knights had his own persona and pageant, relating how he came to hear of the threat to Beauty. Monsieur Nallot of the French embassy described musicians concealed in eagles, musicians with 'wide sleeves, great false beards, and high caps', and processions of trumpeters associated with different knights.[99] Later 'hautbois' (presumably shawms) are specifically mentioned as the knights leave after the tournament.[100] As with the music of the 'rolling trench', hidden musicians aimed to surprise and amaze spectators by giving the appearance that music was magically sounding from nowhere, while the disguises suggest that musicians were meant to represent particular characters and differentiate between the knights' personae (though it seems that Nallot struggled to determine the significance of the costumes).

The defenders' speeches were careful to point out that the knights did not come because they were required – Beauty's fortress was too strong and virtuous to yield to the weapons of love – but rather out of loyalty. Mercury, speaking on behalf of the Knollys sons, declared the fortress invincible and proclaimed that 'Lady Beauty needs no rescue to raise this siege, for that she sits above all reach.' The defenders came only to 'show themselves devout to do her will'.[101] Yet despite these knights' claims that Beauty/Elizabeth is invincible, when the elaborate pageantry and music ended and military action in the tiltyard began, Elizabeth did need her defending knights to compete with the Foster Children of Desire. All Elizabeth could do in this military battle was to watch her 'famous knights'. As *An Apology for Womankind*, one of many books debating the nature of women, declared:

> Their hands are made for music instruments,
> Not for to brandish warlike complements.[102]

This was not the first time music had entered the debate over the military role of nobility at Elizabeth's court. In Edmund Spenser's 'October Eclogue' from *The Shepherd's Calendar* (1579), the shepherd Piers contrasts the different types of song that the poet–shepherd Cuddie might sing:

> Abandon then the base and viler clown,
> Lift up thy self out of the lowly dust:
> And sing of bloody Mars, of wars, of giusts,
> Turn thee to those, that wield the awful crown.

---

[98] Goldwell, *A Brief Declaration*, sig. B1r.

[99] Nallot, 'Tournoi'; Raumer, *History of the Sixteenth and Seventeenth Centuries*, pp. 432–4. Some translations from Nallot's letter are also given in the footnotes in Goldring *et al.* (eds.), *John Nichols's The Progresses*, vol. 3, pp. 66–94; unfortunately these are focused on the appearances of the knights and include few of the details about the musicians.

[100] Nallot, 'Tournoi', fol. 81r.

[101] Goldwell, *A Brief Declaration*, sig. B6v.

[102] I. G., *An Apology for Womankind* (London, 1605), sig. D3r.

> To doubted knights, whose woundless armour rusts,
> And helms unbruised waxen daily brown.
>
> There may thy Muse display her fluttering wing,
> And stretch herself at large from East to West:
> Whither thou list in fair Elisa rest,
> Or if thee please in bigger notes to sing,
> Advance the worthy whom she loveth best,
> That first the white bear to the stake did bring.[103]

The stanzas juxtapose songs about the 'doubted knights', 'woundless armour', and 'unbruised helmets' of Elizabeth's peacetime, with the songs of Mars, wars, and jousts associated with the military ambitions of the Earl of Leicester (the 'worthy' whose badge was a bear with a ragged staff). The commentary tactfully explains to the reader that the shepherd is 'offered of higher vein and more Heroical argument, in the person of our most gracious sovereign ... Or if matter of knighthood and chivalry please him better, that there be many noble and valiant men that are ... worthy of his pain in their deserved praises'.[104] Although the commentator presents the shepherd with a supposedly equal choice of higher subject matter, the stanzas seem to favour the warlike theme. Cuddie is encouraged to sing about Leicester if he wants 'bigger notes', and the peaceful alternative is portrayed through images of decaying tools of war and the waning honour of knights. Piers is critical of the peacetime that leaves knights without occasion to demonstrate their honour.

This line of interpretation also makes sense of the unusual opening to the second day of the tournament, where the four Foster Children began by admitting their defeat. The Foster Children and Desire entered in a chariot accompanied by 'a full consort of music, who played still very doleful music'.[105] This was probably the mixed consort again, with the doleful character perhaps suggesting a prominent role for the flute (which was associated with mourning) or the use of pavan style.[106] In Sir John Davies's *Orchestra or A Poem of Dancing*, the pavan was the dance of the Moon, at whose coming the Earth's 'sad and heavy cheer' was seen.[107] The horses were still decked out in bright red and white, the colours of Desire, so music had the role of signalling the wearied and half-overcome mood of the knights. The contrast between the defiant, aggressive songs from the previous day's entry and this doleful music would be striking, as would the unusually subdued mood for opening a day's tilting.

---

[103] Edmund Spenser, *The Shepherd's Calendar Containing Twelve Eclogues Proportionable to the Twelve Months* (London, 1579), fol. 41r. 'Giusts' is Spenser's Italianate term for 'jousts'.

[104] Ibid., fol. 43r.

[105] Goldwell, *A Brief Declaration*, sig. B8r.

[106] Examples of the association of flutes with mourning are given in John Manifold, 'Theatre Music in the Sixteenth and Seventeenth Centuries', *Music & Letters* 29 (1948), 366–97 (pp. 380–2).

[107] Sir John Davies, *Orchestra or A Poem of Dancing* (London, 1596), sig. B1r–v.

The Foster Children admitted that they were 'fallen lowly' as regards 'summoning this castle to yield' with the 'weaponry of love'.[108] Yet they still invited Beauty/Elizabeth to behold the fighting of the knights. Reading this act of submission in relation to the dual assault of this tournament – one with the weapons of love, and the other with military weaponry – explains this incongruity: they admitted that Elizabeth had defeated their weaponry of love, but suggested that the military battle had not yet been won.

In the final surrender at the end of the day, the four Foster Children acknowledged the supremacy of peace over violence by presenting Elizabeth with an olive branch as token of her 'triumphant peace, and of their peaceable servitude' and conceding that 'they have degenerated from their Fosterer in making violence accompany Desire.'[109] By turning the arts of music and poetry into weapons they had corrupted the conventions of courtly love. While the four Foster Children represented the submission of nobility to peacetime, the actions of the defending knights had also shown the importance of military arts for defence. Like the Unfortunate Knight who left his life of contemplation in a mossy cave to defend beauty, Elizabeth's noblemen must maintain their skills by leaving their courtly entertainments and taking up arms to protect Queen and kingdom. Defending the traditional role of noblemen as a military force, yet acknowledging their need to perform the courtly arts to create a magnificent English court, this event highlighted the compromise of all tournaments in combining musical pageantry with military sport.

SIR HENRY LEE'S RETIREMENT

WHEN old age finally prevented a courtier from participating in martial sports and he came to the end of his active career, a new problem of identity presented itself: how to retire graciously from court life. Elderly noblemen were advised in conduct literature to withdraw from courtly display, as they were not able to perform as gracefully as those in their youth. For Lord Julian in Castiglione's *The Courtier*, feats of arms 'be not comely in age', while 'music, dancing, feastings, sportings, and love, be matters to be laughed at in old men.'[110] As well as physical capability, in tournaments knights performed for the favour of ladies, and courtly love was considered inappropriate in old men (p. 50). This dilemma was particularly tricky for Sir Henry Lee, however, because at the English court a courtier's devotion to women was synonymous with his love of its Queen. Furthermore Lee was the Queen's champion, having initiated the yearly Accession Day tournaments in the 1570s.[111] To make matters worse, he was the same age as Elizabeth, so he needed to retire graciously, but without drawing attention to the age of the Queen.

---

[108] Goldwell, *A Brief Declaration*, sig. B8v.

[109] Ibid., sigs. C1v–C2r.

[110] Castiglione, *The Courtier*, sig. N1r.

[111] As Gabriel Heaton notes, this was a position Lee claimed rather than one that was bestowed on him, and was therefore as much concerned with self-promotion as with celebrating the Queen: Gabriel Heaton, *Writing and Reading Royal Entertainments: From George Gascoigne to Ben Jonson* (Oxford, 2010), pp. 57–8.

In 1590, at the age of 57, Lee staged his resignation and ceremonially transferred his position as Queen's champion to George Clifford, Earl of Cumberland. His carefully designed pageantry initiated a transformation of identity, yet left Elizabeth's position as the object of his devotion unchanged. The fortunate survival of two songs reveals the music to have been infused with the themes, symbolism, and imagery of the occasion and to have played a pivotal role in creating Lee's new persona.

Lee's solution was to turn courtly love into religious devotion. He would no longer style himself as a knight, courtier, and public figure actively serving his monarch, but rather as a hermit, leading a quiet and peaceful life of contemplation and worship of his sovereign in the countryside. The devotion to Elizabeth as a saint seen in earlier pageantry like Sidney's would have offered some inspiration. In addition, as the last of the Four Ages of Man the hermit was an archetypal image of the infirmity old men, providing an excuse for his retirement.[112] The figure also had appropriate chivalric connotations: *The Book of the Order of Chivalry* by Ramon Lull (printed in English by William Caxton, c. 1485) opens with a description of a wise knight who retires to be a hermit after participating in jousts and tournaments for many years.[113] A young squire comes to the hermitage with no knowledge of chivalry. The hermit offers him the book and the squire asks to be instructed in the practice of knighthood. By transforming his identity from Queen's champion to wise hermit, Lee could therefore maintain his reputation as a leader in the revival of chivalric traditions at court.

The first stage in establishing Lee's new identity was his entry into the tiltyard. Peele described how Lee led in the troops with a caparison (a cover spread over the saddle of a horse) depicting a withered running vine, 'as who would say, My spring of youth is past'.[114] He also wore steel armour with grey and white plumes representing old age. These same themes infuse John Dowland's song 'Time's Eldest Son', from *The Second Book of Songs or Ayres* (1600).[115] According to the commonplace book of John Lilliat (a little-known cathedral musician), the verses were said by Lee 'In yielding up his tilt staff'.[116] Lilliat also adds a fourth stanza

---

[112] Anthony Rooley, 'Time Stands Still: Devices and Designs, Allegory and Alliteration, Poetry and Music, and a New Identification in an Old Portrait', *Early Music* 34 (2006), 443–60 (p. 447). The Four Ages of Man were depicted on the title-page of Dowland's *First Book of Songs*, in which one of Lee's songs appears.

[113] Yates, 'Elizabethan Chivalry, pp. 106–8.

[114] Peele, *Polyhymnia*, sig. A2v.

[115] Roy Strong pointed out the connection between 'Time's Eldest Son' and this tilt in *Cult of Elizabeth*, p. 207. Gabriel Heaton also chooses to include 'Time's Eldest Son' in his edition of the entertainments in Goldring *et al.* (eds.), *John Nichols's The Progresses*, vol. 3, pp. 519, 526–7 (though he places it at the end).

[116] GB-Ob: MS Rawl. poet. 148 ['Liber Lilliati'], fol. 75v; Edward Doughtie (ed.), *Liber Lilliati: Elizabethan Verse and Song (Bodleian MS Rawlinson Poetry 148)* (Newark, 1985), p. 77. Lee was to use this hermit imagery again when Elizabeth visited his home at Ditchley in 1592, where devices told of an Old Knight called Loricus who had become a hermit (Lee having appeared as the knight Loricus on Elizabeth's visit to Woodstock in 1575).

which is the same as the last verse of 'His Golden Locks' (known to have been performed during the resignation), thereby suggesting a close connection between these two songs. The specific references to jousts, tilt devices, and martial prowess also make 'Time's Eldest Son' appropriate for a tournament. As Lee did make further appearances at Accession Day tournaments (though not as a participant), it is possible that the song belonged to one of these; yet, either way, the song remains a means of establishing Lee's new hermit persona.

Dowland also set further lyrics from this occasion: the retirement song 'His Golden Locks'.[117] It is even plausible for Dowland's songs to have been the original settings for the occasion, and both would accord well with the accompanying spectacle. Assuming Lilliat's attribution is correct, then 'Time's Eldest Son' would have best suited the entry of Lee into the tiltyard. Like Peele's description, the song's opening words take up the theme of old age and would have proclaimed Lee's knightly persona as he entered:

> Time's eldest son, old age, the heir of ease
> Strength's foe, love's woe, and foster to devotion.[118]

Dowland's music too creates the picture. For Anthony Rooley, 'old age informs every rhythm, as do the easeful harmonies.'[119] Moreover, Dowland's choice of a through-composed setting enabled him to respond more diversely, using madrigalian techniques of word-painting and evoking contrasting musical styles to interact with the intricate themes of the lyrics, speeches, and visual spectacle of the pageant.

Dowland sets the opening statement of 'Time's Eldest Son' to the typical 'long–short–short' dance rhythm of the pavan (Example 4.1).[120] As a processional dance 'used in a masquerade when there is a triumphal procession of chariots of gods, goddesses, emperors or kings', the rhythms and pace of the pavan were well suited to Lee leading a procession of knights into the tiltyard.[121] The pavan's slow tempo – described as 'staid' and 'grave' by Thomas Morley – mirrored the theme of decrepit age in Lee's disguise, while the nocturnal and melancholic associations suggested

---

[117] John Dowland, *The First Book of Songs or Ayres of Four Parts with Tablature for the Lute* (London, 1597), sigs. I2v–K1r. On the wide circulation of these lyrics see Goldring *et al.* (eds.), *John Nichols's The Progresses*, vol. 3, pp. 517–19.

[118] John Dowland, *The Second Book of Songs or Ayres, of 2, 4 and 5 Parts with Tablature for the Lute or Orpharion, with the Viola de Gamba* (London, 1600), sigs. D2v–F1r.

[119] Rooley, 'Time Stands Still', p. 446.

[120] Dowland, *The Second Book of Songs or Ayres*, sigs. D2v–F1r. Full modern edition in: John Dowland, *The Second Book of Songs (1600)*, ed. Edmund Fellowes and Thurston Dart, The English Lute Songs 2 (London, 1969), pp. 21–5. Dowland's title-page indicates that the lower part might be played on the bass viol. As he also adds text, it might be sung.

[121] Thoinot Arbeau, *Orchesography: A Treatise in the Form of a Dialogue Whereby All Manner of Persons May Easily Acquire and Practise the Honourable Exercise of Dancing*, ed. Cyril W. Beaumont and Peter Warlock (London, 1925), p. 58.

Ex. 4.1 Opening of John Dowland, 'Time's Eldest Son' (Part 1), *The Second Book of Songs or Ayres* (London, 1600), sigs. D2v–E1r

Ex. 4.2 Opening of William Byrd, 'The Trumpets',
The Battle, GB-Lbl: MS Mus. 1591 [My Lady Nevell's Book], fol. 21r

in Davies's *Orchestra* (p. 128) signified a man reaching the last part of life and were suitably sombre for the occasion.[122]

The change in Lee's identity is signalled by the words 'heir' and 'foster'. Lee is now estranged from the knightly virtues of 'strength' and 'love', and allied instead with 'ease' and 'devotion'. It is the youths who are 'gallant' and able to please with their 'martial prowess', and with this contrast a new musical style is evoked. Now the music settles into a regular rhythm of repeated semibreves with a static harmony of chords on D until the cadence (bars 8–10). The melody changes from primarily stepwise motion to outlining a triad on D and, for the only time in this song, two dotted rhythms are used consecutively. While not a direct imitation of the sounds of war in the style of pieces like Janequin's *La Guerre*, Dowland employs 'warlike' musical devices such as the *durus* (sharpwards) tonality and lively dotted rhythms.[123] Indeed, the repeated chords, dotted rhythms, and triadic feel are broadly similar to passages in Byrd's multi-movement keyboard piece *The Battle* (Example 4.2).[124]

At the words 'as for himself', the character of the musical setting in 'Time's Eldest Son' returns to a more subdued mood as the bright timbre of the F sharps is temporarily replaced by naturals and an open fifth on the syllable 'self'. The slowing melodic rhythm and the sense of delay created by suspensions on 'he' and 'hath' (and continued on each beat until the cadence in the lute harmonies) capture the knight's lack of 'earthly motion' (Example 4.3).

Illustrating Lee's new life of religious devotion, the second verse begins a series of sacred Latin quotations accompanied by hints of sacred genres in the musical accompaniment. The *Nunc dimittis* (the Canticle of Simeon), the two references to penitential psalms (*De profundis* and *Miserere*), and the *Te Deum* (Hymn of

---

[122] Thomas Morley, *A Plain and Easy Introduction to Practical Music* (London, 1597), p. 181.

[123] Richard Wistreich, 'Of Mars I Sing: Monteverdi's Voicing of Virility', in *Masculinity and Western Musical Practice*, ed. Ian Biddle and Kirsten Gibson (Farnham, 2009), pp. 69–93; Eric Thomas Chafe, *Monteverdi's Tonal Language* (New York, 1992), pp. 20–9.

[124] William Byrd, 'The Trumpets', from *The Battle*, GB-Lbl: MS Mus.1591 [My Lady Nevell's Book], fols. 21r–22v. Full edition: William Byrd, *Keyboard Music II*, ed. Alan Brown, Musica Britannica 28, 3rd rev. edn (London, 2004), p. 177.

Ex. 4.3 John Dowland, 'Time's Eldest Son' (Part 1), bars 11–14

Thanksgiving) are all fitting prayers for an old man making his peace with God.[125] They also contain thinly veiled pleas for Elizabeth to permit his retirement: the opening line of the *Nunc dimittis* is 'Now lettest thou thy servant depart in peace', while the *De profundis* (Psalm 30) begins:

> Out of the deep places have I called unto thee, O Lord.
> Lord, hear my voice: let thine ears attend to the voice of my prayers.[126]

Similarly the opening words of the *Miserere* (Psalm 51) – 'Have mercy upon me, O God, according to thy loving kindness, according to the multitude of thy compassions put away mine iniquities' – are a plea for forgiveness, appropriate perhaps for having broken his vow to be the Queen's champion each year at the Accession Day tilt.[127]

By contrast, a theme of praise is developed through the words '*Te Deum*' and '*Paratum est cor meum*' ('My heart is ready', from Psalm 108). The psalmist's heart is ready to sing the praises of God, just as Lee will praise Elizabeth. Finally, the quotations of the third stanza depict Lee abandoning the 'battle-cries of the godly warrior' and taking up the 'prayers of the hermit'.[128] In his new passive role, Lee must take up '*Noli aemulari*' (Psalm 37, which emphasises God's ability to act without human assistance) and use '*Oremus*' ('let us pray'). The disparity between '*Oremus*' and '*Quare fremuerunt*' (Psalm 20: literally, 'wherefore do they shout') contrasts the busy noise of court or battlefield with the quietness of the hermit's cell.

---

[125] Helen Hackett, *Virgin Mother, Maiden Queen: Elizabeth I and the Cult of the Virgin Mary* (Basingstoke, 1996), pp. 146–54. Hackett has undertaken the most detailed discussion of this song to-date, contextualising the biblical references within Elizabethan religious practice.

[126] William Whittingham, *The Bible and Holy Scriptures* (Geneva, 1561), fol. 234r.

[127] Such a vow is referred to in Sir William Segar, *Honour Military, and Civil* (London, 1602), p. 199.

[128] Hackett, *Virgin Mother*, p. 148.

Ex. 4.4 John Dowland, 'Time's Eldest Son' (Part 2), *The Second Book of Songs or Ayres* (London, 1600), sigs. E1v–E2r, bars 1–5

Musically, the predominantly homophonic feel of the opening stanza is replaced by imitation, both between voice and instrument, and between high and low registers on the lute (Example 4.4). Imitation alone is not enough make the music identifiably sacred in style, even with the religious quotations in these stanzas; however, other musical features also support such sacred connotations. In the third stanza the intoned phrase 'for *Quare fremuerunt* use *Oremus*' is reminiscent of the chant-like style used for psalms or preces and responses in Anglican services (Example 4.5). The words '*Quare fremuerunt*' are declaimed in faster, speech-like rhythms on a single tone supported by one chord until the rhythm and melody broaden out at the cadence in a style similar to Byrd's 'Second Preces' (from the 1560s; Example 4.6).[129] The cadence itself evokes sacred connotations through its

[129] In John Barnard (ed.), *The First Book of Selected Church Music Consisting of Services and Anthems, such as are Now Used in the Cathedral and Collegiate Churches of this Kingdom*, 10 vols. (London, 1641), vol. 1, fol. 89v; vol. 2, fol. 88r;

Ex. 4.5 John Dowland, 'Time's Eldest Son' (Part 3), *The Second Book of Songs or Ayres* (London, 1600), sigs. E2v–F1r, bars 8–10

Ex. 4.6 William Byrd, 'Second Preces', bars 16–19

decorated 4–3 suspension and the delayed movement of the vocal line, comparable to Example 4.7, also from Byrd's 'Second Preces'.

The repeated melismatic 'amens' which end Dowland's song also evoke sacred music (Example 4.8). The 'amens' are set to the so-called 'sacred end' motif, which was used in the refrain of three anthems (Thomas Morley's 'O Jesu Meek', Thomas Weelkes's 'Give Ear, O Lord', and Christopher Tye's 'I Lift My Heart to Thee') all of

> vol. 3, fol. 83r; vol. 4, fol. 84r; vol. 5, fol. 85v; vol. 6, fol. 89v; vol. 7, fol. 89v; vol. 8, fol. 85v; vol. 9, fol. 85v; vol. 10, fol. 85v. For full edition see: William Byrd, *The English Services*, ed. Craig Monson, Byrd Edition 10a (London, 1980), p. 30 (this edition is transposed, whereas the examples given maintain original pitch).

Ex. 4.7   William Byrd, 'Second Preces', bars 21–3

Ex. 4.8   John Dowland, 'Time's Eldest Son' (Part 3), bars 19–22

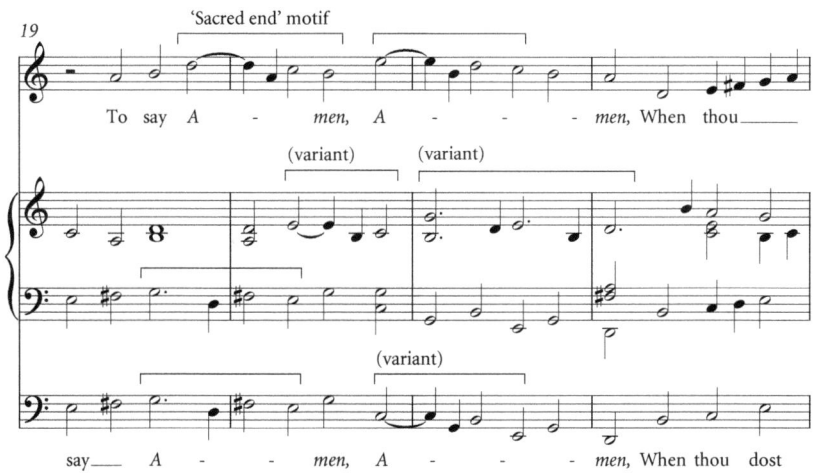

which pray to God for mercy. The motif also appears at the end of Morley's 'sacred end' pavan and Daniel Farrant's 'four-note' pavan, while Dowland also used the same figure in his 'Lachrimae' pavan.[130] This was a motif that signalled a sacred

---

[130] Peter Holman, *Dowland: Lachrimae (1604)*, Cambridge Music Handbooks (Cambridge, 1999), pp. 47–8; Peter Le Huray, *Music and the Reformation in England, 1549–1660*, Cambridge Studies in Music (Cambridge, 1978), pp. 204, 251, 304–5.

Ex. 4.9 John Dowland, 'Time's Eldest Son' (Part 3), bars 1–7

context, and having identified it at its most prominent marking a sacred ending ('amen'), it can also be traced as a motif within the lute part throughout the second stanza, underpinning the religious quotations in the lyrics. Nor was this Dowland's only use of quotation. In the melody of the lute part that opens the third stanza, he also uses the falling fourth motif found in the 'Lachrimae' pavan and 'Flow my Tears' (Examples 4.9 and 2.3). The connotations here are not religious, but melancholic as in the opening pavan, marking the sad end to Lee's reign as the Queen's champion.

'Time's Eldest Son' stands out within Dowland's output for the elaborate musical rhetoric deployed. He created musical parallels for all the key themes of the pageant: the contrast of old age, melancholy, and religious devotion with martial exploits and youth. Nor is the music merely a mirror for the surrounding pageantry. The religious themes explored in the song have not yet featured in the pageantry or speeches; rather, they prefigure the sacred tone of the final resignation tableau.

The retirement device began with a pavilion made to look like the temple of the Vestal Virgins with lights, pillars, and an altar. This temple rose out of the ground to the accompaniment of music 'so sweet and secret, as every one was greatly marvelled'.[131] This was the song 'His Golden Locks', sung by one of

---

[131] Segar, *Honour Military, and Civil*, p. 197.

Elizabeth's favourite court musicians, Robert Hales, and most likely that published in John Dowland's *First Book of Songs or Ayres* (1597).[132] Then the Vestal Virgins brought gifts to Elizabeth before Lee offered up his armour and presented the Earl of Cumberland to be Elizabeth's new champion.[133] As Lee and Cumberland approached Elizabeth, the comparison of age and youth referred to emblematically and in song was enacted in life.

Musically the setting is much simpler than the first song, with a strophic setting, a smooth and largely stepwise melody, and no play of musical styles. It was perhaps intended to reflect the simplicity of the hermit's life. Yet the choice of the galliard style after the pavan rhythms of 'Time's Eldest Son' neatly unites the two songs as the pavan and galliard formed a typical dance pair. The two songs are also linked thematically, continuing the imagery of time, religious devotion, and old age. The vicissitudes of time are depicted in images of 'golden locks' turned to silver, 'lover's sonnets' replaced with 'holy psalms', and the 'man at arms' who 'must now serve on his knees'. Yet despite these physical changes, visibly and audibly displayed, Lee affirms that his devotion and loyalty are constant. 'Beauty, strength, youth' may be 'flowers but fading seen', but 'Duty, faith, love are roots and ever green', and he continues to serve as Elizabeth as 'beadsman' even if he can no longer be her knight.

These poetic contrasts of youth and age are emphasised harmonically, beginning with a false relation (F sharp to F natural) at the exclamation 'O time too swift', which expresses the bitterness the protagonist feels towards time with the coinciding discordant F natural (Example 4.10, bar 6). When youth is described as having tried to spurn time, Dowland employs another striking harmonic shift from F sharp to F natural (bars 9–11). The F natural returns again for the final couplet where beauty, strength, and youth are described as 'flowers but fading seen' (Example 4.11, bars 19–20). Dowland employed similar harmonic changes between F sharp and F natural in his dialogue 'Humour Say What Mak'st Thou Here' in *The Second Book of Songs* (also written for performance to the Queen). Here the sole F natural of the piece marked the 'heavy leaden mood' (Example 4.12, bars 14–15).[134] Although in 'His Golden Locks' these moments of musical melancholy only fit the text exactly in the first stanza, they still suit the overall bittersweet tone of the poem, with its combination of sadness at what is lost in old age and the pleasure to be found in serving Elizabeth.

'His Golden Locks' marked a moment of transformation of both the scene (as the temple mystically rose from the ground) and Lee's identity (as he comes to the end of his tilting career). Following the song he formally presented the Earl

---

[132] Dowland, *The First Book of Songs or Ayres*, sigs. I2v–K1r. Full modern edition in: John Dowland, *The First Book of Ayres (1597, 1600, 1603, 1606, 1613)*, ed. Edmund Fellows and Thurston Dart, The English Lute Songs 1, 2nd edn (London, 1965; rept. 1998), pp. 36–7. Dowland also provides parts for the song to be sung as a four-part ayre.

[133] Segar, *Honour Military, and Civil*, pp. 197–9; Peele, *Polyhymnia*, sig. B3v.

[134] Dowland, *The Second Book of Songs or Ayres*, sigs. M2v–N1r. Full edition in Dowland, *The Second Book of Songs (1600)*, p. 52. A reduced version is presented here for ease of viewing the harmony; the original is for quinto (treble viol), canto (voice), alto, tenor and basso (all voice and/or viol), and lute.

Ex. 4.10 John Dowland, 'His Golden Locks', *The First Book of Songs or Ayres* (London, 1597), sigs. I2v–K1r, bars 1–13

of Cumberland as the new Queen's champion and exchanged his helmet for a 'buttoned cap of the country fashion'. Another of Dowland's songs, 'Behold a Wonder', may have been written for the entry of a knight disguised as an Indian Prince on Accession Day in 1595. It would have similarly marked a moment of transformation: on this occasion Elizabeth's presence turned Blind Love into Seeing Love.[135] Effecting such transformations in scene and identity through

---

[135] Diana Poulton, *John Dowland*, rev. edn (London, 1982), p. 277; 'A Device by the Earl of Essex for the Queen's Entertainment', GB-Lna: SP12/254, Secretaries of State: State Papers Foreign, Elizabeth I ([17 November] 1595), fols. 139r–140v. The speeches were given by a Squire to introduce the Indian prince. The line break in the speech may indicate where the song was inserted. Catherine Bates suggests that the Indian Prince would have been recognised as Cupid, because of his dress of feathers and his bow and arrow (Bates, *Rhetoric of Courtship*, pp. 81–2.) The Prince may have been Sir Robert Dudley, whom Peele described

Ex. 4.11   John Dowland, 'His Golden Locks', bars 18–24

Beau - ty, strength, youth are flowers but fad - ing seen: Du - ty, faith, love are roots and ev - er green.

music allowed a sense of spectacle to be combined with notions of music's power to instigate magical metamorphoses (like those seen at the Bisham progress, pp. 31–3), along with an artful explanation of the pageantry through song lyrics.

Lee's songs, like those of Sidney, evoked the countryside and sacred spaces away from the court and tiltyard. While the military sounds of the trumpets and drums would also have been ever present at the tiltyard, when music was at its most artistic and most political it was the incongruity of courtly music in the military sphere that was the source of inspiration. Lee, Sidney, and the Foster Children used music to underline the strangeness of particular characters in the tiltyard – shepherds, old men, hermits, and Beauty – and through these incongruities tournament pageantry could address broader issues of noble identity beyond the martial arena. For the ideal gentleman-courtier music was a foil to his military display that affirmed his balanced and well-rounded talents; for those with frustrated military ambitions it underlined the limits of beauty, femininity, and courtliness and reaffirmed the importance of martial masculinity and military defence for their protection; for the elderly knight it was a reminder that time could require devotion to take gentler forms. Through the associations of different styles and genres, music could be symbolic of different stages of a knight's life and aspirations.

as entering 'like Venus' son' (Peele, *Anglorum Feriae*, sig. E1r). While this song is a typical tribute to Elizabeth, most of Essex's entertainment was an act of blatant self-promotion which finally caused Elizabeth to leave: Hammer, 'Upstaging the Queen'.

Ex. 4.12 John Dowland, 'Humour Say What Mak'st Thou Here',
The Second Book of Songs or Ayres (London, 1600), sigs. M2v–N1r, bars 14–20

Although only isolated fragments of tournament music survive, Lee's songs demonstrate that music would have been as much a tool as visual spectacle and poetry in these performances of identity. Of course, the subtleties may not have been heard by all spectators. Some musical moments such as Henry Lee's resignation or the songs from the *Four Foster Children of Desire* tournament were performed in front of the Queen's gallery where the ambassadors and noblemen were seated, and were therefore not necessarily audible to the general spectators at the opposite side of the tiltyard. Yet it was perhaps only the Queen and court who needed to understand the details. The transportation of music on pageant cars or musicians accompanying the entering knight allowed the sounds to travel around the tiltyard for all to hear enough to be impressed. For the wider body of paying spectators the aural presence of music was sufficient to create an aura of magnificence and nobility and to symbolise the nobleman's patronage of the arts. As for Elizabeth, she encouraged such display as a sign of the wealth and prosperity of her court. Even if she was, at times, outshone by the pageantry of her noblemen, their tributes continually emphasised her position as the motivation for the elaborate spectacle, and therefore her ultimate authority.

CHAPTER 5

Politics, Petition, and Complaint on the Royal Progresses

THE musicians sound. Queen Elizabeth approaches the gates of the stately house. A procession of courtiers and the long baggage train following her summer progress are snaking away behind her. The noble host and his family have ridden out to meet her. Actors and singers prepare to deliver their lines of welcome. Local people have run to view the spectacle. Poets, playwrights, composers, costume-makers, dancing masters, designers, and builders of scenery, machines, or special effects, have all been busy preparing the entertainments. Vast sums of money have been spent. Such visits were undertakings of considerable complexity for both the Lord Chamberlain, who was responsible for the logistics of moving the court and its possessions, and those preparing to host and entertain. While a nobleman could take part in a tournament in most years from the 1570s onwards, hosting the Queen on one of her summer progresses was a rarer honour. For civic hosts without other access to the court and its entertainments, such opportunities were even scarcer. All those involved in the production, from the Queen downwards, wanted to capitalise on their efforts, so an array personal and political aims vied for prominence.

Itinerant courts were the norm in Renaissance Europe as limited sanitation, the drain on local resources, and the fear of plague forced regular movement between royal palaces. As well as these more localised removes, monarchs undertook longer tours of their realms, making royal entries into multiple towns along the route in order to reinforce their authority across their kingdoms.[1] Other European monarchs travelled further, made longer tours, and enjoyed grander and more classically inspired royal entries (the numerous progresses of Emperor Charles V across his pan-European empire and the two-year Grande Voyage de France by the newly come-of-age Charles IX are examples).[2] Elizabeth's progresses, however,

---

[1] Jeanice Brooks, *Courtly Song in Late Sixteenth-Century France* (Chicago, 2000), pp. 2–5; Mary Tiffany Ferer, *Music and Ceremony at the Court of Charles V: The Capilla Flamenca and the Art of Political Promotion*, Studies in Medieval and Renaissance Music 12 (Woodbridge, 2012), p. 1.

[2] Roy Strong, *Art and Power: Renaissance Festivals, 1450–1650* (Woodbridge, 1984), pp. 44–50, 75–97, 105–11, 115–16; Victor E. Graham and W. McAllister Johnson (eds.), *The Royal Tour of France by Charles IX and Catherine de' Medici: Festivals and Entries, 1564–6* (Toronto, 1979); R. J. Knecht, 'Charles V's Journey through France, 1539–40', in *Court Festivals of the European Renaissance: Art, Politics, and Performance*, ed. J. R. Mulryne and Elizabeth Goldring (Aldershot, 2002), pp. 153–70; Jochen Becker, '"Greater than Zeuxis and Apelles": Artists as Arguments in the Antwerp Entry of 1549', in ibid., pp. 171–95. Also further examples in J. R. Mulryne, Helen Watanabe-O'Kelly and Margaret Shewring (eds.), *Europa Triumphans: Court and Civic Festivals in Early Modern*

were distinguished by the hospitality she received from her nobility, the lavish entertainments they provided, and her deliberate participation and interaction with the crowds during royal entries.[3]

During most summers Elizabeth left the confines of the royal household and spent several months travelling through parts of central, eastern, and southern England, both staying with noble hosts and also making royal entries into towns. She undertook progresses almost every year, except in the 1580s, when political tensions and the threat of invasion made it wiser for her to remain close to London, and from the mid-1590s, when failing health forced her to travel less.[4] While her councillors condemned the progresses as an inconvenient and expensive distraction from serious business, Elizabeth found them politically useful. She took advantage of the chaos of travel to defer decisions, dodge unwanted ambassadorial visits, and maintain her independence of action by keeping her councillors off balance. Some stops were pleasurable stays honouring loyal servants or royal favourites; others were politically calculated to visit potential troublemakers or recusants, to promote religious conformity, or to inspect military defences. Progresses brought her into contact with her subjects and allowed her to cultivate her popularity through both ceremonial dialogue and impromptu interactions with the crowds.[5]

Progress entertainments were a mixture of public and private events with diverse spectators.[6] While indoor events might have a more limited and privileged

Europe (Aldershot, 2004); Pierre Béhar and Helen Watanabe-O'Kelly (eds.), *Spectaculum Europaeum: Theatre and Spectacle in Europe = Histoire du spectacle en Europe (1580–1750)* (Wiesbaden, 1999).

[3] Mary Hill Cole, 'Monarchy in Motion: An Overview of Elizabethan Progresses', in *The Progresses, Pageants, and Entertainments of Queen Elizabeth I*, ed. Jayne Elisabeth Archer, Elizabeth Goldring, and Sarah Knight (Oxford, 2007), pp. 27–44 (pp. 27–9).

[4] Mary Hill Cole, *The Portable Queen: Elizabeth I and the Politics of Ceremony*, Massachusetts Studies in Early Modern Culture (Amherst, 1999), p. 277. Cole provides a table of all Elizabeth's known progresses as well as a detailed analysis of their purposes, logistics, and patterns. David M. Bergeron gives an overview of the royal entries and progress entertainments of Elizabeth's reign: *English Civic Pageantry, 1558–1642*, Medieval and Renaissance Texts and Studies 267, rev. edn (Tempe, AZ, 2003), pp. 15, 17–66.

[5] Cole, *Portable Queen*, pp. 1–5, 36–40, 121–34, 135–71; Bergeron, *English Civic Pageantry*, p. 15; Patrick Collinson, 'Pulling the Strings: Religion and Politics in the Progress of 1578', in *The Progresses, Pageants, and Entertainments of Queen Elizabeth I*, ed. Jayne Elisabeth Archer, Elizabeth Goldring, and Sarah Knight (Oxford, 2007), pp. 122–41; C. E. McGee, 'Mysteries, Musters, and Masque: The Import(s) of Elizabethan Civic Entertainments', in ibid., pp. 104–21.

[6] Many of these entertainments have recently been newly edited in *John Nichols's The Progresses and Public Processions of Queen Elizabeth I: A New Edition of the Early Modern Sources*, ed. Elizabeth Goldring et al., 5 vols. (Oxford, 2014). This was published during the final stages of preparation for this book, and doubtless contains more avenues for new research than I have been able to incorporate here.

audience – the banquets and private evening entertainment at houses like Elvetham, or the masque 'in the Privy Chamber' put on by the civic authorities at Norwich[7] – outdoor entertainments might draw large crowds of people from all social classes. Royal entries into towns saw the streets lined with spectators, while Elizabeth's approach to a nobleman's estate would have been watched by servants of the household, tenants of the estate, and people living in nearby villages. The Earl of Hertford rode out with a train of three hundred men to accompany the Queen to his estate at Elvetham in 1591, while during an elaborate outdoor water pageant the character Sylvanus alarmed a group of 'country people' who caused amusement as they ran away.[8] Sometimes local people or servants were even invited to present their own shows on the nobleman's estate. There were ball games by Somerset men at Elvetham, a bride-ale and hock play at Kenilworth (1575), and a country dance at Cowdray (1591).[9]

During such a public display, Elizabeth's majesty and reputation had to be enhanced in the eyes of her attending subjects, whatever other political aims the host had. Hosts were expected to celebrate the royal visit with a spectacle of lavish praise commensurate with their means, so progress entertainments became displays of extravagant royal image-making. The tributes to Elizabeth as bringer of harmony commissioned by Lady Russell for Elizabeth's visit to Bisham (pp. 31–3) were typical. Elizabeth might be presented as Diana, Venus, Cynthia, or the Fairy Queen, or taken on a staged quest like a Lady of Romance to illustrate her virtues.[10] As such they were important occasions for creating and disseminating Elizabeth's

---

[7] *The Honourable Entertainment Given to the Queen's Majesty in Progress, at Elvetham in Hampshire, by the Right Honourable the Earl of Hertford* (London, 1591), sigs. C1r, D4r–v; B[ernard] G[arter], *The Joyful Receiving of the Queen's Most Excellent Majesty into her Highness' City of Norwich* (London, 1578), sigs. E1r–E3r.

[8] *Honourable Entertainment … at Elvetham*, sig. A4r; Goldring et al. (eds.), *John Nichols's The Progresses*, vol. 3, p. 587.

[9] The bride-ale was the secular festivities following a wedding, in this case including country pastimes such as morris dancing and quintain (a wooden shield on a post that was attacked with a lance either on foot or horseback). The Coventry hock play was performed yearly on Hock Tuesday (the second Tuesday after Easter Day) and celebrated the town's victory over the Danes in 1002. The traditional play had been stopped by Protestant reformers and the townspeople performed it for Elizabeth in the hope of gaining permission to revive it. For these various entertainments see George Gascoigne, 'The Princely Pleasures at Kenilworth Castle', in *The Pleasantest Works of George Gascoigne Esquire* (London, 1587), sigs. A1r–C8v (sig. B2r); Robert Laneham, *A Letter wherein Part of the Entertainment Unto the Queen's Majesty at Killingworth [Kenilworth] Castle in Warwickshire in this Summer's Progress 1575 is Signified* (London, 1575), pp. 26–39; Goldring et al. (eds.), *John Nichols's The Progresses*, vol. 3, p. 560; *Honourable Entertainment … at Elvetham*, sig. D3v.

[10] Jean Wilson, *Entertainments for Elizabeth I*, Studies in Elizabethan and Renaissance Culture 2 (Cambridge, 1980), pp. 15–26; Bergeron, *English Civic Pageantry*, p. 64; Roy Strong, *The Cult of Elizabeth: Elizabethan Portraiture and Pageantry*, new edn (London, 1999), p. 114.

royal image. More recently attention has shifted towards the significance of these events for the hosts: how they manipulated Elizabeth's image to serve their own interests and used the occasion to present petitions and complaints.[11] The poets, artists, copyists, and publishers who produced and circulated details of these shows also looked on these occasions as a chance to sue for patronage, adding further layers of petition.[12] Moreover, not all political messages were necessarily aimed at the Queen: noblemen and towns also competed for status and reputation with their peers and rivals, while landowners and civic leaders performed their magnificence to impress local audiences.

Music was one of the means to which hosts and artists turned to mediate between their duties of praise and entertainment, and their more self-interested ambitions. As with the tournaments, the music-making while the court was on progress was commissioned by the hosts and out of Elizabeth's direct control. Noblemen were responsible for planning their own entertainments for the visit. For musicians they used their own employees as well as loaning musicians from fellow noblemen. The Kytson family, for example, lent Edward Johnson to the Earl of Leicester for the Kenilworth entertainments (1575), and he also went on to compose music for the Earl of Hertford at Elvetham (1591).[13] Noble hosts patronised some of the best musicians of the day, with Lord Chandos employing John Dowland for Elizabeth's visit to Sudeley (1592). On only one occasion, however, is there evidence of Elizabeth's own musicians being employed: Lord Montague used 'her Highness' musicians' at Cowdray (1591). As his was a small-scale entertainment with shows performable by as few as three actors, utilising the Queen's musicians was perhaps

---

[11] For example: Curt Breight, 'Realpolitik and Elizabethan Ceremony: The Earl of Hertford's Entertainment of Elizabeth at Elvetham, 1591', *Renaissance Quarterly* 45 (1992), 20–48; Curt Breight, 'Caressing the Great: Viscount Montague's Entertainment of Elizabeth at Cowdray, 1591', *Sussex Archaeological Collection* 127 (1989), 147–66; Susan Doran, 'Juno versus Diana: The Treatment of Elizabeth I's Marriage in Plays and Entertainments, 1561–1581', *The Historical Journal* 28 (1995), 257–74; Elizabeth Heale, 'Contesting Terms: Loyal Catholicism and Lord Montague's Entertainment at Cowdray, 1591', in *The Progresses, Pageants, and Entertainments of Queen Elizabeth I*, ed. Jayne Elisabeth Archer, Elizabeth Goldring, and Sarah Knight (Oxford, 2007), pp. 189–206; Elizabeth Goldring, 'Portraiture, Patronage, and the Progresses: Robert Dudley, Earl of Leicester and the Kenilworth Festivities of 1575', in ibid., pp. 163–88; Cole, *Portable Queen*, pp. 65–134; Susan Frye, *Elizabeth I: The Competition for Representation* (Oxford, 1993), p. 10.

[12] Gabriel Heaton, *Writing and Reading Royal Entertainments: From George Gascoigne to Ben Jonson* (Oxford, 2010), pp. 7, 29–48; Frye, *Elizabeth I*, pp. 62–3; David M. Bergeron, 'The "I" of the Beholder: Thomas Churchyard and the 1578 Norwich Pageant', in *The Progresses, Pageants, and Entertainments of Queen Elizabeth I*, ed. Jayne Elisabeth Archer, Elizabeth Goldring, and Sarah Knight (Oxford, 2007), pp. 142–62.

[13] David Brown and Ian Harwood, 'Johnson, Edward (i)', *NG2*; David Price, *Patrons and Musicians of the English Renaissance*, Cambridge Studies in Music (Cambridge, 1981), p. 76 n. 5.

an option for those preparing less extravagant entertainments and having more limited means or connections.[14]

When the host was a town the court sent assistance to ensure that appropriate festivities were provided. Thomas Churchyard's payment for an aborted royal visit to Shrewsbury states that he was 'sent hither by my Lord President', while the Lord Chamberlain also appointed authors.[15] These writers were paid by the town, however, so they were no mere mouthpieces for the Queen. The musical employees were similarly a blend of local, aristocratic, and royal personnel. The Norwich waits performed during Elizabeth's entry and supported the cathedral choir.[16] These choristers sang a *Te Deum* on her first evening, and were presumably the 'best voices in the city' who sang during the entry itself.[17] The cathedral also paid Osbert Parsley (singer in the cathedral and composer of both sacred and instrumental music) for compositions, though none survives.[18] Few towns would have had such skilled singers and waits as Norwich – which was England's second city at this time – but they could seek help from elsewhere. Even Norwich augmented its resources with the Queen's musicians, including trumpeters, viols, and cornetts, plus 'the viii musicians that follow the tent' (probably a canopy under which Elizabeth travelled).[19] Towns might also borrow musicians from local noblemen, just as Worcester paid the Earl of Leicester's musicians for services during Elizabeth's visit in 1575.[20]

Reading the extant music and lyrics with a knowledge of each event's political circumstances reveals the ingenuity with which songs were designed to convey numerous competing voices and agendas to diverse audiences. Beginning with the most typical genre – songs of praise – the entertainments commissioned by the somewhat suspect Earl of Hertford and the loyal servant Sir Thomas Egerton demonstrate how such royal tributes might serve as a foil to personal ambitions. Other hosts broke the celebratory mood with laments to make their complaints, relying on the musical fashions of the day to make such melancholy songs appropriate. Such songs could encapsulate the strongest and potentially most offensive statements of an entertainment, a technique employed equally by royal

---

[14] *The Speeches and Honourable Entertainment Given to the Queen's Majesty in Progress, at Cowdray in Sussex, by the Right Honourable the Lord Montague* (London, 1591), p. 3; Wilson, *Entertainments*, p. 86.

[15] McGee, 'Mysteries, Musters, and Masque', p. 112; J. A. B. Somerset (ed.), *REED: Shropshire*, 2 vols. (Toronto, 1994), vol. 1, p. 220. Cole, *Portable Queen*, pp. 40, 68–9.

[16] David Galloway (ed.), *REED: Norwich, 1540–1642* (Toronto, 1984), p. 59. The waits were paid by the Dean and Prebends.

[17] Thomas Churchyard, *A Discourse of the Queen's Majesty's Entertainment in Suffolk and Norfolk with a Description of Many Things Then Presently Seen* (London, 1578), sig. B4v.

[18] Galloway (ed.), *REED: Norwich*, p. 59.

[19] Royal College of Arms, W.C. Ceremonies III, fol. 89r–v, in ibid., pp. 241–2.

[20] Worcester's Chamber Order Book, in Goldring *et al.* (eds.), *John Nichols's The Progresses*, vol. 2, p. 355. There were also payments to the Queen's musicians and to trumpeters.

favourites such as the Earl of Leicester, and the disgruntled Catholic gentleman Lord Montague. The complexity of political motives already in play did not deter musicians from collaborating with their fellow authors and performers in pursuit of employment opportunities or financial reward. Civic hosts, by contrast, showed little concern to soften their political advice with courtly metaphor. They did, however, have to woo their citizens into performing an enthusiastic welcome, enacting the ideal of the harmonious city and kingdom in loyal obedience to its Queen.

PRAISE AND AMBITION

GIVEN the need for royal approval and to affirm Elizabeth's majesty to the diverse crowds, it is not surprising to find that songs of praise were overwhelmingly the primary genre of vocal music for progress entertainments. From the first greeting at the gate, to the tributes made by the various characters, to the farewell song, Elizabeth's beauty, virtues, and goddess-like powers were extravagantly proclaimed. Praising Elizabeth through song rather than speech allowed such flattery to be delivered artfully, often making simple and at times quite stereotypical verses more appealing. But were these tributes always as sincere as they appeared? Doubt has already been cast over the sincerity of printed tributes by Jeremy Smith's re-evaluation of Thomas Morley's *Triumphs of Oriana* (1601). This, he argues, was initially intended in praise of Anna of Demark (Queen of James VI of Scotland) and only later pressed into service in praise of Elizabeth as a gesture of repentance following the treasonous rebellion of the key figure pressing James's claim to be Elizabeth's heir, Robert Devereux, Earl of Essex.[21] The songs commissioned for entertainments during the Queen's progresses had less controversial origins, but were equally politically entangled. It was not just that presenting flattering songs was a means to earn royal approval. The terms of praise might reveal as much about the host's political aims as they did about Elizabeth's qualities.

Elizabeth's entertainment at Elvetham in 1591 is a powerful example of the importance of reading such praises within their wider political context. Elvetham in Hampshire was a minor estate of Edward Seymour, Earl of Hertford, who nevertheless prepared for Elizabeth's visit perhaps the most extravagant and musical programme of entertainments of the reign (the Earl of Leicester's entertainments at Kenilworth in 1575 also compete). The amount of music Hertford commissioned was exceptional– a surprising amount of which survives in some form – while the author of the printed accounts of the entertainment was unusually descriptive when recording the musical aspects of the occasion.[22]

---

[21] Jeremy Smith, 'Music and Late Elizabethan Politics: The Identities of Oriana and Diana', *Journal of the American Musicological Society* 58 (2005), 507–58.

[22] The extant music is described in: Ernest Brennecke, The Entertainment at Elvetham, 1591', in *Music in English Renaissance Drama*, ed. John H. Long (Lexington, KY, 1968), pp. 32–56. See also Susan Anderson, 'Music and Power at the English Court, 1575–1624', PhD dissertation, University of Leeds, 2006, pp. 69–74. The printed account of the entertainment saw two editions, the second of which was labelled as 'newly corrected, and amended'. This second

Almost all of the songs sing Elizabeth's praises. Upon her arrival she was greeted as 'Beauteous Queen of Second Troy' by six virgins representing the Hours and Graces.[23] Admiration for her feminine beauty combined with celebrations of her statecraft as she was portrayed as heir to the legendary Brutus of Troy (a counterpart to Aeneas who supposedly sailed to Britain) establishing a second Golden Age in England. With its May-time imagery and vocal polyphony, 'With Fragrant Flowers We Strew the Way' was probably a madrigal. Its refrain greeting Elizabeth as 'Beauteous Queen of Second Troy' is very similar to that of William Byrd's six-part madrigal 'This Sweet and Merry Month of May' from Thomas Watson's *Italian Madrigals Englished* (1590).[24] Watson was probably the author of both these lyrics, though the overall poetic structure is too different for the Elvetham text to have fitted Byrd's music without considerable alteration.[25] The music for the refrain, however, could potentially have been borrowed, and certainly it is likely that the Elvetham setting would have employed a similar style. Byrd's approach is typically madrigalian, highlighting his direct address to Elizabeth by interrupting the imitative polyphonic flow of crotchets and quavers with a refrain that begins homophonically in minims and semibreves (Example 5.1).

The centrepiece of Hertford's entertainments was a water pageant produced on a specially created crescent-shaped lake (reflecting Elizabeth's image as Cynthia) where Elizabeth received the tributes of Nereus and the sea nymphs, including a song praising her as a 'second sun' (notation not extant).[26] 'In the Merry Month

---

version was believed to be lost and was known only through a composite version in John Nichols (ed.), *The Progresses and Public Processions of Queen Elizabeth: Among which are Interspersed Other Solemnities, Public Expenditures, and Remarkable Events, During the Reign of that Illustrious Princess*, 3 vols. (London, 1823); however it has recently been discovered and edited by H. Neville Davies: Goldring *et al.* (eds.), *John Nichols's The Progresses*, vol. 3, pp. 563–95. There are numerous alterations to the song texts and titles, though few of these make substantial changes to the overall meaning and tone of the performances.

[23] *Honourable Entertainment … at Elvetham*, sig. B4r-v; Goldring *et al.* (eds.), *John Nichols's The Progresses*, vol. 3, p. 579.

[24] Thomas Watson, *The First Set of Italian Madrigals Englished* (London, 1590), no. XXVIII. For a full modern edition see: Thomas Watson, *Italian Madrigals Englished (1590)*, ed. Albert Chatterley, Musica Britannica 74 (London, 1999), pp. 114–19. Francis Pilkington's lute song or four-part ayre using this text – in *The First Book of Songs or Ayres of 4. Parts with Tablature for the Lute or Orpharion, with the Viol de Gamba* (London, 1605) – is probably a later reuse of the lyrics, as 'queen' has been changed to 'king' throughout. Pilkington may also have been too young, as he did not receive his BMus until 1595. Brennecke, 'Entertainment at Elvetham', pp. 39–40.

[25] Anderson, 'Music and Power', p. 70.

[26] Nereus's song is one of the most substantially altered songs: the edition has just two verses, while the 'newly corrected, and amended' edition replaces the second verse with three new verses: Goldring *et al.* (eds.), *John Nichols's The Progresses*, vol. 3, pp. 584–5. Perhaps the creator of the first edition worked from an earlier draft that had been superseded and expanded by the time the entertainment was performed (these revised lyrics as yet still being with the composer).

Ex. 5.1 William Byrd, 'This Sweet and Merry Month of May',
The First Set of Italian Madrigals Englished, ed. Thomas Watson (London, 1590),
no. XXVIII, bars 59–65

of May' was another song in the madrigal vein, most likely set by John Baldwin.[27] It greeted Elizabeth as she opened her windows on the morning of the third day and told the story of two pastoral lovers, Phyllida and Corydon. The author of the printed account was keen to emphasise the quality of the music, praising both the 'worth of the ditty' and 'the aptness of the note thereto applied', perhaps referring to the artful variations in texture that enliven the dialogue between the characters in Baldwin's setting.[28]

The two songs from the day of Elizabeth's departure are also extant. Both were sung 'with the music of an exquisite consort: wherein was the lute, bandora, bass-viol, cittern, treble-viol and flute'.[29] The mixed consort associated the Earl with previous grand progresses such as Kenilworth in 1575, where indeed the composer of these songs, Edward Johnson, had previously been employed (see also pp. 109 and 146). Johnson's settings of the Elvetham lyrics survive in versions for five parts, though signs of the missing sixth part can occasionally be seen at

---

[27] Brennecke, 'Entertainment at Elvetham', p. 47. Baldwin's setting is dated 1592 in Gb-Lbl: rm.24.d2 (fols. 171v–173v), but it is the extant setting closest to the date of the original progress. This is called 'The Ploughman's Song' in one edition (*Honourable Entertainment ... at Elvetham*, sig. D3), and 'The Three-Men's Song' in the 'newly corrected, and amended' version reproduced in Goldring *et al.* (eds.), *John Nichols's The Progresses*, vol. 3, p. 589.

[28] *Honourable Entertainment ... at Elvetham*, sig. D2v. John Baldwin, 'In the Merry Month of May', Gb-Lbl: rm.24.d2, fols. 171v–173v.

[29] *Honourable Entertainment ... at Elvetham*, sigs. E1r–E2v.

cadences.³⁰ The first, 'Elisa is the Fairest Queen', was a galliard danced by the Fairy Queen and her maids as they sang (Example 5.2).³¹ The song provides a clear rhythm for dancing as, similar to other mixed-consort music, it contains none of the imitative counterpoint typical of the earlier consort song. It is often quite homophonic, particularly in bars 13–16 and the concluding couplet (the latter perhaps to emphasise the concluding message). In the original mixed-consort version, however, the lute would probably have played divisions to ornament the melody, especially on the repeat for the second verse.³² The lyrics treat Elizabeth as a fair maiden whose physical beauties are admired: her eyes, hands, breast, and speech. Such an intimate gaze only remains respectful as her physical attributes are read as markers of her hidden qualities: her virtue, piety, and (in a nod to her status as monarch) her powers as one who capable of 'inducing peace, subduing wars'. Her very presence, the singers claim, is a blessing.

The farewell song, 'Come Again Fair Nature's Treasure', was another galliard, but with no dancers this time there seems to have been more interest within the song itself (Example 5.3). The account of the progress describes it as accompanied by a hidden 'consort of musicians' (a mixed consort) and 'sung, with excellent division, by two, that were cunning', suggesting that it was the singers who ornamented the melody here.³³ The opening phrase is a simple canon between the two voices, with the ending modified so that the voices conclude together. The canon is written so that the voices always sing the same words at the same time with identical rhythms, over a relatively homophonic accompaniment. This arrangement conveys the initial statements of the words clearly, while the numerous repetitions of text and melody provided opportunities for the singers to elaborate with divisions. As the printed account suggests, it was talents of the performers that transformed these simple pieces into magnificent performances fitting for their royal audience and Hertford's patronage. As in the water pageant, Elizabeth was again the sun – bringer of joy, delight, and beauty – whose departure would leave 'eternal night'.³⁴

Hertford's extensive and magnificent musical praises appear the very model of how a nobleman should pay tribute to his Queen. His political circumstances, however, suggest potentially ulterior motives. Elizabeth's visit was probably

---

[30] Such as at bar 17 (Example 5.2) where the bare fifth on 'blessed' would usually be decorated with a 4–3 cadence: Edward Johnson, 'Elisa is the Fairest Queen / Come Again', GB-Lbl: Add. MSS 30480–4, vol. 1, fol. 65r; vol. 2, fol. 68v; vol. 3, fol. 63v; vol. 4, fol. 65v; vol. 5, fol. 10v. See also Brennecke, 'Entertainment at Elvetham', pp. 52–5, and the edition of Philip Brett, *Consort Songs*, 2nd rev. edn, Musica Britannica 22 (London, 1974), pp. 58–9, 182.

[31] *Honourable Entertainment ... at Elvetham*, sig. E1r–v.

[32] Matthew Spring, *The Lute in Britain: A History of the Instrument and its Music*, Early Music Series (Oxford, 2001), pp. 163–8; Warwick Edwards (ed.), *Music for Mixed Consort*, Musica Britannica 40 (London, 1977), p. xiv.

[33] *Honourable Entertainment ... at Elvetham*, sig. E2. The two editions present the verses of this song in differing orders. The first edition also has 'o come again', while the second edition omits the 'o', as does Johnson's setting. Goldring *et al.* (eds.), *John Nichols's The Progresses*, vol. 3, p. 595.

[34] *Honourable Entertainment ... at Elvetham*, sig. E2v.

Ex. 5.2   Edward Johnson, 'Elisa is the Fairest Queen',
GB-Lbl: Add. MSS 30480–4, vol. 1, fol. 65r; vol. 2, fol. 68v;
vol. 3, fol. 63v; vol. 4, fol. 65v; vol. 5, fol. 10v

Politics, Petition, and Complaint on the Royal Progresses 153

Ex. 5.3 Edward Johnson, 'Come Again',
GB-Lbl: Add. MSS 30480–4, vol. 1, fol. 65r; vol. 2, fol. 68v;
vol. 3, fol. 63v; vol. 4, fol. 65v; vol. 5, fol. 10v

prompted by a desire to ensure the loyalty of Hertford, who had a chequered past.[35] In 1560 he had secretly married Lady Catherine Grey (whose family were potential claimants to the throne) without royal consent. Elizabeth had sent the pair to the tower, declaring the marriage void and the children (a second followed while they were in the tower) illegitimate. Hertford was judged guilty of rape for dishonouring a royal virgin. Curt Breight has argued that the Elvetham progress was an attempt by the Earl of Hertford to put himself and his sons forward as potential successors to Elizabeth. There were two dimensions to this: first a display of 'familial magnificence' both during the event and through print, and second an emphasis on fertility within an overall theme of desire that sought to 'rewrite the sexual history of Hertford and Lady Catherine Grey'.[36]

The musical provision was one expression of such familial magnificence. Indeed, Susan Anderson suggests that the exceptional expenditure may have exceeded expectation to the extent that it violated decorum.[37] The extravagance was designed to reflect the magnificence not merely of a noble family but of potential royal heirs. Nor was it only the quantity of music that was important. The Earl demonstrated his sophistication as a would-be royal patron by demonstrating awareness of the current musical fashions and wowing spectators with special aural effects.[38] In 1591 only a handful of madrigals by English composers had been published, so 'With Fragrant Flowers' and 'In the Merry Month of May' showed Hertford to be at the forefront of Italianate musical trends. The mixed consort offered a distinctive contrast to the ensembles of the royal household (p. 109). Hidden musicians (as for 'Come Again') and echo effects imitated novelties produced at the most elaborate progress entertainments of the reign so far (Kenilworth in 1575), though with even greater complexities. The song for the water pageant impressed through its novelty and logistical complexity, being sung 'to the lute with excellent divisions' by a trio of sea nymphs, with echoes provided by lutenists and singers in separate boats.[39] Moreover, the attention to musical detail in the published account suggests that Hertford was concerned to have his efforts recorded. The author frequently notes the performers' talents in ornamentation and the composers' effectiveness in creating canons or aptly fitting the music to the lyrics.[40]

The questionable sincerity of Hertford's royal praises comes from the incongruous imagery of fertility he deployed. Such images permeate 'With Fragrant Flowers' and its preceding welcome speech. Elizabeth was continually portrayed as a kind of Venus-figure within the entertainments, inspiring love and fertility in those around her. The sexual connotations of May-time were applied directly to Elizabeth as 'the fairest queen that ever trod upon the green' in Johnson's 'Elisa'. Elizabeth, however, was unmarried, past childbearing age, and approaching sixty. Breight has suggested that the obvious incongruity was calculated to lead

---

[35] Breight, 'Realpolitik and Elizabethan Ceremony', pp. 21–2.
[36] Ibid., pp. 25–7.
[37] Anderson, 'Music and Power', p. 52.
[38] Ibid., pp. 69–74, 80–1.
[39] *Honourable Entertainment … at Elvetham*, sig. C3v.
[40] Ibid., sigs. C2r, D2v, E1r–E2v.

thoughtful spectators into consideration of the much greater appropriateness of the imagery to Hertford's own fruitfulness in producing two potential heirs to the throne. Furthermore, it painted his marriage and the birth of his two sons by Lady Catherine Grey as natural sexuality and fertility inspired by Elizabeth/Venus, not the illegitimacy that was the official judgement.[41]

In this context John Baldwin's seemingly innocuous pastoral song 'In the Merry Month of May' takes on greater political intent. The earlier water pageant had seen Sylvanus's lust for the nymph Nerea comically frustrated by a trick from Nereus that saw him pitched into the water. Breight reads the episode as a frustrated rape designed, with its comic portrayal, to mock and deny the judgement of rape levelled against Hertford.[42] Baldwin's song follows this the next day by implicitly affirming the legitimacy of the marriage and its consummation. Phyllida is a virtuous maiden who tells the shepherd Corydon that maids must 'kiss no men/ Till they did for good and all'.[43] The relationship is only concluded once Corydon has sworn the truth of his love, calling the heavens to witness. It was the language of witnessing that would spur the alert listener to link the pastoral lovers to Hertford and Catherine. The lack of witnesses had been one of the key grounds for annulling their marriage, and a few years later in 1594 the Jesuit Robert Persons would argue for the legitimacy of Hertford's second son on the grounds that when Hertford and Grey both claimed under examination they were married, the examiners became witnesses to the marriage, thereby making it legal.[44]

Despite the subversive undertones that this theme of sexuality might hold, the materials through which it is created are wholly commonplace and therefore beyond reproach. The story of Phyllida and Corydon is typical of light-hearted madrigals and canzonets, and was generic enough to be set again by both Richard Nicolson and Michael East.[45] Pastoral and May-time imagery of shepherds and their lasses was not uncommon in the early 1590s, and nor was the idea of Elizabeth transforming England into a naturally harmonious paradise (pp. 31–6). Similarly 'With Fragrant Flowers' shares with Byrd's 'This Sweet and Merry Month of May' its depiction of countryside holidays, birds singing with joy, and the blossoming natural world (and was also reset by Francis Pilkington for King James I, pp. 149, n. 24). Hertford intended no damage to Elizabeth's authority, as his royal ambitions required the authority of the monarchy to be upheld. Even if Elizabeth suspected Hertford's ulterior motives, she could not complain about the large sums of money being spent in entertaining her, nor her portrayal as a youthful, May-time queen. This was in line with her own attempts to portray an illusion of eternal youth, and she could not criticise it without admitting her old age and failure to secure the succession. Hertford's entertainments were unimpeachable, and a masterpiece in allying his duties as host with his political ambitions.

---

[41] Breight, 'Realpolitik and Elizabethan Ceremony', pp. 28–34.
[42] Ibid., pp. 30–2.
[43] *Honourable Entertainment ... at Elvetham*, sig. D3r.
[44] Breight, 'Realpolitik and Elizabethan Ceremony', p. 38.
[45] Brennecke, 'Entertainment at Elvetham', p. 47.

The splendour of progress entertainments was always aimed at showing off among a nobleman's peers as well as to Elizabeth. Hertford merely took this to an extreme as his long-term ambitions to the succession relied less on Elizabeth (who it was clear was unlikely to name a successor) than on his reputation with courtiers and noblemen who might choose to support his claims. Most hosts were more dependent on Elizabeth for fulfilling their political aspirations. Nevertheless, even her loyal servants were adept at combining royal praise with their own personal petitions. When Elizabeth paid a visit to the home of a trusted advisor or royal favourite it was a great honour, yet still a great expense. Such a host would wish to use the occasion both to enhance his status as one close to the Queen and to bring tangible rewards.

Sir Thomas Egerton and his wife Alice, Dowager Countess of Derby, were two such loyal servants, whom Elizabeth visited at Harefield in 1602 during her final summer progress. Sir Thomas was Elizabeth's Lord Keeper, while Lady Alice was a member of Elizabeth's household. Costing £2000, their entertainments for Elizabeth were some of the most expensive in the latter years of Elizabeth's reign.[46] The entertainments offered a means to address several of their personal interests. Firstly, as an illegitimate son of a minor Cheshire family, Sir Thomas Egerton sought constantly to improve his social status. This was all the more necessary as his wife was the widow of Ferdinando Stanley, Earl of Derby – a great-grandson of Henry VII.[47] As Lady Alice's three daughters needed to be found suitable husbands, a display of magnificence that demonstrated a lavish lifestyle appropriate to the girls' royal lineage and his wife's nobility was essential. Petitioning the Queen for favours would help support this extravagant lifestyle, while the couple also sought Elizabeth's approval for the marriage of Sir Thomas's son John to Frances Stanley, one of Alice's daughters.[48]

A surviving setting for one of the Harefield songs, 'Cynthia Queen of Seas and Lands' offers a rare insight into music's role in enhancing such petitions. The song was sung by a Mariner who entered carrying a box. Afterwards a lottery took place where the ladies of Elizabeth's court drew lots to receive small presents accompanied by verses explaining Fortune's judgement. Written by Sir John Davies, the entertainment was topical in referring to the recent capture of a vessel containing a million ducats off the Spanish coast.[49] In response, Elizabeth is praised as favoured by Fortune and the bringer of bounty and wealth. In a manner typical of post-Armada imagery, she is celebrated as triumphant over land and sea. This combines with conventional 'Virgin Queen' tropes: Cynthia, like Diana, is associated with hunting, the moon, and chastity. Taken at face-value, then, the song

---

[46] Gabriel Heaton, 'Elizabethan Entertainments in Manuscript: The Harefield Festivities (1602) and the Dynamics of Exchange', in *The Progresses, Pageants, and Entertainments of Queen Elizabeth I*, ed. Jayne Elisabeth Archer, Elizabeth Goldring, and Sarah Knight (Oxford, 2007), pp. 225–44 (p. 235).

[47] J. H. Baker, 'Egerton, Thomas, First Viscout Brackley (1540–1617)', *ODNB* (online edn, 2007).

[48] Heaton, 'Elizabethan Entertainments', pp. 237–8.

[49] Francis Davison, *A Poetical Rhapsody, 1602–1621*, ed. Hyder Edward Rollins, 2 vols. (Cambridge, MA, 1931), vol. 2, p. 210.

is a model of royal flattery. Yet the lyrics also contain a note of petition through their emphasis on themes of service and rewards. The song's refrain (given in Example 5.4) was an old saying meaning that just as there is no fishing to be compared to sea-fishing, nor is there any service to be compared to serving the King.[50] These repeated lines draw attention to the status of Sir Thomas and Lady Alice as royal servants, but simultaneously act as a reminder of the remuneration to be expected for such service.

This second layer of meaning is particularly highlighted in a setting of the lyrics in Robert Jones's *Ultimum Vale* (1605).[51] Matching up extant music and Elizabethan entertainments is rarely an easy task and the relationship between the extant version and the original performance at Harefield is not a simple one. The sources do not agree on the details of the original performance. A manuscript copy of the entertainment received by Sir Edward Conway described it as 'sung by 2 mariners', while the text published in Davison's *Poetical Rhapsody* (1608) and a manuscript which belonged to Matthew Hutton, Archbishop of York, indicated only one man.[52] As the verses alone give no indication that two mariners would be present, it seems likely that Conway's manuscript is preserving a detail of the original. Nevertheless, none suggests the four singers, lute, and viol (doubling the bass) called for in Jones's print. Yet Jones's song was published just three years after the progress (much sooner than most of Dowland's entertainment songs) and before the verses were printed and widely available. Furthermore, there would seem little reason to reset such an occasional and topical text so close to the original event. With the accounts of the performance in disagreement, I take the view that Jones's setting was related to the Harefield performance, though it may represent a subsequent arrangement. A vocal duet with lute accompaniment would be the minimum required to partially achieve the effects of the imitative section at 'there is no fishing to the sea' and to maintain interest under the extended held note in the closing bars (Example 5.4).

Jones's setting emphasises the theme of the rewards of royal service by giving particular prominence to the refrain. The refrain makes up seventeen of the thirty-five bars, and with its repetition it occupies two thirds of the total length of the verse. The refrain begins imitatively so that in the four-part ayre the words 'there is no fishing to the sea' are sung eight times. The second half of the phrase, 'nor service to a King', is emphasised by the upper part's decorative scale on 'nor' and a sustained note over four bars on 'service'. Underneath this the lower parts sing the words 'nor service' four times.

---

[50] Ibid., p. 208.

[51] Robert Jones, *Ultimum Vale, with a Triplicity of Music* (London, 1605), sigs. E2v–F1r. The song is also found in GB-Lbl: MS 24665 ['Giles Earle his Book'], fols. 19v–20r (c. 1610–26). For a full edition see David Greer, *Collected English Lutenist Partsongs I*, Musica Britannica 53 (London, 1987), pp. 149–52.

[52] P. Cunningham (ed.), *The Shakespeare Society Papers*, 4 vols. (London, 1844), vol. 2, pp. 65–75; J[ohn] D[avies], 'A Lottery Presented before the Late Queen's Majesty at the Lord Chancellor's House 1601', in *A Poetical Rhapsody Containing: Diverse Sonnets, Odes, Elegies, Madrigals, Epigrams, Pastorals, Eclogues, with Other Poems*, ed. Francis Davison (London, 1608), pp. 4–8; see also Goldring *et al.* (eds.), *John Nichols's The Progresses*, vol. 4, pp. 176–96 (pp. 186–7).

Ex. 5.4 Robert Jones, 'Cynthia Queen of Seas and Lands', *Ultimum Vale, with a Triplicity of Music* (London, 1605), sigs. E2v–F1r, bars 19–35

Ex. 5.4 *continued*

Assuming this setting is broadly similar to the Harefield version, the music highlights both the status of the hosts and the petition that lies behind the royal praise. By emphasising the notion of royal service, the hosts remind the audience of their importance at court and press Elizabeth to acknowledge their service as hosts and over many years at court. In the giving of gifts both through the Mariner in the immediate entertainment and on a grander scale in the provision of this progress, the hosts have performed their noble liberality and magnificence. While the Mariner can distribute only mere 'toys', Elizabeth has received 'many a jewel, many a gem' from sending Fortune on the seas. By presenting Elizabeth's prosperous and bountiful reign the hosts challenge the Queen to live up to her magnificent image and make a show of rewarding them. Fortune is described as having a 'frank and royal hand' in distributing favours, suggesting that the liberal sharing of resources is a princely virtue which Elizabeth should exercise.

Both the Harefield and the Elvetham entertainments illustrate how hosts could use music's ability to communicate on both generic and particular terms to balance their royal duties and personal aims. Write a song in a chosen style and mood and it would immediately create the desired atmosphere. The particular details of its lyrics, however, might add layers of meaning or alter the song's initial connotations, while the musical setting might draw attention to particular lines, or even help to embed repeated phrases in the memory of spectators. Likewise music could communicate broad notions of the magnificence or artistic sophistication of the patron, while simultaneously commenting on specific personal or political issues. Political and social context was also significant: knowledge of the hosts' political history and current circumstances might alter one's initial impression of a song on reflection.

LOVE AND LAMENT

SONGS of praise worked well for self-aggrandisement or petitions for reward, but what if the nobleman had a specific complaint he wished to address to Elizabeth? To achieve this, noblemen used love songs and laments, which could be interpreted in light of the political circumstances of the progress and the relationship between host and monarch. Laments might appear a surprising genre to appear in the celebratory atmosphere of a royal visit, but the farewell song always offered at least one potential opportunity. Furthermore, the popularity of highly stylised, consort song laments in the 1560s–70s and the courtly vogue for the melancholic pose expressed in numerous lute songs of the 1590s admitted these genres on the grounds of current fashion. This technique mirrors the intimate court performances in which complaint was contained within conventional genres (Chapter 2); however, on the more public occasions of the progresses it was even more important that Elizabeth's authority was not threatened nor her image tarnished through the nobleman's expression of grievance. Utilising trends and conventions allowed noblemen to address surprisingly strong criticisms and personal complaints to Elizabeth even at moments when large numbers of spectators would be expected.

When Robert Dudley, Earl of Leicester, hosted Elizabeth at Kenilworth Castle in 1575 he had been a royal favourite and suitor to the Queen for over fifteen years. His entertainments were among the most magnificent of the reign, and were the model for Hertford's extravaganza previously discussed. Music played a prominent role throughout Leicester's entertainment of the Queen, both in welcoming her to the castle and within the many entertainments prepared throughout her stay.[53] It is the final song, however, that presents Leicester's personal complaint most clearly.

The Kenilworth festivities have often been read as an elaborate final attempt at a marriage proposal, though not necessarily one he believed would succeed.[54] They may also have opened the door for Elizabeth to end this pretence at courtship, urging her either to accept Leicester's suit or to liberate him from it and allow him to leave court to fight abroad for the Dutch Protestants.[55] Themes of marriage run throughout the progress, the most blatant statement in the printed account being the show of the nymph Zabeta (clearly representing Elizabeth), which urged her to 'give consent ... to Juno's just desire'.[56] Yet the play was never performed, supposedly due to 'lack of opportunity and seasonable weather', so Leicester's appointed author, George Gascoigne, hurriedly devised a new show for Elizabeth's departure. Acting the part of Sylvanus, he introduced the enchanted wood of Kenilworth made up of lovers turned into trees by Zabeta. Some of these were lovers punished for their inconstancy (the poplar) or ambition (the ivy). Others were victims of a cruel lover, including the oak, a figure of constancy.[57] Leicester is most clearly represented by Deep Desire (a holly bush), who delivers a speech of his continuing love for Zabeta, ending with a song ('Come, Muses, Come'). Leicester might also be seen as personified in the constant oak – whose Latin name *robur* hints at his name – thereby combining sexual and reverential love in a way that illustrated his ambivalent position as both suitor and subject.[58]

On one level Deep Desire's song was a typical lament at the Queen's departure, comparable to other departure songs such as 'What Vaileth Life Where Sorrow Soaks the Heart?', which concluded the Norwich progress (1578).[59] 'Come, Muses, Come' belongs to the genre of consort song laments that was fashionable in the 1570s and frequently performed at court in the plays of the choirboy companies.[60]

---

[53] The courtly texts are printed in Gascoigne, 'Princely Pleasures', while the performances of local, rustic entertainments are described in Laneham, *A Letter*.

[54] For example: Doran, 'Juno versus Diana', pp. 266–8; Marie Axton, *The Queen's Two Bodies: Drama and the Elizabethan Succession*, Royal Historical Society Studies in History 5 (London, 1977), pp. 61–6; Goldring, 'Portraiture, Patronage, and the Progresses', pp. 172–6. Those less certain that Leicester's suit was undertaken with any expectation of marital success include John King, 'Queen Elizabeth I: Representations of the Virgin Queen', *Renaissance Quarterly* 40 (1990), 30–74 (pp. 45–7); Frye, *Elizabeth I*, pp. 70–8.

[55] Doran, 'Juno versus Diana', pp. 266–8.

[56] Gascoigne, 'Princely Pleasures', sig. C2r.

[57] Ibid., sigs. C2v–C8v.

[58] Catherine Bates, *The Rhetoric of Courtship in Elizabethan Language and Literature* (Cambridge, 1992), pp. 59–61.

[59] G[arter], *Joyful Receiving*, sig. E4v.

[60] Philip Brett, 'Consort Song', *NG2*; G. E. P. Arkwright, 'Elizabethan Choirboy Plays and their Music', *Proceedings of the Musical Association* 40 (1913/14), 117–38.

Gascoigne's lament demonstrates all the conventions of the genre: exhortations to the Muses and the landscape to join the lament, exclamations, extensive alliteration ('If death or dole, could daunt a deep desire'), and the rhetoric of death ('I live which seem to die'). The Kenilworth song was novel only in being accompanied by a mixed consort ('consort of Music')[61] rather than the homogeneous consorts used at court. Yet after the numerous references to marriage throughout the visit the resonances with Leicester's relationship with Elizabeth would be unmistakeable, particularly as the Earl had previously presented himself as Desire during revels performed by members of the Inner Temple in 1562.[62]

Gascoigne's lyrics emphasise the long duration of Leicester's suit, and the constancy with which he has maintained it:

> If tract of time, a true intent could tire,
> or cramps of care, a constant mind could taint,
> Oh then might I, at will here live and starve:
> although my deeds did more delight deserve.[63]

He raises the possibility of Leicester staying on his estates rather than returning to court if his suit is not accepted, though stresses the worthiness of his efforts. The song's closing paradox – 'I die in heaven, yet live in darksome hell' – captures Leicester's position in 1575, enjoying high favour but unable to make progress with his suit, yet equally unwilling or unable (one of the farewells is to free will) to leave the heavenly presence of the Queen and make his fortune elsewhere. Leicester is trapped by his position as royal favourite and suitor to Elizabeth. This song is a final petition for her to accept his suit or else free him to marry someone else and to pursue his political ambitions as a soldier. The fashionable and conventional genre of the consort song lament, formulaic in style but designed to represent strong emotion, allowed Leicester to encapsulate his love and his personal complaint within a traditional farewell song on a public occasion.

When in August of the same year Elizabeth was presented with a singing oak tree at the royal manor of Woodstock, she must have recalled the enchanted wood and singing holly bush that had marked her farewell at Kenilworth at the end of July. The poet Sir Edward Dyer's 'The Song in the Oak' was the lament of a constant but unfortunate lover who has been turned into an oak tree. Performed with 'the sound both of voice and instrument', it was either another consort song, or perhaps accompanied with a lute.[64]

---

[61] Gascoigne, 'Princely Pleasures', sig. C8r. The mixed consort had also accompanied 'The Song of Proteus' earlier in the visit: ibid., sig. B1r–v.

[62] Bates, *Rhetoric of Courtship*, pp. 48–52.

[63] Gascoigne, 'Princely Pleasures', sig. D1v.

[64] *The Queen's Majesty's Entertainment at Woodstock* (London, 1585), sig. C2v. For an edition of all the surviving material relating to this progress see Goldring *et al.* (eds.), *John Nichols's The Progresses*, vol. 2, pp. 359–474. The song is not ascribed to Dyer in the printed account of the entertainments, but is attributed to him in several poetic miscellanies (although these miscellanies preserve a variant of the lyrics: p. 408).

Although this song has been interpreted as representing Dyer's personal interests in recapturing the Queen's attention after a period of neglected favour in 1573, recently Dyer's relationship with the Queen has been interpreted more positively.[65] He was still able to act on behalf of clients at court and Elizabeth honoured him in this visit to the royal manor of which he was the Keeper.[66] Dyer had, however, begun his career at court as a member of the Earl of Leicester's retinue and remained closely allied with the Dudley family, suggesting he would be willing to compose verses on Leicester's behalf.[67] The Lieutenant of the Manor of Woodstock was Sir Henry Lee, another member of Leicester's circle.[68]

Arguing that the Queen's reaction convinced Leicester that there was no further possibility of marriage, Doran believes that the Woodstock entertainment used its opening tale of two lovers – a Princess and a Knight forced to separate because a princess has a duty to marry for her state and not for love – to transmit Leicester's acceptance of her rejection of his suit.[69] The singing oak at Woodstock also seems to be a delayed epilogue to the Kenilworth entertainment, mirroring its arboreal theme. Leicester, understanding his suit to have been rejected, recast himself as the unfortunate but constant loyal subject: the oak (his alternative personification in the Kenilworth enchanted wood).

The protagonist of the 'Song in the Oak' associates himself with the lamenting Deep Desire by describing himself as 'the man of woo, the matter of desire'. His song, though, is stripped of further references to desire, focussing solely on the sorrows of an unfortunate man. The cause of the oak's lament remains obscure, left open for those who had travelled with or kept abreast of that summer's progress to interpret. On behalf of his patron, Dyer signalled Leicester's acceptance of the end of their courtship:

> I am most sure that I shall not attain
> the only good wherein the joy doth lie.

Yet 'maintained by firm belief/ that praise of faith shall through my torments grow', Dyer stressed that Leicester's faithfulness would continue as a subject if not as a suitor, and seeks Elizabeth's continued goodwill.

The laments of Gascoigne and Dyer are identical in form (four stanzas of ten-syllable lines with ABABCC rhyme schemes). Dyer's lament, however, avoids the conventional alliterative style and the poem denounces such stereotypical pleas to earth and heaven to join in the lament, asking 'what avails with tragical complaint, not hoping help, the furies to awake?' While this may reflect the comparable merits of the two poets, it is also possible that Gascoigne's poem was

---

[65] Steven W. May, *The Elizabethan Courtier Poets: The Poems and their Contexts* (Columbia, MO, 1991), p. 56.

[66] Ibid. As Dyer's name is not in the published account of the progress we do not know if Elizabeth knew the identity of the author of these lyrics.

[67] Steven W. May, 'Dyer, Sir Edward (1543–1607)', *ODNB* (online edn, 2008).

[68] E. K. Chambers, *Sir Henry Lee: An Elizabethan Portrait* (Oxford, 1936), pp. 17, 33–8, 42, 84–5, 182.

[69] Doran, 'Juno versus Diana', p. 268.

deliberately conventional because the subtext of Leicester's desire to marry the Queen was controversial and because it had to communicate both a public farewell and an intimate petition. While 'The Song in the Oak' had to be deliberately vague about the cause of the woe (Elizabeth), Leicester's acceptance of her rejection of his suit did not need to be contained in a form and style as strictly conventional as Gascoigne's. As Dyer's song did not have the excuse of simultaneously functioning as a farewell lament, the protagonist was aware of the incongruity of the melancholy tone in what should be a celebration:

> Why should I the happy minds acquaint
> with doleful tunes, their settled peace to shake?

The answer perhaps was that not to express regret at the rejection of one's suit by the Queen would give greater cause for offence, and so the protagonist bids the audience see his performance of sorrowful rejection: 'behold infortune's fare'.

CATHOLIC COMPLAINTS

WHILE Leicester successfully issued Elizabeth with an ultimatum over his status as continual suitor, the songs that most openly criticised Elizabeth were commissioned by the Catholic gentleman Anthony Browne, Lord Montague, on her visit to Cowdray in August 1591. The progresses of the 1590s took place in a climate of increasing religious and political tension. Of particular concern were the increased confrontations over the religious nonconformity of both Puritans and Catholics and the war against Catholic Spain (which fuelled anxieties about the loyalty of Catholics).[70] These formed the backdrop to Elizabeth's visit to Lord Montague. He was Catholic, but had enjoyed a reasonable degree of political success early in the reign, serving as an ambassador to Spain and the Netherlands and being Lord Lieutenant of Sussex from 1569 with Lord Buckhurst. In 1585, however, his lieutenancy was not renewed (although Buckhurst's was) and Montague received no further position.[71] Montague's entertainments therefore have a more critical edge than Leicester's: while his efforts were a splendid demonstration of the faithfulness and service of Catholics, he also complained at Elizabeth's failure to recognise the loyalty of her Catholic subjects.[72]

Furthermore, it appears that rumours of Montague's disloyalty were being spread in the summer of 1591. In a speech to Surrey gentry a few months after the progress Montague remarked that 'it hath been told her Majesty that it was dangerous coming for her to my house', and how in early August while staying with the More family at Loseley she had been warned that 'I was a dangerous man to the

---

[70] John Guy, 'The 1590s: The Second Reign of Elizabeth I?', in *The Reign of Elizabeth I: Court and Culture in the Last Decade*, ed. John Guy (Cambridge, 1995), pp. 1–19.

[71] Michael C. Questier, *Catholicism and Community in Early Modern England: Politics, Aristocratic Patronage, and Religion, c. 1550–1640*, Cambridge Studies in Early Modern British History (Cambridge, 2006), pp. 130–6, 140–2, 166–9.

[72] Heale, 'Contesting Terms', pp. 189, 198, 465.

State, and that I kept in my house six score recusants … a wonderful untruth'.[73] The entertainments therefore both asserted Montague's loyalty and criticised all those who questioned it. These grievances were articulated most forcefully in the songs.

The lyrics appear in only one of the two printed versions of the Cowdray entertainments (STC 3907.7); the other (STC 39025) omitted these lyrics but described Elizabeth's actions during the visit.[74] The edition including the lyrics may have been prepared prior to the progress to be given out as a guide to events, while the version without was published afterwards.[75] This raises the possibility that the songs could be deliberately omitted from the second version (presumably for a wider distribution) because of their critical subtexts.[76] The songs were always the least permanent part of the entertainment, for the musical notation never survives as part of the published text. A song which caused offence could be quietly dropped from circulated accounts without much loss, while to omit a whole drama would reduce the magnificence of the entertainment the version portrayed. Their ephemeral nature may be one reason why songs were chosen to communicate complaints.

Although part of separate entertainments and performed on different days, the Cowdray songs seem to follow a narrative of their own. The songs shared a unifying theme of love, which is gradually revealed as a metaphor for the ideal mutual love between monarch and subject. Montague presents himself as the unrewarded admirer and the songs form a progression of increasingly direct complaints that this mutual love is being disrupted by Elizabeth's lack of trust. The first song was primarily a song of royal praise cast as a love song:

> Behold her locks like wires of beaten gold,
> Her eyes like stars that twinkle in the sky,
> The miracle of time, the world's story,
> Fortune's Queen, Love's treasure, Nature's glory.[77]

The hyperbole seen in this first verse is extreme but the model is clearly a lover's

---

[73] Questier, *Catholicism and Community*, p. 176.

[74] *Speeches … at Cowdray*, STC 3907.7; *The Honourable Entertainment Given to her Majesty in Progress at Cowdray in Sussex, by the Right Honourable the Lord Montague, Anno 1591, August 15* (London, 1591), STC 39025.

[75] Wilson, *Entertainments*, p. 88. Gabriel Heaton, however, has proposed the opposite chronology, with the printer acquiring the three songs during the printing and wishing to include them in a revised version. The printer removed the descriptive passages in order to make space for the song texts while enabling the print to still fit on two full sheets of paper: Goldring *et al.* (eds.), *John Nichols's The Progresses*, vol. 3, p. 549. While both are plausible, I am less convinced by Heaton's explanation because the editor of *Speeches … at Cowdray* claims not to be able to set down the final days of the entertainment, though in his chronology these had already been included in *Honourable Entertainment … at Cowdray*.

[76] Churchyard left out the song 'Mistrust Not Truth' from his account of the Bristol entertainments, see p. 178.

[77] *Speeches … at Cowdray*, pp. 3–4.

praise of his beloved. Denying her ageing by labelling her a 'miracle of time', Elizabeth was admired as if she were a beautiful, young woman. Indeed the lyrics seem to have had a second life as a love song when Richard Jones set the first two stanzas in *The Muses' Garden for Delights* (1610), omitting the last verse which was specific to the context of the entertainment.[78]

The mood of the second verse was darker, with its references to 'flattering hopes', 'shadows of delight', 'charms that do enchant', 'false arts deceit', and 'fading joys'. Such complaints were commonly made of courtiers as well as lovers, as seen in *Damon and Pithias* (pp. 98–9). Elizabeth is presented as victorious over these malevolent forces (a claim that was to be undermined in the subsequent songs) and the final verse emphasised the Queen's power over the helpless deer she was hunting:

> Your eyes are arrows though they seem to smile
> Which never glanced but glad the stateliest hart,
> Strike one, strike all, for none at all can fly,
> They gaze you in the face although they die.[79]

Elizabeth's power has a fearsome and disturbing edge to it. Her smiling eyes mask her hidden danger. In performance the wordplay on hart/heart would encourage a dual meaning. Just as the deer are totally dependent on Elizabeth for their life or death, so too the courtiers and noblemen are reliant on her for their welfare.

The second song is a lover's lament, though this genre has no direct connection to the preceding meeting between Elizabeth, a Pilgrim and a Wild Man. The Pilgrim had presented an oak tree hung with the arms of Sussex families, using the tree's association with constancy to stress the loyalty of the shire. The Wild Man's speech that followed ended with this warning about the difference between appearance and reality:

> such a disguised world it is that one can scarce know a pilgrim from a priest, a pauper from a gentleman, nor a man from a woman. Every one seeming to be that which they are not, only do practise what they should not.[80]

The Wild Man's words appear to attack the assumption that Catholics are disloyal to the Queen. Montague admits that he practises what he should not – Catholicism – while the reference to pilgrims and priests may be a daring reference to his hiding of Catholic priests.[81] Yet the assertion that such practices makes people seem 'to be that which they are not' suggests that while Catholicism might make someone seem disloyal, this is not true. Montague complains that he has been misjudged.

Whereas the first song described Elizabeth, the second song concerns Montague's identity. The song presents a faithful lover and compares the protagonist's love to a

---

[78] Robert Jones, *The Muses Gardin for Delights, or Fifth Booke of Ayres 1610*, ed. Edmund Fellowes, English School of Lutenist Song Writers 15 (London, 1925), pp. 44–6. Jones was probably too young to have composed for the original progress.

[79] *Speeches ... at Cowdray*, p. 4.

[80] Ibid., pp. 7–8.

[81] Heale, 'Contesting Terms', p. 201.

phoenix, a bird commonly associated with Elizabeth, suggesting that his constantly renewing love is still more exceptional.[82] The preceding dramatic device pointed to a political rather than amorous interpretation. The song has no clear protagonist in the foregoing drama, and so appears to refer to Montague himself. Whereas the first song demonstrated his love, this second song shows that the love is unrequited:

> My love that makes his nest with high desires,
> and is by beauty's blaze to ashes brought,
> Out of the which do break out greater fires,
> they quenched by disdain consume to nought,
> And out of nought my clearest love doth rise.

Whereas at Elvetham the metaphor of the sun presented Elizabeth as the bringer of life and joys, here the sun destroys, turning love to ashes. The 'high desires' surely referred to Montague's lost position of Lord Lieutenant and his political aspirations, reduced to nought by Elizabeth's decision to appoint another man to the job. Yet his love nevertheless rises from the ashes greater still.

Having drawn a stark contrast between his faithful love and Elizabeth's destructive actions towards him, the final couplet of the song reads like a lesson to the Queen in fostering loyalty:

> Love fancy's birth, Fidelity the womb,
> the nurse Delight, Ingratitude the tomb.

The imagery of the birth, womb, and nurse evokes the idea of Elizabeth as mother to her people. As early as 1559 Elizabeth had told parliament that she wanted to be 'a good mother to my country', and she continued to use the metaphor to legitimise her female authority and construct the monarch–subject relationship as one of mutual love and responsibility.[83] Such love is what Montague claims to have, but the implication in this song is that Elizabeth is not fulfilling her side of the maternal relationship. The lyrics imply that her subject's love for her needs to be nurtured by her own fidelity, or ingratitude will kill it. There is an implicit threat in the suggestion that love for one's monarch can die. Yet it is neutralised by the allegorical language and the conventionality of pleas for death in the rhetorical language of lovers. By ending on such an emotive word as 'tomb', Montague has drawn attention to his unhappy complaint.

The final song puts some concluding wise words on the subjects of love into the mouth of a Fisherman. The song ends the device of the Angler and the Netter/

---

[82] Thomas Churchyard's *A Handful of Gladsome Verses, Given to the Queen's Majesty at Woodstock this Progress* (Oxford, 1592) refers to Elizabeth as 'the only phoenix of this world' (sigs. A2r, C1r). Elizabeth was the phoenix because she had endured the outlawing of her Protestant religion and accusations of treason under Mary to rise as Queen upon Mary's death.

[83] Christine Coch, '"Mother of my Contrye": Elizabeth I and Tudor Constructions of Motherhood', in *The Mysteries of Elizabeth I: Selections from English Literary Renaissance*, ed. Kirby Farrell and Kathleen M. Swaim (Amherst, MA, 2003), pp. 134–61 (pp. 134–6).

Fisherman, whose low social status seems to give them license to speak freely with their 'habits base but hearts as true as steel', as the second verse of the song says.[84] Their dialogue contrasts the simple and virtuous country life with the corruption and rivalry in courts and cities, while the song further explores the theme of appearance versus reality that accompanied the device of the Pilgrim and the Wild Man. The first verse demonstrates how seemingly positive attributes of beauty and wit can mask hidden dangers:

> The fish that seeks for food in silver stream
> is unawares beguiled with the hook,
> And tender hearts when least of love they dream,
> do swallow beauty's bait, a lovely look.
> The fish that shuns to bite, in net doth hit,
> The heart that 'scapes the eye is caught by wit.

The second verse then turns the problem on its head and suggests that true virtues can also be found in unexpected places:

> rich pearls are found in hard and homely shells
> Our habits base, but hearts as true as steel.

Read in the light of Lord Montague's situation, it suggests that loyalty can be found in the unlikely place of her Catholic subjects. Moreover Lord Montague, like other Catholic noblemen, had tended to withdraw from court life and focus on his reputation in his locality. Lord Montague can therefore equate himself with the Fisherman's rural virtues and separation from the corruptions of court politics.

The memorable and prominently positioned lines which end the final two verses contain the clearest expression of Lord Montague's complaint. The third verse ends with the line 'We court them thus, Love me and I'll love thee', summing up Lord Montague's central message on the theme of exchanging service and favours between monarch and noblemen: show love to those who love you.[85] In contrast to the phoenix-like, undying love of the second song, Montague now suggests that love can only be offered if it is returned. The most daringly critical line, however, is the final one and the most prominent in performance: 'We count them lumps that will not bite at love.'[86] It implies Elizabeth is foolish if she will not respond to the love/service that Lord Montague has offered.

Such covert messages and agendas were not subversive subtexts that Elizabeth was expected not to notice. Some interpretations of symbolic threats, or expressions of greater loyalty to Catholicism than to the Queen, forget that Elizabeth was well known for her intelligence. Noblemen can hardly have expected her to miss such treasonous hidden messages.[87] More often, the ambiguity between the joyful,

---

[84] *Speeches ... at Cowdray*, p. 12.

[85] Breight, 'Caressing the Great', pp. 152, 156.

[86] *Speeches ... at Cowdray*, pp. 11–12.

[87] Breight, 'Caressing the Great', pp. 147–66. Elizabeth Heale takes the view that Elizabeth was intended to interpret Montague's complaint: 'Contesting Terms', pp. 189, 198, 465. Writing to his son Robert, after Elizabeth had deciphered a

praising surface and the complaints or political manœuvring beneath was not meant to hide subversive messages, but rather to soften criticisms and requests by simultaneously asserting the nobleman's love and respect for his monarch. By couching complaints and petitions artistically in both poetry and music and serving them with a good dose of flattery and praise, a nobleman could assert his views and plead his petitions in an acceptable form while showing respect for Elizabeth's authority and fulfilling his duty to entertain.

Whether the subtle significance in any of these noble entertainments would have been fully grasped in the immediacy of the performance is doubtful, but the circulation of the materials from these progress entertainments, both informally in manuscript and more officially in published accounts, allowed careful reading, re-reading, reflection, and discussion in the following weeks and months.[88] The anonymous author of the published account of the 1575 Woodstock entertainment specifically directed the reader to examine the text in this way:

> if you mark the words with this present world, or were acquainted with the state of the devices, you should find no less hidden than uttered, and no less uttered than should deserve a double reading over.[89]

While in the printed accounts the songs circulated only as lyrics, those present could compare their detailed readings with their impressions and memories of the performance. Those not present could still discern and draw conclusions from the musical genres and styles employed, just as the musicologist can today. The necessary ambiguity created an intellectual game of decoding political messages but increased the likelihood of messages being either missed or misinterpreted. There was no guarantee that the Queen or fellow noblemen would perceive all the levels of meaning or that they would not interpret the entertainment differently from the nobleman's original intentions. Yet noblemen had to balance the importance of getting their message across with the courtly etiquette required to respectfully petition or even criticise the Queen.

PERFORMERS' PETITIONS

It was not just the nobility and courtiers who wished to petition the Queen. For those who were involved in the devising, composing, and writing of these entertainments there was the opportunity to include personal petitions alongside those themes and messages commissioned by the host. The problem of identifying writers and performers for these entertainments makes interpreting the agendas of the artists – especially musicians – challenging. Nevertheless there are examples of

---

private, allegorical letter concerning his health, William Cecil expressed his belief that 'never a lady beside her, nor a decipherer in the court, would have dissolved the figure to have found the sense as her Majesty hath done.' Thomas Wright (ed.), *Queen Elizabeth and her Times: A Series of Original Letters*, 2 vols. (London, 1838), vol. 2, p. 428.

[88] For an analysis of how the Harefield entertainment circulated in print and manuscript following the performance, see Heaton, 'Elizabethan Entertainments'.

[89] *Queen's Majesty's Entertainment at Woodstock*, sig. B1r.

private requests for patronage or recognition, as well as more general petitions for greater support of the musician's art and profession.

Taking part in a progress gave musicians the opportunity to showcase their talents, not only to the Queen, but also to the host of accompanying noblemen, courtiers, and foreign ambassadors who were all potential sources of employment and rewards. Musicians could expect tips from the spectators for their performances during these occasions. At court, noblemen such as the Earls of Leicester and Essex gave money to the musicians of the royal household during the New Year festivities, while the feeble rewards given by the Duke of Nevers in April 1602 became the subject of court gossip in one of John Chamberlain's letters to Dudley Carleton.[90] For musicians working outside the court, the progresses were an opportunity to display their skills in the hope of gaining a position in the royal household.

Many court musicians were awarded substantial privileges in kind and they also exchanged New Year gifts with the Queen, receiving gilt plate in return.[91] The most common privileges were grants of leases, such as that given to the flautist Gommar van Oostrewijk in January 1590 for 'lands and tenements in Banbury, Barrower, Bagsholt and others in the counties of Worcester, Lincoln and others for 21 years'.[92] Another common privilege was a license for importing or exporting goods: Nicholas Lanier (flute- and cornett-player) received a license to import fifteen tons of French wine duty free in March 1562.[93] Musicians may have used their own contacts abroad or sold on the license to merchants.[94] Some were granted monopolies on particular areas of trade, as with that for printed music and lined music paper given to Byrd and Tallis (p. 3).[95] Other grants included money – £200 was given to violinist Joseph Lupo in January 1601 for his 'long and faithful service' – or offices – Ferdinando Heybourne was given the office of Constable of the castle of Chester in January 1589.[96] Musicians could even enjoy sufficient favour to make petitions on behalf of others: a lease was granted to William Fisher in July 1577 'in consideration of the service of Alfonso Ferrabosco', and another to Cissell Gorges in May 1590 'at the humble suit of Ambrose Lupo' (a long-serving violinist).[97]

---

[90] Peter Holman, *Four and Twenty Fiddlers: The Violin at the English Court, 1540–1690*, Oxford Monographs on Music (Oxford, 1993), p. 48; Paul E. J. Hammer, *The Polarisation of Elizabethan Politics: The Political Career of Robert Devereux, 2nd Earl of Essex, 1585–1597*, Cambridge Studies in Early Modern British History (Cambridge, 1999), p. 318 n. 10; Simon Adams (ed.), *Household Accounts and Disbursement Books of Robert Dudley, Earl of Leicester, 1558–1561, 1584–1586*, Camden Fifth Series 6 (Cambridge, 1995), p. 150 (for 1560), p. 163 (for 1561); John Chamberlain, 'John Chamberlain to Dudley Carleton: 26 April 1602', GB-Lna: SP12/283a, Secretaries of State: State Papers Domestic, Elizabeth I, fols. 177r–179r (fol. 177v).

[91] Holman, *Four and Twenty Fiddlers*, pp. 47–51.

[92] *RECM*, vol. 6, p. 52.

[93] Ibid., p. 10.

[94] Holman, *Four and Twenty Fiddlers*, p. 48.

[95] *RECM*, vol. 8, p. 32.

[96] Ibid., vol. 6, pp. 70, 51.

[97] Holman, *Four and Twenty Fiddlers*, p. 48; *RECM*, vol. 6, pp. 34, 53.

It was these potential rewards (along with the status of the position and gaining the courtesy title 'gentleman') that made the post of court musician so attractive.

During the progresses, most musicians would require the support of the author to make any petition. A few were skilled at both musical and literary composition: Richard Edwards, Master of the Chapel Royal Children, was a writer of court plays, and a composer of consort songs. A subsequent Master of the Chapel Royal Children, William Hunnis, was both a composer of consort songs and an author of devices for the Kenilworth progress, while Thomas Campion also combined poetry and song-writing.[98] More usually, however, poets would collaborate with the musicians, writing both the surrounding dialogue and the lyrics for the composers to set. In such a collaborative production, poets and musicians may have exchanged favours and supported their fellow artists.

One of the entertainments at Sir Julius Caesar's house at Mitcham in 1598 took the form of a debate between a Poet, a Painter, and later a Musician, concerning which was the greater art.[99] While the overall purpose of the show was to flatter Elizabeth, one small scene comically represents the poverty of artists, especially the Musician. The Musician is mocked by the Poet and Painter for his pretensions to high status while living in poverty:

> MUSICIAN: What do you here, you are excluded from the number of arts. I am one of the seven liberal sciences.
>
> POET: Yea; and the liberal'st of them all seven; for thou playest much, and gettest little.
>
> MUSICIAN: I should; for what is ... for melancholy more sovereign?
>
> POET: A sovereign
>
> MUSICIAN: Who breedeth more pleasure then a good musician?
>
> PAINTER: A good cook.
>
> MUSICIAN: Angels frequent musicians.
>
> POET: Look in thy purse and thou wilt prove thy self a liar.[100]

While the Musician draws on popular defences to defend his worth (evoking the angelic music of heaven and music-making as a cure for melancholy), the Poet and Painter employ wordplay to suggest the Musician's poverty. The sovereign and the angel were types of coin (the former with the royal coat of arms and portrait of the monarch, and the latter having a picture of the archangel St Michael killing a dragon), and the Musician is mocked for having neither. Although the scene can be read as a writer's joke at the expense of his fellow musicians, music and poetry are closely connected throughout the device; it is the Poet who performs a 'song' (it is unclear whether it was recited or sung), while in the conclusion the Poet

---

[98] Michael Smith, 'Edwards, Richard', *NG2*.

[99] The identity of the author is unfortunately unclear, though Leslie Hotson suggests John Lyly on the basis of stylistic comparison. Leslie Hotson (ed.), *Queen Elizabeth's Entertainment at Mitcham: Poet, Painter, and Musician* (New Haven, CT, 1953), p. 5.

[100] Ibid., p. 26.

promises to keep his verses for 'seamsters to sing'.[101] Instead, such comic episodes simultaneously entertained and evoked sympathy as subtle nudges to courtly spectators and potential patrons to be generous in their rewards.

Later the Musician's defence of his art was supported by the 'Ditty of the Greek Song', which asserts the music's status and antiquity. The song told how Cupid was stung by a bee and received little sympathy from Venus, who compared the sting to being hit by one of Cupid's darts. Sung in Greek, it reflected the Humanistic credentials of the patron, Sir Julius Caesar, who was one of the Queen's judges. It would also flatter Elizabeth, who was herself well educated with knowledge of Greek. From the musician's point of view, however, the Greek song evoked the ancient origins of the art. Classical Greece was regarded as the golden age of musical excellence, for it was in Greek mythology that the stories of music's power to tame wild beasts and move stones to build cities were told.[102] Perhaps the composer matched the Humanistic impulse of the poet by imitating the latest attempts to recreate the effectiveness of Greek music in Florentine monody? Putting these two entertainments together, they could be said to form an argument that musicians should be given patronage by the nobility so that the high status of their art should not be mismatched with the poverty of their living.

While the Mitcham device promotes the art of music and the status of musicians in general terms, John Dowland's appearance in the entertainments provided by Giles Brydges, Lord Chandos, at Sudeley in 1592 was a personal petition for a court appointment. The Shepherds' Entertainment included the character 'Do.' who sang the song 'Herbs, Words, and Stones', while Dowland probably also set 'My Heart and Tongue were Twins' for the same visit (printed in *A Pilgrim's Solace*, 1612).[103] At the time of this progress Dowland had been seeking employment at Elizabeth's court, and both the songs and their surrounding dialogue can be read as petitions for patronage. The Shepherds' Entertainment was never performed, due to bad weather, but support for Dowland's petition was intended to appear not only in the music and his lines, but also in the speech of other characters. Dowland's spoken lines would have cast him in the persona of the melancholy and ill-rewarded musician: 'I have played so long with my fingers that I have beaten out of play all my good fortunes.'[104] This line must have been composed by the writer rather than

---

[101] Ibid., pp. 24–5, 27.

[102] *The Praise of Music* begins by defining music's birth and antiquity, and cites many stories of music's powers from classical times: *The Praise of Music wherein Besides the Antiquity, Dignity, Delectation, and Use Thereof in Civil Matters, is also Declared the Sober and Lawful Use of the Same in the Congregation and Church of God* (Oxford, 1586), pp. 1–65.

[103] John Dowland, *A Pilgrim's Solace wherein is Contained Musical Harmony of 3. 4. and 5. Parts* (London, 1612), sigs. K2v–L1r. In *England's Helicon* (1600) the song is decribed as 'another song before her Majesty at Oxford', sig. R3r. It was perhaps revived for the Queen's visit to Oxford a fortnight later, after weather had prevented the Sudeley performance. Goldring *et al.* (eds.), *John Nichols's The Progresses*, vol. 3, p. 612 n. 56, and p. 614.

[104] Joseph Barnes (ed.), *Speeches Delivered to her Majesty this Last Progress at the Right Honourable the Lady Russels, at Bisham, the Right Honourable the Lord*

improvised by Dowland during the performance, as it was included in the 'loose papers' which Joseph Barnes collected.[105]

The song Dowland was to sing, 'Herbs, Words, and Stones', lamented a lady who would not be moved by tokens of love as she found all of them potentially deceitful: flowers hide weeds, words tell lies, and gemstones can be fake. This song is appropriate to its dramatic context where the shepherds have been discussing the subject of love; however, the theme of a lady who will not be moved by the petitions of a man was also appropriate to Dowland's continued failure to achieve a position at the English court.[106] The line spoken by Melibaeus after the song also seems to support Dowland's petition: 'Well song and well played, seldom so well among shepherds.'[107] Shepherds were often presented as the opposite to the court and courtiers; therefore Melibaeus's line may have been intended to imply that it was unusual for a musician outside the court to play so well, as one would expect such a talent to be employed there. Dowland's petition required close collaboration with the unknown author, suggesting not only cooperation between writer and composer, but also sympathy and a willingness to help other artists seeking employment.

Dowland's other song for this progress, 'My Heart and Tongue were Twins', shares the theme of unrequited love and reinforces his plea.[108] Apollo is lamenting the loss of Daphne, who was turned into a tree to save her from Apollo's lust, supposedly by the presence of Elizabeth, Queen of Chastity. Dowland's setting is a galliard, though with the lamenting tone set by a Phrygian cadence at the end of the opening line (Example 5.5). The song's theme is encapsulated in the conclusion:

> Engrave upon this tree, Daphne's perfection,
> That neither men nor gods can force affection.[109]

The conclusion (Example 5.6) is marked out by a more declamatory melodic style at its opening, followed by an expansive final line. This repeats the words 'nor gods' while rising to the highest pitch of the piece, over a more contrapuntal and slightly imitative lute accompaniment. Some lines, however, fit the dramatic situation less well: what is meant by the lines describing gods and kings whose

---

Chandos at Sudley, at the Right Honourable the Lord Norris, at Ricote (Oxford, 1592), sig. B4r.

[105] Ibid., sig. A1v.

[106] Poulton also suggests that this song was a petition, but while the dramatic excuse for the song is weak, I do not agree that it was disconnected from the argument of the entertainment: Diana Poulton, *John Dowland*, rev. edn (London, 1982), p. 30.

[107] Barnes (ed.), *Speechs Delivered*, sig. B4r.

[108] Dowland, *A Pilgrim's Solace*, sigs. K2v–L1r. For a full edition see: John Dowland, *A Pilgrimes Solace (1612)*, ed. Edmund Fellowes and Thurston Dart, The English Lute Songs 4 (London, 1969), pp. 54–5. At Sudeley it was performed by 'one that sung', and 'one that played', but it is also arranged as a four-part ayre in *A Pilgrim's Solace* (Barnes (ed.), *Speeches Delivered*, sig. B2r).

[109] Barnes (ed.), *Speeches Delivered*, sig. B2r. In Dowland, *A Pilgrim's Solace*, the first line of the conclusion is 'Then this be sure, since it is true perfection' (sigs. K2v–L1r).

Ex. 5.5 John Dowland, 'My Heart and Tongue were Twins',
A Pilgrim's Solace (London, 1612), sigs. K2v–L1r, bars 1–5

Ex. 5.6 John Dowland, 'My Heart and Tongue were Twins', bars 18–27
(with lyrics from the progress)

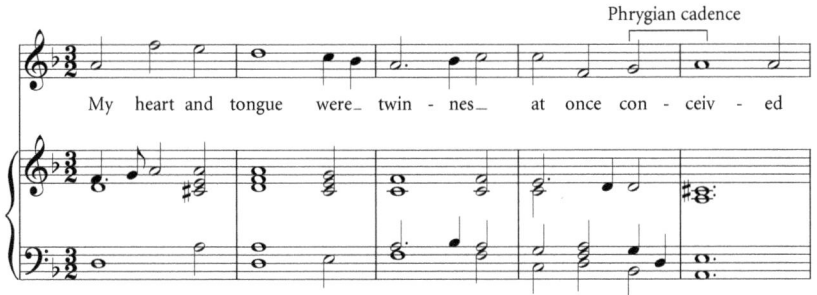

'words are deeds, but deeds nor words regarded?' Apollo's words and deeds were regarded because Elizabeth intervened to save Daphne from them. Nor does there seem any reason for Elizabeth's words or deeds to be described as not regarded, given that both Daphne and Apollo acknowledge her role in the events. This line could be explained as referring to the singer playing the role of Apollo. Dowland's failure to obtain a court position had left him feeling that his words (singing) and deeds (lute playing) were not regarded.[110] Following this alternative layer of interpretation, 'my love with pain, my pain with loss rewarded' can refer not only to Apollo's love for Daphne, but to Dowland's desire to serve his monarch, also unregarded and unrewarded.

Dowland's petitions to the Queen were subtle – they were not the only, nor even the main message of the entertainments or the songs – but they were there to be interpreted, alongside the typical royal imagery of love versus chastity. The deviser's primary task in producing an entertainment for a progress was always to follow the wishes of his employer. Yet in devices that were already mixing the multiple voices of host and monarch, flattery and petitions, there was sometimes space to add a brief appeal from the artists too.

MORAL ADVICE AND POLITICAL COUNSEL

So far the focus has been on the noblemen who played host to the Queen, but Elizabeth also made royal entries into towns on eighty-three occasions during her summer progresses.[111] Her welcome at the town gates would be followed by a procession of pageants stationed at key points along Elizabeth's route through the city. The larger towns such as Bristol and Norwich entertained the Queen for several days, producing daily entertainments similar to those seen on noblemen's estates. Like the noblemen, civic authorities took the opportunity to present their concerns and political views to the Queen.[112] Towns, however, were often more blunt in offering their advice through song.

Political counsel had been offered to Elizabeth on public occasions since the pageantry surrounding her coronation. The citizens of London (or more accurately the civic leaders who organised the shows) believed that Elizabeth needed advice and that they had 'the right, even the duty to offer it'.[113] This belief continued through at least the first two decades of her reign in the advice offered to her at Bristol (1574) and Norwich (1578). Song offered a means of communicating advice in a concise and pleasurable format. As with the courtly choirboy plays of the period, this counsel was often moral as well as political. Elizabeth seems to have graciously accepted the advice offered to her during such entertainments, presenting herself as the traditional wise prince, willing to listen courteously to good counsel.

---

[110] A letter from Dowland to Robert Cecil indicates that this was certainly the case by 1595: Poulton, *Dowland*, pp. 30, 37–8.

[111] Cole, *Portable Queen*, p. 32.

[112] Ibid., pp. 97–134; McGee, 'Mysteries, Musters, and Masque'.

[113] Mary Thomas Crane, '"Video et Taceo": Elizabeth I and the Rhetoric of Counsel', *Studies in English Literature, 1500–1900* 28 (1988), 1–15 (pp. 5–6).

The advice on governance offered to Elizabeth at Bristol (14–21 August 1574) combined general issues of counsel, flattery, and the recognition of virtue, with topical issues related to negotiations surrounding the Treaty of Bristol that was to be signed on 28 August. This treaty settled diplomatic and trade disputes between England and Spain that had been sparked by Elizabeth's confiscation of a ship containing treasure belonging to the Duke of Alva in 1569.[114] The soldier and poet Thomas Churchyard was sent to prepare the pageants and he created a display of English strength that told both her subjects and the foreign ambassadors that Elizabeth was not negotiating out of weakness.[115] War and peace became major themes of the visit, which included both Elizabeth's entry and a three-day mock siege. While this show of strength suited Elizabeth's political needs, Bristol's military readiness was also a source of civic pride. The town had responded enthusiastically to musters in the preceding years and the royal visit was an opportunity to parade the well-trained, well-armed soldiers and sailors the town could provide for the defence of the realm.[116] Bristol's prosperity, however, depended on trade and since 1569 imports and exports between England and the Spanish-ruled Netherlands had been suspended in retaliation for Elizabeth's seizing of the Duke of Alba's gold.[117] Amiable foreign relationships were essential to allow Bristol's merchants to trade successfully, so Churchyard also designed the shows to convey the town's desire for peace, despite the martial tone.[118] A personification of the city tells Elizabeth that, though they have soldiers and courage to fight:

> our joy, be most in peace,
> and peace we do maintain.
> Where on to prince and realm throughout,
> doth rise great wealth and gain.[119]

Later the mock siege of the fort of Peace by the forces of Wars came down firmly in favour of diplomacy as the battle ended with a parley. The forces of Peace declared their best defences not to be bulwarks and curtain walls, but 'the courage of good people, and the force of a mighty prince'.[120]

Two songs were written for this visit. Churchyard wrote the lyrics to 'O Happy Hour All Bliss', which was a 'Hymn … sung by a very fine boy' performed when Elizabeth went to hear a sermon on Sunday.[121] The authorship of a second song,

---

[114] Susan Doran, *Elizabeth I and Foreign Policy, 1558–1603*, Lancaster Pamphlets 20 (London, 2000), pp. 27–33.

[115] Cole, *Portable Queen*, p. 158.

[116] McGee, 'Mysteries, Musters, and Masque', p. 116.

[117] Doran, *Elizabeth I and Foreign Policy*, p. 27; Paul E. J. Hammer, *Elizabeth's Wars: War, Government and Society in Tudor England, 1544–1604* (Basingstoke, 2003), pp. 82–5.

[118] Cole, *Portable Queen*, p. 110; McGee, 'Mysteries, Musters, and Masque', p. 117.

[119] Thomas Churchyard, *The First Part of Churchyard's Chips Containing Twelve Several Labours* (London, 1575), fol. 118r–v.

[120] Ibid., fol. 119v.

[121] Ibid., fols. 103v–104r.

'Mistrust Not Truth', is less clear. Churchyard did not include it in his account of the progress in *Churchyard's Chips* (1575), and it is attributed to 'D. S.' when it appears in the *Paradise of Dainty Devices* (1576).[122] Only later did Churchyard claim authorship of these lyrics in his *Churchyard's Chance* (1580).[123] Its composer, however, was most likely Nicholas Strogers, whose setting survives in the Dow Partbooks which were copied c. 1581–8.[124] The topical nature of the words and their direct message to Elizabeth make it unlikely that a composer would choose to set these words except for the original occasion. This song was probably the 'solemn song by Orphans' sung outside the free school of St Bartholomew during Elizabeth's initial entry into Bristol.[125] Churchyard's omission of both the song and any of the speeches performed at the school might be explained by his falling out with the schoolmaster, whom he claims had obstructed the performances of some of his other devices.[126]

Rather than reflecting the military tone of the entertainments, the two songs emphasise the current threats to England's stability and the need for peace. They offer advice on how the spectators must act to be 'good people' and how Elizabeth should become the 'mighty prince' referred to at the close of the mock siege. The songs address not only peace with foreign nations, but also the problem of traitorous hearts in England.[127] The five years preceding this progress had seen the arrival of Mary Queen of Scots in England in 1568, Elizabeth's excommunication in 1570, and a series of rebellions and plots against Elizabeth: the rising of the Northern Earls in 1569, the Ridolfi plot in 1570–1, and the execution of the Duke of Norfolk for treason in 1572. The descriptive title given by Churchyard to 'Mistrust Not Truth' in *Churchyard Chance* (1580) seems to sum up the mood of both songs: 'written of the Queen, when her highness was in trouble.'

---

[122] D. S., 'A Worthy Ditty, Song before the Queen's Majesty at Bristol', in Richard Edwards (ed.), *The Paradise of Dainty Devices Containing Sundry Pithy Precepts, Learned Counsels and Excellent Inventions* (London, 1576), p. 23. The list of contributors in later editions reveals this to be D. Sand, but his identity is unknown: *The Paradise of Dainty Devices (1576–1606)*, ed. Hyder Edward Rollins (Cambridge, MA, 1927), p. lxi.

[123] Thomas Churchyard, *A Pleasant Labyrinth Called Churchyard's Chance Framed on Fancies, Uttered with Verses, and Writ to Give Solace to Every Well Disposed Mind* (London, 1580), fols. 27v–28r.

[124] GB-Och: Music MSS 984–8 [Dow Partbooks], no. 121 (123 in the modern numbering). Full modern edition in Brett (ed.), *Consort Songs*, p. 38.

[125] 'Adams' Chronicle of Bristol': BRO 13748(4), in Mark C. Pilkinton (ed.), *REED: Bristol* (Toronto, 1997), p. 91. Gabriel Heaton reached similar conclusions in Goldring et al. (eds.), *John Nichols's The Progresses*, vol. 2, p. 220, though he seems unaware of Churchyard's later claiming of the poem as his own.

[126] Churchyard, *Churchyard's Chips*, fol. 110v; Goldring et al. (eds.), *John Nichols's The Progresses*, vol. 2, p. 220. Alternatively this might also explain his later potential plagiarism, depending on how one interprets the song's conflicting attributions.

[127] Churchyard, *Churchyard's Chance*, fols. 27v–28r.

In keeping with the city's desire for peace, the hymn warned against disloyal thoughts and rebellious actions using conventional imagery of dissent and evil intent:

> Away you bosom snakes,
> that sows dissension here:
> Go make your nests, where serpents breed,
> this soil and coast is clear.
> Enchant no man with charms
> ...
> She hateth Hydra's heads,
> and loves the harmless mind.[128]

Taking its place in a church service, the hymn uses poulter's measure (alternating couplets of twelve and fourteen lines). While not the most common metre for psalms and hymns, it was nevertheless used in the 1562 *Whole Book of Psalms* (as in Psalm 67, for example).[129] The short lines provide a strong metre and give its phrases impact. Snakes and serpents evoke man's Fall from the Garden of Eden due to the temptations of a snake, as well as being a symbol of the self-serving flattery among courtiers. In Richard Edwards's *Damon and Pithias* the flattering counsellor Carisophus was called a 'caterpillar', while the more virtuous Eubulus calls flattery 'the serpent that eats men alive'.[130] 'Hydra's heads' refers to the Greek mythological beast with poisonous breath and nine heads; if one of its heads was cut off, two grew back in its place. The Elizabethan aristocracy tended to portray the mass of ordinary subjects as a many-headed monster always in danger of rising up in rebellion (the 'She' who hates them is Elizabeth).[131] The imagery was therefore flexible enough to admonish courtly and lower-class troublemakers alike. The hymn asserts that Elizabeth will survive all such threats through her own virtue and by the grace of God. In short, it was propaganda for a church service.

More obviously advisory was the song 'Mistrust Not Truth', which offered Elizabeth advice on how to achieve a peaceful state.[132] The verses are an acrostic on 'Mi Ladi Elisabeths Grac' [My Lady Elizabeth's Grace], indicating to whom the advice is aimed. The counsel given in the song claimed it would enable Elizabeth to 'stablish long your state/ Continually with perfect peace, in spite of puffing hate'. This hate might be read as referring to either the disloyalty of Englishmen

---

[128] Churchyard, *Churchyard's Chips*, fols. 103v–104r.

[129] Thomas Sternhold et al., *The Whole Book of Psalms Collected into English Metre* (London, 1562), p. 153.

[130] Richard Edwards, *The Excellent Comedy of Two the Most Faithfullest Friends, Damon and Pithias* (London, 1571), sigs. C3r, H3v; Ros King (ed.), *The Works of Richard Edwards: Politics, Poetry, and Performances in Sixteenth-Century England*, Revels Plays Companion Library (Manchester, 2001), pp. 152, 183 [scene 11, line 76; scene 16, line 11].

[131] Christopher Hill, 'The Many-Headed Monster in Late Tudor and Early Stuart England', in *From the Renaissance to the Counter-Reformation: Essays in Honour of Garrett Mattingly*, ed. Charles Howard Carter (London, 1966), pp. 296–324.

[132] Edwards (ed.), *Paradise of Dainty Devices* (1576), p. 23.

or England's difficult relationship with Spain. Other verses, however, seem to refer to Elizabeth's choice of servants and advisors. Elaborating on the hymn's contrast between 'Hydra's heads' and the 'harmless mind', this second song advises Elizabeth to judge each man carefully, avoiding those who merely flatter and identifying the truly loyal hearts who can provide the steadfast ground on which to build her state:

> Avoid from you those hateful heads, that helps to heap mishap,
> Be slow to hear the flatterer's voice, which creepeth in your lap.
> …
> Give faith to those that fear for love, and not that love for fear,
> Regard not them that force compels, to please you everywhere.

The continued unease caused by the rebellions and plots of 1569–72 is evident in the lyrics, which ask:

> How can your seat be settled fast, or stand on steadfast ground,
> So propped up with hollow hearts, whose surety is unfound?

The execution just two years earlier of Thomas Howard, Duke of Norfolk, who had previously been a member of the Privy Council, demonstrated the need to renew such advice. There is a hint of criticism in the suggestion that Elizabeth needs to be instructed in how and how not to govern. The advice to 'Trust not too much unto yourself, for feeble are your stays' reflects typical concerns about the weakness of female rulers and their need to rely on good counsellors.[133] Other lines offer advice on how to encourage loyalty in her subjects, advising her to 'Enforce no fear' and to recognise the efforts of those who express their love for their monarch: 'Embrace their love that wills you good, and sport not at their praise.' This last line in particular seems to ask Elizabeth to appreciate and reward the city of Bristol's efforts in her honour.

Strogers's setting (Example 5.7) begins with a low, narrow-ranged melody (spanning a fourth, c' to f'). This melody is passed imitatively between the voice and treble viol (as is typical of consort songs), and is also repeated for the second line of text. The combination of learned counterpoint, low register, and Dorian mode (the 'grave and staid part of music' according to *The Praise of Music*, 1586)[134] sets a serious and weighty tone.

The third line (Example 5.8) coincides with a distinct change in register to a higher and wider range (d' to c''). There is also a harmonic shift to *cantus durus* (with B natural rather than B flat), a sharpwards shift emphasised by the addition of F sharps and G sharps. The effect is that, as the text moves from the subject of vices to virtues and images of light, the melody reaches higher and the harmony becomes correspondingly sharper and brighter. While the effect is not recreated in every verse, in the final one too this change in register coincides with the hope that

---

[133] John Aylmer, for example, defended Elizabeth's female rule on the grounds that she had chosen wise and experienced counsellors to guide her. John Aylmer, *An Harborowe for Faithful and True Subjects Against the Late Blown Blast, Concerning the Government of Women* (London, 1559), sig. O2r.

[134] *Praise of Music*, p. 55.

Ex. 5.7 Opening of Nicholas Strogers, 'Mistrust Not Truth',
GB-Och: Music MSS 984–8 [Dow Partbooks], no. 121

Ex. 5.8 Nicholas Strogers, 'Mistrust Not Truth', bars 11–14

Elizabeth can maintain peace in her kingdom, despite 'puffing hate'.[135] The syllabic word-setting and the repetition of words and music in the final line are typical of the genre, but nevertheless an aid to communicating the advice clearly even though the vocal part was not the highest in the ensemble.

During Elizabeth's visit to Norwich in 1578, the civic authorities dared to comment on the thorny and personal issue of the Queen's marriage. Rather than addressing a concern for the town's prosperity, here the Norwich élite took the opportunity to present their views on a matter of current political debate. Thomas Churchyard was again the author of *The Show of Dame Chastity*, which was performed on the fourth day of Elizabeth's stay. The show told how Cupid, fleeing from his mother Venus's argument with a Philosopher, is caught by Dame Chastity and her handmaids Modesty, Temperance, Good Exercise, and Shamefastness. They strip Cupid of his carriage, cloak, and bow, and present the bow to Elizabeth as one chaste and wise enough to yield it.[136] Finally a song by Dame Chastity's attendants (probably Churchyard's boy actors)[137] summed up the moral and political content of the show.

The Show of Dame Chastity has been described as 'delicately ambiguous' in presenting Elizabeth with Cupid's arrows, which she might use either to choose her own suitable (Protestant) husband or to preserve her chastity like the archer Diana.[138] The song, however, unequivocally favours chastity. It was intended to persuade Elizabeth against proceeding with marriage negotiations with the Duke of Anjou and to convince the French ambassadors that Elizabeth would not marry.[139] Like Virtue's song from the play *Liberality and Prodigality* (p. 97), Churchyard's lyrics work by contrasting good and bad morals, in this case the virtues and benefits of chastity with the consequences of the vice of lewd life. Using poulter's measure like the 1574 hymn from Bristol, the short lines lend particular emphasis to the repeated keywords, 'chaste' and 'lewd'. It begins:

> Chaste life lives long and looks
> on world and wicked ways,
> Chaste life for loss of pleasures short,
> doth win immortal praise.
> Chaste life hath merry moods,
> and soundly taketh test,
> Chaste life is pure as babe new born,
> that hugs in mother's breast.
>
> Lewd life cuts off his days,
> and soon runs out his date,
> Confounds good wits, breeds naughty blood,
> and weakens man's estate.

---

[135] Edwards (ed.), *Paradise of Dainty Devices* (1576), p. 23.

[136] An account of the show is given in Churchyard, *A Discourse*, sigs. C4v–E1v.

[137] Churchyard, *A Discourse*, sig. C4v.

[138] King, 'Queen Elizabeth I', pp. 47–8.

[139] Doran, 'Juno versus Diana', p. 272.

> Lewd life the Lord doth loathe,
> the law and land mislikes,
> The wise will shun, fond fools do seek,
> and God sore plagues and strikes.[140]

Churchyard describes how the 'common people' flocked to see the entertainment, creating 'as great a train and press about the show, as came with the Court'.[141] For many of these people the song would simply be an edifying moral song; however, clues to its topical meaning would have been discerned by the politically knowledgeable listener. The opening suggestion that chastity brings 'long life' is not the most obvious benefit of this virtue, though it was a common attribute to wish on a monarch. More obvious is the description of 'Chaste life' sitting 'in regal throne' in verse three. Furthermore, many of the metaphors describing chaste life were those commonly applied to Elizabeth. The fourth verse begins:

> Chaste life a precious pearl,
> doth shine as bright as sun

Elizabeth had already been praised as the sun earlier in the progress (in 'The Dew of Heaven', pp. 185–6) and a 1563 broadside had hailed the Queen as 'the pearl/ whom God and man doth love' and 'on earth/ the only star of light'.[142]

The songs performed at Bristol and Norwich illustrate the acceptability of offering direct advice to Elizabeth, even with a hint of criticism. These songs were suitable for public performances because the moral language frequently encapsulated lessons in virtue for the crowds, as well as political comments for the Queen and court. There is over a decade's gap between those civic progresses for which detailed accounts survive (in the 1570s) and those for noblemen's entertainments (mostly from the early 1590s) and doubtless this partly accounts for their different approaches to political song. Nevertheless, this starkly moral and advisory stance was not used by contemporary noble entertainments, such as Leicester's Kenilworth extravaganza or those at Woodstock in 1575, while the contrasting virtues of the suitors in Sidney's *Lady of May* (Wanstead, 1578) were left to Elizabeth's judgement. However, songs of moral advice were still being employed in the device of the fishermen at Cowdray in 1591). Just as the fishermen's device relies on rustic characters, so too the towns utilised their similar outsider status in relation to the social and political élite to analyse the vices of the court. Furthermore, as the morality songs at both towns were sung by children, their connotations of innocence perhaps also granted them a license to speak candidly, comparable again to plain-spoken fishermen. 'Children and fools speak truth' was a popular proverb of the day.[143] This allowed civic leaders to be blunter in their political comment, while aiming to avoid controversy by couching it as goodhearted moral counsel.

---

[140] Churchyard, *A Discourse*, sigs. E1v–E2r.

[141] Ibid., sig. C4v.

[142] *Lo Here the Pearl, whom God and Man Doth Love* (London, 1563).

[143] Michael Shapiro, *Children of the Revels: The Boy Companies of Shakespeare's Time and their Plays* (New York, 1977), pp. 40–1.

STAGING HARMONY

SPECTATING commoners have appeared in passing throughout this chapter as the ordinary people to be impressed with courtly magnificence and royal majesty, the subjects whose popularity Elizabeth wished to court, and the townsfolk who might receive moral edification or be warned against rebellious thoughts. Now I want to focus more directly on these people and how they became objects of political persuasion. Royal entries brought the participation of ordinary people to the forefront of the occasion. While local people who were invited to perform on a nobleman's estates were not the main object of Elizabeth's visit, during the royal entries the townspeople were themselves the hosts, the subjects the Queen had come to see. The people were not mere spectators, but also actors, as their cheering and enthusiasm was a vital part of the spectacle. David Bergeron described town pageants as a 'vast celebratory theatre, constructing community even as this community responded to its creation'.[144] The community constructed was both local – communal celebration fostering a sense of civic identity and pride – and national, enacting a beautiful relationship between Queen, court, and subjects.[145] The unified participation of the crowds served the aims of the civic authorities by demonstrating their good governance and the town's loyalty, while simultaneously enhancing Elizabeth's authority and popularity.

William Leahy, however, has rightly criticised the idea that Elizabeth's entries and processions were unproblematic displays of sovereign power and national unity to suitably impressed and adoring subjects.[146] His examination of the social and cultural conditions surrounding events such as the pre-coronation procession (1559) and the Armada victory procession (1588) suggests that some of Elizabeth's subjects were at best indifferent and at worst opposed to the pageantry.[147] Moreover, although the people were styled in pageant literature as Elizabeth's loving countrymen, they were also viewed as potentially disruptive by those in power, and therefore in continual need of subjecting.[148] So when these events represent in microcosm the ideal social harmony of the kingdom, this was not just designed to flatter Elizabeth with praise for her skilful governance; rather it was intended to educate and persuade the populace. By witnessing displays of the loyalty they should feel, the people might be coaxed into acting their part as Elizabeth's faithful subjects.[149] Through playing their role in a staged entry and acting out an ideal commonwealth, the participants might be instilled with an understanding of their place in the social order along with the behaviours and attitudes expected of them.

---

[144] Bergeron, *English Civic Pageantry*, p. 4.
[145] Cole, *Portable Queen*, pp. 97–8, 107–34.
[146] William Leahy, *Elizabethan Triumphal Processions* (Aldershot, 2005).
[147] Ibid., pp. 65–81.
[148] Ibid., p. 12.
[149] Anderson, 'Music and Power', p. 102.

Music was both the medium of persuasion and the means of enacting this political harmony. Elizabethan beliefs in the connection between sonic and political harmony gave music the potential to play a significant role in this communal instruction. Bernard Garter, one of the authors of the Norwich pageants, described the intended effect of a royal entry in musical terms:

> the majesty of my Prince … gladded the hearts of the people there, as they … laboured to travail forth to view the excellency of their sovereign … Then the abundant clemency of her Highness, receiving the loyal hearts of her loving people in part, as good as their meaning deserved, so enflamed their former desires, as every spark kindled a bonfire. The nobility delighting this harmony, so endeavoured to hold in tune every string of this heavenly music, as there seemed but one heart in Queen, Council, and commonalty. The mayor, magistrates, and good citizens employed their study and substance to hold on this happy beginning.[150]

Garter constructs an image of mutual affection between people and sovereign, and employs the same metaphor of heart strings used in Alciato's *Emblematum liber* and Davies's 'To the Queen' (pp. 9 and 37–8). The city is presented as unified, but its members are not equal, and the varying status of different groups of participants is defined: 1. Queen, 2. nobility, 3. mayor, magistrates, and good citizens (people of the city with education, wealth, and status), 4. 'commonalty'.[151] These hierarchies between court and town, and the governors and the people of the city were supposedly harmoniously united during the civic visit.[152]

Unlike the images of the harmonious kingdom seen in Chapter 1, however, the equation of musical and political harmony during royal entries was not solely metaphorical. Music was essential to creating the celebratory atmosphere that stirred up the watching crowds. Songs could actively encourage participation from the spectators and therefore the literal enactment of musico-political unity. Given the Elizabethan belief that 'the changing of musical notes, hath caused an alteration of the common state' (pp. 6–7) and that music was 'a cause of breeding in us … moral virtues', the songs for these events may have been motivated by a desire to use music to instil social concord.[153]

One song written with the crowds in mind was Thomas Churchyard's 'The Dew of Heaven Drops This Day', written for Elizabeth's royal entry into Norwich in 1578. Sung by an ensemble of 'the waits and best voices in the city' (probably the city waits and the cathedral choir) on 'the great stage that was next the market place', it was designed to be performed by a relatively large number of singers and

---

[150] G[arter], *Joyful Receiving*, sig. A2r.

[151] The *OED* defines the commonalty as 'the general body of the community; the common people, as distinguished from those in authority': 'Commonalty', *OED* online.

[152] For an overview of this whole progress see: Zillah Dovey, *An Elizabethan Progress: The Queen's Journey into East Anglia, 1578* (Stroud, 1996). See also the materials edited in Galloway, *REED: Norwich*, pp. 58–9, and Goldring et al. (eds.), *John Nichols's The Progresses*, vol. 2, pp. 709–833.

[153] *Praise of Music*, p. 62 (quoting Plato).

instruments in one of the most open parts of the city, where crowds could gather.[154] It begins with a long refrain:

> The dew of heaven drops this day
> on dry and barren ground,
> Wherefore let fruitful hearts I say
> at drum and trumpet sound
> Yield that is due, show that is meet,
> to make our joy the more,
> In our good hope, and her great praise,
> we never saw before.[155]

The reference to drums and trumpets – common features in civic festivities – suggested a rousing, public performance.

Churchyard's choice of ballad metre with alternating lines of eight and six syllables also created a popular tone. He used carefully chosen images that would have been meaningful to ordinary people, but were representative of Elizabeth's authority and virtue. The 'dew of heaven' was a recurrent Old Testament metaphor (Genesis 27:28 and 39; Deuteronomy 33:13 and 28; Daniel 4:15, 21–5 and 33; Zechariah 8:12) that was likely to be known through regular church attendance. It often occurs (with the exception of the Daniel passage) in the context of blessings and images of prosperity. The reference to 'fruitful hearts' (also drawing on biblical imagery of bearing fruit, for example Matthew 13:1–23; Matthew 21:43; John 15:1–8) equated showing due reverence to one's sovereign with Christian duty. This was followed in the verses by metaphors of the sun, stars, winter, storms, and wellsprings. As in the opening image of the Queen as heavenly dew nourishing barren ground, many of these metaphors portrayed Elizabeth as giving life and bringing happiness to her people. Whereas winters and storms had filled the years since a sovereign last visited Norwich, she was a second sun, bringing light and springs of virtue where there had been only darkness. In each verse these metaphorical praises of Elizabeth were followed by instructions to her subjects: be loyal to your Queen, show reverence appropriate to her high state, and give her praise.

Contrast this with Garter's earlier song on the route, 'From Slumber Soft', which was performed in a more intimate setting underneath a processional arch using soft instruments (possibly a viol consort).[156] Its audience was not only intended to be exclusive – only those within the arch would hear – but also well educated. The lyrics told a variant of the story of Paris and the Golden Ball and relied on classical goddesses as allegories to enumerate Elizabeth's virtues. Classical gods later appeared in person for a 'princely masque' performed for the Queen and civic dignitaries in the Privy Chamber on the Thursday evening (the entry having

---

[154] Churchyard, *A Discourse*, sig. B4v.

[155] Ibid., sigs. B4v–C1r.

[156] G[arter], *Joyful Receiving*, sig. C3r–v; Anderson, 'Music and Power', pp. 98–100.

taken place on Saturday). Here they brought Elizabeth gifts, including a song from Apollo.[157]

Returning to Churchyard's song, this was also in the form of a carol with the opening refrain repeated between the three following stanzas. While a few other songs in later entertainments at noblemen's houses use repeated couplets at the ends of verses, none uses an extensive refrain like this.[158] There would seem to be little reason to have such a long refrain in a song sung by professional musicians as it added little to the meaning that was not contained in the verses already. The form of Churchyard's song is, however, very similar to a printed broadside by R. Thacker, *A Godly Ditty to be Song for the Preservation of the Queen's Most Excellent Majesty's Reign* (1586).[159] The author might be the Robert Thacker who was a Norwich wait. This song was probably written initially for a civic festivity celebrating either Elizabeth's Accession Day or the foiling of the Babington Plot in 1586, and is a highly unusual broadside because it contains printed music for the tenor part of a four-part song.[160] Like 'The Dew of Heaven', it has verses and a refrain, both with eight lines. The printed music reveals that the refrain was sung to the tune for Psalm 81 found in the *Whole Book of Psalms* (1562), while music for the verses cannot be identified and may have been newly composed.[161] Such a format would allow people to join in with the well-known psalm melody of the refrain, even if they could not read the printed music to perform the new melody of the verse. This may provide an explanation for the unusual, long refrain in Churchyard's song. Perhaps 'The Dew of Heaven' was likewise designed so that, while it was primarily performed by professional singers (the 'waits and best voices'), the crowd could join in with a well-known melody for the refrain. As the tunes in the 1562 *Whole Book of Psalms* are largely set to verses in ballad metre, the refrain could similarly have been performed to a psalm tune (the professional musicians using a harmonised setting).

Towns might also print broadside ballads to mark the Queen's visit. *The First Anointed Queen I Am, within This Town which Ever Came* was prepared for Elizabeth's visit to Rye in 1573 (Figure 5.1). The present-tense exhortations to the people to rejoice, as well as the repetitions of 'now', suggest the lyrics were to be sung during the visit. Other broadsides (not necessarily all sung) were written retrospectively

---

[157] G[arter], *Joyful Receiving*, sig. E1r–E3v. The masque was devised by a Master Goldingham, probably William Goldingham, fellow of Trinity Hall, Cambridge: Goldring et al. (eds.), *John Nichols's The Progresses*, vol. 2, p. 778.

[158] 'With Fragrant Flowers' at Elvetham, and 'Cynthia Queen of Seas and Land' at Harefield, as discussed above (pp. 149 and 158), and the closing song 'Happy Hour, Happy Day' at Ditchley: Wilson, *Entertainments*, pp. 135–6; Goldring et al. (eds.), *John Nichols's The Progresses*, vol. 3, p. 696.

[159] R. Thacker, *A Godly Ditty to be Sung for the Preservation of the Queen's Most Excellent Majesty's Reign* (London, 1586).

[160] John Milsom, 'Music, Politics and Society', in *A Companion to Tudor Britain*, ed. Robert Tittler and Norman L. Jones (Oxford, 2004), pp. 492–508 (p. 497); Katherine Butler, 'Creating Harmonious Subjects? Ballads, Psalms, and Godly Songs for Queen Elizabeth I's Accession Day', *Journal of the Royal Musical Association* (forthcoming).

[161] Butler, 'Creating Harmonious Subjects?'

> *The first anointed Queene I am:*
> *Within this town which euer came.*

⁋ A saying of each good Subiect of Rye.

Happy town, O happy Rye:
that once in thee ye Queen doth ly
Such ioy before was neuer seen
In Rye as now to lodge the Queen.
You filsher men of Rye reioyce:
To see your Queen & hear her voice.
Now clap your hands reioice & sing:
which neuer erst lodged Queen ne king.
Reioyce thou town and porte of Rye:
To see thy souerains Meiestie.
What hart hath he that dwelles in Rye:
That ioyes not now as wel as I:
Oh God that giuest life and breth:
Preserue our Queen Elizabeth.

Viuat Nestorios Elizabetha dies.

Figure 5.1   *The First Anointed Queen I Am, within this Town which Ever Came* [1573], Houghton Library, Harvard University, STC 7582.5

Ex. 5.9 Opening four lines of *A Famous Ditty of the Joyful Receiving of the Queen's Most Excellent Majesty* (London 1584), set to the tune of Wigmore's Galliard

to commemorate civic progresses and enhance the reputation of the town. The Stationers' Register records two broadside ballads that were published after the Norwich progress: *The Receiving of the Queen's Majesty into Norwich*, published by John Charlewood on 24 March 1579 and *A Pleasant Sonnet of the Joyful Receiving of ye Queen's Majesty into Norwich with the Dolour of the Same at Her Departure*, published by Richard Jones on 31 March 1579.[162] An extant broadside, *A Famous Ditty of the Joyful Receiving of the Queen's Most Excellent Majesty, by the Worthy Citizens of London* (1584) is also commemorative, beginning with a description of the procession.[163] The second half of this text may be adapted from a song that was actually sung. At the sixth verse and the line 'the people cri'd with might and main', the lyrics turn to praising Elizabeth and a refrain begins, which is repeated with variations in subsequent verses: either 'a most renowned virgin queen/ whose like on earth was never seen', or 'O Lord preserve our noble queen/ whose like on earth was never seen.'[164] The tone is similar to the prayer ending the Rye ballad: 'O God that givest life and breath: / preserve our Queen Elizabeth.'[165]

According to the broadside, *A Famous Ditty* was to be sung to the tune of 'Wigmore's Galliard'. The courtly connotations of the galliard (a courtly dance) would be particularly appropriate to a royal procession. The tune identified by Claude Simpson does not fit easily to these verses, but the ballad's mildly unusual structure, with eight syllables per line rather than alternating eight and six, does suit the melody (Example 5.9).[166]

---

[162] Edward Arber (ed.), *A Transcript of the Registers of the Company of Stationers of London, 1554–1640*, 5 vols. (London, 1875–94), vol. 2, pp. 349–50.

[163] Richard Harrington, *A Famous Ditty of the Joyful Receiving of the Queen's Most Excellent Majesty, by the Worthy Citizens of London the XII Day of November, 1584 at Her Grace's Coming to St James* (London, 1584).

[164] Harrington, *Famous Ditty*.

[165] *The First Anointed Queen I Am, within this Town which Ever Came* (n.p., 1573?).

[166] Tune adapted from Claude M. Simpson, *The British Broadside Ballad and its Music* (New Brunswick, 1966), pp. 783–5. The original tune may have been simpler than the lute arrangement in William Ballet's Lute Book suggests, and therefore an easier fit to the words. I have added upbeats at the beginning and

Many of these songs specifically encouraged participation from the crowd. Churchyard's 'The Dew of Heaven' instructs the spectators:

> Ring out the bells, pluck up your sprights,
> and dress your houses gay,
> Run in for flow'rs to straw the streets,
> and make what joy you may.[167]

Ringing bells and decorating the streets were all common ways of preparing for and marking a royal visit.[168] Similarly the verses of *The First Anointed Queen* address the people:

> You fishermen of Rye rejoice:
> To see your Queen and hear her voice.
> Now clap your hands rejoice and sing:
> Which never erst lodged Queen ne King.[169]

The ballad exhorts fishermen – ordinary townspeople – to join in, informing them of the significance of the occasion and creating a role for the crowd in the entry of the Queen by inviting them to participate by clapping and singing.

These songs also foster local pride at receiving such a visit from the Queen. The Rye ballad uses the town's name six times within the fourteen lines of the song. Similarly in Churchyard's 'The Dew of Heaven', the final verse captures both Norwich's fortune in having such a visit and the fame that should spring from their efforts in this entertainment:

> The realm throughout will ring of this,
> and sundry regions mo
> Will say, full great our fortune is,
> when our good hap they know.[170]

Such harmony, however, was always an aim rather than a reality. At the pageant following 'The Dew of Heaven' in Norwich, Elizabeth was greeted by 'marvellous sweet and good' music, but Churchyard complains that 'the rudeness of some ringer of bells did somewhat hinder the noise and harmony.'[171] The illusion of perfect harmony was shattered by either the lack of skill or the bad manners of a bell-ringer.[172] Thomas Churchyard also provides some insight into the tensions

---

on the last beats of bars 4 and 8. Rests in bars 4 and 8 both replace a descent to a crotchet *g*.

[167] Churchyard, *A Discourse*, sig. B4v.

[168] Householders had been required to repair and beautify the street-side of their houses for the Queen's visit. On the preparations see: Dovey, *An Elizabethan Progress*, pp. 63–6.

[169] *First Anointed Queen*.

[170] Churchyard, *A Discourse*, sig. C1r.

[171] Ibid.

[172] Rudeness in sixteenth-century English indicated ignorance as much as bad manners: 'Rudeness', *OED* online.

that existed beneath the celebratory surface. At one point he tells us that he was 'not well provided of things necessary for a show (by mean of some crossing causes in the city)'.[173] Churchyard is not explicit about the problem – his comment might refer to civic leaders failing to provide sufficient funds or perhaps the failure of local craftsmen to produce the required props in time – but it is suggestive of tensions between the hired-in devisers and the town. Churchyard also faced such tensions at Bristol where he reports that a local schoolmaster prevented the reciting of several speeches because he 'envied that any stranger should set forth these shows'.[174] Hints of the potential for discord can also be seen the ballads related to royal entries. The Rye ballad acknowledges the potential for people to be less than enthusiastic about the Queen's visit when it asks 'What heart hath he that dwells in Rye/ That joys not now as well as I'?[175] The *Famous Ditty* from Elizabeth's entry in London contains several verses that condemn traitors, and the people are described as crying out:

> O Lord preserve your noble grace:
> and all your secret foes deface.[176]

These anecdotes and verses remind us that the image of harmony was always an ideal, covering up existing local and political tensions while also attempting to bring such a concord into being. In the civic entertainments as in the noble ones, the immediate, joyful musical surface concealed more complex political tensions beneath.

---

[173] Churchyard, *A Discourse*, sig. C4v.
[174] Churchyard, *Churchyard's Chips*, sig. D6v.
[175] *First Anointed Queen*.
[176] Harrington, *Famous Ditty*.

Conclusion

JUST as music and harmony had shaped Elizabeth's image in life, so they did upon her death. Among the tributes from the broadside and chap-book press, Henry Chettle's eulogy reproached all earthly tributes as insufficient for the 'Muses' Patroness', while others pictured Elizabeth singing with the angels.[1] The following year Thomas Bateson's madrigal 'Oriana's Farewell' imagined an all-encompassing musical tribute: Jove playing harmonies upon the spheres, followed by a choir of nightingales, and finally the praises of nymphs and shepherds.[2] In death as in life, musical imagery encapsulated Elizabeth's intelligence, piety, popularity, and power.

Once the glowing tributes faded Elizabeth's musical image was uncertain, as it had been in life. While historian William Camden considered her skill in music 'beseeming a Prince', other seventeenth-century historians saw greater tensions between Elizabeth's image as chaste Virgin Queen and the dancing, music, and frivolous entertainments of her splendid court.[3] Edmund Bohun's *The Character of Elizabeth* (1693) was written in the early years of the reign of another ruling queen, Mary II (as co-monarch with her husband William III). Bohun presented Elizabeth as an exemplary model for Mary and her husband, though he was also prepared to admit her personal faults. He drew particularly heavily on Robert Johnston's *Historia rerum Britannicarum* (posthumously published in 1655), often little more than loosely translating, though claiming to apply his own 'Thoughts, as well as Judgement'.[4] Johnston was a Scot working in London, a Protestant, and a royalist. His belief that history's purpose was to inspire his readers to virtue and wisdom gave his writing a distinctly moral tone in which he strained to moralise Elizabeth's love of music and reconcile it with her image as a diligent ruler.[5] As Bohun similarly

---

[1] Henry Chettle, *England's Mourning Garment Worn Here by Plain Shepherds, in Memory of their Sacred Mistress, Elizabeth* (London, 1603), sig. D2v; I. F., *King James his Welcome to London with Eliza's Tomb and Epitaph, and our King's Triumph and Epitome* (London, 1603), sig. A3v.

[2] Thomas Bateson, *The First Set of English Madrigals to 3, 4, 5 and 6 Voices* (London, 1604), no. XXII. On continued evocations of Elizabeth in later seventeenth-century music see: Leslie C. Dunn, 'Re-sounding Elizabeth in Seventeenth-Century Music: Morley to Purcell', in *Resurrecting Elizabeth I in Seventeenth-Century England*, ed. Elizabeth H. Hageman and Katherine Conway (Madison, NJ, 2007), pp. 239–60.

[3] William Camden, *Annals: The True and Royal History of the Famous Empress Elizabeth* (London, 1625), sig. A1r.

[4] Edmund Bohun, *The Character of Queen Elizabeth, or, A Full and Clear Account of her Policies, and the Methods of her Government both in Church and State her Virtue and Defects* (London, 1693), preface. Both authors also drew on Camden.

[5] W. A. Shaw, 'Johnston, Robert (*c.* 1567–1639)', rev. Shona MacLean Vance, *ODNB* (online edn, 2004); David Allan, *Virtue, Learning and the Scottish Enlightenment: Ideas of Scholarship in Early Modern History* (Edinburgh, 1993), p. 62.

intended to moralise Elizabeth for a contemporary audience, he found Johnston's interpretation of her music-making appropriate to his own aims, and by writing in English he popularised this image for a broader audience.

Though aware of music's capacity to 'adorn and sweeten her Government' in the eyes of both foreign dignitaries and the nobility, Bohun followed Johnston in seeing Elizabeth's personal musical talents as mere ornament.[6] Instead, proof of Elizabeth's extraordinary virtue lay in her ability to maintain her chastity while partaking in musical and courtly pleasures:

> Though she was almost every night tempted to change her resolution [to chastity], by the luxury, cheerfulness, and wantonness of a court which showed itself in interludes, banquets, and balls, and was surrounded on all sides with the enticements of pleasures, and the things which might provoke the most cool and languid lust; yet she preserved herself from being conquered or broken by them. For the fear of God, and a true sense of piety extinguished in her all feminine intemperance and lust.[7]

In a tone as disapproving of courtly opulence and femininity as Salter and Vives in the previous century (pp. 21–2), Bohun presented Elizabeth as the source of reason, piety, chastity, and seriousness in a court given over to sensuous pleasures. He also borrowed Johnston's ploy of blaming its extravagant recreations on her courtiers. After the elaborate entertainments for Alençon's visit, Bohun claims that Elizabeth's courtiers were 'never more to be reclaimed from them', while by contrast 'the Queen herself left off these divertissements, and betook herself, as before to the care of her kingdom.'[8]

Bohun found Johnston's emphasis on Elizabeth's musical temperance useful for the parallels it allowed him to draw between his own monarchs and their illustrious predecessor (a necessary reinforcement of legitimacy for monarchs who had gained the throne by revolution).[9] Although William showed no particular interest in music, Mary played the harpsichord and lute, and was a proficient dancer.[10] She was also cultivating an image of pious virtue and leading a campaign for the reformation of morals across the kingdom. Elizabeth's combination of morality and musical talent therefore provided an illustrious precedent for Mary's, while Elizabeth's supposed restraint in courtly entertainments implicitly justified William

---

[6] Bohun, *The Character of Queen Elizabeth*, pp. 334–5; Robert Johnston, *Historia rerum Britannicarum: ut et multarum Gallicarum, Belgicarum, & Germanicarum, tam politicarum, quam ecclesiasticarum, ab anno 1572, ad annum 1628* (Amsterdam, 1655), pp. 319, 352–3.

[7] Bohun, *The Character of Queen Elizabeth*, pp. 71–2.

[8] Ibid., pp. 345–6; Johnston, *Historia rerum Britannicarum*, p. 353.

[9] John Watkins, *Representing Elizabeth in Stuart England: Literature, History, Sovereignty* (Cambridge, 2002), pp. 191–8. Comparisons between Mary and Elizabeth were also made in contemporary music: Dunn, 'Re-sounding Elizabeth', pp. 248–55.

[10] Tony Claydon and W. A. Speck, *William and Mary*, Very Interesting People (Oxford, 2007), p. 106.

and Mary's moderation in the provision of music at court.[11] Most notable, however, is that despite the changing political climate, the issues of chastity, frivolity, and governance raised by both Johnston and Bohun continued to echo the conflicted attitudes to music held by Elizabeth's contemporaries.

Ultimately Elizabeth's musicality passed fondly into legend. An anecdote published in Paris in 1715 recorded that:

> Queen Elizabeth of England, on her death-bed, remembered the power of music and ordered her musicians to her chamber so that, in her words, she might die as gaily as she had lived. To dispel the horror of death she listened to the music [*symphonie*] with great tranquillity until her last breath.[12]

The story is almost certainly untrue, as most sources agree that Elizabeth could not speak for several days before she died.[13] Yet the persistence of such a story so long after her death reveals the significance of music even in Elizabeth's posthumous reputation.

It was Elizabeth's love of music along with her willingness to allow others to commission entertainments and to tolerate their appropriation for petition and persuasion that had allowed it to play such a rich role in the politics of her court. Noblemen exploited the music for grand, public ceremonies and manufactured intimate, personal performances. They did their duty in singing their monarch's praises, but used every opportunity for their personal benefit and were not afraid to offer counsel or even criticism. So accepted was it that these occasions served multiple interests that even musicians felt able to add their own petitions without fear of reproach.

But how different was music from other courtly arts in its political significance at Elizabeth's court? Tom Bishop has argued that music's function was fundamentally different from that of other cultural modes.[14] He believes that Elizabethans stressed music's 'recoding power' as a distinctive and transformative kind of cultural act. Musical representations were displaced from the ordinary: they were more abstract, oblique in their expression but able to express the inexpressible.[15] Yet claiming music as a separate and unique mode of communication seems to over-exaggerate the differences in function between music and other courtly arts. Most

---

[11] John Van der Kiste, *William and Mary* (Stroud, 2003), pp. 63–4. William and Mary ended the use of string players in the Chapel Royal and reduced the royal household musicians to twenty-four players and a master of music serving on a more occasional basis: Ian Spink, 'Music and Society', in *The Seventeenth Century*, ed. Ian Spink, The Blackwell History of Music in Britain (Oxford, 1992), pp. 1–65 (pp. 56, 63); Roger Bowers, H. Diack Johnstone, Richard Rastall and Peter Holman, 'London (i), II: Music at Court', *NG2*.

[12] Quoted in Peter Holman, *Four and Twenty Fiddlers: The Violin at the English Court, 1540–1690*, Oxford Monographs on Music (Oxford, 1993), p. 22.

[13] Ibid.

[14] T. G. Bishop, 'Elizabethan Music as a Cultural Mode', in *Reconfiguring the Renaissance: Essays in Critical Materialism*, ed. Jonathan V. Crewe (Lewisburg, PA, 1992), pp. 51–75.

[15] Ibid., pp. 56–7, 66.

of the political uses of song in the preceding chapters were not specific to music alone. Courtiers presented poems to the Queen as well as having them set to music. Music might be a means of communicating when spoken appeals were futile, but Robert Carey used competing as the Forsaken Knight on the tiltyard as a different way of attracting royal attention to restore his reputation in 1593.[16] Even the notion of transposition and displacement seems to apply to all courtly arts of persuasion: take, for example, George Puttenham's interpretation of pastoral as a genre in which rustic people and 'rude speeches' are a means to 'insinuate and glance at greater matters'. Through literary fiction, courtly or political matters were displaced to the countryside world.[17] Putting advice, petitions, and complaints into any form of drama, poetry, music, or visual display transported these messages to an artistic realm distanced from the blunt immediacy of real-world events.

Arguably music could create this distance more effectively than spoken arts like poetry and drama. Singing rather than speaking exaggerated the artifice that displaced and contained these messages by being furthest removed from everyday communication. Bishop sees this displacement as stripping music of its polemical force;[18] however, Elizabethans maintained a strong belief in the power of music to move the minds of its hearers and instil harmony and virtue in their souls. Music was not regarded as a neutralising force, but a powerfully effective one. The appropriation of conventional genres such as love songs and laments could convey a courtier's message with considerable emotional and rhetorical force. Verses for music were usually short and succinct, allowing a more concentrated statement of the message of larger dramatic spectacles. Indeed, songs could carry some of the most pointed criticisms. Song was only a safe outlet for dissent because it prevented courtiers from turning to more threatening and violent forms of action, though this is again an argument that has been applied to the courtly arts in general, not just music.[19] It was not the turn to music, but the submitting of their grievances to artistic and rhetorical conventions that showed a courtier's willingness to work within accepted norms of courtly behaviour, containing any subversive potential while allowing the complaint to be strongly expressed.

Moreover, separating out the cultural mode of music from the poetic, dramatic, or visual underplays the frequent blending of music with other arts. Whether setting a poetic text, accompanying dancing, or inserted within a theatrical spectacle, the majority of musical performances were multimodal. It was as a combination of text and music that song could communicate on multiple levels simultaneously, creating an immediate celebratory atmosphere and impressing a crowd while its lyrics contained more pointed political comment for the attentive and politically

---

[16] Robert Carey and Robert Naunton, *Memoirs of Robert Carey, Written By Himself. And, Fragmenta Regalia, by Sir R. Naunton* (Edinburgh, 1808), pp. 56–7.

[17] George Puttenham, *The Art of English Poesy* (London, 1589), p. 31.

[18] Bishop, 'Elizabethan Music', p. 62.

[19] Paul E. J. Hammer, 'Upstaging the Queen: The Earl of Essex, Francis Bacon and the Accession Day Celebrations of 1595', in *The Politics of the Stuart Court Masque*, ed. David Bevington and Peter Holbrook (Cambridge, 1998), pp. 41–66 (p. 58); Louis Montrose, 'Celebration and Insinuation: Sir Philip Sidney and the Motives of Elizabethan Courtship', *Renaissance Drama* 8 (1977), 3–35 (pp. 5–6).

knowledgeable. Indeed, given the greater capacity for precise meaning in song compared with instrumental music, there was perhaps no single cultural mode of music either.

What was most specific to music as a courtly art, however, was how it communicated both as audible, expressive sound and as idea, concept, or metaphor. Music was not only a mode through which to convey a political message persuasively, but also an audible manifestation of personal and political harmony. Even without music's aural presence, a mere image of an instrument or mention of an individual's musicality evoked a host of qualities and connotations. Whether conjuring up notions of harmony that could be equated to social, political, or spiritual order, or the broad spectrum of views on music's feminine or masculine qualities and its merits or dangers, there was considerable flexibility in music's meanings. These were harnessed to create courtly identities and to praise or critique Elizabeth's governance. Such ideas of harmony outlasted the transitory moment of performance, enabling music to have longer lasting political significance.

APPENDIX A

Secular Musicians Employed in the Royal Household of Elizabeth I

The following tables were constructed using: *RECM*, vol. 4: *1603–1625*; *RECM*, vol. 6: *1558–1603*; Andrew Ashbee and David Lasocki, *A Biographical Dictionary of English Court Musicians, 1485–1714*, 2 vols. (Aldershot, 1998); Peter Holman, *Four and Twenty Fiddlers: The Violin at the English Court, 1540–1690*, Oxford Monographs on Music (Oxford, 1993).

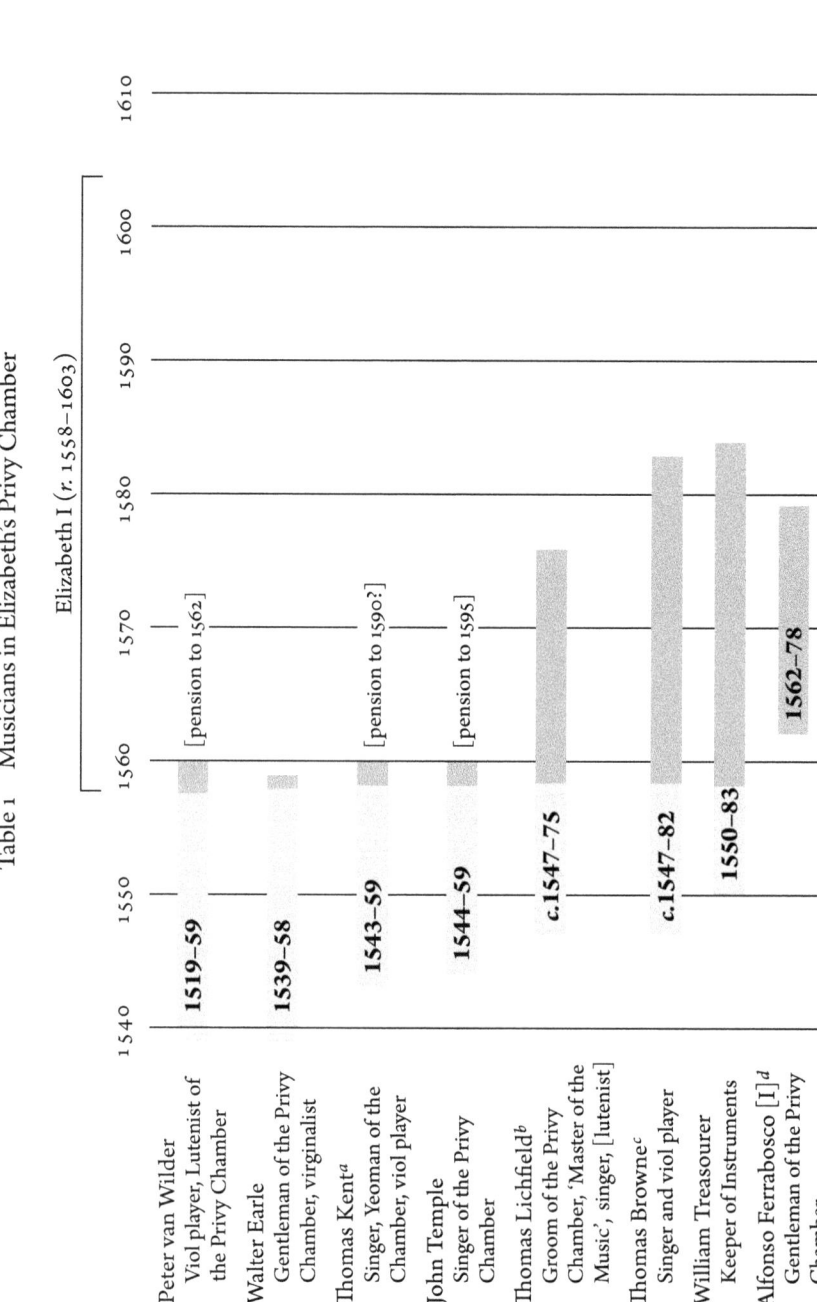

Table 1 Musicians in Elizabeth's Privy Chamber

Appendix A: Secular Musicians Employed in the Royal Household

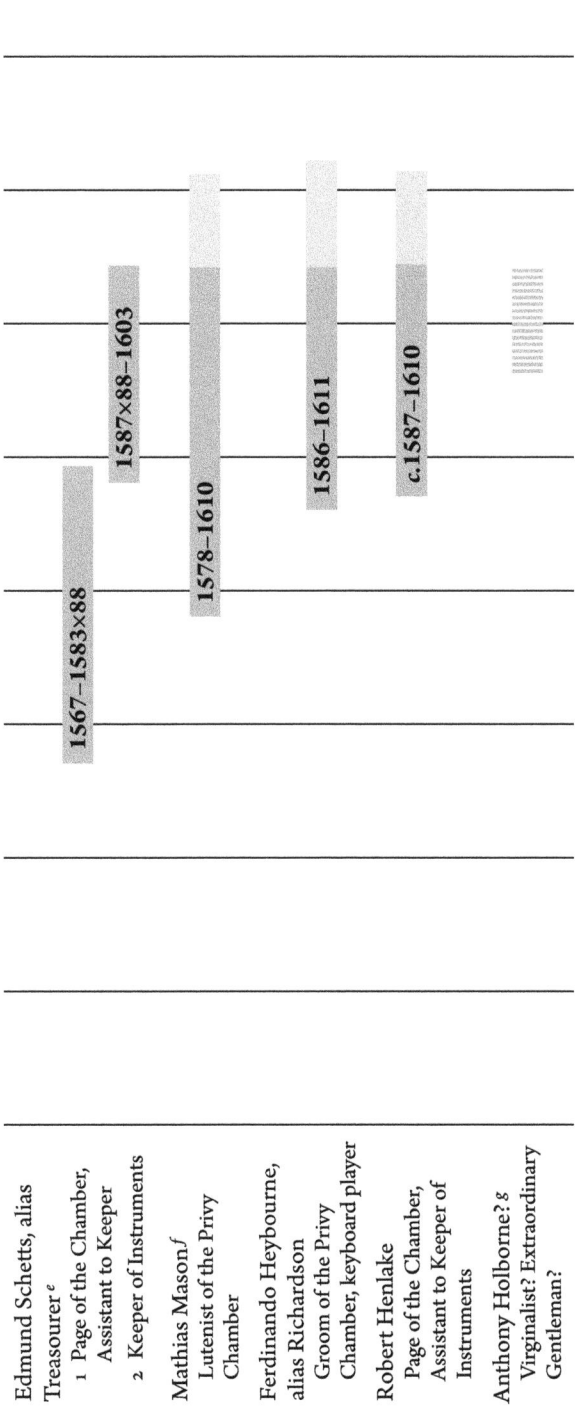

Edmund Schetts, alias Treasourer [e]
1 Page of the Chamber, Assistant to Keeper
2 Keeper of Instruments — 1567–1583×88

Mathias Mason [f]
Lutenist of the Privy Chamber — 1587×88–1603

Ferdinando Heybourne, alias Richardson
Groom of the Privy Chamber, keyboard player — 1578–1610

Robert Henlake
Page of the Chamber, Assistant to Keeper of Instruments — 1586–1611

Anthony Holborne? [g]
Virginalist? Extraordinary Gentleman? — c.1587–1610

a Received an annuity from midsummer 1558; however, if riding charges for a Thomas Kent in 1575, 1576, and 1581 refer to this singer, this would suggest he was still travelling with the Queen and perhaps still performing on occasion.

b Thomas Lichfield surrendered his position as Groom of the Privy Chamber on 9 December 1575; however, in March 1582 he was commissioned to examine the court accounts for unlawful payments for eight years.

c Named as a singing man in the Privy Chamber in 1547. Given a place as a viol player in 1554 in a small viol consort which was probably based in the Privy Chamber. Early in Elizabeth's reign he became the last remaining member of that consort, and so in 1562/3- he was transferred to a newer consort of viols/violins working primarily in the Presence Chamber.

d Ferrabosco left for Paris in 1578 and did not return, though he was paid until 1582.

e Received Treasourer's place in 1587/8.

f Listed as 'lute of the Privy Chamber' in the funeral list, 1603.

g Holborne claimed to be 'gentleman and servant' of the Queen, but there is no record of his payment. He may have been an extraordinary gentleman who served without pay. In 1599 he delivered messages in the Netherlands for Elizabeth: Brian Jeffrey, 'Antony Holborne', *Musica disciplina* 22 (1968), 129–205 (pp. 129, 133–4, 136).

Table 2 Further musicians employed in the royal household

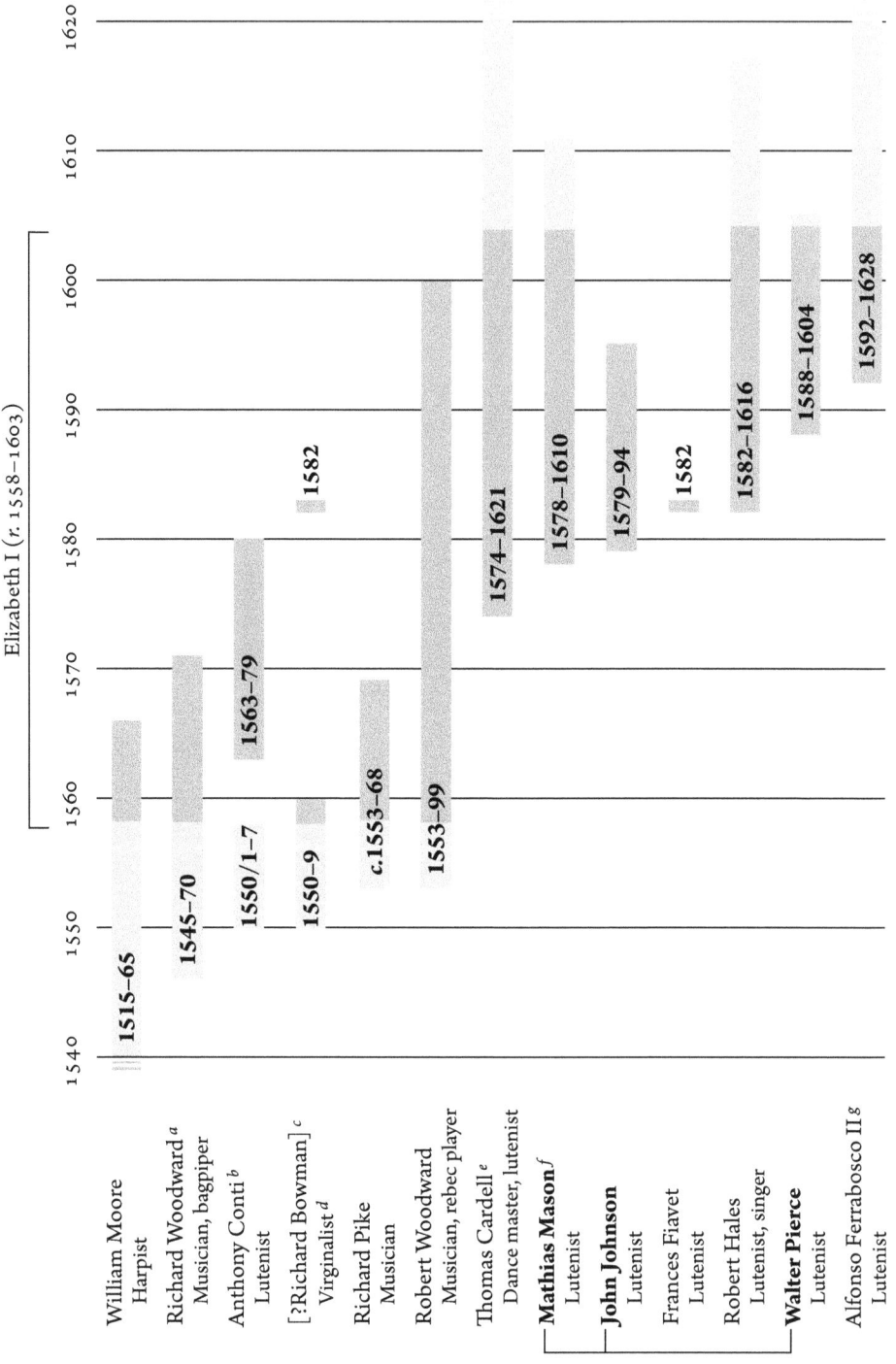

Appendix A: Secular Musicians Employed in the Royal Household

a Listed as a bagpiper in 1553.
b Officially reappointed by warrant in December 1564, but given livery 1563.
c Surrendered his post in February 1559 but was rewarded by Elizabeth in 1582 alongside Mason, Johnson, Woodward, and Browne as her majesty's musicians.
d The list of court offices of 1593 states that there were three virginal-players: *RECM*, vol. 6, p. 63.
e Listed as lutenist 1593–1602.
f Musicians in boldface were listed as 'musicians of the three lutes'.
g Granted an annuity in 1592, but seems to have played little part in court music at this time. Officially appointed to the viols/violins in 1601, but listed with the lutenists in 1593–1603, suggesting he usually worked as a lutenist and not a violinist.

Table 3 Musical consorts at the court of Elizabeth I

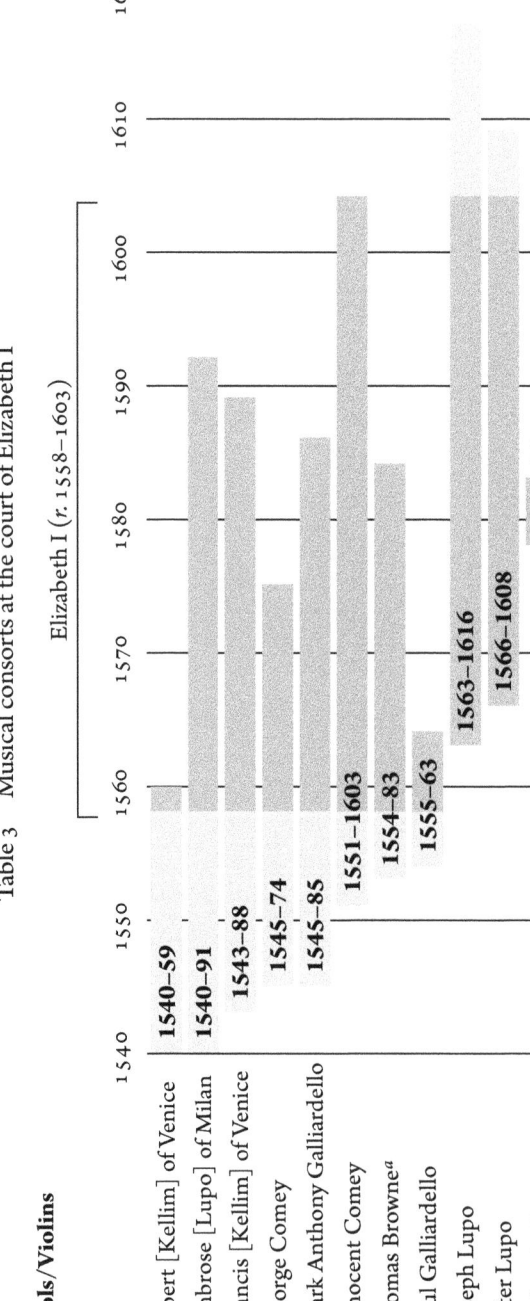

a Named as a singing man in the Privy Chamber in 1547. Given a place as a viol player in 1554 in a small viol consort which was probably based in the Privy Chamber. Early in Elizabeth's reign he became the last remaining member and so in 1562/3 he was transferred to this newer consort of viols/violins working primarily in the Presence Chamber.

b Lupo's was a newly created place, Browne's being formally given to Daniel Farrant in 1607.

c Officially appointed to the Viols/Violins in 1601, but listed with the lutenists in 1593–1603, suggesting he usually worked as a lutenist and not a violinist.

Appendix A: Secular Musicians Employed in the Royal Household 203

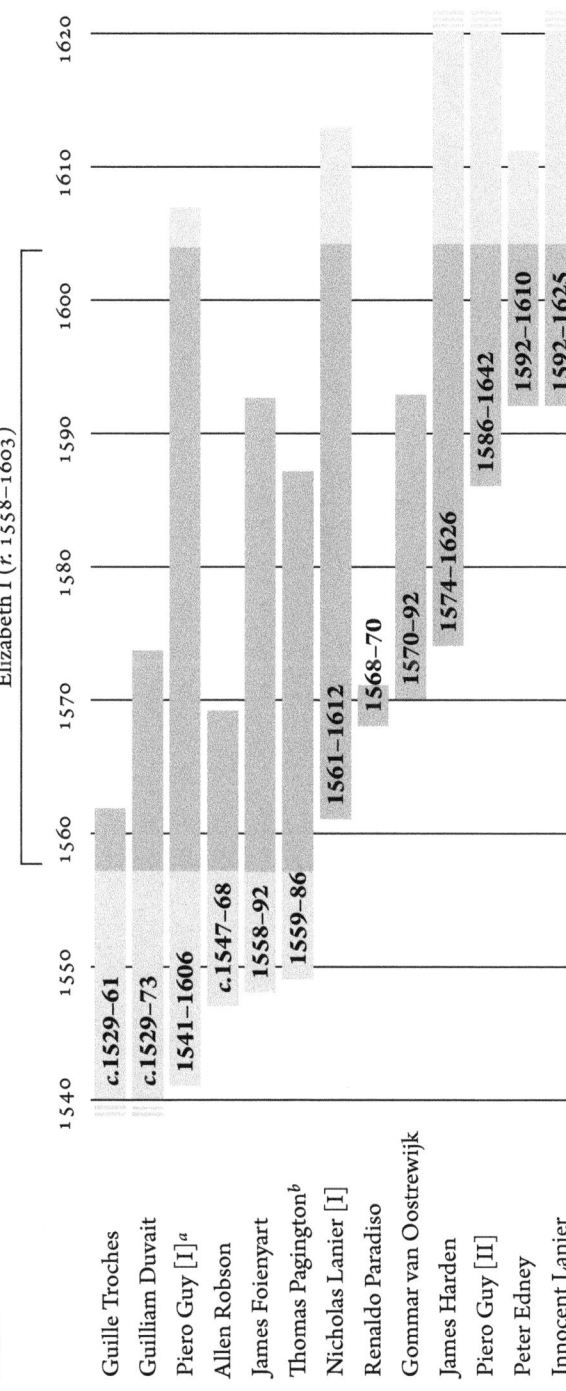

a Payments in 1530 and 1532 may relate to his period of apprenticeship. He was appointed in 1541.

b Served as musician from *c.* 1547. Included among the sackbuts in 1552–3, and the flutes in 1555. Officially appointed to the flute consort in 1559.

Table 3 continued

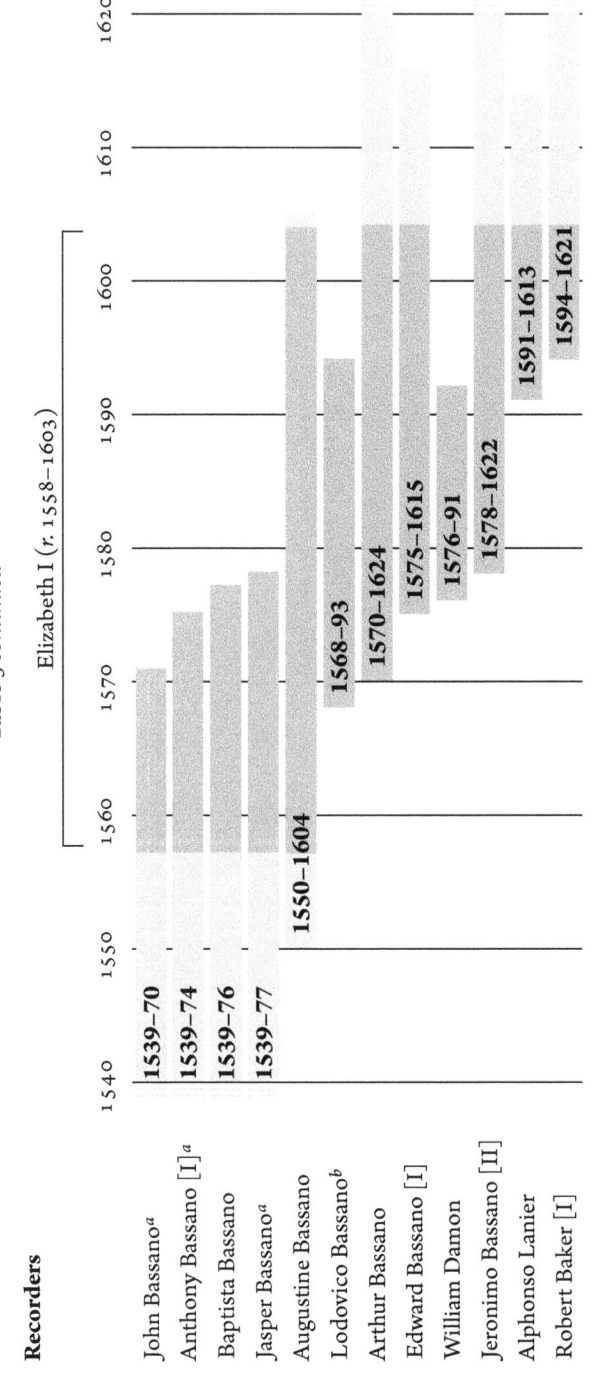

Recorders

Elizabeth I (r. 1558–1603)

Name	Dates
John Bassano[a]	1539–70
Anthony Bassano [I][a]	1539–74
Baptista Bassano	1539–76
Jasper Bassano[a]	1539–77
Augustine Bassano	1550–1604
Lodovico Bassano[b]	1568–93
Arthur Bassano	1570–1624
Edward Bassano [I]	1575–1615
William Damon	1576–91
Jeronimo Bassano [II]	1578–1622
Alphonso Lanier	1591–1613
Robert Baker [I]	1594–1621

[a] Had briefly served in the sackbut ensemble in 1531.

[b] Had probably been serving unofficially since his father's death in 1554.

Appendix A: Secular Musicians Employed in the Royal Household

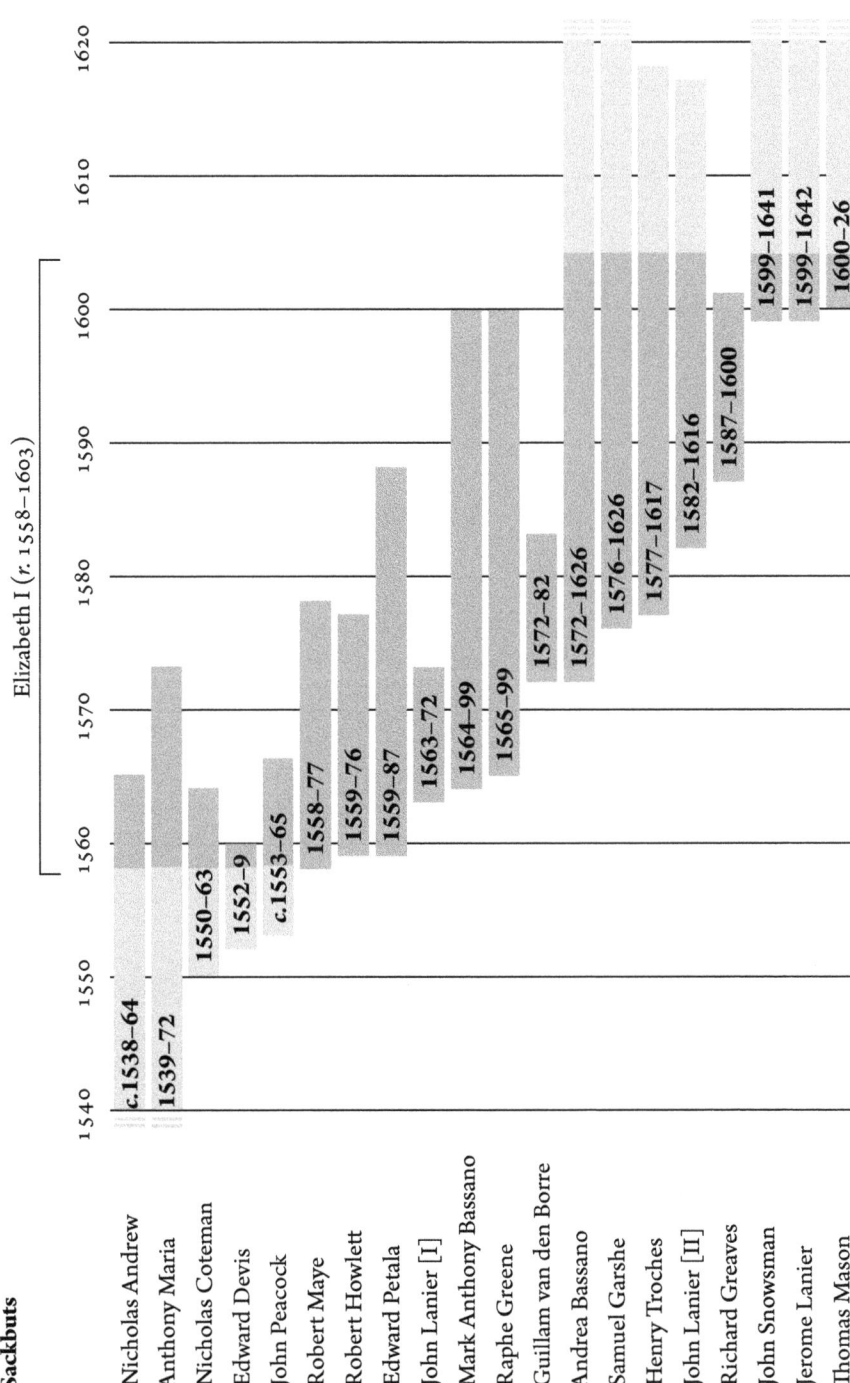

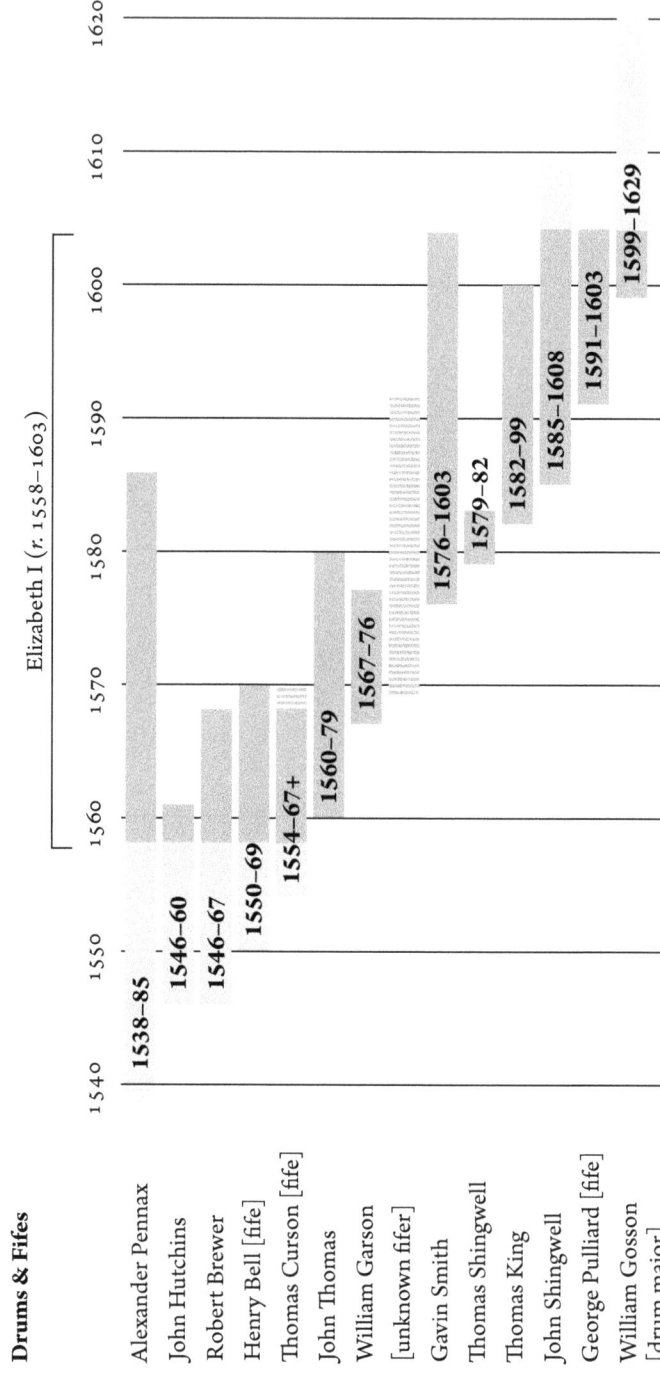

Table 3 continued

APPENDIX B

Extant Secular Songs Connected to Elizabeth and her Court

The following tables were compiled using: Diana Poulton, *John Dowland*, rev. edn (London, 1982); Joseph Kerman's table of 'Madrigals for Queen Elizabeth', in *The Elizabethan Madrigal: A Comparative Study* (New York, 1962), pp. 196–7; Philip Brett (ed.), *Consort Songs*, Musica Britannica 22 (London, 1974); G. E. P. Arkwright, 'Elizabethan Choirboy Plays and their Music', *Proceedings of the Royal Musical Association* 40 (1913/14), 117–38; Joseph Kerman, 'Byrd, William', *NG2*; William Byrd, *Consort Songs for Viols and Voices*, ed. Philip Brett, Byrd Edition 15 (London, 1970); Byrd, *Madrigals, Songs and Canons*, ed. Philip Brett, Byrd Edition 16 (London, 1976); *Psalmes, Sonets and Songs (1588)*, ed. Jeremy Smith, Byrd Edition 12 (London, 2004); *Songs of Sundrie Natures (1589)*, ed. David Mateer, Byrd Edition 13 (London, 2004); Alfonso Ferrabosco the Elder, *Latin Songs, French Chansons and English Songs*, ed. Richard Charteris, Corpus mensurabilis musicae 96 (Neuhausen-Stuttgart, 1984); Richard Charteris, *Alfonso Ferrabosco the Elder (1543–1588): A Thematic Catalogue of his Music with a Biographical Calendar*, Thematic Catalogues 11 (New York, 1984); and other works as referenced. Songs are arranged in approximate chronological order by the event with which the lyrics are connected (if known), or else by publication.

Table 4 Secular songs connected to specific court entertainments

Song[1]	Composer	Source(s)	Genre	Connection with Court
Awake Ye Woeful Wights	Anon. [Richard Edwards?]	GB-Lbl: Add. MS 15117[2]	lute song	Lament from Richard Edwards's *Damon and Pithias*, performed by Children of the Chapel Royal 1564. Original probably a consort song.
Ah, Alas Ye Salt Sea Gods	Richard Farrant (also attributed to Robert Parsons)	GB-Och: Music MSS 984–88 [Dow Partbooks]; US-NNSc: Drexel MSS 4180–5; GB-Lbl: Add. MS 29427; GB-Lbl: Egerton MSS 3665; GB-AB: Brogyntyn MS 27; GB-Lbl: Add. MSS 17786–91; GB-Ob: Tenbury MS 3089; IRL-Dtc: Press B.1.32	consort song	From a story of Panthea and Abradatas. Would fit the final scene of *The Wars of Cyrus*, performed by the Children of the Chapel Royal between 1576 and 1580.[3] Farrant was Master of the Children of Windsor and the Chapel Royal.
Mistrust Not Truth	Nicholas Strogers	GB-Och: Music MSS 984–988 [Dow Partbooks], no. 121; GB-Ob: Tenbury MS 389	consort song	Text given in Richard Edwards, *The Paradise of Dainty Devices* (1576) as 'A Worthy Ditty, Song before the Queen's Majesty at Bristol.'
His Golden Locks	John Dowland	*The First Book of Songs or Ayres*, (1597)	lute song/ 4-part ayre	Sung by Robert Hales on Accession Day 1590 for the retirement pageant of Sir Henry Lee.
Time's Eldest Son	John Dowland	*The Second Book of Songs or Ayres* (1600)	lute song with bass viol	Reportedly said by Sir Henry Lee 'In yielding up his Tilt staff.'[4]
This Sweet and Merry Month of May	William Byrd	*The First Set of Italian Madrigals Englished* (1590)	madrigals (4- and 6-part settings)	'I choose the first for holiday and greet Eliza with a rhyme'. Uses a refrain beginning 'O Beauteous Queen of Second Troy', just as 'With Fragrant Flowers' from the Elvetham progress (1591).[5]
With Fragrant Flowers We Strew the Way	Francis Pilkington	*The First Book of Songs or Ayres* (1605)	lute song/ 4-part ayre	Text from Elvetham progress 1591, modified to 'O gracious King of second Troy'. Probably a later resetting.

Appendix B: Extant Secular Songs Connected to Elizabeth

Song[1]	Composer	Source(s)	Genre	Connection with Court
In the Merry Month of May	John Baldwin	GB-Lbl: rm.24.d2	3-voice song	Text from Elvetham progress, 1591. Dated 1592 in the manuscript.
Elisa is the Fairest Queen	Edward Johnson	GB-Lbl: Add. MSS 30480–4	consort song	Text from Elvetham progress. Printed account suggests originally for mixed consort. Copied with the song below.
Come Again Fair Nature's Treasure	Edward Johnson	GB-Lbl: Add. MSS 30480–4	consort song with 2 voices	Text from Elvetham progress. Printed account suggested originally for mixed consort. Copied with the song above.
Behold Her Locks	Robert Jones	*The Muses' Garden for Delights, or the Fifth Book of Ayres* (1610)	lute song/ 4-part ayre	Text from Cowdray progress, 1591 (omitting last verse). Jones probably too young to have set these for Cowdray.
My Heart and Tongue Were Twins	John Dowland	*A Pilgrim's Solace* (1612)	lute song/ 4-part ayre	Text from Sudeley progress, 1592. Dowland may have been the 'Do.' who sang 'Herbs, Words and Stones' in the same progress.[6]
Behold a Wonder Here	John Dowland	*The Third and Last Book of Songs or Ayres* (1603)	lute song with bass viol	Cynthia has given blind love his sight. Possibly from the entry of a knight disguised as an Indian Prince on Accession Day 1595.
Cynthia Queen of Seas and Lands	Robert Jones	*Ultimum Vale, with a Triplicity of Music* (1605); GB-Lbl: Add. MSS 24665	lute song/ 4-part ayre	Text from Harefield progress, 1602
O the Joys That Soon Should Waste	Anon.	GB-Och: MS Mus. 439	voice and lyra viol	From Ben Jonson's *Cynthia's Revels* (probably performed at court in 1600–1)[7]
Slow, Slow, Fresh Fount	Henry Youll	*Canzonets to Three Voices* (1608)	3-part song	Also from Ben Jonson's *Cynthia's Revels*. Unlikely to be the originally setting.[8]

1 Songs are listed in chronological order by the event to which they relate.
2 The tune is also printed in a broadside, *A New Ballad of a Lover Extolling his Lady. To the Tune of Damon and Pithias* (London, 1568): John Long, 'Music for a Song in "Damon and Pithias"', *Music & Letters* 48 (1967), 247–50 (p. 268).
3 Richard Farrant, *The Wars of Cyrus: An Early Classical Narrative Drama of the Child Actors*, ed. James Brawner (Urbana, IL, 1942), p. 17. Brawner does not believe this play was performed at court; however, it was written at a time when the court was the focus of the choirboy's activities so would almost certainly have been intended for court, even if not actually performed there.
4 Edward Doughtie (ed.), *Liber Lilliati: Elizabethan Verse and Song (Bodleian MS Rawlinson Poetry 148)* (Newark, 1985), p. 165.
5 The songs connected to the Elvetham progress (the next five entries in this list) were identified in Ernest Brennecke, "The Entertainment at Elvetham, 1591", in *Music in English Renaissance Drama*, ed. John H. Long (Lexington, KY, 1968), pp. 32–56.
6 Poulton, *Dowland*, pp. 29–30.
7 Andrew Sabol, "Two Unpublished Stage Songs for the "Aery of Children"', *Renaissance News* 13 (1960), 222–32 (p. 29).
8 David Fuller, 'Ben Jonson's Plays and their Contemporary Music', *Music & Letters* 58 (1977), 60–75 (pp. 61–2).

Appendix B: Extant Secular Songs Connected to Elizabeth

Table 5 Secular songs which address or refer to Queen Elizabeth

Song[1]	Composer	Source(s)	Genre	Connection with Court
Eliza, Her Name Gives Honour	John Bennet	GB-Lbl: Add. MSS 17786–91	consort song	In praise of Elizabeth (1590s)
Blow, Shepherds, Blow	Thomas Morley	*Canzonets or Little Short Songs to Three Voices* (1593)	3-part song	'Fair Eliza see she comes', and, 'All hail Eliza fair, the country's pride and goddess, / long mayest thou live the shepherd's queen and lovely mistress.'
Turn About and See Me	John Mundy	*Songs and Psalms Composed into 3. 4. and 5. Parts* (1594)	3-part song	'A mighty Prince and excellent, Sweet Eglantine the best'
Fair in a Morn	Thomas Morley	*The First Book of Ayres* (1600)	lute song with bass viol	Lyrics by Nicholas Breton. Robin Headlam Wells believes the poem's imagery of the Sun and incomparable beauty refers to Elizabeth.[2]
My Thoughts are Wing'd with Hopes	John Dowland	*The First Book of Songs or Ayres* (1597)	lute song / 4-part ayre	'She doth change and yet remain the same' (possibly a reference to Elizabeth's motto, *semper eadem*). Also 'till Cynthia shine as she hath done before'. Sometimes attributed to the Earl of Cumberland, but unlikely.[3]
Away with These Self Loving Lads	John Dowland	*The First Book of Songs or Ayres* (1597)	lute song / 4-part ayre	Words by Fulke Greville, Lord Brooke (Caelica Sonnet no. 52): 'My songs they be of Cynthia's praise / I wear her rings on holidays.'
Come Gentle Swains and Shepherds	Michael Cavendish	*Ayres in Tablatory to the Lute* (1598); *The Triumphs of Oriana* (1601)	5-part madrigals	Two different settings. 'Then sang the shepherds and nymphs of Diana, / Long live fair Oriana.'[4]

Table 5 continued

Song[1]	Composer	Source(s)	Genre	Connection with Court
Humour Say What Mak'st Thou Here	John Dowland	*The Second Book of Songs or Ayres* (1600)	dialogue for lute, 4 voices and 4 viols	'In the presence of a queen'
?Clear or Cloudy	John Dowland	*The Second Book of Songs or Ayres* (1600)	lute song / 5-voice ayre with treble viol	'Rain on your herbs and flow'rs that truly serve, / And let your weeds lack dew and duly starve.' Possibly addressing the Queen.
Time Stands Still	John Dowland	*The Third and Last Book of Songs or Ayres* (1603)	lute song	'Time stands still', and 'all other things shall change, but she remains the same' – as in Elizabeth's motto, *semper eadem*.
Say Love If Thou Didst Ever Find	John Dowland	*The Third and Last Book of Songs or Aires* (1603)	lute song / 4-part ayre	Love has only found one woman with a constant mind and she is 'Queen of love and beauty'. References to the moon, chastity, and changing yet always staying the same.
By a Fountain Where I Lay	John Dowland	*The Third and Last Book of Songs or Ayres* (1603)	lute song / 4-part ayre	'Was never Nymph more fairly bless'd / Blessed in the high'st degree.' 'Welcome fair Queen of May … Welcome be the shepherds' Queen/ the glory of our green.'
When Phoebus First Did Daphne Love	John Dowland	*The Third and Last Book of Songs or Ayres* (1603)	lute song / 4-part ayre	'Past fifteen none but one should live a maid' – the 'but one' seems to imply Elizabeth.
The Triumphs of Oriana (1601)	Compiled by Thomas Morley		collection of madrigals	All songs end with the refrain 'Then sang the shepherds and nymphs of Diana,/ Long live fair Oriana!'[5]
Oriana's Farewell	Thomas Bateson	*The First Set of English Madrigals to 3. 4. 5. and 6. Voices* (1604)	5-voice madrigal	Refrain: 'then sing the shepherds and nymphs of Diana, / in heaven lives Oriana.'

Appendix B: Extant Secular Songs Connected to Elizabeth   213

Song[1]	Composer	Source(s)	Genre	Connection with Court
I That Sometime a Sacred Maiden Queen	William Byrd	GB-LBl: Add. MSS 29401–5; US-CA: MS Mus.30	consort song	After the death of Elizabeth (same music as for 'When First by Force').
Now We Have Present Made	Anon.	GB-Ob: MSS Tenbury 1162–7, no. 58	consort song with chorus and 2 soloists	Text by Sir Walter Ralegh. Lyrics refer to offering a present to 'Cynthia, Phoebe, Flora, Diana and Aurora', 'princess of world's affection'. The original event was probably in the late 1580–90s; however, this setting survives in a source from c. 1640. Its 'verse and chorus' idiom is more typical of later composers such as Martin Peerson or Thomas Ravenscroft.[6]

[1] Songs are chronologically ordered based either on the date of publication or else by the approximate period of composition for those only in manuscript.

[2] Robin Headlam Wells, 'Thomas Morley's "Fair in a Morn"', *The Lute Society Journal* 18 (1976), 37–42 (pp. 38–9).

[3] Steven W. May, *The Elizabethan Courtier Poets: The Poems and their Contexts* (Columbia, MO, 1991), p. 248.

[4] Jeremy Smith has questioned whether Oriana was originally intended to be understood as Elizabeth: Jeremy Smith, 'Music and Late Elizabethan Politics: The Identities of Oriana and Diana', *Journal of the American Musicological Society* 58 (2005), 507–58. The 1598 collection was dedicated to Arabella Stuart (a possible candidate for the succession), while Smith hypothesises that the *Triumphs* were only hastily adapted as a tribute to Elizabeth following Essex's rebellion, having previously been designed as a tribute for Anna of Denmark (queen of James VI of Scotland, another candidate for succession).

[5] On the doubtful identification of Oriana, see the previous note. However, Thomas Bateson's 1604 madrigal is a farewell to an Oriana who is now in heaven and does seem to represent Elizabeth.

[6] Craig Monson, *Voices and Viols in England, 1600–1650: The Sources and the Music* (Ann Arbor, MI, 1982), pp. 227–30.

Table 6 Other secular songs likely to be from court entertainments

Song[1]	Composer	Source(s)	Genre	Connection with Court
Pour Down, You Pow'rs Divine (second part: No Grief is Like to Mine)	Robert Parsons (also attributed to Nicholas Strogers)	GB-Lbl: Add. MSS 17786–91; GB-Lcm: MS 2049; GB-Ob: Tenbury MS 3089; IRL-Dtc: Press B.1.32; GB-Ckc: MS 2	consort song	Written by a Gentleman of the Chapel Royal. Exclamations to a character called 'Pandolpho'. Possibly from a choirboy play of the 1560s
Come Tread the Paths	Anon.	GB-Lbl: Add. MSS 17786; GB-Och: Music MSS 984–88 [Dow Partbooks]; GB-Lbl: Add. MS 29427; GB-Ob: Tenbury MS 3089; GB-AB: Brogyntyn MS 27	consort song	Exclamations to 'Guichardo'. Could be the story of Tancred and Gismond, performed by the Inner Temple in 1567–8 (though lyrics not included in 1591 printed text), or from a lost choirboy play on the same story.[2]
O Jove from Stately Throne	Richard Farrant	GB-Lbl: Add. MSS 17786–91	consort song	Composed by Master of the Children of Windsor and the Chapel Royal. References to the character 'Altages' suggest possibly from a lost choirboy play of *King Xerxes* (1574–5).[3]
Cease Now, Vain Thoughts	Nathaniel Giles	GB-Lbl: Add. MSS 17786; GB-Lbl: Add. MSS 29372–7; GB-Lbl: Add. MS 29427	consort song	Possibly from a choirboy play. Giles was Master of the Children of Windsor and Chapel Royal.[4] Probably from the 1580s.[5]
Virgo per incertos casus	Alphonso Ferrabosco	GB-Lbl: Add. MSS 30810–5; GB-Lbl: Add. MS 31417; GB-Lbl: Madrigal Soc. MSS.G.21–26; GB-Lcm: Mus. MS 204; GB-Lcm: Mus. MS 2089; GB-Ob: Tenbury MS 389; GB-Ob: Tenbury MSS 340 and 341–4	6-voice Latin song	Possibly from a court drama. Introduces the tale of a Virgin driven over land and sea who reaches Britain. Kerman suggests it might be the story of Io.[6]

Appendix B: Extant Secular Songs Connected to Elizabeth

Song[1]	Composer	Source(s)	Genre	Connection with Court
Where Fancy Fond	William Byrd	*Psalms, Sonnets and Songs* (1588); GB-Och: Music MSS 984–88 [Dow Partbooks]	consort song	Elaborate allegories imply the context of a court entertainment.[7] Byrd was a Gentleman of the Chapel Royal.
Come Ye Heavy States of Night	John Dowland	*The Second Book of Songs or Ayres*, 1600	lute song / 4-part ayre	Poulton suggests from a play or masque. A young woman laments death of her father.[8]

[1] Songs are listed in approximate chronological order by performance.
[2] Brett (ed.), *Consort Songs*, p. 178.
[3] Peter Le Huray and John Morehen, 'Farrant, Richard', NG2.
[4] J. Bunker Clark, 'Giles, Nathaniel', NG2.
[5] Linda Phyllis Austern, *Music in English Children's Drama of the Later Renaissance*, Musicology Series 13 (Philadelphia, 1992), p. 242.
[6] Joseph Kerman, 'An Italian Musician in England', in *Write All These Down: Essays on Music* (Berkeley, CA, 1994), pp. 139–51 (p. 149 n. 1).
[7] Byrd, *Madrigals, Songs and Canons*, pp. 191–2.
[8] Poulton, *Dowland*, p. 268.

Table 7 Further secular songs related to individual Elizabethan courtiers

Song[1]	Composer	Source(s)	Genre	Connection with Court
Musica laeta	Alphonso Ferrabosco	GB-Ob: Mus Sch MSS c.45–50; GB-Ob: Mus.E.1–5; GB-Ob: Tenbury MS 341–44; GB-Ob: Tenbury MS 1018; GB-Och: Music MSS 78–82; GB-Och: Music MSS 463–67; GB-CF: D/DP Z6/1; GB-Lbl: Egerton MSS 2009–2012; GB-Lbl: Madrigal Soc. MSS.G.44–47, 49; US-NH: Filmer MS 1	6-voice Latin song	Farewell song, probably written in 1578. Charteris suggests it was written to Elizabeth, Kerman that it was written to Ferdinando Heybourne/Richardson, Groom of the Privy Chamber.[2]
I Joy Not in No Earthly Bliss	William Byrd	Psalms, Sonnets and Songs (1588)	5-part song	Text attributed to Sir Edward Dyer
My Mind to Me a Kingdom Is	William Byrd	Psalms, Sonnets and Songs (1588)	5-part song	Text attributed to Sir Edward Dyer or Edward de Vere, Earl of Oxford
O You That Hear This Voice	William Byrd	Psalms, Sonnets and Songs (1588)	5-part song	Text by Sir Philip Sidney
If Women Could Be Fair	William Byrd	Psalms, Sonnets and Songs (1588)	5-part song	Text attributed to Edward de Vere, Earl of Oxford
Farewell, False Love	William Byrd	Psalms, Sonnets and Songs (1588)	5-part song	Text attributed to Sir Walter Ralegh in the context of political and poetic rivalry with Sir Thomas Heneage. Setting probably postdates the poetic exchange.[3]
Constant Penelope	William Byrd	Psalms, Sonnets and Songs (1588)	5-part song	Possibly about Penelope Rich (sister of Robert Devereux, Earl of Essex)[4]
Penelope That Longed	William Byrd	Songs of Sundry Natures (1589)	5-part song	Possibly about Penelope Rich (sister of Robert Devereux, Earl of Essex)[5]

Appendix B: Extant Secular Songs Connected to Elizabeth

Song[1]	Composer	Source(s)	Genre	Connection with Court
Weeping Full Sore	William Byrd	Songs of Sundry Natures (1589)	5-part song	Possibly about Penelope Rich (sister of Robert Devereux, Earl of Essex)[6]
O Dear Life	William Byrd	Songs of Sundry Natures (1589)	5-part song	Text by Sir Philip Sidney
What Vaileth It	William Byrd	GB-Lbl: Add. MS 31992	6-part song	Text by Sir Philip Sidney
Were I a King	John Mundy	Songs and Psalms Composed into 3. 4. and 5. Parts (1594)	5-part song	Text by Edward de Vere, Earl of Oxford
My Mistress Had a Little Dog	William Byrd	US-CA: MS Mus.30; GB-Lbl Add. MSS 29401–5	consort song	Pun on 'rich' implies the dog-owner was Lady Penelope Rich.[7] Describes an event that took place between 1596 and 1605.
Who Ever Thinks or Hopes of Love	John Dowland	The First Book of Songs or Ayres (1597)	lute song / 4-part ayre	Love complaint by Fulke Greville, Lord Brooke (an altered version of Caelica sonnet no. 50)
Can She Excuse My Wrongs	John Dowland	The First Book of Songs or Ayres (1597)	lute song/ 4-part ayre	Later instrumental settings are entitled 'The Earl of Essex Galliard'
Now, O Now I Needs Must Part	John Dowland	The First Book of Songs or Ayres (1597)	lute song / 4-part ayre	To the tune of the 'Frog Galliard', whose name may be related to Elizabeth's suitor, the Duke of Anjou, whom she called her 'frog'.
Fly Love That Art So Sprightly	Thomas Morley	Canzonets or Little Short Ayres to Five and Six Voices (1597)	5-part ayre	Bonny Boots[8]
Our Bonny Boots Could Toot It	Thomas Morley	Canzonets or Little Short Ayres to Five and Six Voices (1597)	5-part ayre	Bonny Boots[9]
O Sweet Woods	John Dowland	The Second Book of Songs or Ayres (1600)	lute song / 4-part ayre	Lyrics refer to Wanstead, where Essex often withdrew to from court. (They also quote from Sir Philip Sidney's Old Arcadia.)

Table 7 continued

Song[1]	Composer	Source(s)	Genre	Connection with Court
Faction That Ever Dwells	John Dowland	The Second Book of Songs or Ayres (1600)	lute song / 4-part ayre	Words by Fulke Greville, Lord Brooke (Caelica Sonnet no. 29)
Thus Bonny Boots the Birthday Celebrated	John Holmes	The Triumphs of Oriana (1601)	6-voice madrigal	Bonny Boots
Come Blessed Bird!	Edward Johnson	The Triumphs of Oriana (1601)	6-voice madrigal	Bonny Boots
Wretched Albinus	William Byrd?	GB-Lbl: Add. MSS 29401–5; US-CA: MS Mus.30	consort song	The career of Albinus has striking parallels with the rebellion and execution of the Earl of Essex in 1601.[10]
It Was a Time When Silly Bees	John Dowland	The Third and Last Book of Songs or Ayres (1603)	lute song / 4-part ayre	Lyrics attributed to both Robert Devereux, Earl of Essex, and his secretary, Henry Cuffe
The Lowest Trees Have Tops	John Dowland	The Third and Last Book of Songs or Ayres (1603)	lute song / 4-part ayre	Lyrics attributed to Sir Edward Dyer
Change Thy Mind Since She Doth Change	Richard Martin	Robert Dowland, A Musical Banquet (1610)	lute song with bass part	Words by Robert Devereux, Earl of Essex
My Heavy Sprite	Anthony Holborne	Robert Dowland, A Musical Banquet (1610)	lute song with bass part	Words by the George Clifford, Earl of Cumberland
To Plead My Faith	Daniel Bacheler	Robert Dowland, A Musical Banquet (1610)	lute song with bass part	Words by Robert Devereux, Earl of Essex
O Eyes Leave Off Thy Weeping	Robert Hales	Robert Dowland, A Musical Banquet (1610)	lute song with bass part	Composed by Robert Hales, favourite singer of Elizabeth I

Appendix B: Extant Secular Songs Connected to Elizabeth 219

This list includes songs that set lyrics written by courtiers, and songs written about courtiers. Probably few of these songs were written with the intention of direct political influence. Not all of the lyrics will have had a political meaning, many composers will have set poems written for earlier occasions, and it is not possible to distinguish between those performed at court and those composed for entertainment in aristocratic houses. This list excludes songs dedicated to courtiers, elegies, and seventeenth-century settings unlikely to have been made until after the death of the poet.

[1] Songs are chronologically ordered based either on the date of publication or else (for those only in manuscript) by the approximate period of composition suggested by the event or person to which they relate.

[2] Ferrabosco, *Latin Songs*, p. 1; Kerman, 'An Italian Musician', p. 142.

[3] May, *Elizabethan Courtier Poets*, p. 116.

[4] Byrd, *Songs of Sundrie Natures*, p. xiv.

[5] Byrd, *Psalmes, Sonets and Songs*, p. xxxviii.

[6] Ibid, p. x.

[7] Byrd, *Consort Songs*, p. 177.

[8] Bonny Boots appears to have been a courtier with a talent for singing and dancing. The name has been suggested as a pseudonym for Henry Noel or Christopher Morley (possibly a relation of the composer Thomas Morley): David Greer, '"Thou Court's Delight" Biographical Notes on Henry Noel', *The Lute Society Journal* 17 (1975), 49–59; Sukanta Chaudhuri, 'Marlowe, Madrigals, and a New Elizabethan Poet', *Review of English Studies* n.s. 39 (1988), 199–216.

[9] On the death of Bonny Boots, William Holborne wrote 'Since Bonny Boots Was Dead', which was published in Anthony Holborne, *The Cittern School* (London, 1597).

[10] Byrd, *Consort Songs*, p. 178.

Glossary of Musical Terms

This glossary aims to aid the non-specialist reader by providing some brief definitions for musical terms used within the book.

Almand A court dance in a moderate duple time, originating in Germany and popular from the early sixteenth to the late eighteenth centuries.

Bandora A plucked, bass instrument with wire strings, a scallop-shaped body and a long fretted neck. Invented by John Rose in 1562.

Cantus durus A scale using B natural and the sharpwards side of the harmonic system (*durus* literally meaning hard).

Cantus mollis A scale using B flat and the flatwards side of the harmonic system (*mollis* literally meaning soft).

Canzonet A light-hearted, secular, polyphonic song, imitating the Italian canzonetta but in England not always easily distinguishable from the madrigal. Widespread from the late sixteenth to the late eighteenth centuries.

Carol A song that begins with a refrain that is repeated after subsequent verses. Carols could be courtly or popular, secular or religious, and had been common since medieval times.

Chanson A French, polyphonic song. In the sixteenth century, styles ranged from lyrical melodies over homophonic accompaniments to densely imitative polyphony.

Cittern A plucked instrument with a flat-backed, pear-shaped body, wire strings, and a fretted fingerboard (as a modern guitar has). Most popular in the sixteenth and seventeenth centuries.

Consort A small ensemble of instrumentalists. In modern usage it is frequently applied to groups of instruments of the same family, though in the sixteenth century it more commonly implied a mixed consort of diverse kinds of instruments.

Consort song A modern term to describe a type of English song for solo voice (or, less frequently, voices) and a consort of four instruments (typically viols). Prevalent from the mid-sixteenth to the early seventeenth centuries. The instrumental part was no simple accompaniment, but a rich polyphonic texture.

Contrafacta The writing of a new text to fit pre-existing music.

Cornett Unlike the modern brass instrument of the same name, this was a curved wooden instrument with a lip-vibrated mouthpiece. Most common from the late fifteenth to the late seventeenth centuries.

Divisions Variations created by splitting the tune into shorter notes.

False relation A note in one part sounds simultaneously or adjacent to a chromatically altered version of the same note in a different part, creating a dissonant effect.

Fantasia A freely composed instrumental piece, typically in a contrapuntal style with no fixed form, popular in England from the mid-sixteenth century.

Freemen's (or three-men's) songs Simple polyphonic songs, usually in three parts. Traditionally they were improvised around a well-known melody, although they might also be notated and learned.

Frottola Italian secular song of the late fifteenth or early sixteenth centuries for three to four voices. They were typically strophic and predominantly homophonic with the melody in the upper voice.

Galliard A courtly dance in a lively triple metre, typically paired with the pavan (see below). Probably originating in Italy, it was popular in England the sixteenth and early seventeenth centuries.

Homophony All parts move together at a similar pace and with similar rhythms, producing a chordal texture.

Lute A plucked string instrument with gut strings, a long neck with frets, and a flat-fronted, pear-shaped body. Originating in medieval times, but reaching its heyday in the sixteenth and seventeenth centuries.

Lute song or ayre An English solo song accompanied by the lute or orpharion, and/or bass viol, common in the late sixteenth and early seventeenth centuries. They were usually strophic settings and publications often also included arrangements for performance as four-voice songs.

Madrigal A polyphonic song style usually setting a single verse, often on a pastoral or mythological theme. It originated in Italy in the sixteenth century, but spread to England and Northern Europe. Madrigal style was notable for its copious use of word-painting and diversity of homophonic and imitative polyphonic textures.

Mean The middle voice of a three-part texture and/or an alto voice.

Melisma Multiple notes sung to a single text syllable (in contrast to a syllabic setting, in which there is one note per syllable).

Mixed consort A small ensemble of six instruments from different families that developed in the mid- to late sixteenth century, typically comprising treble viol/violin, flute/recorder, bass viol, lute, cittern, and bandora.

Monody A form of Italian solo song current from *c.* 1600, consisting of a declamatory and expressive vocal line with a simple instrumental accompaniment.

Monophony A melody for a single voice or instrument.

Motet In the sixteenth century this referred to a Latin-texted, sacred, polyphonic song.

Musica humana The inaudible harmony believed to be created in the human soul, or between the soul and the body.

Musica instrumentalis The audible, earthly music produced by instruments and voices.

Musica mundana The inaudible harmony believed to be produced by the motions of the planets.

Orpharion A wire-stringed, plucked instrument with a fretted fingerboard and a scallop-shaped body, similar in size to a lute. Probably invented in England in the late sixteenth century and widely played.

Pavan A courtly dance in a stately, duple time, typically paired with the galliard. Probably originating in Italy, it was popular in England in the sixteenth and early seventeenth centuries.

Phygrian cadence A cadence in which the lowest part descends to the final by a minor second. It has connotations of melancholy.

Poliphant A more unusual and complex type of plucked treble instrument, with wire strings, some of which were unstopped. Invented in England in the late sixteenth or early seventeenth century.

Polyphony A musical texture in which all parts have independently moving melodies. In imitative polyphony the voices enter separately but begin with the same melodic motif.

Positive organ An organ small enough to be movable. Some were free-standing and others designed to be placed on a table.

Rebec A small, bowed instrument with gut strings and a long, narrow body, played on the arm or against the shoulder. Common in the Middle Ages and Renaissance.

Regals A type of small, portable Renaissance organ whose sound was produced by beating reeds.

Roundelay A simple, country song with a refrain, originating in the fourteenth century, probably used for circle dances.

Sackbut An early form of trombone, used from the late fifteenth to the eighteenth centuries.

Shawm A double-reeded wind instrument, a precursor to the oboe. In use from the twelfth to the seventeenth centuries.

Spinet A small, plucked keyboard instrument similar to the virginals. The name was often loosely applied and was used from the late fifteenth to the eighteenth centuries.

Suspension A dissonance created when a note is held over from the previous harmony while the surrounding harmony changes. The dissonant note is then resolved by a descending step to form a consonance again.

Viols A family of bowed, string instruments, played between the legs. Similar to the violin family but with six strings, C-shaped sound holes, and a fretted fingerboard. The viol was brought to England in the early sixteenth century and remained popular in the seventeenth.

Viola bastarda An Italian style of virtuosic bass-viol playing popular from about 1580 to 1630. It condensed a polyphonic vocal piece to a single line and embellished it with elaborate divisions.

Virginals A small keyboard instrument whose sound is produced by a mechanism which plucks the strings, popular in England in the sixteenth and seventeenth centuries. As with the spinet, the name was often loosely applied.

Waits Musicians employed by a town, typically players of wind instruments.

Bibliography

PRIMARY SOURCES, EDITIONS, AND CALENDARS

Adams, Simon (ed.), *Household Accounts and Disbursement Books of Robert Dudley, Earl of Leicester, 1558–1561, 1584–1586*, Camden Fifth Series 6 (Cambridge, 1995)

Albèri, Eugenio (ed.), *Relazione degli ambasciatori Veneti al senato*, 15 vols. (Florence, 1839–63)

Alciato, Andrea, *Emblematum liber* (Augsburg, 1534)

Arbeau, Thoinot, *Orchesography: A Treatise in the Form of a Dialogue whereby All Manner of Persons May Easily Acquire and Practise the Honourable Exercise of Dancing*, ed. Cyril W. Beaumont and Peter Warlock (London, 1925)

Arber, Edward (ed.), *A Transcript of the Registers of the Company of Stationers of London, 1554–1640*, 5 vols. (London, 1875–94)

Aristotle, *The Politics of Aristotle*, trans. Benjamin Jowett (Oxford, 1885)

Ascham, Roger, *Letters of Roger Ascham*, trans. Maurice Hatch and Alvin Vos (New York, 1989)

—— *The Schoolmaster or Plain and Perfect Way of Teaching Children, to Understand, Write, and Speak, the Latin Tongue* (London, 1570)

—— *Toxophilus: The School of Shooting Contained in Two Books* (London, 1545)

Ashbee, Andrew (ed.), *Records of English Court Music*, 9 vols. (Aldershot, 1986)

Ashley, Robert, *Of Honour*, ed. Virgil Barney Heltzel (San Marino, CA, 1947)

Aylmer, John, *An Harborowe for Faithful and True Subjects Against the Late Blown Blast, Concerning the Government of Women* (London, 1559)

Bacon, Francis, *The Works of Francis Bacon*, ed. James Spedding, Robert Leslie Ellis, and Douglas Denon Heath, 14 vols. (London, 1857)

Baldwin, John, 'In the Merry Month of May', Gb-Lbl: rm.24.d2, fols. 171v–173v

Barnard, John (ed.), *The First Book of Selected Church Music Consisting of Services and Anthems, such as are Now Used in the Cathedral and Collegiate Churches of this Kingdom*, 10 vols. (London, 1641)

Barnes, Joseph (ed.), *Speeches Delivered to her Majesty this Last Progress at the Right Honourable the Lady Russels, at Bisham, the Right Honourable the Lord Chandos at Sudley, at the Right Honourable the Lord Norris, at Ricote* (Oxford, 1592)

Bateson, Thomas, *The First Set of English Madrigals to 3, 4, 5 and 6 Voices*, 6 vols. (London, 1604)

Bennet, John, 'Eliza, Her Name Gives Honour', GB-Lbl: Add. MSS 17786–91, fol. 9r–v (MS 17790, fols. 5r–6v)

Boethius, *Fundamentals of Music*, trans. Calvin M. Bower, ed. Claude V. Palisca, Music Theory Translation Series (New Haven, CT, 1989)

Bohun, Edmund, *The Character of Queen Elizabeth, or, A Full and Clear Account of her Policies, and the Methods of her Government both in Church and State her Virtue and Defects* (London, 1693)

The Book of Honour and Arms (London, 1590)

Bourdeilles, Pierre de, Seigneur de Brantôme, 'Vies des dames illustres françoises et étrangères', *Œuvres complètes du Seigneur de Brantôme*, 8 vols. (Paris, 1823), vol. 5, pp. 1–349

Brett, Philip (ed.), *Consort Songs*, 2nd rev. edn, Musica Britannica 22 (London, 1974)

Brewer, J. S., R. H. Brodie, and James Gairdner (eds.), *Letters and Papers, Foreign and Domestic, of the Reign of Henry VIII*, 21 vols. (London, 1864–1920)

Brown, Rawdon, et al. (eds.), *Calendar of State Papers Relating to English Affairs in the Archives and Collections of Venice*, 38 vols. (London, 1864–1947)

Bülow, Gottfried von, 'Journey through England and Scotland made by Lupold von Wedel in the Years 1584 and 1585', *Transactions of the Royal Historical Society* 9 (1895), 223–70

—— and Wilfred Powell, 'Diary of the Journey of Philip Julius, Duke of Stettin-Pomerania, through England in the Year 1602', *Transactions of the Royal Historical Society* 6 (1892), 1–67

Burton, Robert, *The Anatomy of Melancholy, what it is with All the Kinds, Causes, Symptoms, Prognostics, and Several Cures of it* (London, 1621)

Byrd, William, *Cantiones sacrae (1575)*, ed. Craig Monson, Byrd Edition 1 (London, 1977)

—— *Consort Songs for Viols and Voices*, ed. Philip Brett, Byrd Edition 15 (London, 1970)

—— *The English Services*, ed. Craig Monson, Byrd Edition 10a (London, 1980)

—— GB-Lbl: MS Mus.1591 [My Lady Nevell's Book]

—— *Keyboard Music II*, ed. Alan Brown, Musica Britannica 28, 3rd rev. edn (London, 2004)

—— *Madrigals, Songs and Canons*, ed. Philip Brett, Byrd Edition 16 (London, 1976)

—— *Psalmes, Sonets and Songs (1588)*, ed. Jeremy Smith, Byrd Edition 12 (London, 2004)

—— *Songs of Sundrie Natures (1589)*, ed. David Mateer, Byrd Edition 13 (London, 2004)

Camden, William, *Annales rerum Anglicarum, et Hibernicarum, regnante Elizabetha, ad annum salutis M.D.LXXXIX* (London, 1615)

—— *Annals: The True and Royal History of the Famous Empress Elizabeth* (London, 1625)

Campion, Thomas, *Observations in the Art of English Poesy* (London, 1602)

Canning, William (ed.), *Gesta Grayorum, or, The History of the High and Mighty Prince, Henry Prince of Purpoole … who Reigned and Died, A.D. 1594: Together with a Masque, as it was Presented (by His Highness's Command) for the Entertainment of Q. Elizabeth* (London, 1688)

Carey, Robert, and Robert Naunton, *Memoirs of Robert Carey, Written By Himself. And, Fragmenta Regalia, by Sir R. Naunton* (Edinburgh, 1808)

Castiglione, Count Baldassarre, *The Courtier of Count Baldessar Castilio*, trans. Thomas Hoby (London, 1561)

Challoner, Francis, 'Letter to Sir Thomas Challoner: 18 December 1562', GB-Lna: SP70/66, Secretaries of State: State Papers Foreign, Elizabeth I, fol. 94v

Chamberlain, John, 'John Chamberlain to Dudley Carleton: 31 January 1599', GB-Lna: SP12/270, Secretaries of State: State Papers Domestic, Elizabeth I, fol. 41r–v

—— 'John Chamberlain to Dudley Carleton: 26 April 1602', GB-Lna: SP12/283a, Secretaries of State: State Papers Domestic, Elizabeth I, fols. 177r–179r
—— *The Letters of John Chamberlain*, ed. Norman Egbert McClure, 2 vols. (Philadelphia, 1939)
Chambers, E. K., and W. W. Greg (eds.), 'Dramatic Records from the Lansdowne Manuscripts', in *Malone Society Collections*, 16 vols. (Oxford, 1908), vol. 1, pt. 2, pp. 143–215
Charteris, Richard, *Alfonso Ferrabosco the Elder (1543–1588): A Thematic Catalogue of his Music with a Biographical Calendar*, Thematic Catalogues 11 (New York, 1984)
Chettle, Henry, *England's Mourning Garment Worn Here by Plain Shepherds, in Memory of their Sacred Mistress, Elizabeth* (London, 1603)
Churchyard, Thomas, *A Discourse of the Queen's Majesty's Entertainment in Suffolk and Norfolk with a Description of Many Things Then Presently Seen* (London, 1578)
—— *The First Part of Churchyard's Chips Containing Twelve Several Labours* (London, 1575)
—— *A Handful of Gladsome Verses, Given to the Queen's Majesty at Woodstock this Progress* (Oxford, 1592)
—— *A Musical Consort of Heavenly Harmony (Compounded Out of Many Parts of Music) Called Churchyard's Charity* (London, 1595)
—— *A Pleasaunt Labyrinth Called Churchyard's Chance Framed on Fancies, Uttered with Verses, and Writ to Give Solace to Every Well Disposed Mind* (London, 1580)
Clapham, John, *Elizabeth of England: Certain Observations Concerning the Life and Reign of Queen Elizabeth by John Clapham*, ed. Evelyn Plummer Read and Conyers Read (Philadelphia, 1951)
Cunningham, P. (ed.), *The Shakespeare Society Papers*, 4 vols. (London, 1844)
Dallam, Thomas, 'The Diary of Master Thomas Dallam, 1599–1600', in *Early Voyages and Travels in the Levant*, ed. J. Theodore Bent (London, 1893), pp. 1–98
D[avies], [Sir] J[ohn], 'A Lottery Presented before the Late Queen's Majesty at the Lord Chancellor's House 1601', in *A Poetical Rhapsody Containing: Diverse Sonnets, Odes, Elegies, Madrigals, Epigrams, Pastorals, Eclogues, with Other Poems*, ed. Francis Davison (London, 1608), pp. 4–8
Davies, Sir John, *Hymns of Astraea* (London, 1599)
—— *Orchestra or A Poem of Dancing* (London, 1596)
—— *The Poems of Sir John Davies*, ed. Robert Krueger (Oxford, 1975)
—— 'To the Queen', GB-EU: MS Laing III 444, fols. 33v–34r
Davison, Francis (ed.), *A Poetical Rhapsody, 1602–1621*, ed. Hyder Edward Rollins, 2 vols. (Cambridge, MA, 1931)
—— (ed.), *A Poetical Rhapsody Containing, Diverse Sonnets, Odes, Elegies, Madrigals, and Other Poesies* (London, 1602)
'A Device by the Earl of Essex for the Queen's Entertainment', GB-Lna: SP12/254, Secretaries of State: State Papers Foreign, Elizabeth I ([17 November] 1595), fols. 139r–140v
'Devices to be Showed Before the Queen's Majesty by way of Masking at Nottingham Castle After the Meeting of the Queen of Scots', GB-Lbl: Lansdowne MS 5/38 (1562), fol. 126

'The Dialogue between the Squire, Proteus, Amphitrite and Thamesis', GB-Lbl: MS Harley 541, fols. 138r–145r

Doughtie, Edward (ed.), *Liber Lilliati: Elizabethan Verse and Song (Bodleian MS Rawlinson Poetry 148)* (Newark, 1985)

Dowland, John, *The First Book of Ayres (1597, 1600, 1603, 1606, 1613)*, ed. Edmund Fellows and Thurston Dart, The English Lute Songs 1, 2nd edn (London, 1965; rept. 1998)

—— *The First Book of Songs or Ayres of Four Parts with Tablature for the Lute* (London, 1597)

—— *A Pilgrimes Solace (1612)*, ed. Edmund Fellowes and Thurston Dart, The English Lute Songs 4 (London, 1969)

—— *A Pilgrim's Solace wherein is Contained Musical Harmony of 3. 4. and 5. Parts* (London, 1612)

—— *The Second Book of Songs (1600)*, ed. Edmund Fellowes and Thurston Dart, The English Lute Songs 2 (London, 1969)

—— *The Second Book of Songs or Ayres, of 2, 4 and 5 Parts with Tablature for the Lute or Orpharion, with the Viola de Gamba* (London, 1600)

—— *The Third and Last Book of Songs or Airs Newly Composed to Sing to the Lute, Orpharion, or Viols* (London, 1603)

—— *The Third Booke of Songs (1603)*, ed. Edmund Fellows and Thurston Dart, The English Lute Songs 3 (London, 1970; rept. 2005)

Dowland, Robert (ed.), *A Musical Banquet (1610)*, ed. Peter Stroud, trans. Edward Filmer and Keith Statham, The English Lute Songs 16 (London, 1968)

—— (ed.), *A Musical Banquet Furnished with Variety of Delicious Ayres* (London, 1610)

Drayton, Michael, *Idea: The Shepherd's Garland Fashioned in Nine Eclogues. Rowland's Sacrifice to the Nine Muses* (London, 1593)

[Edwards, Richard?], 'Awake Ye Woeful Wights', GB-Lbl: Add. MS 15117, fol. 2

Edwards, Richard, *The Excellent Comedy of Two the Most Faithfullest Friends, Damon and Pithias* (London, 1571)

—— *The Paradise of Dainty Devices (1576–1606)*, ed. Hyder Edward Rollins (Cambridge, MA, 1927)

—— (ed.), *The Paradise of Dainty Devices Containing Sundry Pithy Precepts, Learned Counsels and Excellent Inventions* (London, 1576)

Edwards, Warwick (ed.), *Music for Mixed Consort*, Musica Britannica 40 (London, 1977)

Elyot, Sir Thomas, *The Book Named the Governor* (London, 1531)

Erasmus, Desiderius, *The Education of a Christian Prince*, ed. and trans. Lester Kruger Born, 2nd edn (New York, 1968)

Farrant, Richard, *The Wars of Cyrus: An Early Classical Narrative Drama of the Child Actors*, ed. James Brawner (Urbana, IL, 1942)

Ferrabosco the Elder, Alfonso, *Latin Songs, French Chansons and English Songs*, ed. Richard Charteris, Corpus mensurabilis musicae 96 (Neuhausen-Stuttgart, 1984)

Feuillerat, Albert Gabriel, *Documents Relating to the Office of the Revels in the Time of Queen Elizabeth*, Materialien zur Kunde des älteren Englischen Dramas 21 (Louvain, 1908)

The First Anointed Queen I Am, within this Town which Ever Came (n.p., 1573?)
Fitzwilliam, William, Earl of Southampton, 'About Katharine Howard: 5 November 1541', GB-Lna: SP1/167, State Papers Henry VIII: General Series, fols. 110r–113r, 117r–120v
Foxe, John, *Acts and Monuments of these Latter and Perilous Days* (London, 1563)
Fraunce, Abraham, *Symbolicae philosophiae liber quartus et ultimus*, ed. John Manning, trans. Estelle Haan, AMS Studies in the Emblem 7 (New York, 1991)
Galloway, David (ed.), *Records of Early English Drama: Norwich, 1540–1642* (Toronto, 1984)
G[arter], B[ernard], *The Joyful Receiving of the Queen's Most Excellent Majesty into her Highness' City of Norwich* (London, 1578)
Gascoigne, George, 'The Princely Pleasures at Kenilworth Castle', in *The Pleasantest Works of George Gascoigne Esquire* (London, 1587), sigs. A1r–C8v
GB-Cfm: Mu. MS 734
GB-Lam: The Robert Spencer Collection, MS 601 [Mynshall Lute Book]
GB-Lbl: MS 24665 ['Giles Earle his Book']
GB-Lbl: Royal Appendix MSS 74–6 [Lumley Partbooks]
GB-Oas: MS 155 [Sir Christopher Yelverton's Miscellany]
GB-Ob: MS Don. c. 54 [Richard Roberts's Miscellany]
GB-Ob: MS Rawl. poet. 148 ['Liber Lilliati']
GB-Och: Music MSS 984–8 [Dow Partbooks]
GB-WCc: MS 153 [Winchester Partbooks]
Genet, Jean-Philippe (ed.), *Four English Political Tracts of the Later Middle Ages* (London, 1977)
Gilbert, Sir Humphrey, *Queene Elizabethes Achademy, a Booke of Precedence etc.*, ed. Frederick James Furnivall (London, 1869)
Goldring, Elizabeth, et al. (eds.), *John Nichols's The Progresses and Public Processions of Queen Elizabeth I: A New Edition of the Early Modern Sources*, 5 vols. (Oxford, 2014)
Goldwell, Henry, *A Brief Declaration of the Shows, Devices, Speechs, and Inventions, Done and Performed Before the Queen's Majesty, and the French Ambassadors, at the Most Valiant and Worthy Triumph, Attempted and Executed on the Monday and Tuesday in Whitson Week Last, Anno 1581* (London, 1581)
Graham, Victor E., and W. McAllister Johnson (eds.), *The Royal Tour of France by Charles IX and Catherine de' Medici: Festivals and Entries, 1564–6* (Toronto, 1979)
Grant, Edward (ed.), *Disertissimi viri Rogeri Aschami, Angli, Regiae maiestati non ita pridem a Latinis epistolis, familiarium epistolarum libri tres magna orationis elegantia conscripti* (London, 1571)
Greer, David, *Collected English Lutenist Partsongs I*, Musica Britannica 53 (London, 1987)
Greg, W. W. (ed.), *Gesta Grayorum, 1688*, Malone Society Reprints (London, 1914)
Guazzo, Stefano, *The Civil Conversation*, trans. George Pettie (London, 1581)
Harington, Sir John, *The Epigrams of Sir John Harington*, ed. Gerard Kilroy (Farnham, 2009)
—— *The Most Elegant and Witty Epigrams of Sir John Harington* (London, 1618)

―――― *Nugae Antiquae: Being a Miscellaneous Collection of Original Papers, in Prose and Verse; Written during the Reigns of Henry VIII, Edward VI, Queen Mary, Elizabeth, and King James*, ed. Henry Harington and Thomas Park, 2 vols. (London, 1804)

Harrington, Richard, *A Famous Ditty of the Joyful Receiving of the Queen's Most Excellent Majesty, by the Worthy Citizens of London the XII Day of November, 1584 at Her Grace's Coming to St James* (London, 1584)

Hentzner, Paul, *Itinerarium Germaniae; Galliae; Angliae; Italiae* (Nuremberg, 1612)

Holborne, Anthony, *The Cittern School* (London, 1597)

Holinshed, Raphael, *The Third Volume of Chronicles, Beginning at Duke William the Norman, Commonly Called the Conqueror; and Descending by Degrees of Years to All the Kings and Queens of England in their Orderly Successions* (London, 1586)

The Honourable Entertainment Given to her Majesty in Progress at Cowdray in Sussex, by the Right Honourable the Lord Montague, Anno 1591, August 15 (London, 1591)

The Honourable Entertainment Given to the Queen's Majesty in Progress, at Elvetham in Hampshire, by the Right Honourable the Earl of Hertford (London, 1591)

Hotson, Leslie (ed.), *Queen Elizabeth's Entertainment at Mitcham: Poet, Painter, and Musician* (New Haven, CT, 1953)

Hume, Martin (ed.), *Calendar of Letters and State Papers Relating to English Affairs Preserved Principally in the Archives of Simancas*, 4 vols. (London, 1892)

I. F., *King James his Welcome to London with Eliza's Tomb and Epitaph, and our King's Triumph and Epitome* (London, 1603)

I. G., *An Apology for Womankind* (London, 1605)

The Institution of a Gentleman, 2nd edn (London, 1568)

Johnson, Edward, 'Elisa is the Fairest Queen / Come Again', GB-Lbl: Add. MSS 30480–4, vol. 1, fol. 65r; vol. 2, fol. 68v; vol. 3, fol. 63v; vol. 4, fol. 65v; vol. 5, fol. 10v

Johnston, Robert, *Historia rerum Britannicarum: ut et multarum Gallicarum, Belgicarum, & Germanicarum, tam politicarum, quam ecclesiasticarum, ab anno 1572, ad annum 1628* (Amsterdam, 1655)

Jones, Robert, *The Muses Gardin for Delights, or Fifth Booke of Ayres, 1610*, ed. Edmund Fellowes, English School of Lutenist Song Writers 15 (London, 1925)

―――― *Ultimum Vale, with a Triplicity of Music* (London, 1605)

'Journal des négociations des commissaires et ambassadeurs français de 24 avril au 1er mai 1581', GB-Lna: PRO 31/3/28, fol. 306r–v

King, Ros (ed.), *The Works of Richard Edwards: Politics, Poetry, and Performances in Sixteenth-Century England*, Revels Plays Companion Library (Manchester, 2001)

Klarwill, Victor (ed.), *Queen Elizabeth and some Foreigners: Being a Series of Hitherto Unpublished Letters from the Archives of the Hapsburg Family* (London, 1928)

Knox, John, *The First Blast of the Trumpet Against the Monstrous Regiment of Women* (Geneva, 1558)

―――― *The Works of John Knox*, ed. David Laing, 6 vols. (Edinburgh, 1846–64)

Kyffin, Maurice, *The Blessedness of Britain, or A Celebration of the Queen's Holiday* (London, 1587)

La Primaudaye, Pierre de, *The French Academy wherein is Discoursed the Institution of Manners, and whatsoever else Concerneth the Good and Happy Life of All Estates and Callings*, trans. T. B. (London, 1586)
Laneham, Robert, *A Letter wherein Part of the Entertainment Unto the Queen's Majesty at Killingworth [Kenilworth] Castle in Warwickshire in this Summer's Progress 1575 is Signified* (London, 1575)
Lasso, Orlando di, *Recueil du mélange d'Orlande de Lassus* (London, 1570)
Lloyd, Lodowick, *The Pilgrimage of Princes* (London, 1573)
Lo Here the Pearl, whom God and Man Doth Love (London, 1563)
Lyly, John, *Endimion, The Man in the Moon Played Before the Queen's Majesty at Greenwich on Candlemas Day at Night, by the Children of Paul's* (London, 1591)
—— *Midas Played Before the Queen's Majesty Upon Twelfth Day at Night, by the Children of Paul's* (London, 1592)
—— *Sappho and Phao, Played Before the Queen's Majesty on Shrove-Tuesday by her Majesty's Children and the Boys of Paul's* (London, 1584)
—— *Six Court Comedies Often Presented and Acted Before Queen Elizabeth, by the Children of her Majesty's Chapel, and the Children of Paul's*, ed. Edward Blount (London, 1632)
Maisse, André Hurault de, *A Journal of All that was Accomplished by Monsieur de Maisse, Ambassador in England from King Henri IV to Queen Elizabeth Anno Domini 1597*, ed. Robert Arthur Jones and G. B. Harrison (London, 1931)
Manningham, John, *The Diary of John Manningham of the Middle Temple, 1602–1603*, ed. Robert Parker Sorlien (Hanover, NH, 1976)
Marlowe, Christopher, *Edward II*, ed. Charles R. Forker (Manchester, 1994)
Mason, Sir John, 'Sir John Mason to Challoner: 19 July 1563', GB-Lna: SP70/60, Secretaries of State: State Papers Foreign, Elizabeth I, fols. 99r–100v
Maxwell, John, Lord Herries, *Historical Memoirs of the Reign of Mary Queen of Scots, and a Portion of the Reign of King James the Sixth*, ed. Robert Pitcairn (Edinburgh, 1836)
May, Steven W., 'The Poems of Edward DeVere, Seventeenth Earl of Oxford, and of Robert Devereux, Second Earl of Essex: An Edition and Commentary', *Studies in Philology* 77.5 (1980)
Melville, Sir James, *The Memoirs of Sir James Melville of Halhill*, ed. George Scott (London, 1683)
Montmorency, François de, 'Montmorency to Throgmorton: 14 August 1559', GB-Lna: SP70/6, Secretaries of State: State Papers Foreign Elizabeth I, fol. 76
Morley, Thomas, *Canzonets for Two and Three Voices*, ed. Edmund Fellowes and Thurston Dart, English Madrigalists 1 (London, 1956)
—— *A Plain and Easy Introduction to Practical Music* (London, 1597)
—— *The Triumphs of Oriana, to 5. and 6. Voices* (London, 1601)
Mulcaster, Richard, *Positions wherin those Primitive Circumstances be Examined, which are Necessary for the Training Up of Children* (London, 1581)
Mulryne, J. R., Helen Watanabe-O'Kelly, and Margaret Shewring (eds.), *Europa Triumphans: Court and Civic Festivals in Early Modern Europe* (Aldershot, 2004)
Mundy, John, *Songs and Psalms Composed in 3, 4, 5 Parts*, ed. Edmund Fellowes and Thurston Dart, English Madrigalists 35b (London, 1961)
Nallot, 'Tournoi', F-Pn: MS Dupuy 33 (1581), fols. 77r–81r

Nashe, Thomas, *The Terrors of the Night or, A Discourse of Apparitions* (London, 1594)

Naunton, Sir Robert, *Fragmenta Regalia, or, Observations on the Late Queen Elizabeth, Her Times and Favorites* (London, 1641)

A New Ballad of a Lover Extolling his Lady. To the Tune of Damon and Pithias (London, 1568)

Nichols, John (ed.), *The Progresses and Public Processions of Queen Elizabeth: Among which are Interspersed Other Solemnities, Public Expenditures, and Remarkable Events, During the Reign of that Illustrious Princess*, 3 vols. (London, 1823)

Pears, Steuart Adolphus (ed.), *The Correspondence of Sir Philip Sidney and Hubert Languet: Now First Collected and Translated from the Latin with Notes and a Memoir of Sidney* (London, 1845)

Peele, George, *Anglorum Feriae: England's Holidays Celebrated the 17th Novemb. Last, 1595* (London, 1595; rept. Ipswich, 1840)

—— *The Arraignment of Paris a Pastoral. Presented before the Queen's Majesty, by the Children of her Chapel* (London, 1584)

—— *An Eclogue, Gratulatory. Entituled: To the Right Honorable, and Renowned Shepherd of Albion's Arcadia: Robert Earl of Essex and Ewe for his Welcome into England from Portugal* (London, 1589)

—— *The Life and Works of George Peele*, ed. R. Mark Benbow, Elmer M. Blistein, and Frank S. Hook, 3 vols. (New Haven, CT, 1952)

—— *Polyhymnia Describing, the Honourable Triumph at Tilt, Before her Majesty, on the 17 of November, Last Past* (London, 1590)

Pilkington, Francis, *The First Book of Songs or Ayres of 4. Parts with Tablature for the Lute or Orpharion, with the Viol de Gamba* (London, 1605)

Pilkinton, Mark C. (ed.), *Records of Early English Drama: Bristol* (Toronto, 1997)

Plato, *The Republic*, ed. G. R. F. Ferrari, trans. Tom Griffith, Cambridge Texts in the History of Political Thought (Cambridge, 2000)

Platter, Thomas, *Beschreibung der Reisen durch Frankreich, Spanien, England und die Niederlande, 1595–1600*, ed. Rut Keiser, 2 vols. (Basel, 1968)

Playford, John, *An Introduction to the Skill of Music in Two Books* (London, 1674)

A Pleasant Comedy, Showing the Contention Between Liberality and Prodigality as it was Played Before her Majesty (London, 1602)

Pontaymeri, Alexandre de, *A Woman's Worth, Defended Against All the Men in the World Proving them to be More Perfect, Excellent, and Absolute in All Virtuous Actions, than Any Man of what Quality Soever* (London, 1599)

The Praise of Music wherein Besides the Antiquity, Dignity, Delectation, and Use Thereof in Civil Matters, is also Declared the Sober and Lawful Use of the Same in the Congregation and Church of God (Oxford, 1586)

Puttenham, George, *The Art of English Poesy* (London, 1589)

The Queen's Majesty's Entertainment at Woodstock (London, 1585)

Ralegh, Sir Walter, *The Letters of Sir Walter Ralegh*, ed. Agnes M. C. Latham and Joyce A. Youings (Exeter, 1999)

—— *The Poems of Sir Walter Ralegh: A Historical Edition*, ed. Michael Rudick, Medieval and Renaissance Texts and Studies 209; Renaissance English Text Society 23 (Tempe, AZ, 1999)

Rathgeb, Jacob, *Warhaffte Beschreibung zweier Reisen* (Tübingen, 1603)
Raumer, Friedrich Ludwig von, *History of the Sixteenth and Seventeenth Centuries, Illustrated by Original Documents*, 2 vols. (London, 1835)
Ravenscroft, Thomas, *Deuteromelia: or the Second Part of Music's Melody* (London, 1609)
Razzell, P. E. (ed.), *The Journals of Two Travellers in Elizabethan and Early Stuart England* (London, 1995)
Roberts, R. A. (ed.), *Calendar of the Manuscripts of the Most Hon. the Marquis of Salisbury, Preserved at Hatfield House, Hertfordshire*, 23 vols. (London, 1894)
Rude, Donald W. (ed.), *A Critical Edition of Sir Thomas Elyot's 'The Boke Named the Governour'* (New York, 1992)
Rye, William Brenchley (ed.), *England as Seen by Foreigners in the Days of Elizabeth and James the First, Comprising Translations of the Journals of the Two Dukes of Wirtemberg in 1592 and 1610* (London, 1865)
Salignac, Bertrand de, Seigneur de La Mothe-Fénélon, *Correspondance diplomatique de Bertrand de Salignac de La Mothe Fénélon*, ed. Charles Purton Cooper, 7 vols. (Paris, 1840)
Salter, Thomas, *A Mirror Meet for All Mothers, Matrons, and Maidens, Entitled the Mirror of Modesty* (London, 1579)
Segar, Sir William, *Honour Military, and Civil* (London, 1602)
Shakespeare, William, *The Chronicle History of Henry the Fifth with his Battle Fought at Agincourt in France* (London, 1602)
—— *The Norton Shakespeare*, ed. Walter Cohen et al. (New York, 1997)
—— *Shakespeare's Sonnets*, ed. Katherine Duncan-Jones, Arden Shakespeare, rev. edn (London, 2010)
Sidney, Sir Philip, *An Apology for Poetry* (London, 1595)
—— *The Countess of Pembroke's Arcadia* (London, 1590)
—— *The Countess of Pembroke's Arcadia (The Old Arcadia)*, ed. Katherine Duncan-Jones, World's Classics (Oxford, 1985)
—— 'Dispraise of a Courtly Life', in *A Poetical Rhapsody Containing, Diverse Sonnets, Odes, Elegies, Madrigals, and Other Poesies*, ed. Francis Davison (London, 1602), sigs. B2v–B3r
—— 'Her Most Excellent Majesty Walking in Wanstead [The Lady of May]', in *The Countess of Pembroke's Arcadia* (London, 1598), pp. 570–6
—— *The Poems of Sir Philip Sidney*, ed. William A. Ringler (Oxford, 1962)
Somerset, J. A. B. (ed.), *Records of Early English Drama: Shropshire*, 2 vols. (Toronto, 1994)
The Speeches and Honourable Entertainment Given to the Queen's Majesty in Progress, at Cowdray in Sussex, by the Right Honourable the Lord Montague (London, 1591)
Spenser, Edmund, *The Shepherd's Calendar Containing Twelve Eclogues Proportionable to the Twelve Months* (London, 1579)
Steele, Mary Susan, *Plays and Masques at Court during the Reigns of Elizabeth, James and Charles* (New Haven, CT, 1926)
Sternhold, Thomas, et al., *The Whole Book of Psalms Collected into English Metre* (London, 1562)
Stevenson, Joseph, et al. (eds.), *Calendar of State Papers, Foreign Series, of the Reign of Elizabeth*, 23 vols. (London, 1863–1950)

Stubbes, Phillip, *The Anatomy of Abuses Containing a Discovery, or Brief Summary of Such Notable Vices and Imperfections, as Now Reign in Many Christian Countries of the World* (London, 1583)
Swetnam, Joseph, *The Arraignment of Lewd, Idle, Froward, and Unconstant Women or the Vanity of them, Choose You Whether* (London, 1615)
Thacker, R., *A Godly Ditty to be Sung for the Preservation of the Queen's Most Excellent Majesty's Reign* (London, 1586)
Tyler, Royall, et al. (eds.), *Calendar of Letters, Despatches and State Papers Relating to Negotiations between England and Spain*, 13 vols. (London, 1862–1954)
US-NH: Filmer 2
Valdštejna, Zdeněk Brtnický z, *The Diary of Baron Waldstein, a Traveller in Elizabethan England*, ed. and trans. G. W. Groos (London, 1981)
Victoria and Albert Museum, 'The Glass Virginal', *V&A Collections*, online at <http://collections.vam.ac.uk/item/O58892> [accessed 19 July 2014]
Vives, Juan Luis, *A Very Fruitful and Pleasant Book, Called the Instruction of a Christian Woman*, trans. Richard Hyrde, 7th edn (London, 1585)
Watson, Thomas, *The First Set of Italian Madrigals Englished* (London, 1590)
—— *Italian Madrigals Englished (1590)*, ed. Albert Chatterley, Musica Britannica 74 (London, 1999)
Webbe, William, *A Discourse of English Poetry* (London, 1586)
Wedel, Lupold von, *Lupold von Wedels Beschreibung seiner Reisen und Kriegserlebnisse, 1561–1606*, ed. Max Bär (Stettin, 1895)
Whittingham, William, *The Bible and Holy Scriptures* (Geneva, 1561)
Whythorne, Thomas, *The Autobiography of Thomas Whythorne*, ed. James Marshall Osborn (Oxford, 1961)
Wotton, Henry, *Reliquiae Wottonianae or a Collection of Lives, Letters, Poems with Characters of Sundry Personages and Other Incomparable Pieces of Language and Art*, 3rd edn (London, 1672)
Wright, Thomas (ed.), *Queen Elizabeth and her Times: A Series of Original Letters*, 2 vols. (London, 1838)

SECONDARY LITERATURE

Abraham, Gerald, 'A Lost Poem by Queen Elizabeth I', *Times Literary Supplement*, 30 May 1968, 553
Adams, Simon, 'Howard, Katherine, Countess of Nottingham (1545×50–1603)', *ODNB* (online edn, 2008)
Alexander, Gavin, 'The Elizabethan Lyric as Contrafactum: Robert Sidney's "French Tune" Identified', *Music & Letters* 84 (2003), 378–402
—— 'The Musical Sidneys', *John Donne Journal* 25 (2006), 65–105
Allan, David, *Virtue, Learning and the Scottish Enlightenment: Ideas of Scholarship in Early Modern History* (Edinburgh, 1993)
Anderson, Susan, 'Music and Power at the English Court, 1575–1624', PhD dissertation, University of Leeds, 2006
Anglo, Sydney, '"Image-Making": The Means and the Limitations', in *The Tudor Monarchy*, ed. John Guy, Arnold Readers in History (London, 1997), pp. 16–42

Archer, Ian W., *The Pursuit of Stability: Social Relations in Elizabethan London*, Cambridge Studies in Early Modern British History (Cambridge, 1991)
Archer, Jayne Elisabeth, Elizabeth Goldring, and Sarah Knight (eds.), *The Progresses, Pageants, and Entertainments of Queen Elizabeth I* (Oxford, 2007)
Arkwright, G. E. P., 'Elizabethan Choirboy Plays and their Music', *Proceedings of the Musical Association* 40 (1913/14), 117–38
Asch, Ronald G., *Nobilities in Transition, 1550–1700: Courtiers and Rebels in Britain and Europe*, Reconstructions in Early Modern History (London, 2003)
Ashbee, Andrew, 'Groomed for Service: Musicians in the Privy Chamber at the English Court, c. 1495–1558', *Early Music* 25 (1997), 185–97
—— and David Lasocki, *A Biographical Dictionary of English Court Musicians, 1485–1714*, 2 vols. (Aldershot, 1998)
Astington, John, *English Court Theatre, 1558–1642* (Cambridge, 1999)
Atlas, Allan, *Music at the Aragonese Court of Naples* (Cambridge, 1985)
Austern, Linda Phyllis, '"Alluring the Auditorie to Effeminacie": Music and the Idea of the Feminine in Early Modern England', *Music & Letters* 74 (1993), 343–54
—— *Music in English Children's Drama of the Later Renaissance*, Musicology Series 13 (Philadelphia, 1992)
—— '"Sing Againe Syren": The Female Musician and Sexual Enchantment in Elizabethan Life and Literature', *Renaissance Quarterly* 42 (1989), 420–48
—— 'Women's Musical Voices in Sixteenth-Century England', *Early Modern Women: An Interdisciplinary Journal* 3 (2008), 127–52
Axton, Marie, *The Queen's Two Bodies: Drama and the Elizabethan Succession*, Royal Historical Society Studies in History 5 (London, 1977)
—— 'The Tudor Mask and Elizabethan Court Drama', in *English Drama: Forms and Development: Essays in Honour of Muriel Clara Bradbrook*, ed. Marie Axton and Raymond Williams (Cambridge, 1977), pp. 24–47
Baker, J. H., 'Egerton, Thomas, First Viscout Brackley (1540–1617)', *ODNB* (online edn, 2007)
Bates, Catherine, *The Rhetoric of Courtship in Elizabethan Language and Literature* (Cambridge, 1992)
Beal, Peter, 'Poems by Sir Philip Sidney: The Ottley Manuscript', *The Library* 33 (1978), 284–95
—— and Grace Ioppolo (eds.), *Elizabeth I and the Culture of Writing* (London, 2007)
Becker, Jochen, '"Greater than Zeuxis and Apelles": Artists as Arguments in the Antwerp Entry of 1549', in *Court Festivals of the European Renaissance: Art, Politics, and Performance*, ed. J. R. Mulryne and Elizabeth Goldring (Aldershot, 2002), pp. 171–95
Béhar, Pierre, and Helen Watanabe-O'Kelly (eds.), *Spectaculum Europaeum: Theatre and Spectacle in Europe = Histoire du spectacle en Europe (1580–1750)* (Wiesbaden, 1999)
Ben-Amos, Ilana Krausman, *The Culture of Giving: Informal Support and Gift-Exchange in Early Modern England*, Cambridge Social and Cultural Histories 12 (Cambridge, 2008)

Bergeron, David M., *English Civic Pageantry, 1558–1642*, Medieval and Renaissance Texts and Studies 267, rev. edn (Tempe, AZ, 2003)
—— 'The "I" of the Beholder: Thomas Churchyard and the 1578 Norwich Pageant', in *The Progresses, Pageants, and Entertainments of Queen Elizabeth I*, ed. Jayne Elisabeth Archer, Elizabeth Goldring, and Sarah Knight (Oxford, 2007), pp. 142–62
Berry, Philippa, *Of Chastity and Power: Elizabethan Literature and the Unmarried Queen* (London, 1989)
Bevington, David, 'John Lyly and Queen Elizabeth: Royal Flattery in *Campaspe* and *Sapho and Phao*', *Renaissance Papers* 1 (1966), 56–67
—— 'Lyly's *Endymion* and *Midas*: The Catholic Question in England', *Comparative Drama* 32 (1998), 26–46
—— and Peter Holbrook (eds.), *The Politics of the Stuart Court Masque* (Cambridge, 1998)
Biddle, Ian, and Kirsten Gibson (eds.), *Masculinity and Western Musical Practice* (Farnham, 2009)
Bingham, Caroline, *Darnley: A Life of Henry Stuart, Lord Darnley, Consort of Mary Queen of Scots* (London, 1995)
Bishop, T. G., 'Elizabethan Music as a Cultural Mode', in *Reconfiguring the Renaissance: Essays in Critical Materialism*, ed. Jonathan V. Crewe (Lewisburg, PA, 1992), pp. 51–75
Bornstein, Diane, *Mirrors of Courtesy* (Hamden, CT, 1975)
Bower, Calvin, 'Boethius', *NG2*
Bowers, Roger, H. Diack Johnstone, Richard Rastall and Peter Holman, 'London (i), II: Music at Court,' *NG2*
Brady, Andrea, '"Without Welt, Gard, or Embrodery": A Funeral Elegy for Cicely Ridgeway, Countess of Londonderry (1628)', *Huntington Library Quarterly* 72 (2009), 373–95
Breight, Curt, 'Caressing the Great: Viscount Montague's Entertainment of Elizabeth at Cowdray, 1591', *Sussex Archaeological Collection* 127 (1989), 147–66
—— 'Realpolitik and Elizabethan Ceremony: The Earl of Hertford's Entertainment of Elizabeth at Elvetham, 1591', *Renaissance Quarterly* 45 (1992), 20–48
Brennecke, Ernest, 'The Entertainment at Elvetham, 1591', in *Music in English Renaissance Drama*, ed. John H. Long (Lexington, KY, 1968), pp. 32–56
Brett, Philip, 'Consort Song', *NG2*
Brink, J. R., 'Sir John Davies's Orchestra: Political Symbolism and Textual Revisions', *Durham University Journal* n.s. 41 (1980), 195–201
Brooks, Jeanice, *Courtly Song in Late Sixteenth-Century France* (Chicago, 2000)
Brown, David, and Ian Harwood, 'Johnson, Edward (i)', *NG2*
Bundesen, Kristin, '"No Other Faction But My Own": Dynastic Politics and Elizabeth I's Carey Cousins', PhD dissertation, University of Nottingham, 2009
Burke, Peter, *The Fortunes of the Courtier: The European Reception of Castiglione's Cortegiano* (Cambridge, 1995)
Butler, Katherine, '"By Instruments her Powers Appeare": Music and Authority in the Reign of Queen Elizabeth I', *Renaissance Quarterly* 65 (2012), 353–84

—— 'Creating Harmonious Subjects? Ballads, Psalms, and Godly Songs for Queen Elizabeth I's Accession Day', *Journal of the Royal Musical Association* (forthcoming)

Butler, Martin, *The Stuart Court Masque and Political Culture* (Cambridge, 2008)

Caldwell, John, Edward Olleson, and Susan Wollenberg (eds.), *The Well-Enchanting Skill: Music, Poetry, and Drama in the Culture of the Renaissance: Essays in Honour of F. W. Sternfeld* (Oxford, 1990)

Calogero, Elena, '"Sweet Aluring Harmony": Heavenly and Earthly Sirens in Sixteenth-Century Literary and Visual Culture', in *Music of the Sirens*, ed. Linda Phyllis Austern and Inna Naroditskaya (Bloomington, IN, 2006), pp. 140–75

Chafe, Eric Thomas, *Monteverdi's Tonal Language* (New York, 1992)

Chambers, E. K., *Sir Henry Lee: An Elizabethan Portrait* (Oxford, 1936)

Chan, Mary, 'Cynthia's Revels and Music for a Choir School: Christ Church Manuscript Mus 439', *Studies in the Renaissance* 18 (1971), 134–72

—— *Music in the Theatre of Ben Jonson* (Oxford, 1980)

Chaudhuri, Sukanta, 'Marlowe, Madrigals, and a New Elizabethan Poet', *Review of English Studies* n.s. 39 (1988), 199–216

Clark, J. Bunker, 'Giles, Nathaniel', *NG2*

Claydon, Tony, and W. A. Speck, *William and Mary*, Very Interesting People (Oxford, 2007)

Coch, Christine, '"Mother of my Contrye": Elizabeth I and Tudor Constructions of Motherhood', in *The Mysteries of Elizabeth I: Selections from English Literary Renaissance*, ed. Kirby Farrell and Kathleen M. Swaim (Amherst, MA, 2003), pp. 134–61

Cole, Mary Hill, 'Monarchy in Motion: An Overview of Elizabethan Progresses', in *The Progresses, Pageants, and Entertainments of Queen Elizabeth I*, ed. Jayne Elisabeth Archer, Elizabeth Goldring, and Sarah Knight (Oxford, 2007), pp. 27–44

—— *The Portable Queen: Elizabeth I and the Politics of Ceremony*, Massachusetts Studies in Early Modern Culture (Amherst, 1999)

Collinson, Patrick, 'Pulling the Strings: Religion and Politics in the Progress of 1578', in *The Progresses, Pageants, and Entertainments of Queen Elizabeth I*, ed. Jayne Elisabeth Archer, Elizabeth Goldring, and Sarah Knight (Oxford, 2007), pp. 122–41

Connolly, Annaliese, '"O Unquenchable Thirst of Gold": Lyly's *Midas* and the English Quest for Empire', *Early Modern Literary Studies* 8.2 (2002), 4.1–36, online at <http://purl.oclc.org/emls/08-2/conngold.html> [accessed 19 July 2014]

Council, Norman, '*O Dea Certe*: The Allegory of *The Fortress of Perfect Beauty*', *The Huntington Library Quarterly* 39 (1976), 329–42

Craig-McFeely, Julia, 'The Signifying Serpent: Seduction by Cultural Stereotype in Seventeenth-Century England', in *Music, Sensation, and Sensuality*, ed. Linda Phyllis Austern, Critical and Cultural Musicology 5 (New York, 2002), pp. 299–317

Crane, Mary Thomas, '"Video et Taceo": Elizabeth I and the Rhetoric of Counsel', *Studies in English Literature, 1500–1900* 28 (1988), 1–15

Crane, Susan, *The Performance of Self: Ritual, Clothing, and Identity during the Hundred Years War*, Middle Ages Series (Philadelphia, 2002)

Daniel, Carter, 'The Date of Peele's *Arraignment of Paris*', *Notes & Queries* 29 (1982), 131–2

Davidson, Peter, and Jane Stevenson, 'Elizabeth I's Reception at Bisham (1592): Elite Women as Writers and Devisers', in *The Progresses, Pageants, and Entertainments of Queen Elizabeth I*, ed. Jayne Elisabeth Archer, Elizabeth Goldring, and Sarah Knight (Oxford, 2007), pp. 207–26

Dennis, Flora, 'Music in Ferrarese Festival: Harmony and Chaos', in *Court Festivals of the European Renaissance: Art, Politics, and Performance*, ed. J. R. Mulryne and Elizabeth Goldring (Aldershot, 2002), pp. 287–93

Doe, Paul, and David Allinson, 'Tallis, Thomas', *NG2*

Doran, Susan, *Elizabeth I and Foreign Policy, 1558–1603*, Lancaster Pamphlets 20 (London, 2000)

—— 'Juno versus Diana: The Treatment of Elizabeth I's Marriage in Plays and Entertainments, 1561–1581', *The Historical Journal* 28 (1995), 257–74

—— *Monarchy and Matrimony: The Courtships of Elizabeth I* (London, 1996)

—— 'Three Late-Elizabethan Succession Tracts', in *The Struggle for the Succession: Politics, Polemics and Cultural Representations*, ed. Jean-Christophe Mayer, Astraea Texts 11 (Montpellier, 2004), pp. 100–17

Doughtie, Edward, 'The Earl of Essex and Occasions for Contemplative Verse', *English Literary Renaissance* 9 (1979), 355–63

—— *Lyrics from English Airs, 1596–1622* (Cambridge, MA, 1970)

Dovey, Zillah, *An Elizabethan Progress: The Queen's Journey into East Anglia, 1578* (Stroud, 1996)

Dumitrescu, Theodor, *The Early Tudor Court and International Musical Relations* (Aldershot, 2007)

Duncan-Jones, Katherine, '"Melancholie Times": Musical Recollections of Sidney by William Byrd and Thomas Watson', in *The Well-Enchanting Skill: Music, Poetry, and Drama in the Culture of the Renaissance: Essays in Honour of F. W. Sternfeld*, ed. John Caldwell, Edward Olleson, and Susan Wollenberg (Oxford, 1990), pp. 171–80

—— 'Sidney's Personal Imprese', *Journal of the Warburg and Courtauld Institutes* 33 (1970), 321–4

—— *Sir Philip Sidney: Courtier Poet* (London, 1991)

Dunlop, Fiona, *The Late Medieval Interlude: The Drama of Youth and Aristocratic Masculinity* (York, 2007)

Dunn, Leslie C., 'Re-sounding Elizabeth in Seventeenth-Century Music: Morley to Purcell', in *Resurrecting Elizabeth I in Seventeenth-Century England*, ed. Elizabeth H. Hageman and Katherine Conway (Madison, NJ, 2007), pp. 239–60

Dutton, Richard, *Mastering the Revels: The Regulation and Censorship of English Renaissance Drama* (Basingstoke, 1991)

Eckhardt, Joshua, '"From a Seruant of Diana" to the Libellers of Robert Cecil: The Transmission of Songs written for Queen Elizabeth I', in *Elizabeth I and the Culture of Writing*, ed. Peter Beal and Grace Ioppolo (London, 2007), pp. 115–31

Edwards, Warwick, 'Consort', *NG2*
Empson, William, *Some Versions of Pastoral* (London, 1935)
Fantazzi, Charles, 'Vives, Juan Luis (1492/3–1540)', *ODNB* (online edn, 2008)
Ferer, Mary Tiffany, *Music and Ceremony at the Court of Charles V: The Capilla Flamenca and the Art of Political Promotion*, Studies in Medieval and Renaissance Music 12 (Woodbridge, 2012)
Field, Christopher, 'Fantasia', *NG2*
Fischlin, Daniel, *In Small Proportions: A Poetics of the English Ayre, 1596–1622* (Detroit, 1998)
—— 'The Performance Context of the English Lute Song, 1596–1622', in *Performance on Lute, Guitar, and Vihuela: Historical Practice and Modern Interpretation*, ed. Victor Coelho, Cambridge Studies in Performance Practice (Cambridge, 1997), pp. 47–71
—— 'Political Allegory, Absolutist Ideology, and the "Rainbow Portrait" of Queen Elizabeth I', *Renaissance Quarterly* 50 (1997), 175–206
Forney, Kristine K., 'A Gift of Madrigals and Chansons: The Winchester Part Books and the Courtship of Elizabeth I by Erik XIV of Sweden', *The Journal of Musicology* 17 (1999), 50–75
Fox, Adam, *Oral and Literate Culture in England, 1500–1700*, Oxford Studies in Social History (Oxford, 2000)
Fraser, Antonia, *Mary Queen of Scots* (London, 2004)
Freedman, Richard, *The Chansons of Orlando di Lasso and their Protestant Listeners: Music, Piety, and Print in Sixteenth-Century France*, Eastman Studies in Music (Rochester, NY, 2001)
Freedman, Sylvia, *Poor Penelope: Lady Penelope Rich, An Elizabethan Woman* (Abbostbrook, 1983)
Frieder, Braden, *Chivalry and the Perfect Prince: Tournaments, Art, and Armor at the Spanish Habsburg Court*, Sixteenth Century Essays and Studies 81 (Kirksville, MO, 2008)
Frye, Susan, *Elizabeth I: The Competition for Representation* (Oxford, 1993)
Fuller, David, 'Ben Jonson's Plays and their Contemporary Music', *Music & Letters* 58 (1977), 60–75
Fumerton, Patricia, *Cultural Aesthetics: Renaissance Literature and the Practice of Social Ornament* (Chicago, 1991)
—— '"Secret" Arts: Elizabethan Miniatures and Sonnets', *Representations* 15 (1986), 57–97
Gair, W. Reavley, *The Children of Paul's: The Story of a Theatre Company, 1553–1608* (Cambridge, 1982)
Gale, Michael, 'Remnants of Some Late Sixteenth-Century Trumpet Ensemble Music', *Historic Brass Society Journal* 14 (2002), 115–31
Gerbino, Giuseppe, *Music and the Myth of Arcadia in Renaissance Italy*, New Perspectives in Music History and Criticism (Cambridge, 2009)
Getz, Christine Suzanne, *Music in the Collective Experience in Sixteenth-Century Milan* (Aldershot, 2005)
Gibson, Kirsten, 'John Dowland and the Elizabethan Courtier Poets', *Early Music* 41 (2013), 239–53

—— 'Music, Melancholy and Masculinity in Early Modern England', in *Masculinity and Western Musical Practice*, ed. Ian D. Biddle and Kirsten Gibson (Farnham, 2009), pp. 41–66

—— 'The Order of the Book: Materiality, Narrative and Authorial Voice in John Dowland's *First Booke of Songes or Ayres*', *Renaissance Studies* 26 (2012), 13–33

—— '"So to the Wood Went I": Politicizing the Greenwood in Two Songs by John Dowland', *Journal of the Royal Musical Association* 132 (2007), 221–51

Goldring, Elizabeth, 'Portraiture, Patronage, and the Progresses: Robert Dudley, Earl of Leicester and the Kenilworth Festivities of 1575', in *The Progresses, Pageants, and Entertainments of Queen Elizabeth I*, ed. Jayne Elisabeth Archer, Elizabeth Goldring, and Sarah Knight (Oxford, 2007), pp. 163–88

Goodare, Julian, 'Mary [Mary Stewart] (1542–1587)', *ODNB* (online edn, 2007)

Greenblatt, Stephen, *Renaissance Self-Fashioning: From More to Shakespeare* (Chicago, 1980)

Greer, David, '"Thou Court's Delight": Biographical Notes on Henry Noel', *The Lute Society Journal* 17 (1975), 49–59

Greig, Elaine, 'Stewart, Henry, Duke of Albany [Lord Darnley] (1545/6–1567)', *ODNB* (online edn, 2008)

Guinle, Francis, 'Rude Ditties to a Pipe and Sonnets to a Lute', in *The Show Within: Dramatic and Other Insets: English Renaissance Drama (1550–1642)*, ed. François Laroque, 2 vols. (Montpellier, 1992), pp. 417–26

Guy, John, 'The 1590s: The Second Reign of Elizabeth I?', in *The Reign of Elizabeth I: Court and Culture in the Last Decade*, ed. John Guy (Cambridge, 1995), pp. 1–19

—— 'The Rhetoric of Counsel in Early Modern England', in *Tudor Political Culture*, ed. Dale Hoak (Cambridge, 1995), pp. 292–310

Hackett, Helen, *Virgin Mother, Maiden Queen: Elizabeth I and the Cult of the Virgin Mary* (Basingstoke, 1996)

Hammer, Paul E. J., 'Devereux, Robert, Second Earl of Essex (1565–1601)', *ODNB* (online edn, 2008)

—— 'The Earl of Essex, Fulke Greville, and the Employment of Scholars', *Studies in Philology* 91 (1994), 167–80

—— *Elizabeth's Wars: War, Government and Society in Tudor England, 1544–1604* (Basingstoke, 2003)

—— *The Polarisation of Elizabethan Politics: The Political Career of Robert Devereux, 2nd Earl of Essex, 1585–1597*, Cambridge Studies in Early Modern British History (Cambridge, 1999)

—— 'Upstaging the Queen: The Earl of Essex, Francis Bacon and the Accession Day Celebrations of 1595', in *The Politics of the Stuart Court Masque*, ed. David Bevington and Peter Holbrook (Cambridge, 1998), pp. 41–66

Hanford, James, and Sara Watson, 'Personal Allegory in the *Arcadia*: Philisides and Lelius', *Modern Philology* 32 (1934), 1–10

Hardison, O. B., *The Enduring Monument: A Study of the Idea of Praise in Renaissance Literary Theory and Practice* (Westport, CT, 1973)

Headlam Wells, Robin, 'Elizabethan Epideictic Drama: Praise and Blame in the Plays of Peele and Lyly', *Cahiers Élisabéthains* 23 (1983), 15–33

—— 'Thomas Morley's "Fair in a Morn"', *The Lute Society Journal* 18 (1976), 37–42

Heale, Elizabeth, 'Contesting Terms: Loyal Catholicism and Lord Montague's Entertainment at Cowdray, 1591', in *The Progresses, Pageants, and Entertainments of Queen Elizabeth I*, ed. Jayne Elisabeth Archer, Elizabeth Goldring, and Sarah Knight (Oxford, 2007), pp. 189–206

Heaton, Gabriel, 'Elizabethan Entertainments in Manuscript: The Harefield Festivities (1602) and the Dynamics of Exchange', in *The Progresses, Pageants, and Entertainments of Queen Elizabeth I*, ed. Jayne Elisabeth Archer, Elizabeth Goldring, and Sarah Knight (Oxford, 2007), pp. 225–44

—— *Writing and Reading Royal Entertainments: From George Gascoigne to Ben Jonson* (Oxford, 2010)

Hedell, Kia, 'Musical Contacts of the Swedish Royal Court during the Early Vasa Dynasty (1521–1611): Towards a Changed View of Swedish Particpation in European Cultural Life', in *Early Music: Context and Ideas: International Conference in Musicology, Kraków, 18–21 September 2003*, ed. Karol Berger, Lubomir Chalupka, and Albert Dunning (Kraków, 2003), pp. 103–9

Helms, Dietrich, 'Henry VIII's Book: Teaching Music to Royal Children', *Musical Quarterly* 92 (2009), 118–35

Hill, Christopher, 'The Many-Headed Monster in Late Tudor and Early Stuart England', in *From the Renaissance to the Counter-Reformation: Essays in Honour of Garrett Mattingly*, ed. Charles Howard Carter (London, 1966), pp. 296–324

Hillebrand, Harold Newcomb, *The Child Actors: A Chapter in Elizabethan Stage History*, Illinois Studies in Language and Literature 11 (Urbana, 1926)

Hilliard, Stephen S., 'Lyly's *Midas* as an Allegory of Tyranny', *Studies in English Literature, 1500–1900* 12 (1972), 243–58

Hollander, John, *The Untuning of the Sky: Ideas of Music in English Poetry, 1500–1700* (Princeton, NJ, 1961)

Holm, Janis Butler, 'Thomas Salter's *The Mirrhor of Modestie*: A Translation of Bruto's *La institutione di vna fanciulla nata nobilmente*', *The Library* s6–5 (1983), 53–7

Holman, Peter, *Dowland: Lachrimae (1604)*, Cambridge Music Handbooks (Cambridge, 1999)

—— *Four and Twenty Fiddlers: The Violin at the English Court, 1540–1690*, Oxford Monographs on Music (Oxford, 1993)

Holt, Mack P., *The Duke of Anjou and the Politique Struggle during the Wars of Religion*, Cambridge Studies in Early Modern History (Cambridge, 1986)

Hotson, Leslie, *The First Night of Twelfth Night* (New York, 1954)

Howard, Skiles, *The Politics of Courtly Dancing in Early Modern England*, Massachusetts Studies in Early Modern Culture (Amherst, 1998)

Howatson, M. C., and Ian Chilvers, 'Hermes Trismegistus', in *The Concise Oxford Companion to Classical Literature* (Oxford, 1996), p. 262

Howell, Roger, *Sir Philip Sidney: The Shepherd Knight* (London, 1968)

Hulse, Lynn, 'The Musical Patronage of Robert Cecil, First Earl of Salisbury (1563–1612)', *Journal of the Royal Musical Association* 116 (1991), 24–40

Hunter, G. K., *John Lyly: The Humanist as Courtier* (London, 1962)

Hurstfield, Joel, 'The Succession Struggle in Late Elizabethan England', in *Freedom, Corruption and Government in Elizabethan England*, ed. Joel Hurstfield (London, 1973), pp. 104–34

Jeffrey, Brian, 'Antony Holborne', *Musica disciplina* 22 (1968), 129–205
Kay, Dennis, 'Marlowe, *Edward II*, and the Cult of Elizabeth', *Early Modern Literary Studies* 3.2 (1997), 1.1–30, online at <http://purl.oclc.org/emls/03-2/kaymarl.html> [accessed 19 July 2014]
Kelsey, Sean, 'Davies, Sir John (bap. 1569, d. 1626)', *ODNB* (online edn, 2008)
Kerman, Joseph, 'Byrd, William', *NG2*
—— *The Elizabethan Madrigal: A Comparative Study* (New York, 1962)
—— 'An Italian Musician in England', in *Write All These Down: Essays on Music* (Berkeley, CA, 1994), pp. 139–51
—— 'Music and Politics: The Case of William Byrd (1540–1623)', *Proceedings of the American Philosophical Society* 144 (2000), 275–87
—— 'On William Byrd's *Emendemus in Melius*', in *Hearing the Motet: Essays on the Motet of the Middle Ages and Renaissance*, ed. Dolores Pesce (Oxford, 1997), pp. 329–47
Kesselring, K. J., *The Northern Rebellion of 1569: Faith, Politics, and Protest in Elizabethan England* (Basingstoke, 2007)
Kewes, Paulina, 'Godly Queens: The Royal Iconographies of Mary and Elizabeth', in *Tudor Queenship: The Reigns of Mary and Elizabeth*, ed. Anna Whitelock and Alice Hunt, Queenship and Power (New York, 2010), pp. 47–62
King, John, 'Queen Elizabeth I: Representations of the Virgin Queen', *Renaissance Quarterly* 40 (1990), 30–74
Kottick, Edward L., *A History of the Harpsichord* (Bloomington, IN, 2003)
Knecht, R. J., 'Charles V's Journey through France, 1539–40', in *Court Festivals of the European Renaissance: Art, Politics, and Performance*, ed. J. R. Mulryne and Elizabeth Goldring (Aldershot, 2002), pp. 153–70
Kuchta, David, 'The Semiotics of Masculinity in Renaissance England', in *Sexuality and Gender in Early Modern Europe: Institutions, Texts, Images*, ed. James Turner (Cambridge, 1993), pp. 233–46
Lasocki, David, 'Professional Recorder Players in England, 1540–1740', 3 vols., PhD dissertation, University of Iowa, 1983
—— and Roger Prior, *The Bassanos: Venetian Musicians and Instrument Makers in England, 1531–1665* (Aldershot, 1995)
Lawson, Jane A., 'The Remembrance of the New Year: Books Given to Queen Elizabeth as New Year's Gifts', in *Elizabeth I and the Culture of Writing*, ed. Peter Beal and Grace Ioppolo (London, 2007), pp. 133–72
Le Huray, Peter, *Music and the Reformation in England, 1549–1660*, Cambridge Studies in Music (Cambridge, 1978)
—— and John Morehen, 'Farrant, Richard', *NG2*
Leahy, William, *Elizabethan Triumphal Processions* (Aldershot, 2005)
Lennam, Trevor, *Sebastian Westcott, The Children of Paul's, and The Marriage of Wit and Science* (Toronto, 1975)
Lennon, Colm, 'Burke, Richard, Fourth Earl of Clanricarde and First Earl of St Albans (1572–1635)', *ODNB* (online edn, 2004)
Levin, Carole, *The Heart and Stomach of a King: Elizabeth I and the Politics of Sex and Power*, New Cultural Studies (Philadelphia, 1994)
—— *The Reign of Elizabeth I* (Basingstoke, 2002)

Lindley, David (ed.), *The Court Masque*, Revels Plays Companion Library (Manchester, 1984)
—— 'The Politics of Music in the Masque', in *The Politics of the Stuart Court Masque*, ed. David Bevington and Peter Holbrook (Cambridge, 1998), pp. 273–95
Loades, David, *Mary Tudor: A Life* (Oxford, 1989)
Lockwood, Lewis, *Music in Renaissance Ferrara, 1400–1505: The Creation of a Musical Centre in the Fifteenth Century* (Oxford, 1984)
Long, John, 'Music for a Song in "Damon and Pithias"', *Music & Letters* 48 (1967), 247–50
MacCaffrey, Wallace, 'Carey, Henry, First Baron Hunsdon (1526–1596)', *ODNB* (online edn, 2013)
—— *Elizabeth I: War and Politics, 1588–1603* (Princeton, NJ, 1992)
Manifold, John, 'Theatre Music in the Sixteenth and Seventeenth Centuries', *Music & Letters* 29 (1948), 366–97
Manning, John, 'Continental Emblem Books in Sixteenth-Century England: The Evidence of Sloane MS. 3794', *Emblematica* 1 (1986), 1–11
—— 'Geffrey Whitney's Unpublished Emblems: Further Evidence of Indebtedness to Continental Traditions', in *The English Emblem and the Continental Tradition*, ed. Peter Daly, AMS Studies in the Emblem 1 (New York, 1988), pp. 83–107
—— 'An Unedited and Unpublished Sixteenth-Century English Translation of Some Alciato Emblems: British Library Additional MS. 61822', *Emblematica* 7 (1993), 181–2
Margolin, Jean-Claude, 'Sur un paradoxe bien tempéré de la Renaissance: Concordia discors', in *Concordia discors: Studi su Niccolò Cusano e l'umanesimo europeo offerti a Giovanni Santinello*, ed. Giovanni Santinello and Gregorio Piaia, Medioevo e umanesimo 84 (Padova, 1993), pp. 405–32
Marotti, Arthur F., '"Love is Not Love": Elizabethan Sonnet Sequences and the Social Order', *English Literary History* 49 (1982), 396–428
—— *Manuscript, Print, and the English Renaissance Lyric* (Ithaca, NY, 1995)
—— and Steven W. May, 'Two Lost Ballads of the Armada Thanksgiving Celebration [with texts and illustration]', *English Literary Renaissance* 41 (2011), 31–63
Marsh, Christopher, *Music and Society in Early Modern England* (Cambridge, 2010)
May, Steven W., 'Dyer, Sir Edward (1543–1607)', *ODNB* (online edn, 2008)
—— *The Elizabethan Courtier Poets: The Poems and their Contexts* (Columbia, MO, 1991)
Mayer, Jean-Christophe (ed.), *The Struggle for the Succession: Politics, Polemics and Cultural Representations*, Astraea Texts 11 (Montpellier, 2004)
McCabe, William H., *An Introduction to the Jesuit Theater: A Posthumous Work*, ed. Louis J. Oldani (St Louis, MO, 1983)
McCarthy, Jeanne H., 'Elizabeth I's "Picture in Little": Boy Company Representations of a Queen's Authority', *Studies in Philology* 100 (2003), 425–62

McCoy, Richard C., 'Lord of Liberty: Francis Davison and the Cult of Elizabeth', in *The Reign of Elizabeth I: Court and Culture in the Last Decade*, ed. John Guy (Cambridge, 1995), pp. 212–28

—— *The Rites of Knighthood: The Literature and Politics of Elizabethan Chivalry*, New Historicism 7 (Berkeley, CA, 1989)

—— *Sir Philip Sidney: Rebellion in Arcadia* (Sussex, 1979)

McGee, C. E., 'Mysteries, Musters, and Masque: The Import(s) of Elizabethan Civic Entertainments', in *The Progresses, Pageants, and Entertainments of Queen Elizabeth I*, ed. Jayne Elisabeth Archer, Elizabeth Goldring, and Sarah Knight (Oxford, 2007), pp. 104–21

Mears, Natalie, 'Politics in the Elizabethan Privy Chamber: Lady Mary Sidney and Kat Ashley', in *Women and Politics in Early Modern England, 1450–1700*, ed. James Daybell (Aldershot, 2004), pp. 67–82

Melnikoff, Kirk, 'Jones, Richard (*fl.* 1564–1613)', *ODNB* (online edn, 2004)

Merkley, Paul, and Lora L. M. Merkley, *Music and Patronage in the Sforza Court*, Studi sulla storia della musica in Lombardia 3 (Turnhout, 1999)

Merton, Charlotte, 'The Women who Served Queen Mary and Queen Elizabeth: Ladies, Gentlewomen and Maids of the Privy Chamber, 1553–1603', PhD dissertation, University of Cambridge, 1992

Milsom, John, 'Music, Politics and Society', in *A Companion to Tudor Britain*, ed. Robert Tittler and Norman L. Jones (Oxford, 2004), pp. 492–508

Monson, Craig, 'Byrd, the Catholics, and the Motet: The Hearing Reopened', in *Hearing the Motet: Essays on the Motet of the Middle Ages and Renaissance*, ed. Dolores Pesce (Oxford, 1997), pp. 348–74

—— 'Elizabethan London', in *The Renaissance: From the 1470s to the End of the 16th Century*, ed. Iain Fenlon, Man and Music 2 (London, 1989), pp. 304–40

—— *Voices and Viols in England, 1600–1650: The Sources and the Music* (Ann Arbor, MI, 1982)

Montrose, Louis, 'Celebration and Insinuation: Sir Philip Sidney and the Motives of Elizabethan Courtship', *Renaissance Drama* 8 (1977), 3–35

—— '"Eliza, Queene of Shepheardes", and the Pastoral of Power', *English Literary Renaissance* 10 (1980), 153–82

—— 'Gifts and Reasons: The Contexts of Peele's *Araygnment of Paris*', *English Literary History* 47 (1980), 433–61

—— 'Of Gentlemen and Shepherds: The Politics of Elizabethan Pastoral Form', *English Literary History* 50 (1983), 415–59

—— '"Shaping Fantasies": Figurations of Gender and Power in Elizabethan Culture', *Representations* 2 (1983), 61–94

—— *The Subject of Elizabeth: Authority, Gender, and Representation* (Chicago, 2006)

Morrongiello, Christopher, 'Edward Collard (d. 1600) and Daniel Bacheler (d. 1619): A Critical Study and Edition of their Lute Music', 3 vols., DPhil dissertation, University of Oxford, 2005

Mulryne, J. R., and Elizabeth Goldring (eds.), *Court Festivals of the European Renaissance: Art, Politics, and Performance* (Aldershot, 2002)

Myers, Nick, 'The Gossip of History: The Question of the Succession in the State Papers', in *The Struggle for the Succession: Politics, Polemics and Cultural Representations*, ed. Jean-Christophe Mayer, Astraea Texts 11 (Montpellier, 2004), pp. 49–64

Nelson, Katie, 'Love in the Music Room: Thomas Whythorne and the Private Affairs of Tudor Music Tutors', *Early Music* 40 (2012), 15–26

Nickel, Helmut, 'The Tournament: A Historical Sketch', in *The Study of Chivalry: Resources and Approaches*, ed. Howell D. Chickering and Thomas H. Seiler (Kalamazoo, MI, 1988), pp. 213–62

Norbrook, David, *Poetry and Politics in the English Renaissance*, rev. edn (Oxford, 2002)

North, John, *The Ambassadors' Secret: Holbein and the World of the Renaissance* (London, 2004)

Orgel, Stephen, *The Illusion of Power: Political Theater in the English Renaissance*, Quantum Books (Berkeley, CA, 1975)

—— *The Jonsonian Masque* (New York, 1981)

Osborn, James Marshall, *Young Philip Sidney, 1572–1577*, Elizabethan Club Series 5 (New Haven, CT, 1972)

Palisca, Claude, 'Mode Ethos in the Renaissance', in *Essays in Musicology: A Tribute to Alvin Johnson*, ed. Lewis Lockwood and Edward H. Roesner (Philadelphia, 1990), pp. 126–39

Partridge, Mary, 'Images of the Courtier in Elizabethan England', PhD dissertation, University of Birmingham, 2008

Pattison, Bruce, 'Sir Philip Sidney and Music', *Music & Letters* 15 (1934), 75–81

Payne, Helen, 'Russell, Lucy, Countess of Bedford (bap. 1581, d. 1627)', *ODNB* (online edn, 2008)

Pearl, Sara, 'Sounding to Present Occasions: Jonson's Masques of 1620–5', in *The Court Masque*, ed. David Lindley, Revels Plays Companion Library (Manchester, 1984), pp. 60–77

Perry, Curtis, 'Court and Coterie Culture', in *A Companion to English Renaissance Literature and Culture*, ed. Michael Hattaway, Blackwell Companions to Literature and Culture (Oxford, 2000), pp. 106–18

Pincombe, Michael, *The Plays of John Lyly: Eros and Eliza*, Revels Plays Companion Library (Manchester, 1996)

Pollack, Janet, 'Princess Elizabeth Stuart as Musician and Muse', in *Musical Voices of Early Modern Women: Many Headed Melodies*, ed. Thomasin K. LaMay, Women and Gender in the Early Modern World (Aldershot, 2005), pp. 399–424

Poulton, Diana, *John Dowland*, rev. edn (London, 1982)

Price, David, 'Gilbert Talbot, Seventh Earl of Shrewsbury: An Elizabethan Courtier and his Music', *Music & Letters* 57 (1976), 144–51

—— *Patrons and Musicians of the English Renaissance*, Cambridge Studies in Music (Cambridge, 1981)

Prior, Roger, 'Jewish Musicians at the Tudor Court', *The Musical Quarterly* 69 (1983), 253–65

Prizer, William, 'Una "virtù molto conveniente a Madonna": Isabella d'Este as a Musician', *The Journal of Musicology* 17 (1999), 10–49

Questier, Michael C., *Catholicism and Community in Early Modern England: Politics, Aristocratic Patronage, and Religion, c. 1550–1640*, Cambridge Studies in Early Modern British History (Cambridge, 2006)

Raab, Felix, *The English Face of Machiavelli: A Changing Interpretation, 1500–1700*, Studies in Political History (London, 1964)

Rasmussen, Mary, 'The Case of the Flutes in Holbein's *The Ambassadors*', *Early Music* 23 (1995), 115–23

Raumer, Friedrich Ludwig von, *The Political History of England, during the 16th, 17th, and 18th Centuries*, trans. Hannibal Evans Lloyd (London, 1837)

Ravelhofer, Barbara, *The Early Stuart Masque: Dance, Costume, and Music* (Oxford, 2006)

Roberts, Peter, 'Tudor Wales, National Identity and the British Inheritance', in *British Consciousness and Identity: The Making of Britain, 1533–1707*, ed. Brendan Bradshaw and Peter Roberts (Cambridge, 1998), pp. 8–42

Rooley, Anthony, 'New Light on John Dowland's Songs of Darkness', *Early Music* 11 (1983), 6–22

—— 'Time Stands Still: Devices and Designs, Allegory and Alliteration, Poetry and Music, and a New Identification in an Old Portrait', *Early Music* 34 (2006), 443–60

Ruff, Lillian, and D. Arnold Wilson, 'Allusion to the Essex Downfall in Lute Song Lyrics', *The Lute Society Journal* 12 (1970), 31–6

—— 'The Madrigal, the Lute Song and Elizabethan Politics', *Past & Present* 44 (1969), 3–51

Ruiz Jiménez, Juan, 'From *Mozos de coro* towards *Seises*: Boys in the Musical Life of Seville Cathedral in the Fifteenth and Sixteenth Centuries', in *Young Choristers 650–1700*, ed. Susan Boynton and Eric Rice (Woodbridge, 2008), pp. 86–103

Rygg, Kristin, *Masqued Mysteries Unmasked: Early Modern Music Theater and its Pythagorean Subtext*, Interplay 1 (Hillsdale, NY, 2000)

Sabol, Andrew, 'Two Unpublished Stage Songs for the "Aery of Children"', *Renaissance News* 13 (1960), 222–32

Salomon, Nanette, 'Positioning Women in Visual Convention: The Case of Elizabeth I', in *Attending to Women in Early Modern England*, ed. Betty Travitsky and Adele F. Seeff (Newark, DE, 1994), pp. 64–95

Samson, Alexander, 'Changing Places: The Marriage and Royal Entry of Philip, Prince of Austria, and Mary Tudor, July–August 1554', *The Sixteenth Century Journal* 36 (2005), 761–84

Sarkissian, Margaret, and Edward Tarr, 'Trumpet', *NG2*

Saslow, James M., *The Medici Wedding of 1589: Florentine Festival as Theatrum Mundi* (New Haven, CT, 1996)

Schoen-Nazzaro, Mary B., 'Plato and Aristotle on the Ends of Music', *Laval théologique et philosophique* 34 (1978), 261–73

Scott, David, 'Elizabeth I, Queen of England', *NG2*

Shapiro, Michael, *Children of the Revels: The Boy Companies of Shakespeare's Time and their Plays* (New York, 1977)

Sharpe, Kevin, *Selling the Tudor Monarchy: Authority and Image in Sixteenth-Century England* (New Haven, CT, 2009)

Shaw, W. A., 'Johnston, Robert (*c.* 1567–1639)', rev. Shona MacLean Vance, *ODNB* (online edn, 2004)
Simpson, Claude M., *The British Broadside Ballad and its Music* (New Brunswick, 1966)
Smith, Jeremy, 'Music and Late Elizabethan Politics: The Identities of Oriana and Diana', *Journal of the American Musicological Society* 58 (2005), 507–58
—— ' "Unlawful Song": Byrd, the Babington Plot and the Paget Choir', *Early Music* 38 (2010), 497–508
Smith, Michael, 'Edwards, Richard', *NG2*
—— 'Hunnis, William', *NG2*
Smithers, Don L., *The Music and History of the Baroque Trumpet before 1721*, 2nd edn (Buren, 1988)
Spencer, Robert, 'Bacheler, Daniel', *NG2*
Spink, Ian, 'Music and Society', in *The Seventeenth Century*, ed. Ian Spink, The Blackwell History of Music in Britain 3 (Oxford, 1992), pp. 1–65
Spring, Matthew, *The Lute in Britain: A History of the Instrument and its Music*, Early Music Series (Oxford, 2001)
Starkey, David, *Elizabeth: Apprenticeship* (London, 2000)
—— 'Introduction: Court History in Perspective', in *The English Court: From the Wars of the Roses to the Civil War*, ed. David Starkey (London, 1987), pp. 1–24
Stevens, John, *Music and Poetry in the Early Tudor Court*, Cambridge Studies in Music (Cambridge, 1979)
—— 'Sir Philip Sidney and "Versified Music": Melodies for Courtly Songs', in *The Well-Enchanting Skill: Music, Poetry, and Drama in the Culture of the Renaissance: Essays in Honour of F. W. Sternfeld*, ed. John Caldwell, Edward Olleson, and Susan Wollenberg (Oxford, 1990), pp. 153–69
Strong, Roy, *Art and Power: Renaissance Festivals, 1450–1650* (Woodbridge, 1984)
—— *The Cult of Elizabeth: Elizabethan Portraiture and Pageantry*, new edn (London, 1999)
—— *The English Renaissance Miniature* (London, 1983)
—— 'The Popular Celebration of the Accession Day of Queen Elizabeth I', *Journal of the Warburg and Courtauld Institutes* 21 (1958), 86–103
Tarr, Edward, 'The Trumpet before 1800', in *The Cambridge Companion to Brass Instruments*, ed. Trevor Herbert and John Wallace, Cambridge Companions to Music (Cambridge, 1997), pp. 84–102
Van der Kiste, John, *William and Mary* (Stroud, 2003)
Van Orden, Kate, *Music, Discipline, and Arms in Early Modern France* (Chicago, 2005)
Viroli, Maurizio, *From Politics to Reason of State: The Acquisition and Transformation of the Language of Politics, 1250–1600*, Ideas in Context 22 (Cambridge, 1992)
Von Hendy, Andrew, 'The Triumph of Chastity: Form and Meaning in *The Arraignment of Paris*', *Renaissance Drama* 1 (1968), 87–101
Vredeveld, Harry, ' "Deaf as Ulysses to the Siren's Song": The Story of a Forgotten Topos', *Renaissance Quarterly* 54 (2001), 846–82
Waldo, Tommy, 'Music and Musical Terms in Richard Edwards's "Damon and Pithias" ', *Music & Letters* 49 (1968), 29–35

Walker, Greg, 'Courtship and Counsel: John Lyly's *Campaspe*', in *A New Companion to English Renaissance Literature and Culture*, ed. Michael Hattaway, 2 vols., Blackwell Companions to Literature and Culture (Oxford, 2010), vol. 1, pp. 320–8

—— *Plays of Persuasion: Drama and Politics at the Court of Henry VIII* (Cambridge, 1991)

—— *The Politics of Performance in Early Renaissance Drama* (Cambridge, 1998)

Walls, Peter, *Music in the English Courtly Masque, 1604–1640*, Oxford Monographs on Music (Oxford, 1996)

Warren, Charles, 'Music at Nonesuch', *Musical Quarterly* 54 (1968), 47–57

Watanabe-O'Kelly, Helen, *Court Culture in Dresden: From Renaissance to Baroque* (Basingstoke, 2002)

Watkins, John, *Representing Elizabeth in Stuart England: Literature, History, Sovereignty* (Cambridge, 2002)

Weaver, Andrew H., *Sacred Music as Public Image for Holy Roman Emperor Ferdinand III: Representing the Counter-Reformation Monarch at the End of the Thirty Years' War*, Catholic Christendom, 1300–1700 (Farnham, 2012)

Wegman, Rob C., *The Crisis of Music in Early Modern Europe, 1470–1530* (London, 2005)

Welsford, Enid, *The Court Masque: A Study in the Relationship between Poetry and the Revels* (New York, 1962)

Wienpahl, Robert W., *Music at the Inns of Court during the Reigns of Elizabeth, James, and Charles* (Ann Arbor, MI, 1979)

Wilson, Jean, *Entertainments for Elizabeth I*, Studies in Elizabethan and Renaissance Culture 2 (Cambridge, 1980)

Wilson, Violet A., *Queen Elizabeth's Maids of Honour and Ladies of the Privy Chamber* (London, 1922)

Wind, Edgar, *Pagan Mysteries in the Renaissance*, new edn (London, 1968)

Wistreich, Richard, 'Of Mars I Sing: Monteverdi's Voicing of Virility', in *Masculinity and Western Musical Practice*, ed. Ian Biddle and Kirsten Gibson (Farnham, 2009), pp. 69–93

—— *Warrior, Courtier, Singer: Giulio Cesare Brancaccio and the Performance of Identity in the Late Renaissance* (Aldershot, 2007)

Woodfield, Ian, 'The Keyboard Recital in Oriental Diplomacy, 1520–1620', *Journal of the Royal Musical Association* 115 (1990), 33–62

Worden, Blair, *The Sound of Virtue: Philip Sidney's 'Arcadia' and Elizabethan Politics* (New Haven, CT, 1996)

Woudhuysen, H. R., 'Sidney, Sir Philip (1554–1586)', *ODNB* (online edn, 2005)

Wright, Pam, 'A Change in Direction: The Ramifications of a Female Household, 1558–1603', in *The English Court: From the Wars of the Roses to the Civil War*, ed. David Starkey (London, 1987), pp. 147–72

Yates, Frances Amelia, 'Elizabethan Chivalry: The Romance of the Accession Day Tilts', in *Astraea: The Imperial Theme in the Sixteenth Century* (London, 1975), pp. 88–111

Young, Alan R., *Tudor and Jacobean Tournaments* (London, 1987)

Zecher, Carla, 'The Gendering of the Lute in Sixteenth-Century French Love Poetry', *Renaissance Quarterly* 53 (2000), 769–91

Index

Pages numbers in **bold** refer to musical examples or figures.

Accession Day
   songs, 2, 119, 130–42, **132**, **134**, **135**, **136**, **137**, **138**, **140**, **141**, 187, 208, 209
   musical imagery in poetry, 1, 34–5, 36–7
   tournaments, 34, 65, 67, 106, 107, 115–21, 129–42
Achilles, 111
Alciato, Andrea, 9, 185
Alençon, Francis, Duke of (later Duke of Anjou), 49–50, 104, 114, 123, 124, 182, 193, 217
Alexander the Great, 23
Anjou, Francis, Duke of (formerly Duke of Alençon), *see* Alençon, Francis, Duke of
Anna of Demark, Queen, Consort of James VI of Scotland, 39, 148, 213
Apollo, 1, 31, 32, 83, 101–2, 174, **175**, 176, 187, 212
Aristotle, 6, 7, 8, 9, 33
Armada celebrations, 87–8, 184; *see also* Spain
Arundel, 12th Earl of, *see* Fitzalan, Henry
Arundel, 13th Earl, *see* Howard, Philip
Ascham, Roger, 52, 110
Aylmer, John, 18, 180n133
ayre, *see* lute song

Bacheler, Daniel: 'To Plead My Faith', 67, 69, **71–2**, 72, 73, 118, 218
Bacon, Sir Francis, 55
Baldwin, John: 'In the Merry Month of May', 150, 156, 209
ballads
   printed broadsides, 98n112, 183, 187, **188**, **189**, 190, 191, 210n2
   tunes, 57, 59, 60, 98n112, 187, **189**
Bassano family, 78, 80, 81, 204, 205
Bates, Catherine, 69, 124
Bateson, Thomas, 192, 212, 213
Beauvois, Monsieur de, 46
Bedford, Lucy Countess of, *see* Russell, Lucy
bell-ringing, 36, 82, 85, 190
Bennet, John: 'Eliza, Her Name Gives Honour', 29, 41, 211

Biron, Duke of, *see* Gontaut, Charles de
Bisham, entertainments at, 31–3, 37n94, 142, 145
Bishop, Tom, 194–5
Boethius, 8, 29
Bohun, Edmund, 192–4
Boissise, Monsieur de, 44
Boleyn, Anne, Queen, Consort of Henry VIII of England, 26, 31
Boniface, Joseph, Seigneur de La Mole, 49–50
Bonny Boots, 12n44, 66, 217, 218, 219n8
Breuner, Caspar, Baron of Rabenstein, 43–4, 46, 48, 49
Bristol, entertainments at, 166n76, 176, 177–80, **181**, 182, 183, 191
   'Away You Bosom Snakes', 179
Browne, Anthony, 1st Viscount Montague, 146–7, 148, 165–9; *see also* Cowdray, entertainments at
Browne, Sir William, 62, 63, 64
Brtnický z Valdštejna, Zdeněk, *see* Waldstein, Baron
Brydges, Giles, 3rd Baron Chandos, 146, 173; *see also* Sudeley, entertainments at
Burghley, Lord, *see* Cecil, William
Burke, Richard, 4th Earl of Clanricarde: 'My Love Doth Fly with Wings of Fear', 63–4
Burton, Robert, 20
Burwell, Mary, 44–5
Butler, Sir Philip, 107
Byrd, William
   'The Battle', **133**
   Cantiones Sacrae (1575), 2–3, 6, 29
   Catholicism, 3, 4
   connection with Sidney, 118
   'Look and Bow Down', 87
   monopoly on printed music, 3, 171
   on Elizabeth I as musician, 6, 29
   'Second Preces', 135, **136**, **137**
   secular political songs (additional), 212, 215, 216–17, 218
   'This Sweet and Merry Month of May', 149, **150**, 156, 208

cabinets of curiosity, 84–5
Caesar, Sir Julius, 172, 173
Camden, William, 53, 192
Campion, Thomas, 172
  'Faith's Pure Shield, the Christian Diana', 105, 107, 109
  'Of Neptune's Empire Let Us Sing', 93; *see also Masque of Proteus under* masque
canzonets, *see* madrigals
Carew, Sir Peter, 57
Carey, Henry, 1st Baron Hunsdon, 42, 45
Carey, Robert, 1st Earl of Monmouth, 107, 195
Carey family, 42, 56
carol, 34, 36, 88, 119, 120, 187, 220
Castiglione, Count Baldassarre: *The Courtier* (1528)
  arms, the profession of the courtier, 110
  gentlewoman's duty to entertain, 19–20
  judging each other's merits, 24
  music, 10, 22, 24, 46, 50, 101, 112–13, 114, 129
  reception and readership, 7–8, 13
  shepherd knight disguise, 116–17
Catherine of Aragon, Queen, Consort of Henry VIII of England, 22, 31
Catholics, 3, 4, 31, 33, 36, 47, 50, 53–4, 66, 80, 165–70
Cecil, Sir Robert, 2, 18, 38, 39, 44, 61–3, 64, 68
  'From a Servant of Diana', 62–3
Cecil, William, 1st Baron Burghley, 38–9, 44, 51, 170n87
Challoner, Francis, 27
Chamberlain, John, 38, 51, 86, 171
Chandos, Lord, *see* Brydges, Giles
Chapel Royal, 3, 12–13, 67, 76, 79n18, 80, 82, 98, 172, 194n11
  choirboys, 76, 81, 88, 95, 96n102, 98, 102, 113, 126n94, 208, 214
  see also Byrd, William; Edwards, Richard; Martin, Richard; Morley, Thomas; Tallis, Thomas
Charles II, Archduke of Austria, 47, 48, 49
Charles V, Holy Roman Emperor, 52, 143
Charles IX, King of France, 49, 52, 143
chastity, *see* chastity *under* Elizabeth I; versus chastity *under* love; instilling virtue/chastity *under* music, powers of

Chettle, Henry, 192
chivalry, 46, 123, 128, 130; *see also* courtly *under* love; nobility; tournaments
choirboy acting companies
  Children of the Chapel Royal, *see* choirboys *under* Chapel Royal
  Children of St George's Chapel, Windsor, 88, 95, 208, 214
  Children of St Paul's, 87, 88, 95, 96n102, 100
  plays, 13, 48–9, 81, 88, 89, 94–104, 113, 162, 179
Churchyard, Thomas
  Churchyard's Charity (1595), 39–40
  deviser of entertainments for progresses, 147, 177–8, 182–3, 185–7, 190
  see also Bristol, entertainments at; Norwich, entertainments at
Clanricarde, Earl of, *see* Burke, Richard
Clapham, John, 23
Clifford, George, 3rd Earl of Cumberland, 51, 107, 130, 139–40, 211, 218
Comey family, 80, 202
concordia discors, 28, 32, 33, 34, 41, 110, 114–18, 120, 121, 185
conduct literature, 7–8, 10, 20, 21–3, 45, 50, 109–10, 111–13, 116–17, 117–18, 125, 129; *see also* Castiglione, Count Baldassarre
consort, mixed, 76n1, 108–9, 125, 128, 150–1, 155, 163, 221
consort song, 29, 98, 125–6, 150–4, 161, 162–5, 178, 179–82, 186–7, 208–9, 211–13, 214, 220
Contention Between Liberality and Prodigality (1602), 96–7, 182
contrafacta, 57, 59–61, 187, **189**, 212, 220
counsel, 84
  for courtiers, 94, 96, 97, 99, 102, 179
  for Elizabeth I, 96, 97, 99, 168, 169, 177, 179–82, 182–3
  for subjects, 178–9, 184
  importance of good, 98–9, 180
  in music, 10, 94–9, 168–9, 177–83, **181**, 194
  praise as, 103–4
  and queens, 18, 180
  spirit of, 10, 99, 104, 176, 183

court music
  amateur performance, 3, 43–55, 57–60
  appropriation by, 76, 89, 104
    courtiers/noblemen, 55–75, 92, 106–8, 114–42, 146, 148–70
    musicians, 146, 170–6
    civic authorities, 146, 176–91
    lawyers, 92–4
  ceremonial dinner, 82
  control of by Elizabeth I, 76, 86–9, 105, 106–7, 146
  definition, 3–4
  display of instruments, 82–5
  Elizabeth's tolerance of appropriation, 88–9, 105, 107
  intimate performances, 42–75, 186–7
  manuscripts from royal household, 12n43, 81
  provision of in royal palaces, see Chapel Royal; court musicians; musicians in under Privy Chamber
    external groups, 3, 88, 92–4, 95; see also choirboy acting companies
  see also masques; musical instruments; progresses; tournaments; and individually listed entertainments and musicians
court musicians (royal household)
  bagpiper, 81, 200
  cornetts, 80, 90, 125–6, 147, 171
  diplomatic performances, 81–2, 87
  drums, 76, 77, 80, 81, 82, 90, 206
  development under Tudors, 78–9
  flute consort, 76, 80, 83, 171, 203
  functions, 76–82, 89–90, 146, 147
  harpist, 77, 81, 200
  international connections, 80–1
  lutenists, 61, 77, 78, 81, 87, 198, 199, 200
    three lutes ensemble, 50, 79, 200
  New Year gifts given by, 58
  organisation, 76, 77–8, 79, 86–7, 88
  rebec-player, 77, 200
  recorder consort, 76–7, 78, 80, 204
  reputation of, 3, 82, 86
  rewards given to, 3, 81–2, 171–2
  sackbut (and shawm) consort, 76, 80, 81, 82, 205
  singer, favourite of Elizabeth I, see Hales, Robert
  trumpeters, 77, 80, 81, 82, 147
  viol-player, 77, 78, 198

court musicians *continued*
  viol/violin consort, 76, 78, 79, 80, 81, 147, 171, 202
  virginal players, 27, 77, 198, 199, 200
  see also Chapel Royal; court music; musical instruments; musicians in *under* Privy Chamber; *and* entries for individual musicians and families
courtiers
  collaboration among, 64, 123–9, 163–4
  criticism of, 99, 120, 167, 179, 180
  evils of bad courtiers, 98–9
  importance of good counsellors, 98–9, 180
  perform for Queen, 57, 58, 60
  rivalry among, 38, 42, 60, 64, 65, 68, 75, 146, 169, 216
  write lyrics for Queen, 57–75
  see also counsel; appropriation by courtiers *under* court music; nobility; Privy Chamber; *and* entries for individual courtiers
Cowdray, entertainments at, 33, 145, 146–7, 165–70, 183, 209
  'Behold Her Locks', 166–7
  'The Fish that Seeks', 168–9
  'My Love that Makes His Nest', 167–8
Craig-McFeely, Julia, 48
Cumberland, Earl of, *see* Clifford, George
Cupid, 22, 120, 140n135, 173, 182
Cynthia, *see under* representations *under* Elizabeth I

Dallam, Thomas, 85–6
dance, 13, 53, 54, 76–7, 81, 86n52, 88, 89, 92, 192, 193, 195, 200
  almand, 73, 220
  country dance, 34, 35, 103, 145
  galliard, 51, 52, 59, 66–7, 69, 72, 85, 139, 151, 174, 189, 221
  harmony, image of, 34–5, 90–1, 94, 103
  noblemen, 110, 111, 112–13, 129
  noblewomen, 22, 47, 125
  pavan, 59, 128, 131–3, 137, 138, 139, 222
  see also dance *under* Elizabeth I; masque
Daphne, 174, **175**, 176, 212
Darnley, Lord, *see* Stewart, Henry
Davies, Sir John
  Hymns of Astraea (1599), 29–30, 40–1
  Lottery at Harefield, 157

Davies, Sir John, *continued*
  Orchestra or A Poem of Dancing (1596), 39*n*101, 128, 131–3
  'To the Queen', 37–9, 40–1
Davison, Francis, 92*n*82, 93
Derby, Dowager Countess of, *see* Egerton, Alice
Derby, Lady, *see* Vere, Elizabeth de
Desire (allegorical character), 91, 92, 123–9, 162–3, 164
Devereux, Robert, Earl of Essex
  naval activity against Spain, 68, 93
  political songs related to the Earl, 4, 66–7, 39, 148, 213*n*4, 217, 218
  rivalries with courtiers, 38, 60, 64, 65, 68
  self-promotion at tournaments, 107, 142*n*135
  Sidney's successor, 121
  songs as complaints to Elizabeth I, 65–6, 67–70, **71–2**, 72–3, **74**, 75, 218
  troubled relationship with Elizabeth I, 30*n*58, 65, 66, 68
  writes political poetry, 58, 65, 66, 67–9
  writes lyrics to ballad tunes, 60
  rebellion and execution, 66, 148
  rewards to musicians, 171
Diana, 81, 88–9, 157
  in song lyrics, 63, 81, 211–13
  Penelope Rich as, 39
  see also representations *under* Elizabeth I
diplomacy, 9, 13, 86, 123, 177, 182
  court musicians, 12, 79–82, 87
  instruments displayed, 82–4
  gifts, musical, 85–6
  masques, 91
  royal performances, 12, 42, 44, 45–7, 50–2, 53, 55
  in marital negotiations, 43–4, 47–50
discord, 9, 13, 18, 31, 36–41, 91, 103, 190–1
  see also concordia discors; harmony
Ditchley, entertainments at, 130*n*116, 187*n*158
Dowland, John
  'Behold a Wonder', 140, 209
  'Can She Excuse', 66–7, 217
  compositions for court entertainments, 109, 146, 158, 173–6, 208, 209, 211, 212, 215
  and Earl of Essex, 4, 66–7
  and Sidney family, 118

Dowland, John, *continued*
  creation of songs from pre-existing instrumental dances, 59
  dedication of *Second Book of Songs*, 24–5
  'Earl of Essex Galliard', 66–7
  falling fourth motif, **71**, 72, **73**, **138**, 138
  'Flow my Tears', 72, **73**, 138
  'Herbs, Words, and Stones', 173
  'His Golden Locks', 131, 138–40, **140**, **141**, 208
  'Humour Say What Mak'st Thou Here', 139, **142**, 211
  'It Was a Time When Silly Bees', 67, 218
  'Lachrimae', 72, 137, 138
  'My Heart and Tongue were Twins', 174, **175**, 176, 209
  'My Thoughts are Wing'd with Hopes', 72*n*132, 211
  'O Sweet Woods', 66–7, 217
  Political songs (additional), 211, 212, 215, 217, 218
  seeking court position, 173–6
  'Sorrow Stay', 69, **70**
  'Time Stands Still', 51, 212
  'Time's Eldest Son', 130–8, **132**, **134**, **135**, **136**, **137**, **138**, 139, 208
Dowland, Robert, 61, 67, 68*n*124, **71–2**, **74**, 118, 218
Drayton, Michael, 1, 25
Dudley, Robert, Earl of Leicester
  suitor and royal favourite, 92, 161–5
  rumours about illegitimate children with Queen, 27
  martial reputation, 128
  desire to support Dutch Protestants, 121–2, 122–3, 162
  lends his musicians for entertainments, 125, 147
  rewards musicians, 171
  see also Four Foster Children of Desire; Kenilworth, entertainments at; *Lady of May*; Woodstock, entertainments at
Dyer, Sir Edward, 58, 164, 216, 218
  'The Song in the Oak', 163–5
  see also Woodstock, entertainments at

Eckhardt, Joshua, 62–3, 64
education, music, 7, 8, 17, 19–20, 22, 23, 24, 26, 27, 28, 53*n*50, 78, 102, 111

educational literature, *see* conduct literature
Edward VI, King of England, 53, 106
Edwards, Richard
  The Paradise of Dainty Devices (1576), 60, 178, 208
  Damon and Pithias (1571), 97–9, 100n123, 179, 208
  'Awake Ye Woeful Wights', 98, 208
  composer and author, 172
  Master of the Children of the Chapel Royal, 98, 172
Egerton, Alice, Dowager Countess of Derby, 157–8; *see also* Harefield, entertainments at
Egerton, Sir Thomas, 147, 157–61; *see also* Harefield, entertainments at
Elizabeth I, Queen of England and Ireland
  birth, 30–1
  and Catholic subjects, 3–4, 36, 165–70
  chastity, 15, 102–4, 120, 123–4, 174, 182–3, 192–3; *see also* Cynthia, Diana *and* Virgin Queen *under* representations *below*
  courtly love, strategy of governance, 18–19, 43, 52, 55–6, 61–4
  criticisms of governance, 25, 27–8, 37–41, 68, 178–82
  cult of, 5
  dance, 17, 23, 27, 44, 46, 47, 49, 51–2
  dress, 15, 25
  eternal youth and beauty, 51–2, 92, 123–9, 142, 151, 156, 167
  excommunication, 31, 178
  foreign policy, 39, 47, 50, 85–6, 93, 114, 121–3, 124, 162, 177; *see also* diplomacy; Netherlands; Spain
  gender, impact of, *see* queenship
  intelligence, 1, 29–30, 169–70, 173, 192
    ability to decipher subtexts, 169n87
  legitimacy, 30–1
  marriage and suitors, 47–50, 89, 92, 104, 123–4, 161–5, 182–3
  motto, *semper eadem*, 30, 51, 61, 211, 212
  musicality
    authority, sign of, 15–16, 28, 29–33, 37–8, 40–1, 51–2, 90–1, 102–3
    composer, 17
    criticised, 27–8

Elizabeth I, *continued*
  musicality, *continued*
    education, 17
    favourite piece, 87
    favourite musician, *see* Hales, Robert
    judgement, 29
    performer, 17, 23, 29, 42–52, 54–5, 82–3
    patron, 1, 2, 3, 76, 78–9, 86–8, 171
    painted playing the lute, 15–17, 18, 42
    in her royal image, 1–2, 3, 11, 14, 15, **16**, 17–19, 25–8, 29–33, 36–41, 42–7, 51–2, 54–5, 76, 83, 192–4
    as teenager, 52
    writer of lyrics, 61, 87
    see also diplomacy; *and under* representations *below*
  old age, 40, 50–2, 53, 55, 129, 155–6
  posthumous reputation, 192–4
  relationships with courtiers, 42, 44, 55–75, 157–61
    playfulness, 44, 61, 62
    Earl of Essex, 65–75
    Earl of Leicester, 27, 92, 161–5
  representations
    angel, 44, 63, 192
    Beauty, 92, 123–9, 142
    bringer of harmony, 30–4, 37–8, 39, 102–4, 120–1, 145
    control over?, 3, 5, 17–18, 86–9, 104, 146, 148
    cruel mistress, 60, 67–8, 69, 75, 162, 167, 168, 174
    Cynthia, 32, 51, 93, 145, 149, 157, **159–60**, 209, 211, 213
    Diana (or nymph of), 63, 102–3, 105, 145, 182
    lady of romance, 55, 145
    mother/nurse, 168
    Muses, Queen of, 1–2, 29, 192
    as music/song, 31, 40
    pearl, 183
    Phoenix, 168
    Puritan Maid, 52
    Second Troy, Queen of, 37, 102, 103, 149, **150**, 208
    saint, 119, 130
    sun, 105, 149, 151, 168, 183, 186, 211
    Vanity, 25
    Venus, 145, 155–6, 182

Elizabeth I, *continued*
  representations, *continued*
    Virgin Queen, 15, 31, 104, 120, 157, 189, 192
    see also Oriana
  relations with Mary Queen of Scots, 46–7, 91
  scandalous relationship with Seymour, 52–3
  subjects, mutual love with, 34, 40, 168–9, 184
  succession, 37, 39, 47, 51, 57, 89, 93, 94, 148, 155–6, 157, 213n4
  troubled last decade, 36–7, 38–9, 165
  virtue, 30, 52–3, 68, 94, 97, 151, 179; *see also* chastity *above*
  works dedicated to, 2–3, 6, 8, 19, 29
  see also Accession Day; Chapel Royal; court music; court musicians; England; harmony; monarchy; Privy Chamber; progresses; queenship; rebellion
Elvetham, entertainments at, 144–5, 146, 148–57, 161, 168, 187n158, 208–10
Elyot, Sir Thomas: *The Book Named the Governor* (1531), 7–8, 23n34
  good counsel, 10
  liberality, 97
  musical knowledge necessary for harmonious government, 8–9, 28
  musical judgement, 24
England
  musical reputation, 3, 13, 33, 40, 78, 79–80, 86, 91
  as harmonious kingdom, 33–8, 102–3, 120, 156, 184–5, 191, 192
Erik XIV, King of Sweden, 12n43, 85
Este, Isabella d', Marchioness of Mantua, 24, 52

Fairy Queen, 145, 151
Ferdinand I, Holy Roman Emperor, 43, 48
Ferrabosco, Alfonso (I), 77, 80, 81n25, 171, 198, 199, 214, 216
fishermen, 36, 90, 168–9, 183, 190; *see also* mariner
Fitzalan, Henry, 12th Earl of Arundel, 33
Fortune (allegory), 59, 60–1, 96–7, 157, **159**, 161, 166

Four Ages of Man, 130
Four Foster Children of Desire (1581), 108, 121–9, 142
Foxe, John, 25
freemen's song, 116, 119, 150n27, 221
Fumerton, Patricia, 43

Galliardello family, 80, 81, 202
games of secrecy, 43, 45–7, 64
Garter, Bernard, 185, 186
Gascoigne, George, *see* Kenilworth, entertainments at
gender
  femininity, 30, 61, 125, 127
  masculinity, 108, 111–14, 124, 125, 129
  and music, 11, 13, 19, 28
    effeminacy, 11, 19, 22, 27, 107, 111–12, 114
    masculinity, 22, 107, 111, 112–13
    femininity, 2, 15–17, 19–25, 26–8, 29, 30, 41, 44–6, 47, 48–9, 55, 125, 193
  see also queenship
Gerschow, Frederic, 84
Gesta Grayorum (1594–5), 84; *see also* Masque of Proteus *under* masque
Gibson, Kirsten, 66
gods, classical, *see* individual entries; *see also* various goddesses *under* representations *under* Elizabeth I
golden age, 102, 120, 149, 173
Gontaut, Charles de, Duke of Biron, 50
Greville, Sir Fulke, 65, 123, 211, 217–18
Grey, Lady Catherine, 57n68, 155, 156

Hales, Robert, 61, 62, 65, 88, 109, 139, 200, 208, 218
Harefield, entertainments at, 157–61, **159–60**, 170n88, 187n158, 209
Harington, Sir John, 20
harmony
  diplomatic, 49, 91
  divine/heavenly, 21, 25, 29, 38, 39, 40, 90, 101, 196, 111
  marital/familial, 48–9
  of mind/soul, 8, 19, 24–5, 30, 39, 102, 103, 195–6, 111
  political/social, 6–7, 8–9, 11, 13, 15–17, 18, 19, 28, 30–3, 37–41, 90, 94, 184–5, 191, 196

harmony, *continued*
  of the spheres, 8, 19, 24, 29, 38, 192
  see also concordia discors; discord;
    as harmonious kingdom *under*
    England
Harrington, Richard: *The Famous Ditty of the Joyful Receiving of the Queen's Most Excellent Majesty* (1584), **189**, 191
Henry VII, King of England and Ireland, 78
Henry VIII, King of England and Ireland
  dedicatee of Elyot's *The Governor*, 7
  composer, 24
  as Pan, 30–1
  musical performances, 50, 54, 57
  development of court musical establishment, 78, 19, 80
  participation in tournaments, 106
  'Henry VIII's Book', 24
Hentzner, Paul, 15*n*4, 82, 83, 86*n*52
hermit, 65, 130, 134, 139, 142
Herford, Earl of, *see* Seymour, Edward
Herries of Terregles, Lord, *see* Maxwell, John
Heybourne (alias Richardson), Ferdinando, 77, 171, 199, 216
Hilliard, Nicholas, 15, **16**, 17, 18, 42, 43, 51
Holbein, Hans, the younger, 9, 15, 17
Howard, Katherine, Queen, Consort of Henry VIII of England, 26
Howard, Philip, 13th Earl of Arundel, 123, 125*n*91
Howard, Thomas, 4th Duke of Norfolk, 178, 180
Hunnis, William, 172
Hunsdon, Lord, *see* Carey, Henry
hymn, 133, 177, 179

identity, fashioning of, 11
  civic, 146, 177, 184–5, 190
  court, 78–86
  lawyers, 93–4
  national, *see* England
  noble
    collective, 7, 19–20, 105, 106–7, 108–9, 124–9
    individual, 24–5, 44, 63, 65, 107, 108, 114–21, 123, 129–42, 155–7, 161, 162, 163–4, 167–8
    see also nobility

identity, fashioning of, *continued*
  royal, *see* representations *and* musicality
    under Elizabeth I; Henry VIII;
    queenship
  see also music, connotations of; music, political functions of
Inns of Court, 88, 89, 92, 214; *see also Gesta Grayorum*; *Masque of Proteus* and *Masque of Desire and Beauty under* masque
intimacy, politics of, 42, 44–50, 55–75

James VI and I, King of Scotland, England and Ireland, 39, 93, 148, 156, 213*n*4
Janequin, Clément, 87, 133
Johnson, Edward, 146, 150, 218
  'Elisa is the Fairest Queen', 150–1, **152–3**, 155, 209
  'Come Again', 150–1, **154**, 209
Johnson, John, 79, 200
Johnston, Robert, 192–4
Jones, Robert, 61, 167, 209
  'Cynthia Queen of Seas and Lands', 158, **159–60**, 161, 209
judgement, musical, 21, 24, 25, 29, 101, 110
Juno, 88–9, 102, 103, 162

Kellim family, 80, 202
Kenilworth, entertainments at, 31*n*65, 125*n*91, 145, 146, 148, 150, 155, 161, 172, 183
  'Come, Muses, Come', 162–3, 164–5
Knox, John, 18, 53–4
Kyffin, Maurice, 34, 35, 36
Kytson family, 146

La Mole, Seigneur de, *see* Boniface, Joseph
La Mothe-Fénélon, Seigneur de, *see* Salignac, Bertrand de
La Primaudaye, Pierre de, 8
Lady of May (1578), 115, 118, 122–3, 183
laments, **70**, **73**, 98, 147, 161, 162, 195, 208, 214–18
love complaints, 60–1, 65–75, **71–2**, **74**, 103, 163–5, 167–8, 174, **175**, 176, 209, 214–18
Languet, Hubert, 122
Lanier, Nicholas (I), 80, 171, 203
Lanier, Nicholas (II), 87
Lassus, Orlande de, 33–4
Leahy, William, 184

Lee, Sir Henry
　Queen's Champion, 129
　retirement pageant, 108, 109, 129–42, 208
　as Laelius, 115
　as Loricus, 130n6
　as hermit, 130, 133–8, 139
　association with Robert Dudley, Earl of Leicester, 164
　see also Ditchley, entertainments at; tournaments
Leicester, Earl of, see Dudley, Robert
Lennox, Earl of, his family, see Matthew Stewart
Levin, Carole, 18
liberality, 7, 96–7, 161, 172
Liberality and Prodigality, see Contention Between Liberality and Prodigality
Lichfield, Thomas, 77, 87, 198–9
Lilliat, John, 130–1
Lloyd, Lodowick, 27, 112
London, 36–7, 87, 88, 106, 176, **189**, 191
Lord Chamberlain, 86–7, 88, 143, 147
love
　between monarch and subjects, 34, 168–9
　versus chastity, 30–1, 33, 102–4, 120, 121, 155–6, 174, 176, 182–3, 193
　courtly, 20, 43, 129, 68–9
　courtly versus spiritual, 130, 133, 139, 162
　cruel mistress, 60, 67–8, 69, 75, 162, 167, 168, 174
　effeminacy, 27, 112
　Elizabeth I's style of government, 18–19, 43, 52, 55–6, 61–4
　pastoral, 156, 168–9, 174
　as political metaphor, 43, 59, 60–1, 63–4, 67–9, 75, 120, 129, 130, 167–9, 180
　royal praise via love song, 51, 151–3, 166–7
　versus war, 27, 123, 125, 126, 129
　see also Cupid; love complaints *under* laments; music, connotations of; love *under* poetry; Venus
Low Countries, see Netherlands
Lupo family, 58, 80, 81, 171, 202
lute song, 11, 56, 61, 98, 101, 149n24, 155, 163, 208, 211–12, 215, 217–18, 221; see also Bacheler, Daniel; Dowland, John; Jones, Robert; love complaints *under* laments; Martin, Richard

Lyly, John, 77n10, 100, 102n32, 172n99
　Endimion (1591), 100, 113
　Midas (1592), 100–2
　Sappho and Phao (1584), 48–9, 100, 104n145

Machiavelli, Niccolò, 9, 10
madrigals, 35–6, 36n88, 59, 66, 77, 80, 81, 149–50, **150**, 155, 156, 192, 208, 211, 212; see also *The Triumphs of Oriana* (1601) *under* Morley, Thomas
Mahomed III, Sultan of the Ottoman Empire, 85–6
Maisse, André Hurault, sieur de, 17n6, 30n58, 52, 79
Manningham, John, 64, 91–2
manuscripts, music
　GB-Cfm: Mu. MS 734, 12n43
　GB-Lam: The Robert Spencer Collection, MS 601 [Mynshall Lute Book], 12n43
　GB-Lbl: Add MS 31922 [Henry VIII's Book], 24
　GB-Lbl: rm.24.d2 [Baldwin Commonplace Book], 150n27, 156, 209
　GB-Lbl: Royal Appendix MSS 74–6 [Lumley Partbooks], 12n43, 81
　GB-WCc: MS 153 [Winchester Partbooks], 12n43, 85
　US-NH: Filmer 2, 12n43, 81
mariner, 119, 157, 158, 161; see also fishermen
Marlowe, Christopher, 10–11
Martin, Richard: 'Change Thy Mind Since She Doth Change', 67, 68, 69, 73, **74**
Mary I, Queen of England, 13, 22, 53, 54–5, 78n14
Mary II, Queen of England, Ireland and Scotland, 192, 193–4
Mary, Queen of Scots, 13
　arrival in England, 178
　death warrant signed by Elizabeth I, 93
　meeting planned with Elizabeth I in York, 91
　music and dancing, 46
　criticism of, 53–4
　and singer David Rizzio, 26
　rivalry with Elizabeth I, 46, 47
　and Lord Darnley, 26, 57
Mason, Sir John, 57

Mason, Mathias, 77, 79, 199, 200
masque
　diplomacy, 91
　format, 89, 102, 103, 105, 131
　Jacobean, 89, 90–1
　Masque of Proteus (1595), 92–4
　Masque of Desire and Beauty (1562), 92, 163
　at Norwich, 145, 186–7
　prepared by royal household, 90, 91
　royal image, 90, 91–2, 94
　value for performers and devisers, 2, 88, 89, 90–1, 92, 93–4
　see also dance; harmony
Master of the Revels, 88, 96
Maximilian II, Holy Roman Emperor, 49
Maxwell, John, 4th Lord Herries of Terregles, 26
May, Steven, 58, 60, 62, 66, 68
May-time, 149, **150**, 155–6; see also *Lady of May*; pastoral; shepherds
Medici, Catherine de', Queen, Consort of Henry II, King of France, 13, 52
melancholy, 120, 173, 174
　expressed by music, 56, 72, **73**, 103, 128, 131, 133, 138, 139, 161, 165, 174
　relieved by music, 23, 46, 172
　see also laments
Melville, Sir James, of Halhill, 45–7
Memo, Dionysius, 78
Michieli, Giovanni, 53
military sphere and music, 107, 110, 111–13, 125, 126
　musical styles, 6, 14, 27, 87, 107, 111, 125, 126, **133**, 141
　see also nobility; war versus peace
Mitcham, entertainments at, 172–3
monarchy
　divinely appointed, 29, 30, 38, 39, 40
　musical monarchs, 26, 41, 46–7, 50, 52–5, 57, 193; see also Elizabeth I
　musicality important for, 24, 101
　two bodies, theory of, 41, 45
　see also counsel; court music; political/social under harmony; Privy Chamber; queenship; *and* entries for individual kings and queens
Monoxe, Henry, 26
Montague, Lord, *see* Browne, Anthony
Montmorency, François de, 85

Montrose, Louis, 18–19, 102
morality
　as a language of politics, 10, 95, 96–7, 182–3
　as means to royal praise, 1, 52–3, 94, 102, 145, 182–3
　plays, 95, 96–104
　songs, 95–6, 97, 99, 169–70, 179–80, **181**, 182–3
　see also counsel; of mind/soul *under* harmony; versus chastity *under* love; various entries *under* music, connotations of *and* music, powers of
Morley, Thomas, 61, 118, 131, 136, 137, 211, 217
　'Blow, Shepherds, Blow', 36n88, 211
　The Triumphs of Oriana (1601), 39, 148, 211, 212–13, 218
Mulcaster, Richard, 1–2, 19–20
Mundy, John, 12n44, 217
　'Turn About and See Me', 35–6, 211
music, connotations of
　authority, 15, 17, 18, 19, 23–4, 28, 29–33, 378, 40–1, 47, 90; see also political/social *under* harmony
　beauty, 19, 20, 54, 55
　courtly love, 20, 22, 27, 50, 56, 63
　culture and fashion, 3, 7, 13, 24, 76, 78, 79–81, 108–9, 118, 147, 155, 161
　eloquence and learning, 1–2, 7, 11, 15, 19, 25, 30
　flexibility of, 11, 13, 19, 22–4, 25, 28, 41, 49, 50, 111–12, 196
　foolishness, 11, 22, 27, 53
　frivolity, 19, 21, 22, 27, 53–4, 112, 192, 193
　intimacy, 20, 43–5, 54
　lust, 11, 15, 21, 22, 26–7, 193
　magnificence, 13, 54, 76, 79, 82, 84, 86, 104, 142, 155
　marriage/marriageability, 15, 19, 20, 47–9, 55
　rationality, 13, 19, 21, 24–5, 28
　religion/piety, 13, 20, 21, 25
　or lack of, 53–4
　sensuality, 13, 15, 18, 19–22, 25, 26–7, 43, 44–5, 54
　status, 7, 19, 24, 101, 102, 108–9, 142; see also nobility
　virtue, 19, 24, 25, 102, 103, 111
　youth, 50–2

music, connotations of, *continued*
　see also *concordia discors*; discord; and music *under* gender; harmony; love; melancholy; military sphere and music; morality; music, powers of; pastoral; religious imagery/themes
music, political functions of, 1–2, 3, 11–12, 14, 121, 141–2, 146
　both sound and idea, 11, 17, 41, 196
　compared to other arts, 194–6
　complaint, 59–60, 65, 161, 162–3, 168–70, 163
　　criticism, 68–9, 75, 147–8, 166–70, 180, 194
　concision of message, 97, 99, 100, 176, 195
　diversity of functions, acting simultaneously, 3–4, 14, 76, 90–1, 93, 94, 96, 104, 147, 148, 158, 161, 170, 176, 183, 195–6
　draw attention, 10, 58, 92, 99
　gift, 12n43, 58–9, 85–6, 187
　harmony, creation of political, *see* political/social *under* harmony
　imagery/ideas, *see* harmony; music, connotations of; symbolism *under* musical instruments
　memory, 73, 100, 161, 169, 170, 196
　novelty, 83–4, 85–6, 108–9, 125, 127, 155; *see also* musicians, hidden
　persuasion, 2, 10–11, 12, 14, 92, 93, 119, 122, 124, 184–5
　petition for reward/patronage, 3, 158, 161, 171, 173–6
　praise, royal, 91–2, 93–4, 103, 119, 148, 149, **150**, 151, 155, 157–8, 166–7, 186–7, 192, 194
　quick preparation, potential for, 69, 72–3
　reflective versus active political song, 12, 66–7
　relationships, fashioning of, 2, 13, 42–5, 55, 56–7, 59–60, 61, 63–4, 65, 67–8, 130, 163–4
　safe outlet, 11, 169–70, 195
　　containment/displacement, 69–75, 74–5, 170, 194–5
　　convention, 46, 59, 65–6, 68–9, 156, 161, 163, 164–5, 168, 195

music, political functions of, *continued*
　safe outlet, *continued*
　　ephemerality, 58–9, 166
　　ambivalence of expression, 69
　self-promotion (by courtiers/noblemen), 64, 104, 105, 107, 156–7, 161; *see also* nobility; identity, fashioning of
　theories about, 6–11, 95–6
　topical issues, 93, 96, 101, 103–4, 123–4, 157, 182
　see also counsel; court music; diplomacy; musicality *and* representations *under* Elizabeth I; identity, fashioning of; morality; music, connotations of
music, powers of
　affective, 2, 10–11, 20, 45, 95, 195
　civilising, 7, 31, 32
　didactic, 10, 95
　instilling virtue/chastity, 7, 33, 10–11, 95–6
　transformative, 31–3, 139–42
　see also harmony; music, connotations of; music, political functions of
musical contests, 31–2, 97, 101–2, 116, 122
musical instruments
　bagpipes or pipes, 30, 31, 32, 54, 101, 116, 118, 119
　cornetts, 31–2, 54, 80, 125–6, 220
　diplomatic gifts, 85–6
　drums, 36, 107, 111, 116, 125, 126, 142, 186
　flutes, 9n.31, 83, 109, 128, 150, 221
　lutes, 15, **16**, 17, 20, 30, 32, 42, 43–5, 46, 53n50, 54, 56, 57, 78, 80, 85n49, 88, 101, 111, 125, 151, 155, 193, 221
　　lute strings, 9, 38, 48–9, 185
　　see also consort, mixed; lute song
　organ, 54, 78, 83, 85–6
　orpharions and wire-stringed plucked instruments, 17, 78, 109, 125, 150, 220, 221, 222
　rebec, 77, 222
　recorders, 54, 109, 116, 204, 221
　regals, 98, 200, 221
　symbolism of, 9, 15, 17, 30, 38, 44, 48–9, 125
　trumpets, 36, 85, 107, 116, 126, 127, 133, 142, 186
　viol/violins, 20, 73n135, 85, 88, 109, 131n120, 150, 158, 180, 186

musical instruments, *continued*
  virginals and spinets, 17, 20, 42, 43, 45–6, 49, 50, 53n50, 54, 55, 78n14, 83–4, 85n49, 222
  wind instruments, attitudes to, 101
  see also bell-ringing; consort, mixed; court musicians; instruments displayed *under* diplomacy
musicians, hidden, 108, 125, 127, 151, 155, 161
musicians, status of, 172–3

Nallot, Monsieur, 108n16, 127
Nashe, Thomas, 9–10
Naunton, Robert, 59
Netherlands, 177
  military support for, 39, 114, 121, 122–3, 124, 162
Nevers, Charles Gonzaga, Duke of, 171
New Year gifts, 58, 171
Nine Worthies, 1, 2n5
nobility
  arms versus arts/letters, 108, 110, 111, 120–1, 122
  courtier versus knight, 109–10, 111–13, 122, 142
  honour, 109, 110, 117–18
  military role, 110, 111, 122, 124, 127, 129, 142; *see also* war versus peace
  music and, 7, 14, 19–20, 24, 101, 102, 108–9, 110, 111–13, 114, 146–7, 155
  performance of, 108–9, 116–18
  royal service, 127, 145, 161, 167–8
    versus personal ambition, 105, 107–8, 114, 124, 129n111, 146, 157, 194
  women, 19–20, 23, 24–5, 46, 47
  see also counsel; courtiers; music, connotations of; noble *under* identity, fashioning of
Noel, Sir Henry, *see* Bonny Boots
Norbrook, David, 55
Norfolk, 4th Duke of, *see* Howard, Thomas
Norwich, entertainments at, 89, 105n3, 145, 147, 162, 176, 182–3, 185–7, 189, 190–1
  'From Slumber Soft', 186
  'The Dew of Heaven', 183, 185–6, 190
  'Chaste Life Lives Long', 182–3

old age, 40, 50–2, 55, 129–42, 155, 156
Oostrewijk, Gommar van, 81n25, 171, 203
Opiciis, Benedictus de, 78

Oriana, 39, 148, 192, 211, 212, 213n4, 213n5
Orsino, Don Virginio, Duke of Bracciano, 44, 45, 50, 51–2
Oxford, Earl of, *see* Vere, Edward de

Pan, 30–2, 101–2, 103; *see also* pastoral; shepherds
Parsley, Osbert, 147
pastoral, 1, 34–6, 101–3, 114–21, 149–56, 173–4
  court versus country, 32, 101–2, 119–20, 169, 174
  English version of, 1, 35
  virtue/innocence, 119–20, 169
  estrangement from court, 122
  music, 1, 34–6, 116–17, 101, 102–3, 150, **152–3**, 155–6; *see also* madrigals
  licence to speak plainly, 169
  political issues within, 37n84, 195
  fertility, 36, 155–6
  see also Lady of May; Pan; Philisides; ploughmen; shepherds; Spenser, Edmund
Pavia, Battle of, 87
Peele, George
  Anglorum Feriae (1595), 35, 36–7, 40, 106
  The Arraignment of Paris (1584), 81, 90, 102–4
  Polyhymnia (1590), 106, 107, 121, 130, 139, 140n135
  An Eclogue, Gratulatory (1589), 121
Pierce, Walter, 79, 200
Philip II, King of Spain, 48, 53, 101, 102
Philisides, 114–21
  sources in which appears, 115
  lovesick shepherd, 115, 120
  shepherd knight
    fusion of courtly arts and military sport, 114, 121
    incongruity, 116, 142
    relation to Sidney's biography, 114–15, 118
    managing audience expectations, 117
    as mask, 117–18
    inspired by Castiglione's *The Courtier*, 116–17
    and royal praise, 120–1
    representative of Sidney's estrangement from court, 22
    and frustrated martial ambition, 122
    imitated by Earl of Essex, 121

Philisides, *continued*
   see also pastoral; shepherds; Sidney,
      Sir Philip; tournaments
Pilkington, Francis, 149n24, 156, 208
Plato, 6–7, 8, 33, 34, 185n153
Platter, Thomas, 82, 83
plays, *see* choirboy acting companies;
   plays *under* morality; *and* individual
   entries for plays or playwrights
Playford, John, 17
ploughmen, 1, 36, 115, 116, 118, 119, 120,
   150n27
poetry, 122, 127, 130–1, 142, 172–3
   acrostic, 25, 29–30, 179–80
   answer poem, 61
   critical, 37–41, 120, 127–8
   didactic, 95–6
   by Elizabeth I, 87, 88n59
   love (complaint), 59–61, 67–9
   love (happy), 20, 63–4, 123
   musical imagery in, 1, 20, 25, 30–1, 34–5,
      36, 37–41
   pastoral, 1, 115, 116, 118, 120, 34–5
   political occasions, about, 34–5, 105, 107,
      109
   royal image, 30–1, 37–41, 51
   'utilitarian poetics', 11, 43, 56, 57–8, 59–61,
      63–4, 65, 67–9, 115, 117, 170, 195
   see also individual entries for poets
portraiture, 9, 15, 17, 25, 43, 51, 62–3, 64, 76
   miniature of Elizabeth I playing the lute,
      15, **16**, 17, 18, 42, 43
Poulton, Diana, 66–7
printing, music, politics of, 2–3, 4, 33, 66,
   67, 119
Privy Chamber, 82
   access to, for male courtiers, 26–7, 44,
      56
   musicians in, 26–7, 77–8, 79, 87, 194,
      198–9
   performance space, 43–4, 45–6, 49–50,
      78, 145, 186, 194
   women in, 2, 42, 44, 53n50, 56, 78
progresses, entertainments for, 14, 143–91
   audience, 144–5, 146, 157, 161, 183, 184,
      185–7
   circulation in print and manuscript, 148,
      150, 158, 166, 176, 178, **188**, **189**
   reading and reflection, 161, 170
   civic hosts, aims of
      counsel, 148, 176–83

progresses, entertainments for, *continued*
   civic hosts, aims of, *continued*
      civic pride/reputation, 146, 177, 184–5,
         189, 190
      comment on topical issues, 177, 183
      outsider status, 183
   Elizabeth I, motives of, 144, 145, 148
   European monarchs, 143–4
   expense, 156, 157
   extent, 144, 176
   farewell song, 161, 162–3
   itinerant courts, a necessity, 143
   local people, participation of, 145, 147,
      178, 182, 184, 185, 187–9, 190
   meaning, layers of, 147, 148, 151–7, 161,
      169–70, 176, 183
   music
      organisation of, 146–7, 148
      political roles of, 146, 147–8, 155–6,
         158–61, 163, 165, 166, 169–70, 176,
         180–2, 183, 184–5, 190, 191
      imagery/metaphor, 172, 185, 190
   musicians
      benefits for, 146, 170–6
      collaboration with authors, 172, 173–4
      named, 149, 150, 158, 173–6, 178, 180
   noble hosts, aims of, 146, 147–8
      political ambition, 151, 155–6, 157
      rewards for service, 157–61
      criticism/complaint, 162–3, 167–70
      magnificence/status, 155, 161
   preparations, 143, 146, 147
   royal entries, 176–91
   tensions within, 178, 190–1
   see also individual entries for specific
      entertainments and hosts
Protestantism, 13, 33, 50, 52–3, 57, 80, 114,
   121–3, 124, 145n9, 162, 165, 168n82, 182
psalms, 133, 134, 135, 139, 179, 187
Puttenham, George, 34, 61n86, 99, 195

queenship
   concerns regarding, 18, 30, 53, 180
   distinctiveness of, 2n5, 5–6, 11, 44, 54,
      55–7, 78, 106, 124, 125, 127
   image, 18, 25, 43, 51, 102–3, 121, 125, 128,
      149, 151, 155–6, 166–7, 168
   music and, 13, 15, **16**, 17, 19, 25, 29–33,
      37–41, 44–52, 53–5, 55–7, 192–3
   criticism of musical queens, 26–8,
      53–4

queenship, *continued*
　see also counsel; court music; musicality *and* representations *under* Elizabeth I; gender; *and* entries for other individual queens

Ralegh, Sir Walter, 12, 39, 44, 58, 68–9, 213, 216
　'Fortune Hath Taken Thee Away My Love', 59–61
Ravenscroft, Thomas, 116, 119, 213
rebellion, 47, 179, 180, 191
　Babington Plot, 35, 48, 187
　Essex's Rebellion, 66, 148, 213n4
　lower classes as dangerous, 179, 184
　Northern Rising, 36, 178
　Oxfordshire Rising, 179
　Ridolfi Plot, 178
　social unrest, 36, 37, 39, 179
　traitors, 178, 191
religious imagery/themes, 18, 29, 35, 101, 119, 130, 133–9, 167, 186
　angels, 20, 38, 44, 63, 172, 192
　'sacred end' motif, 136, **137**, 138
　sacred musical styles, 2–3, 119, 135–8, 147
　see also saint *under* representations *under* Elizabeth I; divine/heavenly *under* harmony; divinely appointed *under* monarchy
Rich, Lady Penelope, 20n19, 39, 78, 216–17
Richardson, Ferdinand, *see* Heybourne, Ferdinando
Ridgeway, Cicely, Countess of Londonderry, 78
Rizzio, David, 26
Roberts, Richard, 64
royal household, musicians of, *see* court musicians
Ruff, Lillian, and D. Arnold Wilson, 66
Russell, Lady Elizabeth, 31, 145; *see also* Bisham, entertainments at
Russell, Lucy, Countess of Bedford, 24–5
Rye, entertainments at, 187, **188**, 189, 190, 191

sacred music, *see under* religious imagery/themes
Salignac, Bertrand de, Seigneur de La Mothe-Fénélon, 49–50
Salter, Thomas, 21, 23, 46

Schifanoya, Il, 86
Seymour, Catherine, Countess of Hertford, *see* Grey, Lady Catherine
Seymour, Edward, 1st Earl of Herford, 57n68, 145, 146, 148, 151, 155–7, 162; *see also* Elvetham, entertainments at
Seymour, Thomas, Baron Seymour of Sudeley, 52
Shakespeare, William, 8n30, 28, 48
Shepherd Knight, *see* Philisides
shepherds, 1, 35, 36, 37, 94, 103, 141, 156, 192, 211–12
　musicality of, 34, 35, 36n88, 116, 118, 127–8
　idealised in Classical and Italian literary models, 118
　king as shepherd, 118
　biblical connotations, 119
　natural honesty versus deceitful courtiers, 119–20
　represent contemplative life, 122
　Shepherds' Entertainment at Sudeley, 173–4
　see also Lady of May; Pan; pastoral; Philisides; Spenser, Edmund
Shrewsbury, Earl of, *see* Talbot, George
Sidney, Sir Philip, 67, 95, 110, 114–21, 123, 141, 216, 217
　political career, 114, 121–2
　literary outputs, 115, 118
　and music, 60, 118
　'Sing, Neighbours, Sing', 119
　posthumous reputation, 121
　supportive of military action in Netherlands, 114, 122–3
　see also Four Foster Children of Desire; *Lady of May*; Philisides
Silva, Guzman da, 49, 87, 89
Sirens, 21–2, 23–4
Smeaton, Mark, 26
Smith, Jeremy, 39, 148
Spain
　diplomatic relations, 48, 50, 52, 53, 87, 102, 122, 124, 177, 180
　war with England, 39, 40, 68, 93, 101, 124, 157, 165
　see also Armada celebrations; Philip II
Spenser, Edmund: *The Shepherd's Calendar* (1579), 30–1, 118, 127–8
Stanhope, John, 1st Baron Stanhope, 51
Stanley, William, 6th Earl of Derby, 2

Stewart, Henry, Duke of Albany and Consort of Mary Queen of Scots [known as Lord Darnley], 26, 57
Stewart, Matthew, 4th Earl of Lennox, his family, 57; *see also* Stewart, Henry, Duke of Albany
Strogers, Nicholas: 'Mistrust not Truth', 178, 180–2, **181**, 208, 214
Sudeley, entertainments at, 146, 173–4, **175**, 176, 209
Sylvanus, 145, 156, 162
Syrinx, 30–1; *see also* Pan

Talbot, George, 6th Earl of Shrewsbury, 62
Tallis, Thomas, 3, 171
  Cantiones Sacrae (1575), 2–3, 6, 29
Thacker, R.: *A Godly Ditty to be Sung for the Preservation of the Queen's Most Excellent Majesty's Reign* (1586), 187
Thacker, Robert, 187
three-men's song, *see* freemen's song
Throckmorton, Sir Arthur, 2, 11, 92
Throckmorton, Elizabeth [Bess], 2
Time (allegory), 51, 67, 92, 130, 131, **132**, 133, 208, 212
tournaments
  aims of nobility in, 14, 105, 106–7, 114, 124, 129–30, 141
  format, 14, 105–6, 117, 123, 143
  incongruous characters, 116–17, 125, 133, 141
  knightly personae, 105, 107, 108, 114–21, 123, 129–41
  music
    roles of, 108, 113–14, 116, 125, 131, 141–2
    songs, 116, 117, 119, 125–6, 130–42, **132**, **134**, **135**, **136**, **137**, **138**, **140**, **141**
    musicians, 109, 116, 127, 130–1, 139
    instrumental, 105, 107, 116, 118, 125, 128, 128
    musical pageantry versus military sport, 107, 110, 114, 120–1
  publication of, 106
  royal image, 105, 106, 114, 119–21, 123, 142
  spectators, 106, 107, 142

tournaments, *continued*
  see also Four Foster Children of Desire; Lee, Sir Henry; Philisides; Sidney, Sir Philip
tyranny, 10, 98–9, 100–1, 102

Vautrollier, Thomas, 33–4, 36, 37
Venus, 22, 27, 32*n*71, 102, 103, 145, 155–6, 173, 182
Vere, Edward de, 17th Earl of Oxford, 2, 8, 58, 96*n*102, 216, 217
Vere, Elizabeth de [later Lady Derby], 2, 62
virtue, *see* morality; *see also* virtue *under* Elizabeth I; music, connotations of; music, powers of
Vives, Juan Luis, 22, 23, 45

waits, 88, 147, 185, 187
Waldstein, Baron, 83, 85
Wanstead, 67, 217
  entertainments at, *see Lady of May*
war versus peace, 6–7, 38–9, 40, 91, 92, 94, 107, 110, 111, 113, 120–3, 124, 125, 127–9, 151, 177
Watson, Thomas, 149
Webbe, William, 59–60
Wedel, Lupold von, 83, 86*n*52, 106
Werrecore, Hermann Matthias, 87
Whythorne, Thomas, 47*n*47, 58–9
Wilder, van, family, 78, 79*n*18, 198
Wilson, D. Arnold, *see* Ruff, Lillian
Wild Man, 31, 32, 123*n*81, 167
William III, King of England, Ireland and Scotland, 192, 193, 194*n*11
Windsor, Lord Frederick, 123
Woodstock, entertainments at, 10, 130*n*116, 163–5, 168*n*82, 170, 183
Worcester, entertainments at, 147
Wotton, Sir Henry, 65, 66, 67
Württemberg, Frederick, Duke of, 17*n*7, 46, 50, 83

Zwetkovich, Adam, Baron of Mitterburg, 49

Studies in Medieval and Renaissance Music

VOLUMES ALREADY PUBLISHED

Machaut's Music: New Interpretations
edited by Elizabeth Eva Leach

The Church Music of Fifteenth-Century Spain
Kenneth Kreitner

The Royal Chapel in the time of the Habsburgs:
Music and Court Ceremony in Early Modern Europe
edited by Juan José Carreras and Bernardo García García

Citation and Authority in Medieval and Renaissance Musical Culture:
Learning from the Learned. Essays in Honour of Margaret Bent
edited by Suzannah Clark and Elizabeth Eva Leach

European Music, 1520-1640
edited by James Haar

Cristóbal de Morales:
Sources, Influences, Reception
edited by Owen Rees and Bernadette Nelson

Young Choristers, 650-1700
edited by Susan Boynton and Eric Rice

Hermann Pötzlinger's Music Book:
The St Emmeram Codex and its Contexts
Ian Rumbold with Peter Wright

Medieval Liturgical Chant and Patristic Exegesis:
Words and Music in the Second-Mode Tracts
Emma Hornby

Juan Esquivel: A Master of Sacred Music during the Spanish Golden Age
Clive Walkley

Essays on Renaissance Music in Honour of David Fallows:
Bon jour, bon mois et bonne estrenne
edited by Fabrice Fitch and Jacobijn Kiel

Music and Ceremony at the Court of Charles V:
The *Capilla Flamenca* and the Art of Political Promotion
Mary Tiffany Ferer

Music and Meaning in Old Hispanic Lenten Chants:
Psalmi, Threni and the Easter Vigil Canticles
Emma Hornby and Rebecca Maloy

Music in Elizabethan Court Politics
Katherine Butler

Verse and Voice in Byrd's Song Collections of 1588 and 1589
Jeremy L. Smith

The Montpellier Codex: The Final Fascicle. Contents, Contexts, Chronologies
edited by Catherine A. Bradley and Karen Desmond

A Critical Companion to Medieval Motets
edited by Jared C. Hartt

Piety and Polyphony in Sixteenth-Century Holland:
The Choirbooks of St Peter's Church, Leiden
Eric Jas

Music, Myth and Story in Medieval and Early Modern Culture
edited by Katherine Butler and Samantha Bassler

www.ingramcontent.com/pod-product-compliance
Ingram Content Group UK Ltd.
Pitfield, Milton Keynes, MK11 3LW, UK
UKHW020053100426
11791UKWH00008B/496